American Negro Folk-Songs

NEWMAN I. WHITE

AMERICAN NEGRO
FOLK=SONGS

BY

NEWMAN I. WHITE

FOREWORD BY
BRUCE JACKSON

FOLKLORE ASSOCIATES, INC.
HATBORO, PENNSYLVANIA
1965

Reprinted in facsimile from the original
edition of 1928 by permission of the
Harvard University Press

FOREWORD

I

Little folksong collecting is done among American Negroes now. There are occasional sorties by blues fanatics into southern swamps for long-lost names, and a few of us have been exploring some lesser-known areas of Negro folk activity—but that's about all. The blues fetish has helped distort our conception of what Negro folksong is and has helped stifle conversation on the topic. If one mentions Negro folk music, three activities generally come to mind: blues, prison work-songs and spirituals.

But there is more, much more. Much of it, in its delightful variety, has been gathered and preserved in this superb book by Newman White—who, at the other extreme, understood blues not at all.

One of White's major themes, one that the current blues monism obfuscates, deals with the vital interrelationship between Negro folk-song and minstrel and later white commercial music. He assumes and demonstrates white influence on Negro folksong, and it is to the detriment of neither. Our modern romance of the bluesman—Robert Johnson, Skip James, John Hurt, Charlie Patton, Son House and the others—has him rising autochthonous out of a Mississippi morass like a musical Venus on the six-string half-shell. Of course he is doing different things than the white hillbilly, but there is a danger in the tendency to disassociate him from the mainstream of western culture.

Our Negro problem nowadays is operative on several fronts, some of the most difficult being the ones closest to home. Obviously we do not know the Negro, we do not know what he wants and we do not know how we should help him get it. We know things are not right, by far, but too often the Negro the white man talks about in his theoretical discussions has little if anything to do with the Negro who walks and eats and wears shirts and goes to work and listens to the radio.

Perhaps nowhere is this myopia more apparent than among many fans of Negro blues. We often find among them a curious negrophilia such that every Negro utterance, however trite, or every Negro musical activity, however incompetent, is more valuable than any statement by anyone anywhere, ever. It is, I suppose, one of the more offensive forms of patronage fostered by our times.

White's attitudes reflect his times, but to a large extent he transcends them by—surprising as it may sound—hard work. We can pick up in these pages attitudes we can date or locate geographically, but only a few—and they appear in his chapter introductions, not in his selection of what to print. Other than the few songs he thought too bawdy for publication, he prints everything.

To go by the original manuscript,[1] the bawdy verses he omitted comprised a minute portion of the collection. Few of them would cause much concern or be the object of much interest now. I rather suspect that the few items in the original MS are all there were. From what I've read of Newman White, in various publications and in letters from his wife and friends, I doubt he was the kind of scholar who would have destroyed parts of his collection simply because he did not approve of them. The collecting was done mostly by students, much of it in 1915-16, and that alone would account for a paucity of really obscene material.

Perhaps the best way to appraise the excellence of this volume is to juxtapose it with some of its more notable contemporaries. The twenties were, in retrospect, an incredible decade for the publication of major folklore collections in America,[2] just as the previous decade

---

1. The original MS is in the Houghton Library, Harvard University (catalog #27256.38.1F*), 3 volumes, holograph MS and typed copy. Volumes I and II were gathered by White when he taught at Alabama Polytechnic Institute in Auburn, 1915-16, and were presented to Harvard College Library in June 1918 at the suggestion of George Lyman Kittredge. The donation bookplates in these two volumes had read, "From the compilor," but the last word was crossed out—in a hand I think is Kittredge's—and replaced by "collector." Volume III, submitted several years later, reads "collector."

2. Among them: N. Howard Thorpe, *Songs of the Cowboy* (Cambridge, 1921); Louise Pound, *American Ballads and Songs* (New York, 1922); R. W. Gordon, "Old Songs that Men Have Sung," in *Adventure* (July 10, 1923 to November 10, 1927); J. H. Cox, *Folk-Songs of the South* (Cambridge, 1925); Howard W. Odum and Guy B. Johnson, *The Negro and His Songs* (Chapel Hill, 1925) and *Negro Workaday Songs* (Chapel Hill, 1926); Dorothy Scarborough, *On the Trail of Negro Folk-Songs* (Cambridge, 1925); Franz Rickaby, *Ballads and Songs of the Shanty-boy* (Cambridge, 1926); W. Roy Mackenzie, *Ballads and Sea Songs from Nova Scotia* (Cambridge, 1928); Phillips Barry, Fanny Ecktorm, and Mary Smyth, *British Ballads from Maine* (New Haven, 1929); A. K. Davis, Jr., *Traditional Ballads of Virginia* (Cambridge, 1929).

had been an incredible one for accumulating them. In all probability, neither has ever been duplicated.

Dorothy Scarborough's *On the Trail of Negro Folk-Songs* is a charming book with delightful texts that rambles and wanders in a pleasantly schoolmarmish way and ultimately tells us more about Dorothy Scarborough than it does about the American Negro. Miss Scarborough was an interesting woman with interesting interests, and we can go along, but it is a personal rather than scholarly accompaniment.[3]

The work of Howard W. Odum and Guy B. Johnson, in particular *The Negro and His Songs and Negro Workaday Songs,* is vitiated, for our purposes, by their purposes. They were so interested in sociology and causes and conditions that they failed to include the kind of information that might have made their texts of more general use. In the process they demonstrate one of the dangers of a sociological method applied without qualification to folklore materials—sociology is a new science and it often dates quickly. Few sociological discussions of the twenties written *in* the twenties mean much now.

Newman White gathered a lot of facts, then attempted to assay their meaning and value. Odum and Johnson, I suspect, had some ideas, and collected and selected facts to demonstrate them.[4] This shouldn't demean their work—it was important and valid enough for 1925 and the texts they include are interesting—but they should be viewed in some historical perspective. Historical hindsight always gives one an unfair advantage, perhaps, but still their two books on Negro folk-songs read like a Music of the Darkies with a bit of enlightened sociological body English. Here is one example: " . . . It may be affirmed that all that has been said of the spirituals is true. They are beautiful, childlike, simple and plaintive. They are the Negro's own songs and are the peculiar expression of his own being" (*The Negro and His Songs,* 19). Even in 1925 one could consider that singularly imperceptive.

---

3. For a dissenting view, one much more favorable to Miss Scarborough, see Roger Abrahams' preface to the reprint edition of *On the Trail of Negro Folk-Songs* (Folklore Associates, Hatboro, 1963).

4. For a dissenting view, one much more favorable to Odum and Johnson, see Roger Abrahams' preface to the reprint edition of *The Negro and His Songs* (Folklore Associates, Hatboro, 1964). I understand his position generally, and think the book should be read. But I find treatment of the material and the manner of presentation so epidermal that the texts are never really useful.

They examined and I believe selected texts, and then discussed them, in what are essentially white terms; their whole framework was white, they read protest where a white man would have been protesting, they read simplicity where a white man would have been simple. It is all very nice, but it isn't necessarily the way things are. As Melville and Frances Herskovits later put the problem, "Lacking a knowledge of the cultural matrix, the interpretation of narrative must rest on the surface of expression, since attempts to derive meaning inevitably follow standards set by the culture of the student rather than of the people being studied."[5] It is confusion about the nature of that cultural matrix that dates books like *The Negro and His Songs,* for not only has the Negro learned new things in the last forty years but so has the white man.

Consider the differences between Newman White's essay on spirituals and theirs. The difference consists of more than the fact that one was done by a careful, painstaking scholar and the other by two enthusiastic sociologists. There is a gap in perspective, a time gap. The books of Odum and Johnson stand for us now as period pieces, more interesting for the attitudes they embody than the facts they reveal. *American Negro Folk-Songs* is as valuable as ever it was. Scarborough never really kept her texts away from herself; Odum and Johnson never kept them away from their cant. White kept his material separate and was better able to see what it contained.

His method is to accept nothing, nothing at all save his raw data, and he sometimes questions even that. He constantly harks back to earlier sources and his scholarship is a model for us still. "It is high time," he writes at one point,

> that these points be removed as far as possible from the realm of opinion and prejudice, and that an effort be made to examine the evidence judicially. I am cheerfully suspicious that my own attempt will seem in some quarters to be tinged with the racial prejudice of the white man; nothing more could be expected in the state of acute race-sensitiveness that involves the discussion of anything pertaining to the Negro. (p. 19)

One would like to be able to calmly and honestly insert such a remark in a preface to a book of one's own; it is the kind of comment one wishes had been inserted in many others that, high-spirited enough for their time, have begun to date as the enthusiasms which supplied

---

5. *Dahomean Narrative* (Evanston, 1958), 8.

most of the books' binding energy have become realities and no longer necessary. White writes introductions and he presents material; he always keeps the two activities apart. As a result, both have worn well.

More than anything else his ability to derive diligently rather than prescribe (and proscribe) patently has contributed to the volume's viability. Here is one example, by no means the most exhaustive, of his diligence:

> A curious mixture of secular and religious song traits. Lines 5, 6, 7, and 8 are stanza 7 of "Jerusalem, My Happy Home" as printed in *Zion Songster,* second edition, 1827, but omitted from the hymn as printed in the *Christian Psalmist,* tenth edition (1856) and *Methodist Hymnal,* 1854 and 1905. The same lines occur as stanza 7 of another hymn in John C. Totten's *Selection of Hymns and Spiritual Songs as Usually Sung at Camp Meetings,* etc. (19th edition, New York, 1927), p. 83.
>
> Lines 11, 12, and 13 occur in many spirituals as a stanza, and the last two lines as refrains.
>
> The connection with "Home, Sweet Home" is obvious. (p. 129)

He labors no less for his theoretical discussions:

> A proper consideration of [the originality of Negro song] involves more than a study of the songs and the testimony of the singer. It requires at least a cursory examination of the books of travellers and sojourners in the slave states, including those travellers away from the South—the fugitive slaves; the pro-slavery and anti-slavery propaganda literature of the eighteen-forties and fifties; the early minstrel books; the records of early church-workers among the Negroes; and the religious songs of the white people in the South. No writer has hitherto considered all these sources of information. Some of them have been ignored altogether. . . . The use of these materials in the present volume is very far from exhaustive, but I have at least considered all of them thoughtfully before attempting to reach any conclusions. (pp. 19-20)

He does the same with music. His discussion of the available scholarship, some of it extremely esoteric, is perceptive and sensitive (v. 22 ff.).

He questions the then-generally accepted notion of *double-entendre* in the spirituals. His response to the question is initially one of common sense:

> I do not believe that slaves, even with the freedom of speech sometimes allowed them, would have ventured to compose

and sing openly many of the songs about ole massa's stinginess or ole missis' promises of freedom, before the black-face minstrel had made them harmless commonplaces. Originating such songs would be a rather heavy presumption on ole massa's tolerance. (p. 149)

The contrary argument claims that the Negro material antedated the white, and that the white slaveholders never understood the *doubles*. This may be reverse prejudice: if the Negro slaves were verbally clever, it is not necessarily true that the white planters and farmers were all, without exception, stupid. However convenient that might be for third-grade history books, I fear it does not bear up under examination, or thought. One can argue White's point, but one would be hard put to dismiss it.[6]

II

There are a few qualifications with which this book should be read and a few possible objections that should be qualified. I shall list and discuss briefly the most important of these.

1. *He sometimes waxes rather moralistic.* In his discussion of Women Songs, for example, he at once attempts to point out and justify what is wrong with the male Negro's attitude toward his women. White didn't really have the sociological background to do either and would have better left both alone. But he keeps such comments to his introductions, and they are rare. The songs themselves stand with headnotes, not editorials.

---

6. Mark Miles Fisher, in his *Negro Slave Songs in the United States* (New York, 1953, paperback reprint N. Y., 1963), a revision of his 1945 Ph.D. thesis in the Department of Church History, University of Chicago, argues against the white-to-Negro hypothesis of the origin of the spirituals. Although Fisher's book is excellent, his logic is sometimes questionable, and this is one of the points he resolves more by implication than fact. Although there is not room here to go into his argument, let me point out that it does present the other side—but it does not by any means win its case.

The problem of influence in the spirituals is not quite the same as the problem of influence in Negro folksong in general. In the twenties concern was more with text than tune and White's point, which deals with texts, has not been adequately countered. It has been qualified, however, in the broader context of American Negro and African folksong, by the fruits of subsequent investigations of African and South African folk music. For more balanced views of the problem, one might consult Herskovits' *Myth of the Negro Past* (New York, 1941), chapter VIII, particularly pp. 216-269, and Harold Courlander's frequently perceptive calm study, *Negro Folk Music, USA* (New York, 1964), chapters I and II.

*2. He laments the paucity of songs dealing with "racial conscious-
ness," or rather observes how small a portion of his collection they
comprise.* These songs were recorded by white men, southern white
men. What would a Negro have collected? Perhaps exactly the same
thing, perhaps not. We'll never know. We won't even know how
things stand now because there are few Negroes in folklore—maybe
because most folklorists come from a middle-class background and the
urban Negro is too new to that status to want to spend his adult life
ferreting about lower class enclaves. In any event, collection by
Negroes is not being done to any great degree.

3. Many of the texts appear to be fragmentary. There are several
reasons for this, none of them to White's dishonor. We have been
conditioned by collectors of white folksongs, whose raw material tends
to arrive in long, coherent versions, and editors of Negro folksong,
who try to make their collections look that way by lumping, editing,
melding and otherwise bastardizing their material. Of all the volumes
purporting to present Negro folksong as it is, we can accept as valid
the texts in only a few—Scarborough and Odum and Johnson among
them. Negro folksong is different than white folksong. This has been
said before and it needs repetition. Negro song is not so alien a thing
as bluesophiles would have it, but there are important differences one
must consider.

The structural units in Negro folksong are the metaphor and line,
not the plot or part of plot. Instead of weaving narrative elements to
create a story, the Negro song accumulates images to create a feeling.
Certain configurations obtain sufficient currency to be recognizable
by title, but these are fewer in number and far more various in mani-
festation than any comparable white material. Even those Negro
songs that have been extensively recorded, such as "John Henry,"
have never gone rigid among the folk, as have many white folksongs.
One could compile a useful motif- and type-index to native American
ballads and many native white American lyrics, but this would be
impossible with Negro songs. Negro songs *are* formulaic, however,
and a study of the incidence and configurations of formulae would be
profitable, if arduous.

Which brings us to the next point in White's favor: many of the
short verses he includes *are* complete. After some experience in the
field, one recognizes their authenticity. And these are just what most
other editors usually combine (without telling us) or omit altogether.

4. *He does not understand blues at all,* and considers them rather degenerate. In light of our current imbalance in the opposite direction, that is no great hurt, and, again, he keeps his comments in his introduction and presents the texts as they came to him. We cannot reasonably ask for more.

5. *Much of the material was gathered by students.* It has become fashionable to snicker at material gathered by students. For some mystic reason the material is deemed tainted if the master's hand has not itself done the dipping. It can also be that the master directs. Student collections are bad or useless only if the teacher sending his students out hasn't bothered to instruct them in what to look for, how to look for it, how to preserve it. If he instills in his students something of the same principles he himself follows, there is no reason to assume the resulting collection is any less valid than a collection edited from the personal archives of a number of more doctorally endowed collectors. Some of the texts here obviously have been distorted—some by memory, some by the inability of many whites to hear what a Negro is saying when he is saying something a white man wouldn't. This is no novelty—compare transcriptions of tapes to what is in print and you'll find few published collections without error of this kind. But we can spot most of these; they stand out like the proverbial sore thumb, even to the least medically oriented reader. And by contrast they help us see how valid the others are.

III

Harvard's print order ran one thousand five copies in 1928.[7] The edition did not run out of print until 1949. A large portion of the thousand that went out is no doubt in university libraries, so it is not likely that this book is in very many homes, even folklorists', right now. This reprinting is a happy one.

Reviews on publication were excellent. There was one rather specious mixed review by Arthur Huff Fauset in *Opportunity* (May 1929). Others, from the *Seattle Town Crier* (November 2, 1928) to

---

7. I want to thank Harvard University Press (in particular Mark S. Carroll, Associate Editor of the Press) for giving me access to its files concerning *American Negro Folk-Songs.*

the *Bookman* (February 1929, by Abbe Niles), were perceptive and positive. A sensitive review by R. P. Harriss appeared in the *Baltimore Evening Sun* (June 26, 1929). The book was never reviewed in *Journal of American Folklore,* I'm not sure why. One of the reasons might be that most of the logical people were reviewing it else-where. Louise Pound, reviewing it for *Saturday Review of Literature* (October 13, 1928), said that *American Negro Folk-Songs*

> is not an anthology merely, or even primarily, though it includes innumerable texts. It is a thorough and independent treatment of Negro folk-song, its origins, history, types, and its relation to the poetry of the whites. It is well and sympathetically written and may be accepted at once as authoritative.
>
> Nearly sixty books dealing with Negro song, about nineteen of them by Negroes, have appeared since the beginning of the World War. . . . Of the books concerned with folksong, that of Professor White is the widest-ranging and the profoundest. He utilizes what has been done by others, subjects the available material to careful examination, and interprets it in a manifestly unprejudiced way. Not the least valuable feature of his work is its fine bibliography.

And, we might add, not the least impressive feature now is that both the book and its bibliography are still useful, and Miss Pound's review is still valid.

IV

Newman White was one of those devoted amateur folklorists who have done so very much for the field. His own area was English Romanticism, Shelley in particular. His production of this impressive volume and his selection as editor of the *Frank C. Brown Collection of North Carolina Folklore* are indications of how deeply rooted his private interest was. Mrs. White recently wrote me that

> When I first met Newman in the fall of 1918 (I was a graduate student at Washington University) he had already collected the bulk of the material in *American Negro Folk-Songs*. His preface to the book tells all this better than I can, or that I need to repeat.
>
> The bibliography shows that he published a number of Shelley articles in the 20's. He also constantly reviewed

books in the Romantic field. During the years 1928-43 he worked mostly on Shelley, but he never retired from folklore. He loved it; he sang Negro songs all his life. He took up the monumental task of editing the Brown collection partly, I think, because there was an understanding between him and Dr. Brown that he would do it, and largely because Newman was a passionate, devoted North Carolinian. His mother's people, the Iveys, are still a large, well-distributed, well-known family in the state; his father's family (his grandmother was a Barringer from Pennsylvania) are also in various offshoots and largely under other names important citizens of N. C. I don't think Newman ever wanted to live anywhere but in N. C.; he was a part of it. He had other offers, but happily settled back afterwards, content to be here. He made an adopted Tar Heel out of me!

I am sure that no one but Newman could have brought order and system out of the Frank C. Brown collection. It was a chaotic mass of material, contributors often indicated only by initials or last names. Some of the necessary detective work brought interesting, even hilarious results, such as a letter addressed to a contributor last heard of in Greensboro, which came back with two official P. O. stamps: *Deceased, Address unknown.*

Newman White was born in Statesville, North Carolina, on February 3, 1892; he died December 6, 1948. Save for summers teaching out of state (Texas in 1930, Harvard in 1939 and Minnesota in 1941), a year each at Alabama Polytechnic Institute (1915-16) and Washington University in St. Louis (1918-19) and his three years as a graduate student at Harvard (M.A. in 1915, Ph.D. in 1918), he was a lifelong resident of North Carolina. He entered Trinity College (later Duke) in the fall of 1909 and graduated four years later *magna cum laude* and with highest honors in English. He remained at Trinity as graduate student and assistant in English and obtained an M.A. there in 1914. He returned in 1919 and continued teaching in Durham for the rest of his life. In 1943, at the death of Frank C. Brown, he assumed both the chairmanship of Duke's English Department and the general editorship of the Brown Collection. He was a member of numerous professional organizations, among them the American Folklore Society, North Carolina Folklore Society (two terms president), Modern Humanities Research Association, Modern Language

Association (on the Committee on Monographs, advisory editor for articles on Shelley scholarship.)[8]

These are academic facts and do not tell us very much. Mrs. White kindly put me in touch with a number of Professor White's friends and former students. The parts of their warm and detailed letters that follow need little comment.

Guy Davenport, now teaching at the University of Kentucky, was an assistant on the Brown project. He writes:

> I remember him as a tall, leaning man—as if his hat had weight. (And it was usually somebody else's hat he put on whatever his hand, never his eyes, found on the stand). His absentmindedness was well-known. I remember the afternoon that he lit a matchfolder rather than the intended cigaret, causing a burn that required a bandage for days. He was apt to call people by any name that came to mind; I got used to answering to any monosyllabic name.
>
> He wept when the atomic bomb was dropped on Hiroshima.
>
> His tobacco manners were Rooseveltism: long holder, chain-smoking, a slight grimace of his lips in putting the holder into his mouth. He smiled almost constantly, especially with his eyes. . . . .
>
> His enthusiasms: this was most useful to me. I remember an evening at his home when he got out his relics (Shelley's snuff box, his edition of J. Gordon Cougler which he read from with poker-faced irony, many books and curios); I saw the deep quality of his affection for these things. He was, at least once an afternoon, struck by some phrase or absurdity in the Brown Collection, and would read it aloud to anyone about (blank-faced but polite typists, usually) until he'd had his satisfaction of it.

---

8. I have drawn these facts *passim* from James Cannon, III and Lewis Patton, "Newman Ivey White: Scholar and Humanitarian, February 3, 1892—December 6, 1948," *Library Notes: A Bulletin Issued for the Friends of Duke University Library,* #24 (Newman Ivey White Memorial Issue) (July 1950), 5-14.

I would like to express my gratitude to the others who graciously helped me prepare this section: the writers of the letters cited in the text, Miss Esther Evans of Duke University Library, and in particular Mrs. Newman White, who not only took time to write me at length, but also helped me locate the others. Mrs. White also supplied the photograph of Professor White. It appeared in the Durham *Morning Herald,* April 21, 1945, in a feature article by Lucile K. Boyden, "Duke Scholar Editing Famous Brown Collection."

His kindness: this was proverbial. He was never mean, and his patience went a long way before it became a slow burn. He was a splendid satirist, of course, but never a petty one.

He was an old-fashioned, courtly gentleman, without, I think, ever being aware of it. He conducted over the years a poetry seminar for the poetlings about, and I think it pained him to see the kind of verse that was attractive to them, but he was determined not to be conservative and would listen with the most cultivated attention to the worst kinds of ineptitude.

[These remarks are not at all what I thought I might say about Newman White. I realize that his memory is much more personal and close than I had suspected. I found him a kind friend and teacher, and must have been more dependent on him than is usual in even the best teacher-pupil alliances. He made the relationship seem perfectly natural, and only later, with wider experience of college life, did I realize how extraordinary it was. If I had to say specifically what I learned from him, I'd say that it was what a scholar's devotion is, the very idea—one I'd never been exposed to— that scholarship was a completely engaging, whole life.]

Mr. Ashbel G. Brice, editor at Duke University Press, first met Newman White in 1937 when he enrolled in White's graduate seminar in the romantic poets. He discusses another aspect of White's personality:

. . . During the later depression years he did volunteer work downtown for the needy. He was liberal in every sense of the word. This extended to his fighting for a greater faculty voice in the administration of the university. A Trinity alumnus and a North Carolinian, he was devoted to the institution, but he did not hesitate to say what he thought was wrong. In those days the group in control was still the one that had been in control when Trinity became Duke. I think it pretty clear that some of them felt White should have been on their side in their attempt to keep things as they had always been.

One minor revolution he early fought for was sensible academic dress. The older generation here tended to be a bit starchy in such matters—even when the thermometer was in the upper nineties. The era was the era of the "slack suit" shirt and trousers of the same light material. I can still see Dr. White in one of these, the omnipresent cigarette holder in his mouth, as he hurried across to his office.

W. F. Twaddell, now chairman of the Linguistics Department at Brown, first met Newman White in 1922 when he enrolled in a section of freshman English White was teaching. Professor Twaddell, then in his mid-teens, was greatly impressed by White and their relationship continued for many years.

> He somehow avoided any of the overt signs of being *soigné* and yet was impressively urbane and cosmopolitan. The man from west-Piedmont North Carolina could take or leave the trappings of what we would now call the jet set. The talk was partly literary, and he started me off on readings in out-of-the-way corners that I have treasured. . . .
>
> Ni [White's nickname] was the anchor of a most unlikely organization that I recall as from 1924-26 and maybe a bit later called the Cat's Head Club. (The Cat's Head was part of a dormitory where several of its members lived, and where we normally foregathered.) This had ca. nine members, was extremely forward-looking, saved its nickels to buy the *Mercury,* read Cabell, Hergesheimer, Donn Byrne, Paul Morand, Rainer Maria Rilke, etc. Somehow this group captured Duke's journalism in 1925-26—the *Archive* (literary) and the *Chronicle* (usual college newspaper). The editor of the *Archive* was R. P. Harriss. . . . The *Chronicle* editor Gay Allen, of Walt Whitman specialization.—Even now, I can think back with pride at what our bunch did way back there in the consulship of Cal Coolidge. . . .
>
> His tennis-playing was legendary. Left-handed, he was a demon to serve to, or receive from. I never dared venture onto the same court with him, but often watched him play. . . .
>
> The kid's-eye view I had of him and Marie convinced me that it must be wonderful to be married to a pretty, smart girl. The obvious fun in just being married to each other was overpowering pro-matrimony propaganda.

Mr. R. P. Harriss, mentioned in Professor Twaddell's letter, is a novelist and journalist, currently with the Baltimore *News American.* His long and delightful letter not only added specific information to the letters of the others, but also summed up much of what they said. To conclude, then, here is a long excerpt from Mr. Harriss' letter:

> Entering his classroom as a freshman, in 1921, I found his manner a little formal; later, as I came to know him well, I discovered a warmth and humor I had not suspected, with infinite kindness and understanding. This, I know, was the

experience of other students of his. He was scrupulously fair, unfailingly courteous, instinctively a gentleman.

I had imagined he could help me become a journalist, a calling for which I hotly panted. As it turned out, he had little practical guidance to offer in that direction. Instead, he imparted something more valuable. And although I left at the end of my sophomore term to take a newspaper job, thanks to his influence I returned after a riotous Wanderjahr to resume study, edit the student literary magazine, and graduate respectably. . . .

He was tall, angular, strong, but without an athletic swagger; wore glasses, looked rather schoolmasterish. I was surprised to learn he had been a noted athlete, still played a smashing game of tennis and was coach of the varsity tennis team.

He had somewhat hawklike features. His unruly, grayish light-brown hair was brushed straight back, and it seemed to hackle-up in front whenever he was intensely moved, by mirth or (more guardedly) by a great line of poetry. I always had a feeling that under provocation he might blaze with anger, but never knew that to happen; instead, he remained even-tempered. Yet, while always approachable, he had a certain reserve which probably was impenetrable. Of his intellectual honesty, integrity and courage there was never any doubt.

His classroom procedures were relaxed but not slipshod; there was much good humor, always within a serious framework. Outside his classroom he sometimes startled his students, notably at the initiation meeting for new members of the Fortnightly Literary Society, when his parody of the initiates' writings was devastating. . . .

In my time at Duke University, White was better known as a Shelleyan than as a folklorist, partly because Dr. Frank C. Brown had preëmpted the folklore field, partly because White's teaching was in English literature and he preferred to combine literary research with teaching. If at that time he placed literary publication ahead of folklore work, that did not preclude an intense and growing concern on his part for the latter. This was made evident during his compilation and editing (in collaboration with Walter Clinton Jackson) of *An Anthology of Verse by American Negroes* published by the Duke University Press in 1924. At that time he frequently spoke of the importance of the Negro folksongs he was gathering, sometimes stopping whatever work he was doing at the moment to sing one and relate something of its history and the manner in which it was come by.

White also was recognized, at least on the Duke campus, as a poet. Extremely modest about his poetry, he never saw fit to collect it into a volume. (Certainly it would have made a respectable, even a distinguished, small collection, had he done so.) He seemed far more interested in bringing the poetry of others to his students, in his lectures, and in furthering their own poetry production, in his verse-writing class.

During my last two years as an undergraduate I was a member of a small group which attended informal literary gatherings at his home, these often being presided over by his wonderfully good-natured, intelligent and high-spirited wife, Marie. Newman and Marie White were a well-matched pair. Their conversation sparkled, they always knew the latest and best campus stories and related them delightfully. Both of them hugely enjoyed really dreadful poesy: their collection of superbly bad verse surely must have been one of the liveliest in the English language. So an evening at the White's home usually had its hilarious moments, though it was a more serious concern with poetry that brought us together.

Not long after graduating, I got a newspaper job in Baltimore which brought me into the company of Mencken. When my first signed article appeared in print on the same page, side by side, with one by Mencken, I proudly mailed a tearsheet to Dr. White. He responded to my ephemeral journalistic item by sending me a reprint of his latest scholarly publication. My newspaper work took me to Paris and London for several years, yet we continued to exchange samples of our work, he always treating my newspaper trivia as if it were on a par with his folklore or Shelley papers. I imagine he was disappointed in my very skimpy literary output—one successful novel, a few short stories and poems —over and above the large bulk of my workaday journalistic production. But I like to think that he realized to a degree how my private world of imagination and experience had been enlarged and brightened by having known him.

V

What follows is not by any means a complete bibliography of the writings of Newman White. He published extensively on Shelley and the English Romantics; his massive *Shelley* (2 vol., New York, 1940, rev. 1946) still stands as the major compilation of the documentary evidence relating to the poet's life. The folklore items cited here are drawn from a list kindly supplied by Mrs. White and from Robert W. Christ, "The Published Writings of Newman Ivey White," in *Library Notes*, #24, pp. 53-60.

"The Collection of Folk-Lore," *Proceedings of the Alabama Educational Association*, XXXV (June 1916), 119-26. (White's first published scholarly essay.)

Folk-Lore Primer. Auburn, 1917. 20 pp. Published by the Folk-Lore Committee of the Alabama Association of Teachers of English; White was chairman of the Committee 1917-18.

"Racial Traits in Negro Song," *Sewanee Review*, XXVIII (July 1920), 396-404.

"American Negro Poetry," *South Atlantic Quarterly*, XX (October 1921), 304-22.

"Racial Feeling in Negro Poetry," *South Atlantic Quarterly*, XXI (January 1922), 14-29.

An Anthology of Verse by American Negroes. Ed. with a critical introduction, biographical sketches of the authors and bibliographical notes by Newman White and Walter Clinton Jackson, introduction by James Hardy Dillard. Durham, 1924.

American Negro Folk-Songs. Cambridge, 1928.

"The White Man in the Woodpile; some Influences on Negro Secular Folk-Songs," *American Speech*, IV (February 1929), 207-15.

Twenty-three mimeographed catalogues of materials in the Frank C. Brown Collection of North Carolina Folklore, not published but issued privately for the associate editors and for North Carolina libraries. Ranging from 3-257 pp., and classifying and organizing over 30,000 folklore items, and several thousand auxiliary items. Durham, 1943-1946.

"Organization of the Frank C. Brown Collection of North Carolina Folklore," *Yearbook of the American Philosophical Society, 1945* (Philadelphia, 1946), 218-19.

"General Introduction," *Frank C. Brown Collection of North Carolina Folklore*, Vol. I. Durham, 1952. Pp. 3-28. (Written in 1948.)

BRUCE JACKSON

Cambridge, Massachusetts
November, 1964

PREFACE

PERHAPS a few words are needed about the present collection and how it has been brought together and presented. It was begun in 1915, at the Alabama Polytechnic Institute, Auburn, Alabama. During the two years of my teaching at the Alabama Polytechnic Institute I collected some songs directly from Negro singers, but the bulk of my songs came from students who had learned them from the Negroes. I added a number, both then and later, from my own recollection. I am indebted also to the manuscripts and memories of a number of my friends, white and colored. My colleague at Alabama Polytechnic, Professor C. C. Certain, gave me an interesting collection of gang work songs, and Mr. and Mrs. J. J. W. Harriss, of Greensboro, North Carolina, enlivened a Christmas vacation for me with songs of an older generation in North Carolina. Among my colored friends I am most indebted to Ed Lloyd, janitor of the apartment house in which I live. With Ed I have swapped songs (the only infallible method of collection) during many a golden afternoon when Ed was supposed to be washing windows or cleaning floors for my wife, and I was supposed to be attending to grave professorial duties. Ed refers to this book, justly, as "our book."

When I left Alabama in 1917, I had collected perhaps one half of the songs in my collection. For the next two years, in Cambridge, Saint Louis, and Maine, my major interests were elsewhere and I added to my collection only sporadically. In 1919 and 1920, however, I collected a considerable number of songs through my students at Trinity College, now Duke University, Durham, North Carolina. The original manuscripts of my Auburn and Trinity collections, together with typed copies, were presented to the Widener Library through Professor Kittredge, who had them bound for preservation. From 1920 to 1927 I have added a few songs to the collection from various sources.

All of the songs were given to me either in manuscript or by word of mouth. In each case I have consistently stressed the point, particularly with students, that I wanted no materials from printed sources. A careful collation of the songs thus obtained with printed songs obtained directly from the singers has convinced me that there are very few indeed about whose genuineness there can be any justifiable doubt. On the contrary, it authenticated several songs I had been on the verge of discarding as suspicious. And why not? It has always been easier for a Southern youth, as I know from my own experience, to recall a Negro song than to get one from a book.

In each case the donor was asked if the song was complete, if he could sing it, when and where it was heard, and the circumstances under which it was sung. The songs, with the information thus furnished, were immediately typed and proof-read. As they stand in the printed collection, some of the information furnished with the songs has been omitted as unnecessary, particularly the first two items; for I have learned that no Negro folk-song is ever complete, and it is now too late to return with a phonograph and collect the tunes from the original contributors.

The notes with which these songs are accompanied seek first to provide a history of the particular version here printed — where and from whom it was procured by me, where and when it was sung, and under what particular conditions; secondly, by pointing out parallels to the song (or more generally, parts of the song) in other collections, to provide information as to its age and geographical range. Together with the cross-references to songs in my own collection, they illustrate, as no mere assertion could make clear, the incredible cross-breeding and inbreeding of the Negro song. To the student they should give more than a hint as to how Negro songs develop — how, probably, most folk-songs develop. They show also, more definitely than could be shown in the pages of a preface, to what extent and in what manner the folk Negro, America's most conservative citizen, has preserved tags from nineteenth-century religious songsters and minstrel books, even as he has preserved older tags of English speech. The references and cross-references by which these facts are indicated are not all that could have been made; to have listed all correspondencies would have been impossible. I believe, however, that they are sufficient, and I can imagine many a genial reader to whom they will seem even superfluous. If any such should feel his geniality waver under the mass of tediousness they present, I shall bear his reproaches meekly; in fact, I shall almost be inclined to participate in them, as Charles Lamb did in the damning of his own play. I should myself have sunk under the tediousness of such minute annotations as this work necessitated, but for my conviction that only in such a way could the materials be brought together to enable the Negro song to be seen as it actually is.

The grouping of the songs can hardly be called strictly logical. After several attempts to arrange a large number of Negro songs into groups that would be clearly discrete, I have concluded that such an achievement is an impossibility. Even a logical division into Religious Songs, Work Songs, and Social Songs, which would seem to be satisfactory, shows numerous overlappings of religious songs used as work songs, work songs used as social songs, and *vice versa*. The division I have finally hit upon as most satisfactory is based upon a combination of two principles — the function of the song as used by the Negro, and the function to which the song may be arbitrarily put as a revelation of the Negro's state of mind on various subjects. There are numerous overlappings from one group into another; these are unavoidable under any system and are somewhat rectified by cross-references. The work songs are so numerous that they are best presented in three groups, those dealing with gang laborers, those dealing with rural workers, and those dealing with miscellaneous occupations. To these might also be added most of the songs in all the remaining sections of the book. In fact, there is scarcely a group of songs in my classification from which songs might not be taken to illustrate any other class. But obviously some sort of classification must be attempted if the songs are to be presented at all; and the present classification, after repeated experiments, seems the one best adapted for practical presentation of the present collection.

Most Negro songs are without titles that are universally recognized. Many editors have sought to remedy this defect by inventing titles or giving a local title as a general one, with the unfortunate result that many songs essentially the same are known by half-a-dozen different names. In this volume I have sought to avoid adding to the confusion of arbitrary titles and have given only local titles and such general titles as seem to have won acceptance already.

I have reduced the bulk of my annotations by giving only the name of the author and date of the volume for books that are frequently cited. For full information about these books the reader may consult my bibliography.

For permission to reprint short passages (more specifically acknowledged in the proper context), I am indebted to the courtesy of G. P. Putnam's Sons, G. Schirmer and Co., A. and C. Boni, the *Journal of American Folk-lore*, and *Contemporary Verse*.

To all the students and other friends by whom this collection was augmented I am deeply grateful. I wish also to express my thanks to the Alabama Polytechnic Institute, Duke University, and Harvard University for material assistance, and to Miss Ethel Davis, who typed my final manuscript, for her intelligent help in checking and indexing. I am deeply indebted to my wife for recording the tunes given in Appendix I, and — to conclude as nearly all American students of folk-lore must conclude — to Professor George Lyman Kittredge for encouragement, coöperation, and suggestions.

N. I. W.

CONTENTS

I. The Negro Song in General 3

II. Religious Songs 31

III. Upstart Crows — The Reaction From Religion . . 130

IV. Social Songs — Dance and Banjo 148

V. Social Songs — Narrative Songs and Ballads . . 185

VI. Songs about Animals 224

VII. Work Songs — Gang Laborers 250

VIII. Rural Labor 281

IX. General and Miscellaneous Labor 290

X. Songs about Women 311

XI. Recent Events 341

XII. The Seamier Side 356

XIII. Race-Consciousness 376

XIV. Blues and Miscellaneous Songs 387

Appendices:

    I. Specimens of Tunes 405

    II. Specimens of Negro Ballets and Related Songs . . . 413

    III. Specimens of Spiritual Songs and Camp-Meeting Songs of the White People. 427

    IV. Specimens of Songs from the Old Minstrel Books. . . 443

    V. Specimens of Songs from Ante-Bellum Novels, Travel Books, Slave Autobiographies, etc. 454

Bibliography 467

Index of Titles 483

Index of First Lines 485

American Negro Folk-Songs

I

THE NEGRO SONG IN GENERAL

THE Negro has always been a great singer, but the Caucasian peoples have had to be reminded of this fact again and again before they were convinced, or attached any importance to the conviction. The Negro himself was convinced last of all. Except in a few places like Fisk University, Hampton Institute, and Tuskegee Institute, only backward "country niggers" were ever caught singing spirituals between the eighteen-eighties and the second decade of the twentieth century. As late as 1909 Negro students at Howard University rebelled and refused to sing them. (By the more progressive and aggressive elements in the race the spiritual was frowned upon as a reminder of slavery and ignorance. Now that the white race has been suddenly converted to the beauty of the spiritual, Negro churches are using the old songs more and more.) Some choirs have even relearned them from the numerous recently printed versions, so that the folk-song collector can no longer be certain in every case that his spiritual is a flower of purely oral tradition. When I asked a member of one of the Durham Negro congregations if spirituals were sung much at his church he replied, "Yes, suh, we sings 'em — any time the white folks 'quests 'em. Miss C——, she sings 'em. She was trained at the Chicago Conservatory."

The popularity of Negro work songs and blues that has sprung up in the wake of the revived interest in spirituals has increased the Negro's own interest in even these songs; but they are so much more spontaneous and incidental than the spiritual that the Negro is hardly likely ever to sing them from a book when they come so much more easily out of his head.

The Negro will go on singing, of course, but he will never be quite as unconscious of his great gifts as heretofore. Several times previously the Negro song has had its day on the minstrel and concert stage and in the printed book, only to retire into its original fastnesses among the illiterate folk-group, not entirely unchanged, but without fundamental alteration.

Constantly, from the very first, it has been influenced by the songs of the white people, much more than current writers on the subject seem to realize. In the early days (and to some extent still) almost the whole life of the Negro was conditioned upon his acceptance and partial imitation of the white man's ideas of life.) The compliant and imitative tendency thus developed has become a racial trait and is no doubt responsible for the introduction into his songs of many touches from the songs he heard about him. A camp-meeting tune or a secular stanza here, a whole song there, isolated lines and phrases everywhere — the whole body of Negro folk-song is shot through with unmistakable signs of this influence. But it cannot be doubted that the folk-song assimilated these influences and retained its essential homogeneity. (The Negro possessed a very limited English vocabulary, an invincible racial indifference to the meaning of words and verbal structure in songs as compared with the meaning of rhythms and melody, an inherited saturation with a music fundamentally different from that of the white man both in its pentatonic characteristics and in the marvellous rhythms caught from the African drum.) Though he probably did his best to imitate faithfully, fortunately he failed. He *had* to modify the white man's songs. All the music that he originally possessed and all that he acquired fused into a new body of folk-song, fundamentally homogeneous, but neither African nor Caucasian.

It will probably be a long time still before the piney-woods singer of spirituals or the illiterate Negro gang-laborer loses his folk-songs or modifies them beyond recognition. As I write these very lines, I hear every day the work songs of Negroes building a new university for the white man. Twelve miles away, more than one hundred and twenty-five years ago, ancestors of these same workmen sang other work songs as they labored on the walls of the first state university in America. But the cases are different. The race itself is different; it has already partly fulfilled its destiny of eventual negroidization, and some of its leaders have even discarded the word Negro for the more accurate Aframerican. Many Negro laborers to-day have phonographs, and some even radios. There are about four hundred Negro newspapers in America to-day and several magazines, including such excellent ones as *The Crisis* and *Opportunity*. More and more the Negroes are learning from the printed page. White people in Charleston have been teaching spirituals to Negro schoolchildren. The Negroes are becoming less and less a folk-group. Even while their racial leaders are slowly teaching them independence and self-respect, Negroes are following the white man in their new respect for the Negro folk-song, and in many other ways that are not the ways of folk-song. The Negro is told to be himself, even to be proud of himself; but he is also told to be ambitious, to "rise."

can novelist quotes an extemporaneous song sung under similar circumstances.[3]

When the religious songs of the Negro arose, mainly as a result of the missionary activities of the Methodists and Baptists, many slave-owners were at first opposed to religious instruction for slaves. In 1834, Mr. Kingsley charged that "religion" had ruined the morale of his Florida slaves. Fanny Kemble several times alludes to the hostility of Georgia overseers to religious instruction for slaves.[4] From Bishop Capers, the Methodist pioneer in slave missions, we learn both of the early hostility of planters to religious instruction for slaves and of their change of heart when it was demonstrated that religious instruction "paid."[5] In 1845 a meeting that convened at Charleston, South Carolina, to consider religious instruction for Negroes, recorded its conviction that religion "helps production and discipline";[6] and in the *Annals of Southern Methodism* for 1856 we find that the planters are showing great interest in the slaves' religion. It would be a gross injustice to conclude that most of these planters, orthodox church members as they were, had no genuine religious interest in their slaves. Contemporary evidence shows that they had. The consistency of religion, as it is sincerely practised, with a desire for profit is hardly to be denied without rejecting the concept Paradise itself. But the fact remains that the Negro spiritual, in which so much of his religion is bound up, is in origin a product of exploitation.

Dance songs and other songs of amusement, while generally used spontaneously as a means of recreation, were also encouraged by the planters as a means of keeping the Negro happy and contented. Sir Charles Lyell found the slaves passionately fond of dancing and music,[7] and one of the books by fugitive slaves gives several examples of common dancing songs.[8] Fanny Kemble was told that many plantation overseers prohibited melancholy tunes among the slaves and encouraged nothing but cheerful music and senseless words, because of their better effect upon the disposition of the workers.

[3] Thomas Bangs Thorpe, *The Master's House, A Tale of Southern Life*, 1854, p. 77.
[4] Frances Anne Kemble, *Journal of a Residence on a Georgia Plantation, 1838–1839*, New York, Harper and Brothers, 1863.
[5] William Wightman, D.D., *Life of William Capers, D.D., One of the Bishops of the Methodist Episcopal Church, South; including an Autobiography*, Nashville, Tenn., Southern Methodist Publishing House, 1859.
[6] *Proceedings of the Meeting in Charleston, S. C., May 13–15, 1845, on the Religious Instruction of the Negroes*, etc., Charleston, S. C., 1845.
[7] Sir Charles Lyell, *A Second Visit to the United States*, New York, 1849.
[8] David Wilson, ed., *Twelve Years a Slave — Narrative of Solomon Northup*, New York, 1853. See Appendix v, p. 454.

Mr. Kingsley, as we have already seen, encouraged dancing and merriment among his Florida slaves for similar reasons.

Work songs, of course, have always received practical encouragement. Booker T. Washington, in his preface to S. Coleridge-Taylor's *Twenty-Four Negro Melodies*, says that "Oftentimes in slavery, as to-day in certain parts of the South, some man or woman with an exceptional voice was paid to lead the singing, the idea being to increase the amount of labor by such singing,"[9] and Lafcadio Hearn noted the same practice among the Negro cane-cutters in the French West Indies.[10] Julien Tiersot says that the efficiency of the corn songs is so well recognized that plantation owners give extra pay to the song leaders.[11] In the Mississippi River region an observer noticed this practice as follows:

The planter who has any piece of emergency work on hand, like a long, quick pull in a boat or the repair of a levy, always resorts to the device of getting his men to start some rhythmic plantation melody; and a superintendent of some Southern mining works — involving labor peculiarly hard for Negroes — once told me that his hands once "struck" summarily, when for some reason he was forced to stop their singing.[12]

I myself have seen gangs of Negro laborers in North Carolina and Alabama working to songs started by a song-leader, and have been told by several men who have been in charge of construction gangs in various Southern states that it is a common practice to give the leader extra pay.

In the eighteen-forties Negro music, for the first time, spread beyond the plantation. Negro dances, dance songs, and songs of merriment, such as we have seen that the planters were encouraging, came upon the minstrel stage and achieved widespread popularity. The religious songs were certainly in existence, or developing, at this time, as we know from the presence in the minstrel songs of a few tags from the spirituals,[13] but they were practically ignored by the minstrels, either because they seemed inappropriate for minstrel purposes, or because they had not reached a state of prominence comparable with that of the livelier secular songs.

[9] Quoted by Henry Edward Krehbiel, *Afro-American Folk Songs; a Study in Racial and National Music*, New York and London, G. Schirmer, 1914, p. 47.
[10] Lafcadio Hearn, *Two Years in the French West Indies*. Quoted by Krehbie *op. cit.*, p. 47.
[11] Julien Tiersot (Jean Baptiste Elisee Julien), *La musique chez les peuples indigenes de l'Amérique du Nord (Etats-Unis et Canada)*, Paris and New York, 1911, p. 203.
[12] Clarence Deming, *By Ways of Nature and Life* (New York and London, 1884), p. 378.
[13] See p. 53.

This movement started with the popularity of the "Jim Cro[w]
dance, so called from the name of the Louisville Negro who is sai[d]
have invented it in the early eighteen-thirties. It came upon
New York stage in 1832, and is described by a practically conte[m]
porary writer as follows: "Weight thrown alternately upon the h[eel]
of one foot and the toes of the other; left hand rested upon hip, rig[ht]
extending aloft, turning around as the song required."[14]   Abo[ut]
1914, in New York, I saw it simultaneously acted, sung and d[e]
scribed in the play, Lilac Time, as follows:

> Jump, jump, jump, Jim Crow,
> First upon your heel-tap and around you go;
> Slide, slide, point your toe
> You're as naughty as the devil when you jump Jim Crow.

Its popularity was enormous. It permeated the American vaude-
ville stage, was taken up in England, was heard by travellers in
Egypt and India, and returned to the plantation to find an echo in
Uncle Remus's:

> Make a bow to de rabbit an' a bow to de crow,
> Takes a limber-toed gemmun for to jump Jim Crow.

Its name is alive to-day in such phrases as the Jim-Crow car and
Jim-Crow legislation.

"Jim Crow" had been preceded in 1829 by "Zip Coon" and
"Long Tail Blue"; it was closely followed by such popular songs as
"Ole Virginny Nebah Tire, Settin' on a Rail," and numerous other
songs which the writer of the article in *Putnam's*, who speaks as a
plantation-owner and slave-holder, pronounces genuine. A little
later, about 1841, came the even more popular "Old Dan Tucker,"
which is sung in Negro minstrel shows to-day.

Numerous companies, such as the Ethiopian Serenaders, the Virginia Minstrels, the Kentucky Minstrels, and the New Orleans
Serenaders, sang these songs all over the country. If any of the
original singers were Negroes, — and I find no proof that they were,
— burnt cork soon came to take the place of natural pigmentation,
just as spurious songs largely supplanted the genuine Negro songs
that had given these companies their first impetus. Certainly the
principal performers, such men as Charles White, "Jim Crow" Rice,
Dan Emmett, Henry H. Paul, T. G. Booth, and "Pickaninny"

[14] "Negro Minstrelsy, Ancient and Modern," in *Putnam's Monthly* (Jan., 1855),
v, 72–79.

Implicit in most of the exhortations of Negro leaders is the inevitable "Imitate the white man" — carrying coals to Newcastle still,
though in a different cart.

The mass of Negroes are still nearer to the folk stage than they
are to their leaders, but one can foresee even now the end of the old
Negro folk-song. James Weldon Johnson's fine poetic tribute to the
spirituals in *O Black and Unknown Bards*, like the singing of spirituals by talented Negro concert singers, is essentially a sentimental
tribute to the past. The Negro has awakened to the beauty of his
folk-songs, but he admires them as the white man does. The very
perspective that he has achieved is ominous for his songs, however
auspicious it may be for the general progress of the race. His belated hail is really hail and farewell. The last chapter in the appreciation of Negro folk-song is an ironical one.

The whole history of the Negro song is ironical. Travellers in
Africa have almost universally commented upon the native African
fondness for music. The slave coffles coming from the interior to the
coast may or may not have indulged in song. Nor have I seen any
testimony in the grim accounts left by the slave-traders as to
whether or not the resident agents of the Royal African Company
and others encouraged the slaves to sing during their confinement
in barracoons, awaiting the arrival of slave ships. But from that
time on, the Negro song saw queer uses. Slave captains were finan-
cially concerned to deliver to America as many slaves as possible,
and in as sound condition as the horrors of the passage permitted.
Accordingly, slaves were encouraged, sometimes forced, to dance
and sing during the daylight hours allowed them on deck. There
are old prints which show cargoes of slaves being whipped into song.
It was thought to have prevented many a slave from jumping overboard or from grieving himself into sickness and death.

There is little or no record of Negro singing in America in the
eighteenth century, but during the early nineteenth century there is
plenty of evidence that this strange practical exploitation of Negro
song continued. One Southern slave-holder states that he kept his
new African Negroes happy and productive by encouraging "as
much as possible dancing, merriment, and dress."[1] An English
traveller, in describing a slave coffle, says that the drivers kept up
the spirits of the migrating slaves by good food and by encouraging
them to sing "Ole Virginny Neber Tire."[2] An ante-bellum Ameri-

[1] Z. Kingsley, *A Treatise on the Patriarchal System of Society as it exists . . . under the
Name of Slavery, By an Inhabitant of Florida* (4th edition), 1834.
[2] G. W. Featherstonehaugh, *Excursion through the Slave States* (London, 1844), i, 123.

Coleman, were white men and wrote many of their own songs. Charles White offered a reward of fifty dollars to any one who could make it appear that he was not the author of some forty of the most popular "Negro" songs, including several that were claimed by other celebrated minstrels. Clad in conventional evening clothes, or in exaggerated plantation costume, these artists rattled the tambourines and bones, twanged the banjo, and lifted their voices in halls of their own, or wherever a theatre or concert hall was to be had.

Popular artists occasionally retired, or pretended to retire, to the plantations for new material; but by 1855 the author of the article in *Putnam's* found the parodies of "Jim Crow" so common that he could nowhere obtain a copy of the original version. In a volume of so-called Negro songs that he examined he could "find only ten with any trace of genuineness." My own examination of many such volumes convinces me that less than ten per cent of the songs are genuinely Negro. New versions of the original songs ran rampant; sometimes with the name of a white man (for example, that of a captain in the United States navy) given as the author. Parodies and original songs celebrated such current topics of interest (to the white man) as Dickens's visit to America, Nullification, 54-40 or fight, Harrison, Taylor, Jackson, Van Buren, and Tyler, as well as the very sentimental and conventionalized charms of every black or yellow girl for whom an unnatural name could be found. The case is best dismissed in the words of the writer already quoted:

The names even have lost their marked significance. The questionable taste which has given birth to appellations like "Fannie Fern," "Lottie Lee," "Minnie Myrtle," and their long retinue of vegetable alliterations, has crept into this department of poetry, and exhibits itself in such Africo-romantic fancies as *Rosie Lee, Minnie Dale, Flora May, Nellie Bell,* or *Eddie Way.* Poetasters who never saw an alligator or smelt the magnolia blossom in their lives sit coolly down to write an African ditty as a pleasant after-dinner pastime, or a daily task; and as a natural consequence of this reprehensible assumption, we find the banana growing wild in Tennessee, South Carolina slaves gorging themselves with pumpkin pie, a deceased Negress buried upon the Lawrence River in the midst of a furious snow, and a Kentucky sugar-mill in full blast in the month of June.

These songs got back to the plantation, largely spurious as they were, and were undoubtedly among those which the plantation-owners encouraged the Negroes to sing. They persist to-day in isolated stanzas and lines, among the songs handed down by plantation Negroes, as will be seen by the notes to many of the secular songs in this volume.

Fanny Kemble wrote that the Jim Crow dancing of the minstrel stage was tame compared with that on her husband's Georgia plantation. Whether this be true or not, — her book is too passionate to be thoroughly trustworthy, — an examination of several volumes of these early minstrel songs leads to a strong conviction that other things were tamed down. They contain nothing of the strong passions found in the narratives of escaped slaves. There are very few references to punishment and escape from slavery, and the more frequent mention of abolition and Harriet Beecher Stowe is generally either indifferent or scornful. The masters are kindly to an almost suspicious degree. Plantation life is pleasantly presented as a compound of singing, loafing, attending massa or missis, making love, fishing, and hunting the coon or 'possum, with a strange silence as to rabbit-hunting. Some individual songs are definitely pro-planter in their point of view. Beyond doubt, the Negro minstrel song, like many of the novels of ante-bellum Southern life, was commonly used as an instrument of propaganda against the interests of the Negro himself.

The next public appearance of the Negro song was under entirely different auspices, and in a new guise. During the Civil War a number of Northern white men came into much closer contact with the Southern Negro. After the war a number of Northern officers remained in the South during the military occupation preceding the reëstablishment of state government. A number of Northerners especially interested in the Negro came to the South to assist in the operation of the Freedman's Bureau and in the religious and educational development of the Negro. Almost all the Negro songs published between 1860 and 1870 were evidence of the sympathetic interest of these men. A chaplain of "contrabands" at Fortress Monroe published *O Let My People Go* as early as 1861.[15] In June, 1867, Major T. W. Higginson, who had been in charge of Negro troops in South Carolina, published his often-quoted *Atlantic Monthly* article on "Negro Spirituals."[16] Later in the same year appeared the well-known collection of W. F. Allen and others,[17] gleaned from the Negroes among whom the compilers were working.

[15] *The Song of the "Contrabands," "O Let My People Go." Words and music obtained through the Reverend L. C. Lockwood, Chaplain of the "Contrabands" at Fortress Monroe,* New York, 1861.

[16] T. W. Higginson, "Negro Spirituals," *Atlantic Monthly,* xix (June, 1867), 685–694.

[17] W. F. Allen, C. P. Ware, Lucy M. Garrison, and others, *Slave Songs of the United States,* New York, 1867.

John Mason Brown's article, "Songs of the Slave," appeared in
Lippincott's Magazine in December of the following year, but I am
unable to say whether or not it was the outgrowth of similar activities among the freedmen. A belated example of a similar product
is Barton's *Old Plantation Hymns*,[18] which were noted down while
the author was doing religious and educational work among the
Negroes between 1880 and 1887.

The authors of these articles and volumes were almost exclusively
men with an incomplete acquaintance with the Negro, to whom the
Negro was primarily an object of sympathy and pity. Probably
none of them had had daily and intimate contact with Negroes before the Civil War. Consequently all except John Mason Brown
practically ignored the lighter side of Negro song, which the minstrels had stressed exclusively, and which the ante-bellum travellers
had noticed much more often than the spirituals. Their sympathies
misled them, easily and often, into supposing that the "wild, sad
strains" of the hymns reflected the Negro's idea of the unutterable
sadness of slavery. To them "freedom" meant freedom from slavery; "the Promised Land," freedom; "the year of Jubilee," the year
of emancipation; "the Egyptian bondage," physical slavery. It
cannot be denied that these interpretations were accepted by Negroes and white people during and following the Civil War. In his
"Song of the Negro Boatman," Whittier wrote:

> O praise an' tanks — de Lord has come
>   An' set de people free;
> An' Massa tink it day ob doom,
>   An' we ob jubilee.

The chorus of a song of individual white authorship introduced
among the freedmen by Northerners concludes:

> Well it must be now de kingdom's comin',
>   In de year ob Jubilee.

Probably similar interpretations were taught the ante-bellum slaves
by such Abolitionists as could gain access to them. One pro-slavery
writer charges roundly that Abolitionists sought to furnish slaves
with a key to the Bible which would pervert it into an instrument
of "despair, hatred, and blood." [19] Fanny Kemble said as early as

---

[18] William Eleazar Barton, *Old Plantation Hymns*, Boston and New York, 1899.
First published in the *New England Magazine*, Dec., 1898, and Jan. and Feb., 1899.

[19] J. H. Hammond, *Two Letters on Slavery in the United States, addressed to Thomas
Clarkson, Esq.* (Columbia, S. C., 1845), p. 19.

1839 that the slaves considered their case analogous to that of the oppressed Israelites of song and sermon.—

But what these sympathetic interpreters overlook is that precisely the same imagery was common in the religious songs of white people during the early nineteenth century and down to the present day. The point is so vital to the question of the originality and true meaning of the spirituals that it will have to be discussed more fully in the chapter devoted to religious songs; for the present, it will be sufficient to point out that these expressions were all originally religious in their significance, that they have been sung by white people for at least one hundred years without thought of other than spiritual meaning, that they were especially common in the early camp-meeting songs that influenced the Negro most, and that these expressions were actually taught in the manuals composed by Methodists and Baptists for the early training of slaves. Whatever they may have come to mean to some Negroes at a later time, they were never originally, or even generally, the expression of the Negro's longing for physical freedom.

The really valuable contribution to our knowledge of Negro song made by such men as Allen, Barton, and Higginson is not to be minimized. They were not ignorant of some influence upon the Negro song from the songs of white people. No one of them, probably, could have made the mistake made by General Armstrong, later president of Hampton Institute, when he heard his Negro troops singing a song which he supposed to be a Negro creation and named the *Negro Battle Hymn*, but which in reality was a song of militant Christianity that had been printed and sung by white men at least thirty years before.[20] A little knowledge of the popular religious songs of early Baptists, Methodists, and Christians would have enlightened General Armstrong; further research in the same materials would undoubtedly have corrected a mistaken tendency in such writers as Higginson and Allen. The point I am here making is that these men, too, were unconsciously warping the Negro song somewhat to their own sympathies. And since most subsequent opinion of the Negro song has been greatly influenced by these writers, the point requires making. An example of its effect on such an excellent commentator as Major Higginson may be seen in his concluding sentences:

By these they could sing themselves, as had their fathers before them, out of the contemplation of their low estate, into the sublime scenery of

---

[20] See page 46, and Appendix III, p. 427.

the Apocalypse. I remember that this minor-keyed pathos used to seem
to me almost too sad to dwell upon while slavery seemed destined to last
for generations; but now that their patience has had its perfect work,
history can afford to lose this portion of its record. There is no parallel
instance of an oppressed race thus sustained by religious sentiment alone.
These songs are but the vocal expression of their faith and the sublimity
of their long resignation.

Of this it may be said that the Negro slave seldom contemplated
his low estate; Major Higginson's fellow townsman, Charles Eliot
Norton, wrote that it was difficult to induce him to do so.[21] "Minor-
keyed pathos" involves the fallacy, long exploded, that music in a
minor key is sad because it seems so to the alien listener. It is also
a mistake to suppose that most Negro music is in a minor key, and
that there is not a great deal of jubilation and glory hallelujah in the
spiritual. "An oppressed race sustained by religious sentiment
alone" ignores the fact, made evident enough by planters and travellers, that the Negro slaves were "sustained" fully as much by their
lively secular songs as by their spirituals. It assumes that the oppression is that of slavery, although for half a century the white
race, in the popular religious songs which the Negro sang and from
which his songs started, had been proclaiming itself oppressed in
precisely the same terms. At camp-meetings both races, sometimes
together, seemed actually to enjoy this oppression. For both races
it was the same, the oppression of sin, which in other songs both
races were joyfully confident of overcoming.

Possibly it was the moderate success of these post-war publications that suggested the idea that the Negro might exploit his own
songs to the advantage of the Negro race. At any rate the idea was
broached in 1872 at Fisk University (Nashville, Tennessee), a Negro
college then entirely under white control. The institution was desperately in need of money. As a part of its efforts to raise funds it
formed a choir of "Jubilee Singers," who gave concerts in the North
and East and finally in Europe. Their story is told in two books.[22]
Although they were sometimes insulted and humiliated by hotel-
keepers and Northern audiences, their tours were spectacularly
successful. They sang before Queen Victoria, breakfasted with
Gladstone, and sent home $60,000 from one of their trips. Fisk Uni-
versity as it exists to-day is largely a result of their singing. Before
1874 Hampton Institute (Hampton, Virginia) also had a group of

---

[21] *Letters* (Boston, 1913), i, 121.

[22] G. D. Pike, *The Jubilee Singers of Fisk University*, Boston, 1873; and J. B. Marsh,
The Story of the Jubilee Singers, London, 1877, — both with appendices of songs.

singers raising money in the North.[23] Tuskegee Institute (Tuskegee, Alabama) and other Negro colleges followed suit. All have found the device a most successful means of getting money and desirable publicity, and have continued its use to the present day. Although they used the spirituals mainly to obtain the interest of the white man, these colleges all made a practice of singing them at home, and no doubt contributed greatly to the preservation of the spiritual during the time when most of the literate and semi-literate members of the Negro race were desirous of forgetting it.

The Negro race in general was not yet ready to take up the racial songs, but certain elements in the race had become keenly aware of their financial value. The appreciation of Northern and foreign audiences soon convinced them, perhaps at first a little to their surprise, of the musical value of their songs. All their earlier song-books, most of which, by the way, were edited by white people, show a full realization of the essential dignity and value of the Negro spiritual. Instead of being regarded, as Paul Laurence Dunbar regarded Negro dialect, as "the broken language of a broken race," the spirituals came to be regarded in most of the Negro colleges as an object of pride. But the editors of these song-books followed the earlier post-war writers in disregarding the secular song almost entirely, and stressing the spiritual as a record of the feelings of the race under slavery. It was good propaganda, and it was undoubtedly what the editors themselves thought — or rather felt — to be the truth, for they made even less effort than Allen and Higginson to get at the real origin and early connections of the Negro spiritual. As for the secular songs, no one since the early minstrels had considered them as of any significance.

Since the Negro colleges first put singers on the road, the Negro song has never been allowed to fall back into obscurity. The song collections originally published from Negro colleges have gone through successive editions, generally with an increase in the number of songs included. New collections have come from the Negro schools, some of them from schools that were never prominent for their travelling singers.[24] Fisk University and Hampton Institute have continued to be the most prominent centres of this activity and, since 1914, have broadened their interest beyond the predominantly financial one with which they started. The former has pro-

[23] Mrs. M. F. Armstrong and Helen W. Ludlow, *Hampton and Its Students*, New York, 1874.

[24] E. g., Emily Hallowell, *Calhoun Plantation Songs*, Boston, C. W. Thompson and Co., 1905.

duced the song collection of Frederick J. Work,[25] the historical and critical discussion of John Wesley Work,[26] and Thomas Washington Talley's book of secular songs.[27] The latter has produced successive editions of the collection by Thomas P. Fenner and others,[28] and the excellent series of studies by Mrs. Natalie Curtis Burlin.[29] Graphophone records of Negro quartettes and choruses enjoyed a moderate popularity from the first. Various collections and articles appeared from miscellaneous sources, most of them following the early post-war tradition of neglecting the secular songs and emphasizing the spirituals as a record of racial sufferings.

Serious students both of folk-lore and of music became interested, the latter, perhaps, being somewhat influenced by Dvořák's enthusiastic praise of Negro music. Between 1888 (volume I) and 1914 the *Journal of American Folk-lore* published over one hundred articles and notes dealing with the Negro, a large proportion of which had to do with his songs. A well-known British musician, S. Coleridge-Taylor, the son of a native African, published a volume containing some bits of authentic and reliable musical analysis.[30] Negro folk music was subjected to the analysis of such critics of music as Richard Wallaschek, Carl Engel, and Julien Tiersot.[31]

In 1914 Henry Edward Krehbiel published his *Afro-American Folk Songs*.[32] As music critic for the New York *Tribune*, Mr. Krehbiel had become interested in the Jubilee Singers. His conclusions in some respects seem slightly warped by his sympathies and by the fact that his analyses are based upon the early song-

[25] Frederick J. Work, *Folk Songs of the American Negro*, Nashville, Tenn., Work Brothers, 1907.

[26] John Wesley Work, *Folk Song of the American Negro*, Nashville, Tenn., Press of Fisk University, 1915.

[27] Thomas Washington Talley, *Negro Folk Rhymes, Wise and Otherwise, with a Study*, New York, Macmillan, 1922.

[28] Thos. P. Fenner, Fred. G. Rathbun, and Miss Bessie Cleveland, *Cabin and Plantation Songs as Sung by the Hampton Students* (3d edition), New York and London, G. P. Putnam's Sons, 1901.

[29] Natalie Curtis Burlin, *Hampton Series Negro Folk-Songs* (4 vols.), New York and Boston, G. Schirmer, 1918–1919. Also *Songs and Tales from the Dark Continent*, New York and Boston, G. Schirmer, 1920.

[30] S. Coleridge-Taylor, *Twenty-Four Negro Melodies*, Boston, Oliver Ditson and Co., 1905.

[31] Richard Wallaschek, *An Inquiry into the Origin and Development of the Music, Songs, Instruments, Dances and Pantomimes of Savage Races*, London, 1893. Carl Engel, *An Introduction to the Study of National Music; comprising Researches into Popular Songs, Traditions and Customs*, London, Longmans, Green, 1866. Julien Tiersot (Jean Baptiste Elisee Julien), *La musique chez les peuples indigènes de l'Amérique du Nord* (*Etats-Unis et Canada*), Paris and New York, 1911.

[32] Henry Edward Krehbiel, *Afro-American Folk Songs; a Study in Racial and National Music*, New York and London, G. Schirmer, 1914.

collections, which in themselves were naturally somewhat propagandistic. Nevertheless, in spite of his neglect of the secular songs, Mr. Krehbiel's book remains the standard study of Negro folk-music.

The interest of the student of folk-lore is best represented by Mr. Perrow's scholarly and well-informed articles; [33] while Mr. H. W. Odum's Clark University studies [34] broke new ground both in giving the secular songs adequate attention and in studying the Negro song from a social point of view.

Thus at the beginning of the World War the Negro song had for some years been the object of study from several points of view. It was no longer merely a tool for the exploitation of the Negro for the white man's benefit or the white man for the Negro's. The Negro himself, outside of the Negro colleges, was still blissfully unconscious of his songs as anything peculiar or remarkable.

The present lively interest in Negro folk-song seems to have begun about 1914. Within the thirteen years since the beginning of the World War (this is written in 1926) there have appeared 59 books dealing with the Negro folk-song. Most of these are collections. In some cases a number of separate publications as sheet music have been catalogued by the Library of Congress under one general title. Counting the individual titles under which they originally appeared, the total number of publications, including books and sheet music, recorded in the Library of Congress, is 137. Whether the computation is based on the general titles only or is expanded to include all individual titles later assembled under one general title, the result shows a greater number of titles published within the last thirteen years than in the sixty-eight years preceding. Of the 59 general titles, 19 are the work of Negro authors, compilers, or editors. One of the 19 comprises under one title, 43 separate sheet-music "folios" of one song each, and another comprises six, making the total number of publications by Negroes 67 out of 137. Among the eleven Negroes responsible for one or more of these volumes occur the names of such well-known Negro musicians and singers as Roland Hayes, Harry Thacker Burleigh, J. Rosamund Johnson, and W. C. Handy. Mr. Burleigh's 48 volumes, mostly sheet-music "folios" of single songs, constitute a most extensive

[33] E. C. Perrow, "Songs and Rhymes from the South," *Journal of American Folk-lore*, xxv (1912), 137–155; xxvi (1913), 123–173; xxviii (1915), 129–190.

[34] H. W. Odum, "Religious Folk-Songs of Southern Negroes," in *American Journal of Religious Psychology and Education*, 1908–1909, iii, 265–365; and "Folk-Songs and Folk-Poetry as found in the Secular Songs of Southern Negroes," in *Journal of American Folk-lore*, xxiv, 255, 351; both separately published by Clark University Press.

musical rendition of Negro songs. The first book of spirituals edited by James Weldon Johnson,[35] Secretary of the Society for the
Advancement of the Negro Race in America, became a "best seller"
immediately, and was included in most of the magazine lists of
"best books" for 1925.

A significant change occurred in the attitude of the Negro colleges.
The old song collections continued, as we have seen. But from
Hampton came the volumes of Mrs. Natalie Curtis Burlin, consti-
tuting a genuine and excellent study of the nature and background
of Negro song. From Fisk University came two studies by Negroes,
the first [36] a study of the nature and the history of the spiritual; the
second [37] a collection of secular songs, with a study of their nature
and background. Manifestly the Negro is no longer merely the
singer of his folk-songs.

There is plainly evident a continued and increasing interest on the
part of the white man, both from a Negrophile point of view, such
as that shown by a number of magazine writers and attachés of
Negro colleges, and from a more objective and scientific one. From
the point of view of the folk-lore scholar, for example, Professor Cox
has annotated a number of Negro songs.[38] Professor Odum and Mr.
Guy B. Johnson, starting from Professor Odum's little-known Clark
University study of years ago, have published two considerable collections of Negro folk-song, presented and analyzed from a sociological point of view.[39]

A new element had entered into the history of the Negro folk-song.
The white man's interest was now for the first time predominantly
objective and scientific, no longer patronizing or purely sentimental.
The Negro song had gained enormously in dignity among the white
people. Among the Negroes themselves its prestige had extended
far beyond college circles and its value far beyond the money-value
that had first appealed to the Negro colleges. Negro singers like
Roland Hayes and Paul Robeson have made the singing of Negro
folk-songs popular on the concert stage. Taking note of the white
man's interest in his songs, the Negro has become more interested
himself, and has invested his songs with a new dignity. By an ironic

[35] James Weldon Johnson, *The Book of American Negro Spirituals*, New York, The
Viking Press, 1925.

[36] John Wesley Work, *op. cit.*

[37] Thomas Washington Talley, *op. cit.*

[38] John Harrington Cox, *Folk-songs of the South*, Harvard University Press,
Cambridge, 1925.

[39] Howard W. Odum and Guy B. Johnson, *The Negro and His Songs*, Chapel Hill,
North Carolina, 1925; and *Negro Workaday Songs*, Chapel Hill, North Carolina, 1926,
University of North Carolina Press.

turn, the relics despised in the eighteen-seventies have become ob-
jects of pride. The Negroes have taken over the opinions of the
earlier collectors, that the spirituals are a record of suffering and
forbearance under slavery. Naturally they emphasize the purely
Negro origin and character of the songs.

There was still another purpose for the Negro folk-song to serve.
When the voice of racial minorities came to be heard in the land,
following President Wilson's most far-reaching utterance, the voice
of the Negro was not least. Numerous books and articles demonstrated the worth and the truly remarkable progress of the Negro in
business, science, and the arts. The folk-song, especially the spiritual, is now a part of this demonstration. No one who has ever
heard them sung will assert that racial pride in these songs is not
just, even though the dispassionate student must make some dis-
count for the sensitive race-consciousness which has adopted them
as one of its instruments. It is a double pity, in the circumstances,
that the pride of the "New Negro" in his racial songs should have
been taught him by white men. But that is only a part of the general
irony that makes the history of Negro song so innately poignant.
Compelled to sing amid the horrors of the slave ship, encouraged on
the plantation to sing first secular songs, then spirituals — all for
the white man's profit; taking over and handing down many of his
secular songs from the pseudo-Negro minstrels who sometimes used
them as a part of the pro-slavery propaganda; profiting somewhat
by the sympathetic but not entirely comprehending interest of
Northern uplifters, the Negro at length learned from the white
man the money-value of his songs and built colleges out of them.
Finally he learned to be proud of them and to use them as propaganda of racial self-respect. Once the white man's instrument, they
are now the Negro's, having swung a full circle from Negro scorn to
Negro pride. Of all this, educated Negroes are at least partially
aware. But the backwoods farm laborer and the illiterate gang
laborer, who will keep Negro folk-songs alive for several generations
yet, are still aware of little about the Negro song except, unconsciously, that it is a part of themselves.

One fact that stands out very clearly in the history of the Negro
song is that its use predominantly as a tool of immediate interests
has encouraged the growth of mistaken notions as to its origin and
meaning. The objective truth about these songs has never been
sought very earnestly by the great majority of people who have been
interested in the songs themselves. The matter has been greatly
complicated by a surrender of dispassion, on both sides, to race

prejudice. White people are too prone to assume without investigation, that everything the Negro has achieved is the result of imitating the white man and is therefore to be dismissed as trifling — a conclusion that ministers but strangely to the Nordic conviction of race superiority. This attitude, it is true, is seldom encountered in print. One often encounters denial of the imitation theory, and searches in vain for any printed statement of the theory so often controverted. That is because nearly all the writers on the subject have been Negrophile. The theory does exist, in the mind of nearly every average white man to whom I have talked on the subject. Despite some elements of truth, this assumption is fully as unjust and inaccurate, in the final analysis, as the Negro's assumption that his folk-song is entirely original.

In the foregoing pages I have already said enough to indicate my own opinion on most of the points in question. It is high time, however, that these points be removed as far as possible from the realm of opinion and prejudice, and that an effort be made to examine the evidence judicially. I am cheerfully suspicious that my own attempt will seem in some quarters to be tinged with the racial prejudice of the white man; nothing more could be expected in the state of acute race-sensitiveness that involves the discussion of anything pertaining to the Negro. I am fully aware that the white man has certain inescapable prejudices and that I am writing as a white man; but I also know that I greatly respect the Negro race for its character and accomplishments, and have had from childhood a positive affection for many individual Negroes. I shall at least examine some evidence that has hitherto been ignored or not fully considered, and shall try to reach fair conclusions. This last may be the more easily achieved because of my conviction that, no matter how it developed, the Negro song is now definitely and peculiarly Negro, and that it is no more discrediting the Negro race to point out certain alien elements in its origin than it is a discredit to English poetry to have borrowed its rhyme from the French.

The main point to be settled, if possible, is the originality of the Negro song. On this depend somewhat such questions as whether or not the Negro songs represent the Negro's racial feelings toward the white man and the white man's exploitation of the Negro.

A proper consideration of this matter involves more than a study of the songs and the testimony of the singers. It requires at least a cursory examination of the books of travellers in Africa and students of native African folk-lore; the narratives of travellers and sojourners in the slave states, including those travellers away from the South — the fugitive slaves; the pro-slavery and anti-slavery propaganda literature of the eighteen-forties and fifties; the early minstrel books; the records of early church-workers among the Negroes; and the religious songs of the white people in the South. No writer has hitherto considered all these sources of information. Some of them have been ignored altogether, while such as have been considered have generally been handled so casually as not to prohibit a reëxamination. The use of these materials in the present volume is very far from exhaustive, but I have at least considered all of them thoughtfully before attempting to reach any conclusions.

In most of the numerous books written by travellers in Africa, one finds the Negro song mentioned only casually, if at all. Naturally the writers were mainly engrossed in more thrilling matters. However, if we did not possess several books devoted specifically to the study of African music and folk-lore, we should be certain from the travel-books alone that the native African was particularly fond of music. On this point the travellers are practically unanimous. Whatever else he may have got from his white masters, the Negro brought his love of music with him. Mungo Park tells how the Negroes improvised a song about him, which the Duchess of Devonshire later turned into English verse for him.[40] The song itself has no significant resemblances — after the Duchess had worked on it — to American Negro songs, but the manner of its origin is significant. W. Winwood Reade observed that his people always began to sing when he compelled them to overcome their natural laziness and continue rowing.[41] George Francis Lyon observed Negro women singing while pounding wheat, always in time with the music.[42] Another traveller noted that, after harvesting grain, the women "sang and beat the grain to a chorus."[43] Mary Kingsley records her Bantu boatmen's love of singing, and remarks that the tunes are "far superior" to the words. She describes the words as superficial, consisting of monotonous repetition of a phrase or line, referring sometimes to a recent occurrence, sometimes to a person, as for example, "The shark bites the Bubi's hand."[44] In another book she gives an interesting account of the Bantu song-net minstrel, who

[40] Mungo Park, *Travels in the Interior Districts of Africa* (4th edition, London, 1800), p. 151. The song is quoted in my Appendix V, p. 465.

[41] W. Winwood Reade, *The African Sketch Book* (London, Smith, Elder and Co., 1873), i, 32.

[42] George Francis Lyon, *A Narrative of Travels in Northern Africa, 1818–1820* (London, Murray, 1821), p. 336.

[43] James Augustus Grant, *A Walk Across Africa* (Edinburgh, Blackwood, 1864), p. 86.

[44] Mary Kingsley, *Travels in West Africa*, London, Macmillan, 1897.

carries a net to which various articles are attached, and sings a song about the article designated by the listener.[45] A. B. Ellis gives six examples of African airs, and describes the songs as recitative with short choruses. The recitative is often improvised comment on the peculiarities of any passing stranger, especially if the stranger is a European.[46] From the Bantus of Northern Rhodesia J. Torrend quotes folk-tales in which were interspersed short songs of five or six lines. The song is an integral part of the story, and is often sung by the listeners as a chorus. The story takes its name from the first line of the song. Although the words of the songs do not resemble American Negro songs, their use is very similar to the use of songs in the Uncle Remus stories.[47] Mrs. Burlin has carefully recorded a number of African songs with the music,[48] but the words and meaning are quite different from those of American Negro songs, though there are work songs that perform the same function as the American Negro work song and are similarly short and trivial in meaning. The same dissimilarity in meaning and slight kinship in function is to be found in the songs quoted by Mr. Talley,[49] both in the seven from Africa and in the five from Jamaica, Venezuela, Trinidad, and the Philippines. And the same may be said of the words of the various African songs quoted from travel-books in Carl Engel's *Introduction to the Study of National Music*.[50]

Miss Scarborough prints two or three songs as being native African songs brought to this country by African slaves and handed down in the original language.[51] Mrs. Jeannette Robinson Murphy quotes an African song brought from Africa by the nurse of Mrs. Jefferson Davis, a full-blooded African who continued singing the song long after she had forgotten the meaning of the words.[52] The songs noted down for Sir Hans Sloane in Jamaica in 1688 were largely pure African.[53] But such songs, even when known to be genuine,

[45] Mary Kingsley, *West African Studies* (London, Macmillan, 1899), p. 149.

[46] A. B. Ellis, *Studies in Tshi-, Ewe-, and Yoruba-Speaking Peoples* (1887), chap. 22.

[47] J. Torrend, *Specimens of Bantu Folk-lore from Northern Rhodesia*, London and New York, Dutton, 1921.

[48] Natalie Curtis Burlin, *Songs and Tales from the Dark Continent, recorded from the singing and the sayings of C. Kamba Simango and Madikane Cele*, New York and Boston, G. Schirmer, 1920.

[49] *Negro Folk-Rhymes*, etc., New York, Macmillan, 1922.

[50] London, Longmans, Green, 1866.

[51] Dorothy Scarborough, *On the Trail of Negro Folk-Songs*, Cambridge, Harvard University Press, 1925.

[52] *Southern Thoughts for Northern Thinkers* (New York, Bandanna Publishing Co., 1904), p. 25.

[53] Walter Jekyll, *Jamaican Song and Story* (London, B. Nutt, 1907), p. 281.

are so extremely rare that they have slight bearing on the question
of how much of his songs the Negro brought with him from Africa.

So far as the words of his songs go, there is practically no connection between the American Negro and Africa. Nor is there any reason for supposing that there is any connection in subject matter,
with possibly some slight exception for Br'er Rabbit. I have seen
no translations of African songs that seem in the slightest to resemble American Negro songs in the actual words that were sung.

In some respects other than the music, however, there is a connection between the two. There are native African work songs
which, like those of the American Negro, are short improvised
snatches about the work or some trivial subject of passing interest.
Constant repetition of a phrase or a line are common to both. The
use of short songs in animal stories evidently comes from Africa.
Native Africans, like the American Negro before the supremacy of
railroads, seem always to have been especially fond of boat songs.
In America the former African continued his songs in two of their
most important functions, to accompany his rowing and to aid him
at his other work; and his song retained its old characteristics of
brevity, triviality, repetition, and improvisation. Further than this,
except for the music there seems to be no connection.

As for the music, it seems probable that there is a much stronger
connection, but on this point I have insufficient technical knowledge
to do more than summarize and balance what has been said by
trained musicians. Dr. Wallaschek denies any originality whatever
to Negro music, and Tiersot accepts the opinion that Negro music
is largely the result of imitation. Krehbiel dismisses Wallaschek's
opinion with contempt, and argues that the considerable use in
Negro songs of the minor mode and the pentatonic scale, both of
which characterize African music, could have originated only in
Africa. He admits that both these elements exist in old Scotch and
Irish music, but thinks there was too little of this music in the South
to have influenced the Negro. On this point he ignores the great
popularity of Scotch and Irish songs in all the early nineteenth-
century "songsters," as well as the fact that in the slave-breeding
states of North Carolina and Virginia there was a strong Scotch
element, and that here, during most of the eighteenth century,
slaves worked side by side with indentured men, a considerable
number of whom had been sent from Scotland after the Jacobite
uprisings. Krehbiel's position on this point was strenuously echoed
by J. W. Work, and seems to have been pretty generally accepted
by writers on Negro music. Both C. S. Myers and Miss Lucy

Broadwood, who analyzed the music of Mr. Jekyll's Jamaican Negro songs, agreed that most of the tunes were of European origin, but they do not deny an African element in the music. Mrs. Burlin, whose work with Negro music seems on the whole to be more careful and reliable than that of most other critics, is of the opinion that, though American Negro music absorbed much from the music of the white man, all of its really distinctive features were brought from Africa. "That Negro folk-song is indeed an off-shoot from an African root, nobody who has heard Africans sing or even beat the drum can deny." [54] This is practically the same as Mrs. Murphy's conclusion, some years before, after hearing an African sing. It is supported by the analysis of a large number of spiritual tunes recently made by Mr. Fisher and summarized in the preface to one of the most valuable of the recent collections of spirituals. [55]

Many slaves and ex-slaves have believed that their tunes came from Africa, and have so informed white people. In most cases this is mere guess-work, and like a great deal of folk belief about folk-songs, has little weight as evidence unless otherwise supported. Thus Mrs. Murphy's conviction that the tunes were African was buttressed by the statement of an old Negro: "But the tunes was brung from Africa by our granddaddies. Dey was just 'miliar songs, but in de old days dey call 'em sperituals case de Holy Spirit done revealed 'em to 'em." [56] Anyone who has examined many of the early nineteenth-century collections of hymns knows that the Negro got the word spiritual from one of the regular divisions of these books.

It seems fairly evident that a thorough and reliable investigation of the relations of American Negro and native African music is yet to be made. As Mr. C. S. Myers maintains in his appendix to *Jamaican Song and Story*, our present knowledge of African music is chiefly ignorance. The obscurity may be somewhat clarified by the labors of Mr. George Julius Ballanta. Mr. Ballanta is a native of Sierra Leone, a graduate of The Institute of Musical Art, who has already edited a collection of spirituals with an analysis of their music. [57] Since 1925 he has been studying African music in West Africa. One of the most distinguished critics of music in America,

[54] *Hampton Series Negro Folk-Songs* (New York and Boston, G. Schirmer, 1918–1919), ii, 4.

[55] William Arms Fisher, *Seventy Negro Spirituals*, Boston and New York, Oliver Ditson and Co., 1926.

[56] *Southern Thoughts for Northern Thinkers*, New York, Bandanna Publishing Co., 1904, p. 23.

[57] G. J. Ballanta, *Saint Helena Island Spirituals*, New York, G. Schirmer, 1925.

writing to a friend of Mr. Ballanta, says: "So far as I know, he is the first musician who has undertaken to give us the *essence* of African music, in place of the Europeanized products which pass as Negro music, but are usually about as African as a Mozart opera."

Meanwhile, one or two common-sense considerations may be advanced pointing toward a tentative conclusion. The slave had to change his language because it was the medium through which he must accommodate himself to the white man's world; but his music was his own, at least until he joined the white man's church. It was practically his only private affair, and it was deeply inbred wherever he went. He clung to his native drums, triangles, jawbones, and quills, long after his language was forgotten. In the mid-nineteenth century, according to Carl Engel, Brazilian Negroes could still be related to their particular ancestral regions of Africa through their musical instruments. If the Negro had desired to forsake his own music for that of the white man, it is difficult to see how he could have done so. Hawaiian singers, with no particular musical heritage of their own, could not help making something quite different out of missionary hymns that they had no intention of altering. Even to the non-technical ear, there are fundamental and distinguishing differences between Negro music and Caucasian music in America. Knowing these facts, and knowing the innate conservatism of Negro character as we do, it seems reasonable to conclude that the Negro brought African music with him to America, and that it is a considerable element in the songs he sings to-day.

No effort, however, to settle the originality of Negro music can be conclusive without studying the religious life of the whites which enveloped the Negro once he had "come through" and "got religion." Since this is a matter belonging properly to the study of only one branch of Negro song, the spiritual, its details will have to be reserved for the chapter on Religious Songs. In that chapter I hope I have made it plain not only that the Negro spiritual was originally the same as the camp-meeting song and spiritual song of the white man, but that it grew out of the same primitive religious practices that produced the cruder religious songs of white people, and that it still preserves, along with parts of the old "spiritual songs" of the whites, a faithful picture of the more familiar and unrestrained side of the white man's religion in the first half of the nineteenth century. This impression is confirmed by the numerous accounts of religious expression of the slaves found in the old novels of the ante-bellum South. "The general excellence of the Negro ear for music" was a subject of common remark in the United States in

1854, according to Charles Pickering;[58] but the testimony of all the travellers and novelists is significantly confined to the music. Apparently they all take it for granted that the slave was doing his best to sing the white man's hymns. The evidence is similar as to the secular song. The snatches quoted by the ante-bellum travellers, diarists, and novelists, and by the fugitive slaves in their autobiographies, all show two strong tendencies at work — the improvising tendency and the imitative tendency. The improvisations were the Negro's own, and have largely died out (if we can base so general a conclusion on the fact that none of those actually quoted seems to have survived), to be supplanted by other improvisations which are certainly genuinely and originally Negro, and which, as we have seen, are but the continuation of a habit brought from Africa. The earlier imitations survive in the occasional echoes of Mother Goose and other traditional folk-songs of the white people and in the really astonishing number of snatches from the early black-face minstrels.

There is but one conclusion toward which all of this evidence tends. The American Negro song was not at first original with the Negro. It originated in an imitation frustrated by imperfect comprehension and memory, and by a fundamentally different idea of music. One of the means by which new Negro folk-songs are being created to-day, as the notes to this collection should demonstrate, is by variational imitation of the popular songs of the white man. Three great waves of the white man's song have beat upon it, namely, the revival songs of the early nineteenth century, the early minstrel songs, and (fortunately with no great force) the coon songs of the late nineteenth and early twentieth centuries. At the present time it is in the peculiar position of being modified by the blues, which were originally Negro folk material but which come back to the Negro, through phonographs, sheet-music, and cabaret singers, as a factory product whose dubious glory may be attributed to both white and Negro "authors."

But this, after all, is but one side of the conclusion, and the least significant. The songs of the Negro to-day are beyond question the Negro's songs, not the white man's. The music alone makes them something quite different, and the words, even where they were originally the white man's words, have in most cases been so profoundly modified as to be unrecognizable. They have become thoroughly naturalized as vehicles of the Negro imagination. The

---

[58] Charles Pickering, *The Races of Man* (London, 1854), p. 190; quoted by Carl Engel.

current of Negro song habits has made of them something quite
different from anything the white man has ever made of them or
could make of them. In fact it has made of them in individual
cases, something different from anything other Negroes have made
of them; for it is a peculiarity of Negro song that the same singer
seldom sings the same song twice exactly the same, and almost
always sings it a little differently from the way in which others
sing it.

I think the notes to the more than eight hundred songs in this
volume make fairly clear all the most characteristic ways of the
Negro folk-song, so far as the text of the song is concerned. One of
the most important of these is improvisation, which has already
been discussed. Improvisation is not peculiar to Negro folk-song, of
course, but it is highly characteristic; it is a racial trait, and it is
carried to much greater length than by white people. The next
great characteristic is that of variation. Stanzas which have become firmly fixed in Negro song often recur in variously modified
forms. This, too, is common to most folk-song; but in no type of
English folk-song that I know is it so marked as in the Negro song.
Finally, there is the accumulative tendency. In English folk-song it
is nothing extraordinary to find a stanza or fragment of one song
drawn into another by some accidental attraction; in Negro folk-
song, however, there is hardly any such thing as a stanza belonging
particularly to one song and to that alone. Generally speaking,
practically any stanza is at home in practically any song. Since the
tune is variable and the stanza is variable, any song is prolonged to
almost any length desired, simply by fishing stanzas out of a spa-
cious but none too accurate or discriminating folk memory, aug-
menting them by improvised lines or stanzas if it seems desirable,
and accommodating stanzas and tunes to each other. Any song may
be stretched upon this Procrustes bed of infinite possibilities and
become either a variant or a new song. Few songs have a fixed beginning and almost none has a definite end. Practically the only
fixed element is the stanza or phrase, and that is only relatively
fixed. From this point of view the Negro song, in spite of its simple
metrical structure, is veritably an Old Man of the Sea. Although I
have heard Negroes singing since I was a small boy, I was so astonished at the extent of this phenomenon in the present collection that
I distrusted it, until examination showed the same thing to be true
of all other collections in comparison with each other and with mine.

These three traits are common to all types of Negro folk-song.
Other traits not so fundamental are the extensive use of refrains and

the fondness for parody. The latter is merely a more sophisticated phase of the tendency to variation and is seldom to be encountered in the truly religious songs. The former is common in both religious and secular songs, but the refrains of one group, while freely shuffled from song to song within the group, are seldom shuffled from religious to secular songs and *vice versa*. Wherever a refrain is so borrowed, it tends to become exclusively identified with the type of song for which it is borrowed.

Dialect may be considered a characteristic of the spirituals and the older secular songs; but Negro dialect was never so standard or consistent as dialect writers have made it; and it is now so obviously on the wane and so obviously (where it exists at all) merely a mixture of ordinary illiterate English with a few dialect survivals, that it is no longer a very significant element, except in a few localities such as eastern South Carolina. The dialect of the spirituals is very capably discussed by Mr. James Weldon Johnson in the preface to the *Book of American Negro Spirituals*.

Underlying the more important traits of Negro folk-song there is a sort of balance between the conservatism of the singer, which leads him to preserve many of the old conventional ideas, forms, and expressions, and his desire for novelty, which leads him to improvise. But the improvising is due partly to an inherited convention and sometimes, no doubt, to a failure of memory, as well as to an extraordinary indifference to the meaning of words. To the Negro the meaning of a song is not the sum of the meaning of its individual sentences. His sense of logic, at least in his songs, is different from the white man's. From the white man's point of view this difference may be expressed as the predominance of *feeling* over *meaning*. It often leads the Negro into absurd collocations and sequences, ridiculous expressions, meaningless words, and whole lines of nonsense. So it seems to the white man, but not necessarily to the Negro, who goes by the general feel of the song (words and music merged) and not by precise rules of English. Thus it makes little difference to the singer of spirituals whether all God's chillun got shoes or all 'at's got chillun got shoes; whether Sister Mary wore three links of chain, wove three links of chain, or merely had three links of chain. In the secular songs, where the singer is not under such strong personal emotion, this transcending of verbal meaning is not so noticeable.

The tradition of Negro folk-songs, like both their origin and structure, is badly mixed. If the Negro song owes a great deal of its origin to the white man's songs, it has not been without its counter influence on the white man. It would be impossible for the Negro to be in daily association with the white man for three centuries, in the field, on the construction job, in the kitchen, and in the nursery, without having some of his songs caught up and repeated by white people. The first time I heard "Alabama Bound" and "Dr. Cook's in Town," they were sung by white men on the vaudeville stage. "Casey Jones," which has been called a Negro creation (certainly the song is in extensive tradition among the Negroes) was once as much at home in the white man's vaudeville as on a "six-eight driver where he won his fame." When I first heard "Little David," it was sung by a college room-mate who had picked it up as a dance-song in the North Carolina mountains. Another mountaineer first made me acquainted with "Mourner, you Shall Be Free." Some of the old revival hymns, like "The Old-Time Religion," I have received from both white and Negro sources. The song, "Well de Good Book say dat Cain killed Abel," enters this collection *via* a Jewish student of the College of the City of New York, who taught it to me as a current campus song. He is the only person I ever heard sing it, yet the same song was reported by Professor Perrow as sung by Virginia Negroes. The well-known song of the Creation, beginning "Lord he thought he'd make a man," has come to me from several Negro sources, but the only times I have heard it sung were, first, by a lady who had learned it from students at the University of Alabama, and second, by several students of Randolph-Macon Woman's College, in Virginia, who did not seem to regard it in the least as pertaining exclusively to the Negro. "Swing Low, Sweet Chariot" was the favorite song of the fifth grade in the grammar school that I attended. As an undergraduate at Trinity College I used to help sing a popular baseball rally song which was introduced by one of the cheer-leaders as his own composition. With tactful variations in the fourth line, it ran as follows:

> Wake Forest, Wake Forest
> Yo' face mighty long dis mornin', dis mornin',
> Oh yo' face mighty long.
> — Yes, my God, it was put on wrong,
> This mornin', this evenin', so soon.

Years later, in Mr. Perrow's collection, I found its original. With Bre'r Rabbit for Wake Forest and ears for face, it was a Negro folk-song. Similarly the stanza:

> I'm a Tar Heel born, I'm a Tar Heel bred,
> And when I die I'm a Tar Heel dead,

sung for generations as a part of the regular University of North Carolina song, has a suspicious kinship to a number of stanzas printed in various Negro spirituals, in which the singer is sometimes Methodist "bawn" and sometimes Baptist.

Instances of this kind could be multiplied indefinitely. The "Keemo Kimo" refrain used in several Negro songs occurs also in a number of college and preparatory school "yells." The Montgomery *Advertiser* of April 4, 1916, contained an editorial pointing out that the "delightful essay in verse" which a writer in *Harper's Magazine* had found on the fly-leaf of one of Mark Twain's books and attributed to him, was in fact nothing but a well-known Negro stanza comparing the ladybug, firefly, and bedbug. Mr. Perrow's collection, already several times referred to, contains a considerable number of Negro songs sung by white people.

An attempt to account for all these circumstances would be hopeless. Some, doubtless, are the result of a common song ancestor. Others may be borrowings by the Negro, who is one of the best borrowers in the world. But some, beyond question, are borrowings by the white singers. However this may be, their significance in one respect is very plain and is emphasized by the other peculiarities of origin and nature exhibited by the Negro folk-song. They show that whoever undertakes to interpret the Negro from his songs must walk as delicately as Agag.

No true Southerner would ever be deterred by this consideration, however. Every Southern white man, as a well-known Southern speaker once remarked, considers himself an authority on the "Race Question." He knows that the Negro does not say all he means or mean all he says; he is aware of a secretive strain in the Negro which attempts to keep certain things strictly within the race. He may even suspect, what is certainly the truth, that the Negro knows the white man better than the white man knows the Negro. Nevertheless he feels that he "knows the Negro"; and, if there is anything in constant daily association for three centuries, he does, especially the things the Negro wants him to know. My own conviction of free grace in this field has wavered rather than increased in the twelve years since I first became interested in Negro folk-song, and the desire to evoke a clear picture of the folk Negro from his songs has yielded rather disastrously to minute annotations of the songs themselves. However, I am as a confident as ever that the songs reveal the singer, if they are only read aright. From time to time throughout this volume I have indulged myself in various comments on the character of the folk Negro. He is a person invincibly likable.

In his songs I find him, as I have found him elsewhere, a most naïve and unanalytical-minded person, with a sensuous joy in his religion; thoughtless, careless, unidealistic, rather fond of boasting, predominantly cheerful, but able to derive considerable pleasure from a grouch; occasionally suspicious, charitably inclined toward the white man, and capable of a gorgeously humorous view of anything, particularly himself.

II

RELIGIOUS SONGS

NOT all religious songs of the Negroes are spirituals, for the Negro sings the same songs that the white man sings, and he also has his chanted prayers and chanted sermons. Nor is spiritual the only name by which they have been called. They have sometimes been called plantation songs or melodies; and in Louisiana they have been called "mellows," a corruption of melodies, from plantation melodies. The recent extensive interest in these songs has fixed the word spiritual, however, as the commonly accepted word meaning Negro religious folk-song.

Travellers in the South and novelists of Southern life noticed the religious singing of the Negro from the earliest years of the nineteenth century down to the Civil War, but the first comment on the Negro religious songs as something distinctively a Negro possession occurs in a brief article called "Contraband Singing," signed C. W. D., published in *Dwight's Journal of Music* (Boston) in 1861. From that time on, their history may be found in the preceding chapter. At the present writing (August, 1927), the great recent interest in the spiritual shows no sign of abatement. Collections still come from the press. Last year an American opera based on the spiritual "Deep River" aroused considerable interest in New York; this year two plays of Paul Green and (within the last month) Ziegfeld's Follies, keep the spirituals alive on the New York dramatic stage.

Cast in the simplest of metrical patterns and clothed in the most beautiful folk melodies that America has produced, they richly deserve their popularity. They are valuable, not only as music, but as a complete expression of a race to whom religion is still more of a vital reality than to any other element of the American population.

The religion that the spirituals set forth is a very clear and definite one. It is at bottom the camp-meeting religion of the ante-bellum South, to some extent the revivalist religion of the South to-day — early nineteenth-century fundamentalism. To be sure, it has received some racial modifications. Seemingly, it is modified considerably by the great freedom with which a spiritual may allow itself to become mixed with other spirituals and with extraneous material;

but this appearance largely vanishes when we regard the stanza, and not the whole song, as the real unit. We are then able to evoke a very clear notion of the religious ideas underlying the song. The Negro has never been able, as fully as the white religious enthusiast of the early camp-meeting songs, to regard the jóyousness of present living as of no account; but he has adopted the great idea underlying many of the old hymns that this life is only a pilgrimage to eternity. Though he is at bottom too pagan for this idea to be much more than a convention, it is a very firm convention. Christians, as in the early religious songsters of white people, form a band of the elect, the "union band," who are journeying to heaven, their "souls set free" from sin.

The journey begins with the desire to be saved. "I wa-ant to go up dere," sing the elect and the mo'hner, with a yearning emphasis on the "want." "I want to go to heab'n and I want to go right." I have a mother, sister, brother, or deacon in the promised land or "way in de glory," whom I want to take by the hand. "If you get there before I do, Tell all my folks I'm a-comin' too." The backslider and the sinner are asked, "Don't you want to go to heaben?" and are urged to "come on," and "join in this band." In order to go, you must "lay down dis world" and "shoulder up" your cross; you must "keep yo' hand on de gospel plow." More specifically, you must "get all yo' business right," "get religion," "stop your tongue from telling lies," and "hold your light." You must know the way — "Show me the way, oh, show me the way."

Once "my feet been taken out de miry clay" (here the first personal pronoun takes a significant precedence of the second) I'm "on mah journey now." There is still "one wide river to cross," and old Satan, who is a "snake in the grass," "a liar and conjuror too," besets the path (as he did that of "John de Bunyan"). I may climb Jacob's ladder or travel over a "rough rocky road" as a pedestrian; a sweet chariot swings low to carry me home, or I take passage on the "Old Ship of Zion"; but if I go with the majority I go on the gospel train. There is even a "little black train," not a Jim Crow train, but "death's black train." When I enter heaven I am to be "all dressed in white."

"When I get dere," I know quite definitely what I am going to do. I am going to ride on "two white horses" or in "a golden chariot." I am going to "wear that starry crown," "walk and talk with Jesus," "set down 'side de Lamb an' Father Abraham," "eat at de welcome table," "jine de happy angel band," "set in de Kingdom and hear sweet Jordan roll." Fully accoutred with shoes, robe, derby, crown, and harp, I'm "gonna walk all over God's heab'n." Realizing an earthly aspiration to be a coachman or race rider, I shall "whip them golden horses." It is a heaven worth having. "Everybody talk about heab'n ain't goin' dere," but I have no doubt as to myself. Hell is another matter. It is "dark and dismus," but it is mainly a lurid warning to the sinner man who is sitting on its gates. The mourner is invited to "rise and tell" how he "shurned" it. The elect, climbing Zion's hill, mos' done sufferin', and with "good news" ringing in his ears, is not seriously worried by its threat, for he knows he has "come through," and that the "Lord's gonna meet you on half-way ground." But Hell is far from being something simply of the mind itself. It is approached by a road "fair and wide," a road kept fairly warm with people who "walk on the cross," liars, crap-shooters, drunkards, back-biters, and schemers. You can't scheme into heaven, you can't "shoot 'er" into heaven; "God 'll ketch you with no excuse."

As for the sinner, he had better row his boat one side. "Death comes slippin' in the house at night"; let him take warning. "Yo' house on fire" (here the pronoun changes back to the second person). "I'm goin' to leave you behind." In the Last Judgment, "when the first trumpet sound" and "when the rocks and the mountains shall all melt away," the elect will find a new hidin' place, but the sinner is asked, "What you goin' to do when the world's on fire?"

God is a much more indefinite figure than Satan; Jesus ("Marse" Jesus) is a baby chile, a companion, and a familiar friend, the driver of the heavenly chariot, the captain of the gospel ship, and conductor of the gospel train.

The spirituals are most solidly based upon "de good Book." The number of Biblical characters mentioned is more astonishing even than their actions. In the present collection we find Jacob, Moses, Noah, Jonah, David, the two Marys, Martha, Luke, John, Ananias and Sapphira, Cain, Abel, Daniel, Nicodemus, Paul, Silas, the "Hebrew children," John, Jesus, Joseph, Josiah, Ezekiel, and Pharaoh's daughter. Some of them are merely mentioned in passing or as witnesses "to my Lawd." Others are dealt with very erratically by the Negro memory and imagination. Mary's three links of chain are curiously unscriptural. The discovery of Moses by a young lady who stumped her toe looking for roses is a bit startling. John the Baptist and John the Apostle become amalgamated. Ezekiel's wheel becomes a childish marvel; Jonah is cast up very unorthodoxly in a "sweet 'tater patch." Cain kills Abel in what must have been a rough-house, with the leg of a table. Paul and Silas "had to run." Daniel spoke strange words in the lion's den. It becomes her own feet, instead of Christ's, that Mary washed — "and washed 'em clean." The stories of Creation, of the Ark, and of the Garden of Eden all receive graphic alterations.

It is not only in the Biblical incidents and characters of the spirituals that the Negro displays his fondness for reading and explaining the Bible. Many spiritual stanzas are based upon favorite texts. Anyone who will compare a large body of Negro spirituals with the books of Ezekiel, Isaiah, and Revelation will be astonished. I cite a few examples below, drawing upon some spirituals not found in this collection, but easily recognizable by anyone familiar with other collections.

Biblical Passages	*Spiritual Passages*
Ezekiel, xxxvii, 1–11. Thus saith the Lord God unto these bones; Behold, I shall cause breath to enter into you and ye shall live (5).	Dry bones gwine to rise again; Dese bones gwine rise again.
Ezekiel, i and x.	Zika made a wheel.
Daniel, ii, 34. Thou sawest that a stone was cut off without hands.	Daniel saw the stone.
2 Kings, ii, 1–11. Elijah's translation.	Swing low, sweet chariot, comin' for to carry me home.
Jeremiah, viii, 22. Is there no balm in Gilead; is there no physician there?	There is a balm in Gilead.
Jeremiah, xlvii, 3. At the rushing of his chariots and at the rumbling of his wheels.	I heard a mighty rumbling up in the sky Well it must have been my Lord a passing by.
Isaiah, xiii, 10. And the moon shall not cause her light to shine.	And the moon refuse to shine.
Isaiah, xlii, 10. We will sing unto him a new song. (Cf. Psalm xl, 3, Rev., v, 9, and xiv, 3.)	We will sing a new song.
Isaiah, ii, 10. Enter into the rock and hide thee in the dust. (Cf. Isaiah, ii, 20, 21.)	Hide me over in the Rock of Ages. Went down to the rock to hide my face.
Isaiah, vi, 11. Then said I, Lord, how long. — xxvii, 13. And it shall come to pass in that day that the great trumpet shall be blown. (Cf. also the seven successive trumpet blasts of destruction in Rev., viii and ix.)	Lord, how long shall I blow? What shall I do when the first trumpet sound?

Isaiah, x, 6. I will send him against an hypocritical nation.

Hypocrite, hypocrite, de Lawd despise.

Isaiah, lx, 1. Arise, shine, for thy light is come, and the glory of the Lord is risen upon thee.

Rise, shine and shout your jubilee.

Den my little soul gwine to shine shine.

Isaiah, *ad. lib.* Many verses beginning "In that day."

In that day.

2 Corinthians, v, 1. For we know that if our earthly house of this tabernacle were dissolved, we have a building of God, an house not made with hands.

Not made with hands.

I know I have another building.

2 Peter, iii, 10. But the day of the Lord will come as a thief in the night, in the which the heavens shall pass away with a great noise and the elements shall melt with fervent heat.

When de star from de elements is fallin'

Revelation, vi, 12, 13. And the sun became black as sack cloth of hair and the moon became as blood and the stars of heaven fell unto the earth. (Cf. also Isaiah, xiii, 10, xxiv, 23, and lxi, 19.)

An' de sun an' de moon dip in blood.

What you gwine do when de world's on fire?

Rev., vii, 13. What are these that are arrayed in white robes, and whence came they?

Who's that comin' all dressed in white?

Must be the children of the Israelite.

Rev., xix, 11. And I saw heaven opened and behold a white horse, and he that sat upon him was called Faithful and True. — Also xix, 14. And the armies which were in heaven followed him upon white horses.

I'm goin' to ride the milk-white horse.

Two white horses side by side

Them's the horses I'm a-gwine to ride.

Rev., xx, 12. And another book was opened which was the book of life. — xx, 15. And whosoever was not found written in the book of life was cast into the lake of fire.

My name's been written in de book of life.

Rev., xxii, 2. In the midst of the street of it and on either side of the river was there the tree of life.

Over all trees in Paradise
The Christians call it the tree of life.

Thus much of the folk Negro's religion is reflected by his religious songs. If we supplement the record of the songs by the accounts left by different observers, both the religion and the songs in which it is expressed should be more fully comprehended.

Bishop Asbury, the founder of American Methodism, left a voluminous journal in which he several times mentions the religious zeal and enthusiasm of the "blacks" during the period of his contact with them — the last third of the eighteenth century. His own body-servant sometimes exhorted, and it is a matter of record that he was not always regarded as inferior to the bishop. Lorenzo Dow, whose journal [1] constitutes such an interesting record of primitive Methodism from the early seventeen-nineties to 1816, often spoke to mixed audiences. He showed an interest in the condition of the Negroes, and in Savannah in 1802 spoke from the pulpit of the black preacher, Andrew, "he [that is, Andrew] being the only preacher in town." [2] The earliest reference to Negro religious singing that I have found occurs in Dow's account of a visit to New Orleans in 1816:

Governor C. invited me to dine — observed how many of his colored people were religious, and the satisfaction he took in hearing them *sing* [sic] and pray at devotion at night; one who was not religious was of more trouble on the plantation, than all the rest.[3]

It is evident from these excerpts that the Negro was religious long before the Methodists and Baptists undertook regular Negro missions.[4] But Black Andrew was at one time whipped from his flock in Savannah, and Fanny Kemble gives evidence both of the planters' opposition to religious instruction for Negroes and of their dawning realization of its value.[5] In the same passages and elsewhere she gives much stronger evidence of the interest the slaves held in religion. During all this century, however, and even to the present day (in the cases of a few ante-bellum left-overs) Negroes were freely accepted as members of the white churches. In slavery times a large proportion of the membership of the white Baptist and Methodist congregations were Negroes.

The efforts of Bishop Capers to secure special attention to Negro religious instruction were begun in South Carolina in 1821, and won the support of South Carolina planters in 1829. From the time, some years later, that the influence of these efforts came to be felt

[1] Lorenzo Dow, *History of Cosmopolite, or the Four Volumes of Lorenzo's Journal concentrated in One, containing his experience and travels from childhood to near his fortieth year, also his polemical writings*, etc. (3rd edition corrected and enlarged), Philadelphia, 1816.

[2] *Ibid.*, p. 124.

[3] *Ibid.*, p. 343.

[4] For further historical details, see Carter G. Woodson's *History of the Negro Church*, Washington, The Associated Publishers, 1921.

[5] Frances Anne Kemble, *Journal of a Residence on a Georgia Plantation in 1838-1839* (New York, 1863), pp. 57, 71, 90.

generally throughout the South, opposition to religious education for Negroes may be said to have become negligible. After the slave insurrections of the eighteen-twenties and thirties most of the slave states passed laws either forbidding the Negroes to preach or requiring the presence of at least one white man at every Negro religious gathering. Nevertheless, the Negroes could and did avail themselves of the fullest opportunities for religious expression, in meetings of their own, in the white man's church, and, most enthusiastically, in the white man's camp-meeting. In 1845 a South Carolina gentleman wrote proudly to Thomas Clarkson that a majority of Southern Methodists and Baptists were colored, and that "almost everywhere they have precisely the same opportunities of attending worship that the whites have, and besides, special occasions for themselves exclusively." [6]

Most of the earlier descriptions of Negro religious meetings in which white people participated stress the decorum with which they were conducted. A little later, when Negroes had churches of their own, they allowed themselves greater scope. A foreign observer thus describes one of the services he conducted in a Negro church:

The poor blacks manifested great feeling. . . . After the sermon the people sang some of their own peculiarly soft and mellow airs. This excited them and we had a remarkable scene. They leaped, I know not how high, and in a manner one would have thought impossible. But, more than this, they danced to their own melody, and in perfect time, and exhibited the signs of the most rapturous happiness.[7]

Two descriptions of Negro church services in the eighteen-eighties give fuller details. The first is a service in Tennessee as seen between 1880 and 1887 by William E. Barton, a Northern missionary; the second, as seen about 1883 by Clarence Deming, represents the religion of the Negroes of the Mississippi Bends, one of the most isolated groups of Southern Negroes. Though neither is typical of Negro church services to-day, which seek to be as much like those of white people as possible, both are representative of the services in which the spirituals developed and flourished:

The company has long been swaying back and forth in the rhythm of the preacher's chant, and now and then there has come a shout of assent to the oft-repeated text. Each time the preacher's almost incoherent talk becomes articulate in a shout, "I have trod de wine-press"; there

---

[6] *Two Letters on Slavery in the United States, addressed to Thomas Clarkson, Esq.*, by J. H. Hammond (Columbia, S. C., 1845), p. 25.

[7] James Dixon, D.D., *Personal Narrative of a Tour through a Part of the United States and Canada* (3rd edition, New York, 1850), p. 94.

are cries of "Yes!" "Praise de Lawd!" and "Glory!" from the Amen
corner, where sit the "praying brethern," and the Hallelujah corner,
where sit the "agonizing sistering." In the earlier demonstrations the
men rather lead, but from the time when Aunt Melinda cries out, "Neb-
bah mind de wite folks! My soul's happy! Hallelujah!" and leaps into
the air, the men are left behind. Women go off into trances, roll under
benches, or go spinning down the aisle with eyes closed and with arms
outstretched. Each shout of the preacher is the signal for some one else
to start; and, strange to say, though there are two posts in the aisle, and
the women go spinning like tops, I never saw one strike a post. I have
seen the pastor on a day when the house would not contain the multitude
cause the seats to be turned and take his position in the door with a third
of the audience inside and the rest without, and have heard him provoke
the most ecstatic response to a reference to his wife such as this, "O, I
love dat yaller woman out dar in dat buggy, but I love my Jesus bettah!"
I have seen the minister in grave danger of being dragged out of the pulpit
by some of the shouters, who in their ecstasy laid hands on him. I have
seen an old man stand in the aisle and jump eighty-nine times without
moving a muscle of his thin, parchment-like face, and without disturbing
the meeting.[8]

The services witnessed by Clarence Deming were equally vivid:

Next comes the sermon. The elder almost always opens in an apolo-
getic tone, deprecating his own physical condition. He is either "drefful
hoarse from a good deal of preachin'" or "a mighty bad cold got right
into de lung"; a "mool has kicked him," or some other ailment has made
him feel so badly that his auditors "mus' n't 'spect much dis time."
Then he chooses his text, usually from Job or from "de Book of de
Rebelations," the fiery metaphor of which is an inexhaustible mine for
the exhorters. Usually the sermon consists of a review of some of the
metaphorical pictures of the Scripture, which the preacher describes himself as seeing. As the frenzy grows on him he becomes louder in utterance
and more demonstrative in movement. He prances back and forth from
edge to edge of the platform, now with vibrating hands in air, now bend-
ing forward or leaping as high as he can toward the roof to express his
soaring exaltation. Perspiration pours in streams down his dusky skin.
At the end of every sentence he utters a loud, indescribable noise, half-
way between a snort and a groan, or drops his voice into a sort of paren-
thetical chant, made up of set phrases like "O what a sight!" or he gives
a tremendous snort, followed by a hissing expectoration. When I first
saw this amazing expectoration I supposed it due to a genuine cold; but
since then I have discovered that it is a studied embellishment of Negro
oratory in the Bends. All through the sermon the preacher is stimulated

---

[8] William Eleazar Barton, *Old Plantation Hymns*, etc. (Boston and New York, Lamson, Wolfe and Co., 1899), p. 41.

by the chants of the sisters, the shouts of the brethern, and a swaying, rhythmical movement which swings the whole congregation in unison. Particularly if the elder describes some figurative combat of his own with Satan, the shouts of "Gib it to him!" "Shoot him down!" and once, "Cut him wid a big razor!" urge on the preacher to combat and almost lift the roof. His sermon usually lasts a full hour, with a short interval about the middle of the discourse for rest, during which the congregation chant a hymn. Instead of closing with a peroration the sermon is finished off with a sort of anti-climax, the preacher's voice sinking suddenly from a yell to a few colloquial words, thanking his congregation for their attention and hoping his words will "beneficiate" them. Words must fail utterly to depict the absurd effect of this closing apology, or the combination of shouts, spitting, chants, and pastoral contortions which lend their peculiar emphasis to one of these negro discourses.[9]

At the present time such manifestations as these are most often met with at camp-meetings, baptizings, and protracted meetings. A contemporary baptizing in Louisiana is thus described by Mr. Kennedy:

Baptizings formerly took place in the river or bayou or stream of water that was nearest at hand; but of recent years nearly all the churches have pools dug in the churchyards, and they are filled with water at the appointed time, and the ceremonies are held on the grounds. The night before baptizing the "candidates for the pool" assemble before the church, and after much subdued humming and singing in chorus, one after another the candidates glide up the aisle, swaying in rhythmic dance-movements, murmuring the burden of some hymn tune in an undertone, until they reach the altar where the deacons and the elders are seated, and there they stand and relate their fantastic experiences to the congregation. After a while the harmonious monotony and the exacting rhythm exert their intoxicating power over the congregation and their emotion grows more intense as the narrations go on. Like the chorus of the ancient Greeks, their exclamations and responses lend poetic fervor and religious elation to the enactment of the archaic drama; and sometimes from a state of mild hysteria the condition resolves itself into an incoherent frenzy, with loud shouting, wild jumping, bench-walking, and acrobatic feats beyond belief.[10]

Shouting, which accompanies most of the meetings just described, is of two kinds. Sometimes it is a ceremony as described by a writer in the *Nation* for May 30, 1867.

[9] Clarence Deming, *By Ways of Nature and Life* (New York and London, G. P. Putnam's Sons, 1884), p. 361. Quoted by permission of the publishers.
[10] Robert Emmet Kennedy, *Black Cameos*, (New York, A. and C. Boni, 1924), p. xvii. Quoted by permission of the publishers.

When the "sperichil" is struck up, they begin first walking, and by and by shuffling around, one after the other, in a ring. The foot is hardly taken from the floor, and the progression is mainly due to a jerking, hitching motion, which agitates the entire shouter, and soon brings out streams of perspiration. Sometimes they dance silently, sometimes as they shuffle they sing the chorus of the spiritual, and sometimes the song itself is also sung by the dancers. But more frequently a band, composed of the best singers and of tired shouters, stands at the side of the room to "base" the others, singing the body of the song and clapping their hands together or on their knees.[11]

This form of shout, I believe, is not often to be met with to-day. A commoner form, however, has been general in camp-meetings, Holy Roller meetings, baptizings, and revivals from the early nineteenth century to the present time. In this form the shout is a strictly individual performance. Several of the redeemed may be shouting at the same time, but with no conception of team work. Whenever one of the audience is so overcome by the exhorter as to lose all self-control he may go into a frenzy of incoherent utterance, sometimes walking over the benches or falling on the floor and writhing, with frequent loud exclamations such as "Saved," "Safe in Jesus," "Redeemed," "Mount Zion," "O Lordy," "Holy Ghost," or "Hallelujah." Some of these shouts are preserved in the spirituals as refrains or exclamations at the end of lines. They need not always be strictly appropriate. A story is told of one colored sister at a baptizing near Augusta, Georgia, who came up from the water, dazed from too long immersion, shouting "Christmas Gift!"

But what of the spiritual during this development of Negro religious practice which has just been sketched? Up to the eighteen-sixties we have had some mention of Negro religious singing, but little of spirituals as something peculiar to the Negro; after 1860 we hear a great deal of Negro spirituals. It would seem that the testimony at this point requires a little closer scrutiny.

A New England Latin professor, who visited Negro congregations in Baltimore in 1836, was deeply impressed with their singing, but failed to mention any difference between the hymns themselves and those of the white people, a point in common with the references already given from Lorenzo Dow and Fanny Kemble.[12] Nehemiah Adams, a Boston minister who visited the South in 1854, remarks on

[11] Quoted by Charles Lincoln Edwards, *Bahama Songs and Stories* (Boston and New York, Houghton, Mifflin and Co., 1895), p. 108.

[12] E. A. Andrews, *Slavery and the Domestic Slave Trade in the United States*, Boston, 1836.

the way in which the hymns (those of Watts being the favorites) were always lined out to the Negro congregation, two lines at a time, from memory,[13] a practice also recorded of prayer meetings by Mrs. Schoolcraft.[14] In 1854 John Russell commented on the special delight of the Negroes in "spiritual songs and hymns" sung in country churches of mixed congregation. "The favorite subjects are Jordan's banks and the happy land to which the singers are travelling."[15] An English war correspondent refers to the same songs, sung by his Negro rowers, as "wild Baptist chants about the Jordan, in which they delight."[16]

Thus it would seem that at this interesting point the Negro was singing both regular hymns and "wild Baptist chants"; also that his hymns were lined out to him from memory, two lines at a time. The lining out was a common practice among white congregations in the eighteenth and early nineteenth centuries. It was adopted from the white people by the Negroes, and was much more important for the Negro because of his difficulty with the language and his inability to read. Some of the Negro spirituals to-day seem to be only composites of unrelated two-line stanzas, probably as a result of the old lining-out process. The contemporaneous existence of regular hymns and "wild chants" has always been true of the religious songs of both Negroes and white people. With the white people the "wild chants" were camp-meeting songs, which were seldom even printed and which faded into the background with the decline of camp-meetings; with the Negroes they flourished long after their use among the whites was relegated to the backwoods. Less illiterate songs of this type, however, were frequently printed for use in the religious meetings of the whites. They were called "spiritual songs." Almost all the hymn-books of the evangelical and dissenting sects of the whites prior to 1860 were called "hymns and spiritual songs"; the spiritual songs being of a much more informal character and occupying a separate section in the back of the hymn-book. They are the songs which John Russell, in the passage quoted above, says were the favorites of the Negro communicants. Here, undoubtedly, we have the origin of the word "spiritual" as applied to Negro songs, and here, too, begins to take form a suspicion that the connection of the Negro spiritual with the more

13 Nehemiah Adams, *A Southside View of Slavery, or Three Months in the South in 1854* (Boston, 1854), p. 54.

14 Mrs. Henry R. Schoolcraft, *The Black Gauntlet: A Tale of Plantation Life in South Carolina* (Philadelphia, 1860), p. 419.

15 John Russell, *The Hireling and the Slave* (Charleston, 1854), p. 97.

16 William H. Russell, *My Diary North and South* (Boston, 1863), p. 207.

primitive forms of the white man's religion in the nineteenth century
is considerably stronger than is generally realized. Any attempt to
see clearly the background of the Negro spiritual must take into
consideration the religious practice of the Southern white man during the first half of the nineteenth century. Once this is done, a
number of traits in the Negro spiritual assume a decidedly un-
Ethiopian aspect.

Starting with religious meetings a little before the beginning of the
century, let us compare a few extracts from the journal of Lorenzo
Dow with the accounts of Negro meetings already quoted. Here is
an impression of a meeting in 1796:

> Here, after S. Hutchinson had finished his sermon, J. Mitchell began to
> exhort, when there commenced a trembling among the wicked; one, and
> a second, and a third, fell from their seats; and the cry for mercy became
> general; and many of the backslidden professors were cut to the quick;
> and I think for eleven hours there was no cessation of the loud cries; no
> business of a temporal nature could be done at this quarterly meeting
> conference. . . . In this love feast the cry began again and continued till
> within two hours of sun-setting.[17]

In 1803 or 1804 Dow first encountered the "jerks," in eastern
Tennessee. "I began to speak to a vast audience, and I observed
about thirty to have the *jerks;* though they strove to keep still as
they could, these emotions were involuntary, and irresistible." [18]
When Dow preached at Knoxville on February 19, "the Governor
being present," about a hundred and fifty appeared to have the
jerking exercise," one of whom "had them powerfully; and I believe
he would have fallen over three times had not the auditory been so
crowded that he could not, unless he fell perpendicularly." Quakers,
who had opposed the jerks, had them "as keen and powerful as any
I had seen, so as to have occasioned a kind of grunt or groan when
they would jerk."

I have passed by a meeting house [he comments the day after this
meeting], where I observed the undergrowth had been cut up for a camp-
meeting, and from 50 to 100 saplings left breast high; which to me appeared so slovenish that I could not but ask my guide the cause, who
observed that they were topped so high, and left for the people to jerk by:
this so excited my attention that I went over the ground to view it; and
found where the people had laid hold of them and jerked so powerfully,
that they had kicked up the earth as a horse stamping flies.[19]

[17] Dow, *History of Cosmopolite*, etc., p. 51.
[18] *Ibid.*, p. 182.   [19] *Ibid.*, p. 183.

Bishop Capers, who was the founder of Methodist missions among slaves, thus describes a revival at which he was present in his youth, in South Carolina:

But what was most remarkable both at this camp-meeting and the following one, a year afterwards (1803), as distinguishing them from the present meeting of 1806, and much more from later camp-meetings, was the strange and unaccountable bodily exercises which prevailed there. In some instances, persons who were not before known to be at all religious, or under any particular concern about it, would suddenly fall to the ground, and become strangely convulsed with what was called the jerks; the head and neck, and sometimes the body also, moving backwards and forwards with spasmodic violence, and so rapidly that the plaited hair of a woman's head might be heard to crack. This exercise was not peculiar to feeble persons, nor to either sex, but, on the contrary, was most frequent to the strong and athletic, whether man or woman. I never knew it among children, nor very old persons. In other cases, persons falling down would appear senseless, and almost lifeless, for hours together; lying motionless at full length on the ground, and almost as pale as corpses. And then there was the jumping exercise, which sometimes approximated dancing; in which several persons might be seen standing perfectly erect, and springing upward without seeming to bend a joint of their bodies.[20]

In his "Songs and Rhymes from the South," Professor E. C. Perrow describes a typical religious meeting of the Southern mountaineers, our "contemporary ancestors" who have preserved the folk ways of the whites almost as faithfully as the Negroes:

At least once a year, every church has a big "meetin'." The preacher usually delivers, on these occasions, an interminable amount of what seems to the uninitiated a mass of emotional rant. If there is more than one preacher present, each of them is expected to preach a sermon. I have known services to last from half-past ten to half-past two on Sundays. Sometimes the evening services are prolonged until nearly daybreak. Sometimes two or three exhorters are talking at one time. Often the sermons are not very intelligible; but the seed falls on good ground, and soon the whole congregation is in an uproar of religious frenzy. I have seen, at these meetings, dozens of people on the floor at one time wildly gesticulating, and at the top of their voices shouting the praises of the Lord. This sort of thing is kept up for hours, usually until the shouters, especially the women, are exhausted almost to the point of fainting,

---

[20] William M. Wightman, D.D., *Life of William Capers, D.D., One of the Bishops of the Methodist Episcopal Church, South; including an Autobiography* (Nashville, Tenn., Southern Methodist Publishing House, 1859), pp. 53–54 in Autobiography.

although fainting is an accomplishment of which these sturdy mountain-women know little.[21]

Here we may well pause, recall the accounts of Negro religious observances given in the preceding pages and wonder (or shall we wonder?) just how much of the orgiastic emotionalism which we commonly consider typical of Negro religion came from Africa and how much from the white brethren from whom the religion was derived. The white man of to-day might very well modify his tone of patronage toward the Negro's religious primitivism; it is mainly his own last year's clothes. I can well fancy old Alonzo Dow, back from the days of the Great Awakening, exclaiming, "Who been here since I been gone?" And the answer is, the colored brother, with his lamp still trimmed and a-burnin'.

If the framework and setting of the Negro spiritual smack so strongly of the white man in the woodpile, we may well carry the comparison further. Going back to the songs that the white man sang at the religious occasions described above (and be it remembered, the Negro was always there, too, singing with him), are the songs like the Negro spirituals in their ideas and form, are they in any cases the same songs, and do they have stanzas in common? Since the Negro often worshipped at white churches where regular hymns were used instead of spiritual songs, do his spirituals preserve any traces of the hymns?

The most folksy of all the religious folk-songs of white people in the early nineteenth century were seldom written at all. They were a folk possession, perfectly well-known by all true professors; and besides, why print songs for congregations the majority of whom cannot read? Moreover, there is more than a suspicion that most editors of religious songsters, like John C. Totten, the editor of a *Selection of Hymns and Spiritual Songs — as Usually Sung at Camp-Meetings* (19th edition in 1827, New York) bore down a little consciously on the selection, not wishing to include ungrammatical and undignified songs which everyone knew, anyhow. However, the spiritual songs that were deemed worthy of print carry much the same expressions that the Negro spirituals do, and differ from the regular hymns in exactly the same way. Turning back to the previous exposition of the content of Negro spirituals and comparing it with the songs contained in the many religious songsters of the early nineteenth cen-

---

[21] E. C. Perrow, "Songs and Rhymes from the South," in *Journal of American Folklore* (1913), xxvi, 145-146.

tury,[22] we find in the latter the same emphasis on the heavenly
journey, the union band, and freedom in the sense of freedom from
sin. The backslider and the "witness" occur constantly in the same
way as in the Negro spirituals. The gospel plough, the gospel ship,
the gospel train, the wily Satan, the chariots, the angel band, the
relatives in the promised land, the Judgment Day — all are in the
"spiritual songs" and revival songs sung by white people in the
early nineteenth century. "Such expressions as 'Cross Jordan,'
'O Lord remember me,' 'I'm going home,' 'There's room enough in
Heaven for you,' we find abundantly in Methodist hymn books,"
wrote the editors of the first collection of Negro spirituals.[23] Even
the white robes and the white horses exist in the white man's spirituals, and the shoes on which the Negro walks all over God's
heaven are really the shoes of faith which we encounter in *Zion
Songster* (1827) in the following lines:

> What kind of shoes are those you wear
> On which you boldly stand?

The similarity of structure is so marked in many of the songs that
it is necessary only to refer the reader to the several songs reprinted
from old religious songsters in the appendix to this volume. There
is also a marked similarity in the Biblical basis of the two groups of
songs. The spiritual songs of the white people prefer much the same
sections of the Bible as those of the Negroes; they differ from the
regular hymns, just as the Negro spirituals do, in a much greater
emphasis upon the Apocalypse, the personal devil, and the narrative
parts of the Old Testament.
    Also, they improvise in the same way. In the old camp-meeting
song, "Canaan, Bright Canaan," which is attributed to John Moffit,
about 1829,

the hymn lines were either improvised or picked up miscellaneously from
memory, the interline, "I am bound for the land of Cana-an," occurring
between every two. John Wesley's "How Happy is the Pilgrim's Lot"
was one of the snatched stanzas swept into the current of the song. An
example of the tune-leader's improvisations to keep the hymn going was,

---

[22] Such as William Walker, *The Southern Harmony and Musical Companion*, new
edition, Philadelphia, 1847; J. D. Cates, *The Sacred Harp*, Philadelphia, 1867; *The
Christian's Companion*, n. d., but printed before 1836; Leavitt's *Christian Lyre*, 1830;
William Hunter's *Minstrel of Zion*, 1845; *The Revivalist*, Philadelphia, 1868; *Zion
Songster*, 2nd edition, 1827; etc.
[23] William Francis Allen, *Slave Songs of the United States* (New York, 1867), p. ix.

> If you get there before I do, —
>   I am bound for the land of Cana-an!
> Look out for me, I'm coming too —
>   I am bound for the land of Cana-an! [24]

Professor Perrow has recorded his observation of a similar improvised extension of "The Old Time Religion" at a "big meetin'" of
mountain whites;[25] and an ante-bellum novelist has shown the
same practice among the slaves in the following account of a funeral:

All night the Negroes watched over her body, singing, in choral
strains, of the triumph of redeeming love. They even added another
verse to the immemorial hymn of good old Daniel, enrolling Dilsy among
the immortal worthies who have entered the promised land, —

> Where now is good old Dilsy?
> Where now is good old Dilsy?
> Where now is good old Dilsy?
>   Safely in the promised land, etc.[26]

This is the same song as "Where Are Now the Hebrew Children?"
quoted by Brown and Butterworth [27] as an old camp-meeting song
of the white people.

The presence of so much improvising is perhaps one reason why
so few of the Negro spirituals are traceable in their entirety to
spiritual songs of the white people. The editors of *Slave Songs* noted
that "Climb Jacob's Ladder" was to be found in the song-books [28]
and that the second part of "Go in the Wilderness" was "the
familiar Methodist hymn, 'Ain't I Glad I Got Out of the Wilderness.'" [29] Professor Louise Pound has traced another to an early
camp-meeting song of the white people.[30] To these may be added
the "Negro Battle Hymn" included in successive editions of the
spirituals published by the Hampton Institute, and edited by
Thomas P. Fenner. It is found in the 1847 edition of *The Southern
Harmony and Musical Companion* (p. 301) as "The Trumpeters,"
and also in *The Christian's Companion* (p. 288) minus the refrain
and with additional stanzas, the only difference being that where

---

[24] Theron Brown and Hezekiah Butterworth, *The Story of the Hymns and their
Tunes* (New York, 1906), p. 273.

[25] *J. A. F. L.*, xxvi, 148.

[26] Caroline Lee Hentz, *The Planter's Bride* (Philadelphia, 1854), p. 55.

[27] *Op. cit.*, p. 270. The song is printed in Appendix III to this volume, p. 429.

[28] W. F. Allen, *Slave Songs of the United States*, p. xviii.

[29] *Ibid.*, p. 4.

[30] The Ancestry of a "Negro Spiritual," *Modern Language Notes*, 1918, xxxiii, 442–
444.

the Negro song has "We want no cowards in our band," the song of
the whites has, very significantly, "tories" for "cowards." There
are also a number of songs, like "The Old Ship of Zion," "A Great
Camp Meeting," "Put John on the Island," "Where Now are the
Hebrew Children?" and "The Old Time Religion," which have always been used as camp-meeting or spiritual songs by both races,
and are still so used.

Rather frequent examples occur in the spirituals, of passages from
regular hymns that have been absorbed piecemeal. These stanzas
have almost all been taken two lines at a time or four lines at a time,
mixed with material from other hymns or from spirituals, and broken
up by the use of interlines and refrains, in a way that suggests very
definitely how the hymns were first learned, by lining out. This
suggestion is borne out by the fact that some of the hymn fragments
thus adopted into the Negro spiritual appeared in the ante-bellum
hymnals of the whites and have since been dropped, except by the
Negroes. Illustrations from the present collection are numbers
51A and B and number 86. I note the same phenomenon in most of
the other collections, particularly in Barton's. In Barton's collection and in one volume each of the Fisk University and Hampton
Institute collections (Marsh, 1877, and Fenner, 1901), a very cursory examination reveals over thirty such fragments.

Not to tax the reader's patience with too many tables of parallel
passages, let us consider only the mutations of one of Watts's hymns,
the first stanza of which occurs twice without alteration in a spiritual
in Barton's collection (pp. 27 and 29):

> Am I a soldier of the cross,
>   A follower of the Lamb,
> And shall I fear to own his cause
>   Or blush to speak his name?

In another spiritual in the same collection (p. 27) only the first and
third lines of this stanza are used. In still another (p. 7) the following arrangement occurs:

> Am I a soldier of the cross
> Am I a soldier of the cross
> Am I a soldier of the cross
>   A follower of the Lamb?

followed by three stanzas similarly composed of the first two lines of
stanzas two, three, and four of Watts's hymn. In the Fisk University spirituals we find:

> Am I a soldier of the cross,
> When death shall shake this frame
> Or must I count this soul as lost
> When death shall shake this frame? [31]

and the same two lines, in another spiritual (p. 214) with "Yes, My Lord," for the interline. The most frequent of all echoes from this hymn, however, is the first line alone, which occurs in almost all the collections of spirituals. Other hymns most constantly echoed in similar manner are "Amazing Grace," "I'll be There," Jesus my All to Heaven is Gone," "When I Can Read my Title Clear," "Happy Day," "Alas and Did my Saviour Bleed," and "Onward Ride in Triumph, Jesus." These echoes, taken together, prove the truth of the observers who, in describing the lining out of hymns by the slaves, remarked that the hymns of Watts and Wesley were favorites.

The same freedom of arrangement and adaptation shown by the Negroes in the use of hymn lines is found also in the camp-meeting songs of the white people, though in the latter case it is more generally the folk-song stanza rather than the hymn-fragment that is so used. Nevertheless, the practice in both cases is the same.

At length we come to the question, how many passages in the Negro spirituals have been taken from the "spiritual songs" of the white people. Here, where it would at first seem that demonstration should be easiest, a considerable difficulty is encountered. Not that such parallels do not exist; on the contrary, they are fairly plentiful; but the clearness of the connection thus far establishes an expectation that more of such parallels should exist than are to be found. Some thirty or forty such parallels I can establish from half a dozen such books as *Zion Songster, The Revivalist, The Christian Lyre, The Christian Psalmist*, and *The Southern Harmony and Musical Companion*. Such specimens as the following occur, either identically or with characteristic variations, in a number of Negro spirituals:

> Oh he's taken my feet from the mire and clay
> And he's placed them on the rock of ages.

> I hope to praise him when I die
> And shout salvation as I fly.

> This world is not my home,
> This world is not my home,
> This world is all a wilderness,
> But heaven is my home.

---

[31] J. B. T. Marsh, *The Story of the Jubilee Singers, with their Songs* (London, 1877), p. 164.

I have some friends before me gone
And I'm resolved to follow on.

Who are those arrayed in white?

I am bound for the land of Canaan

If you get there before I do
Look out for me, I'm coming too.

These and other lines occur in the "spiritual songs" in various
combinations and with various interlines, just as they (and the
hymn-fragments also) occur in Negro spirituals. A more common
phenomenon, however, is illustrated by such stanzas from the
"spiritual songs" as

The tree of life my soul has seen
Loaded with fruits and always green;

and

What kind of shoes are those you wear
On which you boldly stand,

which, in the spirituals, become

Over all trees in Paradise
The Christians call it the tree of life;

and

What kind o' shoes you goin' to wear?
Golden slippers!

Such stanzas have almost "crossed over," to use a Negro expression,
with reverse intention. There are many others like them, and there
are still more, undoubtedly, which have crossed over so completely
as to be no longer recognizable under their original color. These
passages, originally colloquial, are not nearly so easy to isolate in a
colloquial *milieu* as the bits from regular hymns. Even in their
original habitat they are not definitely fixed and immutable. When
adopted into Negro song they were rapidly changed by the dialect,
by the habit of improvising which was part and parcel both of the
white revival song and of Negro song-habit, by the limited memory
and knowledge of the slave, and by the racial carelessness of verbal
meaning which often converted Noah into Norah, Nicodemus into
Nigger Demus, Sapphira into Sapphias, "live-a humble" into "live
a humbug," and under Major Higginson's direct observation during
the Civil War, "gird on the armor" into "guide on de army." When
"Sister Mary took a hop out de willow tree" and "hopped right
over into Galilee" the real hop was only from the New Testament

to the 137th psalm, where "we hanged our harps on the willow tree."
Still another difficulty is the fact that most of the cruder religious
songs of the white people do not exist in printed form. The reten-
tion in the spirituals of so many expressions from the spiritual songs
and revival songs of the white people is clear evidence, under these
conditions, of the many more that must have been there originally.
"Their tunes are all psalm tunes and the words are from hymn
books," said a Richmond slave-holder to William Cullen Bryant in
March, 1843.[32]

At this point, at least in my own mind, the last element of doubt
concerning the origin and development of the Negro spiritual vanishes. The identity of the word spiritual with the "spiritual song"
of the white people, the identity of the religious background of the
two in practice, the presence to-day of revival songs in both groups
which have been in both groups from the first, the peculiar use of
hymn-fragments in the spirituals, the continued existence in the
spirituals of fragments from the old revival songs of the white people,
the sporadic cases of old spiritual songs of the whites that have survived in the Negro spirituals after being forgotten by white people —
all these facts lead to the inevitable conclusion that the Negro spiritual is simply a continuation and development of the white spiritual.

Before 1860, apparently, there was no remarkable difference between the words sung by the Negroes and whites, or some of the
observers who commented on the different *singing* of the Negroes
would have commented on the difference in what was sung. The
word "spirituals" did not apply particularly to Negro songs because it was still somewhat in use by the whites for similar songs.
The missionary activity of the Methodists and Baptists among the
Negroes, at its height during the period 1830–1850, spread the kind
of songs that missionaries generally spread among simple and illiterate people. The lapse of time before 1860 gave plenty of opportunity
for the Negro spiritual to develop variations, at the same time that
the white man was tending away from the main body of his spiritual
songs. The Northern welfare workers who took up the spiritual in
the eighteen-sixties as an instrument of propaganda were further
away from the white spirituals than Southern white people were;
furthermore, they were looking for something else. Thus they made
the honest, characteristic mistake of assuming the fundamental

---

[32] *Prose Writings of William Cullen Bryant.* Edited by Parke Godwin. New York:
D. Appleton & Co., 1901, II, 26. Bryant also quotes two secular songs in describing
a South Carolina corn-shucking, pp. 31–33. These were called to my attention by my
colleague, Dr. Jay B. Hubbell.

originality of the Negro spiritual. They had to, or what would have become of their preconceived notion that the Negro was constantly singing of his desire for freedom and that the Negro spiritual was the "sorrow-song" of slavery? As a matter of fact, the very catechisms compiled expressly for the Negroes by such Methodist and Baptist ministers as William Capers and E. T. Winkler contained the same references to freedom — from sin — that the spirituals of both races contained; and among the thousands of Negro songs that I have read I have encountered less than a dozen songs,[33] several of which appear to have been composed *for* the Negro, which contain unequivocal references to the desire for freedom from physical slavery. The folk Negro was never so foolish as his benefactors thought him, even in the first flush of emancipation.

It thus becomes plain why it is that some of the religious songs of the mountain whites [34] contain stanzas found in the Negro spirituals (though there are very few Negroes in the mountains) and not found in the religious songs sung by other white people to-day. The mountaineers were simply conserving their own. And the most puzzling of all the books of spirituals, Marshall W. Taylor's *Revival Hymns and Plantation Melodies*,[35] becomes a little less of an enigma to the student of Negro folk-song. According to his introduction, Taylor's songs are of two classes: (1) revival songs sung in white congregations and memorized and altered by Negro singing, and (2) "Plantation songs," that is, songs sung by the Negroes on the plantations, also religious. The first group he says he learned from his mother, a former slave. He neglected to isolate the Negro songs and he ignored the dialect, with the result that the two groups are utterly indistinguishable. Some may be definitely pronounced not Negro, but few can be definitely classified as not white. The book is more like *The Revivalist* than like any collection of spirituals. The answer

---

[33] Namely, *Kingdom Coming* (IV, no. 27 in this collection); *Freedom Over Me* (Barton, 1899, p. 25; Marsh, 1877; Fenner, 1906, p. 114); *Babylon Is Fallen* (Fenner, 1901, p. 76; referred to by Barton, 1899); *Before I'd Be a Slave* (J. W. Work, 1915, p. 2); *No More Auction Block for Me* (Marsh, 1877, p. 146; Fenner, 1901, p. 95); *Massa Gwine to Sell us Tomorrow* (Fenner, 1901, p. 86); and the *My Ole Massa Promised Me* songs (IV, no. 2 in this collection). Of these songs the first two were written by Henry C. Work, a white abolitionist, as war songs and did not take a very lasting hold upon popular tradition. Indeed the only traditional version of *Babylon Is Fallen* which I have seen has no apparent connection with freedom. I have never encountered *Bobolishun's Coming* except for a reference to it by Barton in 1899. Krehbiel (p. 17) has pointed out that the musical basis of *Freedom Over Me* is two popular white tunes, one of them *The Battle Cry of Freedom*. Such songs, therefore, are not only few in number and tenuous in tradition, but suspicious in origin.

[34] See E. C. Perrow, *J. A. F. L.*, xxvi, 145–148.

[35] Cincinnati, Marshall W. Taylor and W. C. Echols, 1882.

is both simple and easy. The songs are indistinguishable in the book, without the aid of dialect, because without dialect they were so in actual fact.

The "spiritual song" of the white people still lives, after a fashion. It is no longer the folk-possession of whole communities, but it is vigorously alive in the various manila-bound volumes of religious songs used in revival meetings. A volume of such songs popular in the eighteen-nineties [36] contains many of the old familiar phrases, slightly altered, the same familiar methods of developing songs from stock lines with interline refrains and of varying stanzas by the variation of only a small number of words. The book still in use by two popular Southern revivalists [37] contains "The Old Ship of Zion," "The Old Time Religion," "Old Fashioned Grace," "Outshine the Sun," "Life's Railway to Heaven," "I Have a Mother in the Promised Land," etc. One song (No. 306) illustrates the old method of repetition, with slight successive variations, better than any of the older songs I have seen. This song ("words and music by Robert Matthews, copyright 1915 by William J. Ramsay") begins:

> My religion's not depending on the weather, Lord,
>   let it rain
> Chorus: I'm glad we're all here together, Lord,
>   let it rain, Lord, let it rain, Lord,
>   let it rain.

In the next four stanzas simply substitute *praying, singing, blessing,* and *coming* for religion, and *his* for *my* in the last two stanzas, and we have the complete hymn of one hundred and forty-five words, with only six verbal variations! [38] Mr. Ham, according to the newspapers, has several times relieved drought-stricken communities by producing rain.

The fact that the Negro spiritual is an outgrowth of the revival

---

[36] Sankey, etc., *Gospel Hymns*, numbers 5 and 6 combined, Bigelow and Maine Co., 1892.

[37] *The Ham-Ramsay Revival Hymns: A collection of high class Gospel Music for use in Evangelical Meetings, Church Services, Sunday School and Young People's Societies,* edited and compiled by William J. Ramsay; Associate Editor, Evangelist M. F. Ham, William J. Ramsay, Chattanooga, Tennessee; n. d., but contains songs copyrighted individually as late as 1917.

[38] In their town churches the Negroes make rather extensive use of similar volumes under such titles as *Heavenly Praises, Gates of Praise, The Perfect Praise, Gems of Love,* and *Notes of Gold.* In some of these volumes I find songs very much like the spirituals. There is also a more fugitive type of religious song-book, generally composed or compiled by irregular Negro preachers and revivalists for their own use, which contains a good deal of material in every way very similar to the spirituals, showing that the production of Negro spirituals is still going on. See Appendix II.

song of the white people does not mean that it was not subject to other influences, nor does it explain the manner in which individual songs originate. The spiritual sometimes borrows stanzas from secular songs, though not nearly so often as it lends. A few of the spirituals show traces of the early minstrels; but the spirituals as a whole are much less subject to outside influences than any other type of Negro song.

Numbers 7, 10B, and 25 in this chapter seem to show an influence from the minstrel stage on the spirituals. Also the humorous treatment of Noah in the old minstrel "Creation Song" may have set the key for III, no. 30, V, no. 25, XIII, no. 17, and similar songs in this collection. On the other hand, several conventional spiritual expressions occur in the minstrel songs; for example, "Good News, Hark, good news," [39] "Ring dem Bells," [40] "Jordan is a Hard Road to Travel." [41] In the Negro Singers' Own Book, the song "A Few Days" (p. 96) has all the earmarks of a complete spiritual, with the chorus:

> For I've a home out yonder; few days, few days!
> For I've a home out yonder; I am going home.
> For I can't stay in the wilderness; few days, few days!
> For I can't stay in the wilderness; I am going home.

It seems plain enough that in these cases the influence was from the spirituals to the minstrels. Incidentally this shows that during the eighteen-forties and fifties the Negro spiritual had assumed sufficiently definite form to attract some slight attention from the minstrels as something characteristic of the Negro.

As to the individual origins, there are two methods, both well authenticated by observers. Mr. James Weldon Johnson gives an account of one of these, that of individual composition. [42] Spirituals were composed by regular bards who spread them from congregation to congregation. "Singing" Johnson was one of these composers whose methods James Weldon Johnson describes. Mr. Kennedy gives a similar account of spirituals in Louisiana, adding that when the songs become popular they are printed by the authors and sold as "ballets." [43] The ballet writers are common all over the South

---

[39] Negro Singers' Own Book, 1846 (?), p. 150, and Christy's Nigga Songster, n. d., p. 150.

[40] Negro Singers' Own Book, pp. 111, 173, 425.

[41] George Christy and Woods Melodies, copyright 1854, p. 66.

[42] James Weldon Johnson, The Book of American Negro Spirituals (New York, The Viking Press, 1925), pp. 21–23.

[43] Robert Emmet Kennedy, Black Cameos (New York, A. and C. Boni, 1924), p. xxiii. For specimens of such "ballets," see Appendix II.

and do not always confine their writing to spirituals. When their songs are new, it is fairly easy to tell them from the other spirituals. Spirituals in this collection which are probably of ballet origin are numbers 6, 15, 24, 85, and 86.

The other method of origin is that of communal composition. A particular song might take its origin from a chanted prayer or sermon, several of which are given in this collection. The process was thus explained to Mrs. Murphy by an old Negro:

We'd all be at de Prayers House de Lord's Day and de preacher he'd 'splain de word and read whar Ezekiel done say —

"Dry bones ter lib ergin."

And, honey, de Lord would come a-shinin' thoo dem pages and revive dis ole nigger's heart, and I'd jump up dar and den and holler and shout and sing and pat, and dey would all catch de words and I'd sing it some ole shout song I'd heard 'em sing from Africa, and dey'd all take it up and keep at it, and keep a-addin' to it, and den it would be a speribuals.[44]

Mrs. Burlin describes the same process as she observed it in Virginia:

Service had already begun before we came and the congregation, silent and devout, sat in rows on rough, backless benches. The preacher now exhorted his flock to prayer and the people with one movement surged forward from the benches and down onto their knees, every black head deep-bowed in an abandonment of devotion. Then the preacher began in a quavering voice a long supplication. Here and there came an uncontrollable cough from some kneeling penitent or the sudden squall of a restless child; and now and again an ejaculation, warm with entreaty, "O Lord!" or a muttered "Amen, Amen," — all against the background of the praying, endless praying.

Minutes passed, long minutes of strange intensity. The mutterings, the ejaculations, grew louder, more dramatic, till suddenly I felt the creative thrill dart through the people like an electric vibration, that same half-audible hum arose, — emotion was gathering atmospherically as clouds gather — and then, from the depths of some "sinner's" remorse and imploring came a pitiful little plea, a real Negro "moan," sobbed in musical cadence. From somewhere in that bowed gathering another voice improvised a response: the plea sounded again, louder this time and more impassioned: then other voices joined in the answer, shaping it into a musical phrase: and so, before our ears, as one might say, from this mol-

---

[44] Jeannette Robinson Murphy, *Southern Thoughts for Northern Thinkers* (New York, Bandanna Publishing Co., 1904), p. 23.

ten metal of music a new song was smithied out, composed then and there by no one in particular and by every one in general.[45]

This communal composition was the same process that Mr. Perrow observed among the Southern mountaineers, except that in his case it was a matter of adding new stanzas to an old song. But the difference is not so great as it appears, for the spontaneous generation of song within a folk-group must follow the channels already marked out for songs of that group if the group is to take part in its generation. Much of the actual material spontaneously produced might come from the folk memory and be, in the final analysis, not even original with the folk who produced it spontaneously. An excellent example of this is the lines:

> Matthew, Mark, Luke and John
> Killed Old Lead and home he run.
> Old Lead was eat and Tom was beat
> And Mary ran brawling down the street.

This stanza was given to Miss Scarborough by Hatcher Hughes as an improvisation about an occurrence which took place immediately before the song was composed.[46] Yet there is nothing really original about it; the first line is part of a traditional English folk-rhyme quoted by Wordsworth in "The Redbreast" in 1834, and the rest is "Tom, Tom, the Piper's Son," from Mother Goose.

Mr. J. W. Work has given the circumstances under which about a dozen of the better-known spirituals are said to have originated, with the statement that others have known origins "just as romantic." [47] The trouble is that the origins are too romantic; nearly all of them deal with escaping slaves or slaves bowed down with the cruelty of some particular persecution. No doubt the narrators believed their own stories. They "gin the tale as 't was gin to them." But some of them are improbable from the very circumstances. How is a slave mother to start a new communal song ("Swing Low, Sweet Chariot") in the act of escaping; and what is the sense of slaves who were forbidden to worship singing "Steal Away" to advertise their intention of doing so? The two songs are much more likely to have originated respectively from Peter Cartwright's hymn,

---

[45] Natalie Curtis Burlin, *Hampton Series Negro Folk Songs* (New York and Boston, G. Schirmer, 1918–1919), iv, 4. Quoted by permission of the publishers. See also Mrs. Burlin's article, "Negro Music at Birth," *Musical Quarterly*, 1919, v, 86–88.

[46] Dorothy Scarborough, *On the Trail of Negro Folk-Songs* (Cambridge, Harvard University Press, 1925), p. 75.

[47] John Wesley Work, *Folk-Song of the American Negro* (Nashville, Tenn., Press of Fisk University, 1915), pp. 76–89.

> Then my soul mounted higher
> On a chariot of fire,

which was in print as early as the eighteen-thirties; and from the hymn,

> I love to steal an hour away
> From every cumbering care
> And spend the hours of setting day
> In humble, grateful prayer,

which occurs in a Presbyterian hymn-book printed in 1843. Neither of these suggestions is demonstrable, but they are not inherently improbable or contrary to the demonstrable historical background of the spirituals, as most of the individual "origins" are. The editors of *Slave Songs* discovered in the eighteen-eighties how unreliable such origins are; they erred only in supposing that their informant was deliberately lying when he claimed the authorship of a song they later found in Methodist song-books. The ease with which members of a folk-group propagate honest errors about folk-origins is too well known to require more than passing comment.

In pointing out the heavy indebtedness of the Negro spiritual to the religious songs of the white people, I have had to expose several erroneous beliefs long cherished by those who have regarded the Negro song *in vacuo*, without reference to its religious milieu. This is not to allege that the Negro spiritual is really "white." Most decidedly the Negro spirituals of to-day are the Negro's own. The Negro has been singing them as his own for three generations. In the separate religious meetings allowed him before the Civil War, and in the separate churches which sprang up in the eighteen-fifties and sixties, he has been free to do as he would with them. They have always been the greatest single outlet for the expression of the Negro folk-mind. Under these conditions the marvel is that the spiritual has preserved so much of what the white man had given it. The strong element of improvisation in the white man's crude religious songs was alone sufficient to ensure that the Negro, in applying the same practice to the same song, would very soon develop something different. The way in which most of the stanzas from the white man's song would "cross over" has already been illustrated. This transformation would take place rapidly under the influence of the Negro's misunderstanding or even carelessness of the exact meaning of the white man's lines. Even to-day few Negroes ever sing the same song precisely alike. A powerful aid to this variation existed in the Negro's inheritance of a music fundamentally different in basis from that of the white man and in his much more highly developed sense of rhythm.[48] These circumstances would affect not only the music, but the words which accompanied it. The result would be a body of hymns fundamentally different in music from those of the white man, while preserving some echoes of Caucasian tunes; and a body of words "a long ways from home," though in spots still as true to home as Wordsworth's skylark. The devil would become a little more of a conjure-man; Christ would become Marse Jesus in the image of an ideally perfect earthly master. Biblical history would undergo transformations unlikely to happen in the white man's songs. The vivid imagery of the Apocalypse would impress itself a little more vividly upon the naïve imagination of the slave than upon that of the white man. Logical sequence of thought would have less weight with him. Both from his inferior earthly station and from his more intense and naïve emotional nature, he would savor the joys of heaven a little more keenly; and these joys, definitely marked out by tradition as they were, would receive some surprising additions.

All this is exactly what happened. Originals for the better-known Negro spirituals have never yet been discovered in the white man's songs. If they are, they will probably be of the nature of those I have just suggested for "Swing Low" and "Steal Away," mere starting-points from which the Negro has developed the most impressive religious folk-songs in our language. Originally the Negro spiritual was a sincerely intended, if erratic, imitation, but the white man would be both stupid and prejudiced if he failed to see that the Negro has long since made it his own.

[48] I recently served as one of the judges of a singing contest between Negro choirs from two country churches. The choirs first sang every song through, without the words, to show that the song had been properly learned by notes. Then each song was repeated, with the words. When the judges had retired (as the master of ceremonies said, "to make up their rebuttal"), my colleagues, who were trained musicians, commented on the marked difference between the two renditions.

SONGS, WITH ANNOTATIONS

The following songs classified in other groups might also be included with religious songs: III, 13, 17, 24, 25; XII, 20; XIII, 4.

I

PHARAOH'S ARMY [1]

THE song occurs in variant versions in most of the printed collections, beginning with Higginson (*Atlantic Monthly*, 1867, vol. xix, p. 685).

Reported from South Carolina in *J. A. F. L.*, 1914, p. 249. Perrow, 1913, pp. 156, 157, gives three variants from East Tennessee and Mississippi in 1905 and 1909, with comment that there are many absurd and obscene stanzas.

Odum, 1926, pp. 190, 191, gives three variants of "Pharaoh's Army" used as work songs.

For one of the tunes, see Appendix I, p. 406.

A

Reported from Auburn, Ala., 1915-1916, anonymously. It is also sung around Durham, N. C.

Stanzas 1 and 2 are apparently a refrain and closely resemble printed versions of "Pharaoh's Army." Stanzas 3, 4, 5, and 6 are common individually to a number of printed songs in almost all collections. Stanza 7 is an original expression of a rather common admonition. Cf. Fisher, 1926, p. 127.

> Pharoh army got drowned in the sea;
> I am so thankful it was not me.
>
> Pharoh army got drowned —
> O Mary, don't you weep.
>
> O Lord, Pharoh army got drowned —
> O Martha, don't you moan.
>
> If you wants to get to Heaven when you die,
> Stop your tongue from telling lies.
>
> Mary weep and Martha moan,
> Weeping about brothers dead and gone.
>
> Two white horses side by side;
> Them am the horses I am going to ride.
>
> When I go to Heaven I want to go right,
> I want to go to Heaven all dressed in white.
>
> Sinners, you all take my advice
> And try to get religion for this is nice.

[1] No local title given.

𝓑

Reported from Columbia, Tenn., 1925, MS. of Mrs. O. B. Thompson, who says
it has been sung in that part of the state for many years.

O MARY, DON'T YOU WEEP! [1]

O Mary, don't you mourn,
O Mary, don't you weep, don't you mourn;
   Pharoh's army got drown-ded,
   O Mary, don't you weep!

The way of evil doing is wide and fair,
And many, many, many they who perish there;
   Pharoh's army got drown-ded,
   O Mary, don't you weep!

There was a mighty man who came on earth to save,
Thro' Him we stem the tide of tribulation's wave;
   Pharoh's army got drown-ded,
   O Mary, don't you weep!

2

CLIMBING JACOB'S LADDER [2]

𝓐

REPORTED from Cherokee County, Ala., 1915–1916, MS. of R. C. Bradford.
Heard at a Negro "protracted meeting."

The refrain is common to a number of printed songs, as are lines 1 and 7 as
first lines of successive stanzas (for example, Fenner, 1901, pp. 1 and 118).
There are several printed versions of "Climbing Jacob's Ladder," beginning
with T. W. Higginson's "Negro Spirituals" in *Atlantic Monthly*, June, 1867,
p. 685; for example, *Southern Workman*, xxix, 288; Hallowell, 1905; Fenner
(reprint of 1924), p. 118; Perrow, 1913, p. 156. "Climb Jacob's Ladder" was
one of the three songs rejected by Allen (*Slave Songs*, 1867, p. vi, footnote) as
spurious because found in Methodist hymn-books.

The song has become the basis of a work song given by Odum, 1926, p. 111.

Cf. Perrow, 1913, p. 156 (as from Mississippi in 1909), and Marsh, 1877,
p. 190.

     I am climbing up Jacob's ladder,
     Don't you grieve after me;
     I am climbing up Jacob's ladder,
     Don't you grieve after me;
     Fer I'm climbing up Jacob's ladder,
     Kase I don't want you to grieve after me.

---

[1] Local title.   [2] No local title given.

Ebry round goes higher and higher,
Don't you grieve after me;
Ebry round goes higher and higher,
Don't you grieve after me;
Ebry round goes higher and higher,
Don't you grieve after me;
Kase I don't want you to grieve after me.

ℬ

Reported from Durham, N. C., 1919, MS. of Walter J. Miller, as heard "back in the 'sixties." The refrain and first half of line 3 are common to several printed spirituals.

Climb up Jacob's ladder, higher and higher,
'Way in de Kingdom;
Satan is a liar and you need n't d'pend upon him,
'Way in the Kingdom.

3

SIS MARY WORE THREE LINKS OF CHAIN [1]

𝒜

REPORTED from northern Alabama, 1915–1916, MS. of G. E. Lumpkin. The first line and the refrain are found in most printed versions of this song and occur separately in other songs. The variant versions show how a common line may be varied in Negro singing, how almost any line may be attracted into a song. Stanza 5 is the only one peculiar to this song and version.

"Going away on the mountain" (stanza 2) is generally connected with the idea of shouting, just as "down in the valley" connotes praying. "Coming through" represents the end of the spiritual ferment preceding shouting, and comes from the early Methodist and Baptist preachers.

Sis Mary wore three links ob chain,
Sis Mary wore three links o' chain,
Sis Mary wore three links o' chain,
Glory, glory, to his name,
All my sins been taken er way, taken er way.

Chorus

All my sins er taken away,
All my sins been taken er way,
All my sins been taken er way,
Glory, glory, to his name,
All my sins been taken away, taken er way.

[1] No local title given.

I'm gwine er way on the mountain,
I'm gwine er way on the mountain,
I'm gwine er way on the mountain,
Glory, glory, to his name,
All my sins been taken er way, taken er way.

Sis Mary had one baby child,
Sis Mary had one baby child,
Sis Mary had one baby child,
And every time that child would cry
All my sins been taken er way, taken er way.

O! you oughter been there when I come through,
O! you oughter been there when I come through,
O! you oughter been there when I come through,
I believe ter my soul you'd er shouted too,
All my sins been taken er way, taken er way.

O! Mary, Mary de Mag-delene,
O! Mary, Mary de Mag-delene,
O! Mary, Mary de Mag-delene.
She washed her feet and she washed 'em clean,
All my sins been taken er way, taken er way.

B

Reported from Clarke County, Ala., 1915–1916, MS. of W. A. Cammack.
Sung by field hands. The last stanza, with a different refrain, belongs to most
printed versions of "Little David." Sung around Durham, N. C., with line 3,
"Every link was my God's name." I have seen every line in other spirituals.

Sister Mary wore three links ob chain (twice repeated)
All dem links had Jesus name,
All my sins done taken away, taken away.

Bin to de riber and I bin baptized (twice repeated)
All my sins done taken away, taken away.

Going to heben on de morning train (twice repeated)
All don't hear me'll hear me sing,
All my sins done taken away, taken away.

Little David was a shepherd boy (twice repeated)
Killed Goliath and leaped for joy,
All my sins done taken away, taken away.

C

ALL MY SINS BEEN TAKEN AWAY [1]

Reported from Auburn, Ala., 1917; MS. of W. S. Lindsey.

Stanza 2 is a variation of the stanza found in various printed spirituals (for example, *Century Magazine*, August, 1899, p. 580, as from South Carolina):

> Over all trees in Paradise
> The Christian calls it the tree of life;

found also in the Bahama Islands (Edwards, 1895, pp. 41, 57).

Sister Mary wore three links of chain,
Sister Mary wore three links of chain,
Sister Mary wore three links of chain,
All my sins been taken away, taken away.

Over all trees in Paradise,
Over all trees in Paradise,
Over all trees in Paradise,
That ain't all and more besides,
All my sins been taken away, taken away.

I've been to the river and I been baptized,
I've been to the river and I been baptized,
I've been to the river and I been baptized,
That ain't all and more besides,
All my sins been taken away, taken away.

D

Reported from Auburn, Ala., 1915–1916, MS. of A. M. Kearly.

Mary wore three lengths of chain,
Every length was in Jesus name,
All my sins done taken away.

He give me the horn and told me to blow,
He give me the 'ligion and told me to go,
All my sins done taken away.

That ain't all, I got more besides,
I have been to the river and have been baptized,
And all my sins are taken away.

[1] Local title.

E

Reported from Auburn, Ala., 1915–1916, MS. of J. B. Christian, as heard in Tallahassee, Fla.

Cf. *J. A. F. L.*, 1910, p. 438 (as from Virginia and Maryland), for a combination of this song and "No Hidin' Place" (no. 74, in this chapter).

> Sis Mary had three links of chain
> Sis Mary had three links of chain
> Sis Mary had three links of chain,
> And called each one in Jesus name,
> All my sins done taken away, done taken away.

F

Reported from Durham, N. C., 1919, MS. of Blake B. Harrison.

> Mary wore a golden chain,
> Mary wore a golden chain,
> Mary wore a golden chain,
> Every link in Jesus' name.

Refrain

> All my sins been taken away, been taken away.

G

Reported from Auburn, Ala., 1915–1916, MS. of R. Langdon. "Sung at a Negro baptizing."

Same as stanzas 1 and 3 of *B*, with slight variations. "Going to heben on de morning train" becomes the more conservative "I'm goin' to leave," etc.

H

Reported from Auburn, Ala., 1915–1916, MS. of J. B. Christian, as heard in Tallahassee, Fla. The tune is the same as *E*.

> I'm gwine ter leave on de mornin' train,
> I'm gwine ter leave on de mornin' train,
> I'm gwine ter leave on de mornin' train,
> Kase Jesus is done heard me sing.

4

THAT GOSPEL TRAIN IS COMING [1]

THE gospel train is only one of several kinds of Negro train songs, a number of which are given in Miss Scarborough's chapter, "Railroad Songs," *On the Trail of Negro Folk-Songs*, 1925, pp. 238–264; and in Odum, 1925, pp. 112–115.

See also H. T. Burleigh, *Negro Spirituals*, 1917–1924; Ernest Newton, *Twelve Negro Spirituals*, 1925; Johnson, 1925, p. 123; and in this volume, Appendix III, p. 440.

The gospel train is by no means confined to the Negroes; it makes its regular runs to-day from the revival meetings of the whites. Cf. the *Ham-Ramsay Revival Book* (1917–1925), no. 58, "Life's Railway," and no. 144, "Life's Railway to Heaven"; and "The Beulah Railway," Appendix II, p. 422.

The refrain, "Get on board," is common to many of the gospel-train songs.

A

Reported from Auburn, Ala., 1915–1916, MS. of S. A. Allen, as heard in Shelby County, Ala. — "Incomplete." Stanza 2 is common to a number of songs. Sung around Durham, N. C., with "There's room for many more" as line 2 of refrain.

Cf. Edwards (Bahama), 1895, p. 26; Marsh, 1877, p. 150; Kennedy (as from Louisiana), 1924, p. 74; Odum, 1925, p. 114; Scarborough, 1925, pp. 239, 253 (as from Texas); Ibid., p. 254 (as from South Carolina).

> That gospel train am coming,
> I hear him just at hand,
> Come and get your ticket
> And be ready for the band.

Refrain

> Oh, get on board, all you little chillun,
> Get on board and ride for many a mile.

> That gospel train am coming,
> I hear him just at hand,
> I hear them car wheels moving
> And rumbling through the land.

> Oh, get on board, etc.

---

[1] Local title for *A* around Durham, N. C.

ℬ
IT AIN'T NO HARM TO TRUST IN JESUS [1]

Reported from Durham, N. C., 1919, MS. of Austin L. Elliott.
    Every line is found in printed versions of other songs, but the combination is
original.

> Oh, don't you hear that whistle blo'n',
> Oh, don't you hear that whistle blo'n',
> Oh, don't you hear that whistle blo'n'?
> Get on board, get on board.
>
> Oh, it ain't no harm to trust in Jesus,
> Oh, it ain't no harm to trust in Jesus,
> Oh, it ain't no harm to trust in Jesus;
> Get on board, get on board.
>
> Jesus is the conductor,
> Jesus is the conductor,
> Jesus is the conductor;
> Get on board, get on board.
>
> Oh! have you got your ticket ready,
> Oh! have you got your ticket ready,
> Oh! have you got your ticket ready?
> Get on board, get on board.

5

Reported from Marshall County, Ala., 1915–1916, anonymously.
    Similar stanzas are found in printed versions of "Dat Gospel Train" and by
intrusion in other spirituals. Cf. Fisher, 1926, p. 51.

> De Lord's train jus' got one track
> Rat [2] straight to heben and rat straight back.

6
THE LITTLE BLACK TRAIN [3]
𝒜

Reported from Durham, N. C., 1925, as sung to me by Ed Lloyd, who says it
has been printed and is a favorite at Creedmoor, N. C., where he has heard it
sung for some years.
    The chorus and stanzas 1 and 3 occur, with some verbal differences, in
Scarborough, 1925, pp. 260–261 (11 stanzas, as from Texas "Holy Rollers").

---

[1] Local title. [2] Right. [3] Local title.

A variant called "Business Affairs," Kennedy, 1925, p. 17 (as from Louisiana) contains lines 1, 2, 3, 4, and 13, all in different combinations.

Chorus

There's a little black train a-comin';
  Get all your business right;
Get your house in order;
  The train may be there to-night.

God spoke to Hezekiah
  In a message from on high,
Said prepare yourself for dying,
  For the little black train to-night.

Hezekiah got in earnest,
  Turned to the walls and prayed;
God heard Hezekiah prayin',
  Spared him fifteen years.

Go and tell the ball room ladies
  Who's filled with worldly pride,
Death's little black train is comin',
  Get prepared to take a ride.

B

Reported from Durham, N. C., 1919(?), MS. of W. L. Hampton, as heard in Durham County, N. C., in 1909.

Look here, nigger, do you figger on going up dar;
If you get your business right, get your heart in order;
For the little black train is going to come at night.

7

LITTLE DAVID, PLAY YO' HARP [1]

"LITTLE DAVID" occurs under various titles in a number of collections: for example, Perrow, 1913, p. 161; Kennedy, 1925, p. 160, as from Louisiana; Johnson, 1925, p. 65; Work, 1907, p. 64; Fenner (reprint of 1924), p. 139; Burleigh, 1917-1924; *Southern Workman*, xxix, 104, xxx, 196, and xlix, 340; G. Schaefer, *Songs from the South*, 1925; De Loss Smith, "Little David," 1925. Cf. Appendix II, p. 426.

---

[1] Local title.

A

Reported from Durham, N. C., 1925, MS. of N. I. White. "Heard in North Carolina in 1912 as a song sung by the mountain whites." Similar to the printed versions of "Little David." The music is similar to that sung by the Fisk University Quartet. Sung by Negroes around Durham, N. C. That this version is descended from an old secular song sung by slaves in the early eighteen-fifties is strongly indicated by Solomon Northup's song, given in the Appendix V, p. 454.

Line 7 is found in "Clar de Track" (*Negro Singers' Own Book*, 1846[?], p. 111), "Old Pee Dee" (*Ibid.*, p. 173), and "The Raccoon Hunt" (*Ibid.*, p. 425).

> Little David, play on yo' harp, Hallelu,
> Hallelu, Little David, play on yo' harp, Hallelu.

> Who's been here since I been gone?
> A big black nigger wid a derby on,
> Little David, play on yo' harp, Hallelu,
> Hallelu, etc.

> Never see the like since I been born,
> The people keep comin' an' de train done gone,
> Little David, play on yo' harp, Hallelu,
> Hallelu, etc.

> Away up yonder, beyond the sun,
> A big black nigger wid a derby on,
> Little David, play on yo' harp, Hallelu
> Hallelu, etc.

B

Reported from Auburn, Ala., 1915–1916, MS. of T. H. Bonner, as heard in Clay County, Ala.

Although common as variant stanzas of "Little David," this couplet and those following it might easily belong to different songs according to the principle, clearly exemplified by every published collection, that almost any stanza is at home in almost any song.

> Haven't seen the like since I been born,
> People keep comin' and the train done gone.

C

Reported from Auburn, Ala., 1915–1916, anonymously.

> Who's been here since I been gone?
> Great big nigger with a derby on.

D

Reported from Auburn, Ala., 1915–1916, anonymously, as from Marshall County, Ala. "Sung at Negro religious meetings together with 'Amazing Grace' and others."

Lines 1 and 3 are often used as the first lines of couplets in various spirituals, and the two couplets, as here given, occasionally occur separately. With "blue" for "red," the first couplet occurs in a secular song, "Pretty Little Girl," Talley, 1922, p. 172. Cf. also "The Frog in the Well," a secular song of the whites, Campbell and Sharp, 1917, p. 319, as from western North Carolina. It was in a song of the mountain whites that I first heard this couplet (or a variant), about 1911.

> Who's been here since I been gone?
> Pretty little girl with a red dress on.
> Nebber saw the like since I been born,
> People keep coming and train done gone.

E

Reported from Auburn, Ala., 1915–1916, MS. of S. A. Allen, as from Shelby County, Ala. Same as lines 1 and 2 of *D*.

F

Reported from Durham, N. C., 1919, MS. of W. J. Huckabee, Jr., as from eastern North Carolina. "Sung by Negroes working in street."

> David had a harp with a thousand strings,
> He'd touch one string an' a thousand would ring.

Refrain
> Little David, play on your harp, Halle-halle-lu-yeh.

G

Reported from Durham, N. C., 1925, MS. of N. I. White. Sung to me by Ed Lloyd as additional stanzas of "Little David," sung by his father in Creedmoor, N. C. Tune different from Victrola records.

> Some come cripple and some come lame,
> But they went away walkin' in my God's name.
>
> Some come deef and some come dumb,
> But dey went away talkin' in my God's tongue.

8

I GOT SHOES [1]

WITH the usual variations, the song occurs in several of the printed collections; for example, Work, 1907, p. 60; Fenner (reprint of 1924), p. 168; Edna Thomas, *Negro Spirituals*, London, 1924; Odum, 1926, p. 60; H. T. Burleigh, 1921. It is also sung by college glee clubs. I have heard practically the same as stanza 1, with an amplified refrain, sung by the students at Trinity College, N. C., 1909–1914. A version of it is even featured in Ziegfeld's Follies, opening in 1927.

A

Reported from Durham, N. C., 1925, MS. of N. I. White. Sung to me by Ed Lloyd as current around Durham. The tune is somewhat different from that of the Fisk University Quartet's rendering.

The second line is often sung as: "All 'at 's got chillun got shoes."

Line 3 occurs in a number of other spirituals; for example, Fenner, 1901, p. 140.

Stanzas 1, 4, and 5 are as in Kennedy, 1925, p. 156, as from Louisiana. A parody of the song occurs in Odum, 1926, as "All Us Niggers 'Hind de Bars."

> You got shoes, I got shoes,
> All God's chillun got shoes,
> When I git to Heb'n goin' to put on my shoes
> Goin' to walk all over God's Heb'n.
> Heb'n, Heb'n, goin' to walk all over God's Heb'n.
>
> I got a derby, you got a derby,
> All God's chillun got a derby,
> When I git to Heb'n goin' to put on my derby
> Goin' to walk all over God's Heb'n,
> Heb'n, Heb'n, goin' to walk all over God's Heb'n.
>
> I got a robe, you got a robe,
> All God's chillun got a robe,
> When I git to Heb'n goin' to put on my robe
> Goin' to walk all over God's Heb'n,
> Heb'n, Heb'n, goin' to walk all over God's Heb'n.
>
> I got a crown, you got a crown,
> All God's chillun got a crown,
> When I git to Heb'n goin' to put on my crown
> Goin' to walk all over God's Heb'n,
> Heb'n, Heb'n, goin' to walk all over God's Heb'n.

[1] No local title given.

I got a harp, you got a harp,
All God's chillun got a harp,
When I git to Heb'n goin' to put on my harp
Goin' to play all over God's Heb'n,
Heb'n, Heb'n, goin' to play all over God's Heb'n.

B

Reported from Auburn, Ala., 1915–1916, MS. of M. S. Perdue. "Sung by Negro nailing lathes on a building."

Substantially the same as stanzas 1 and 2 of *A*, with the "you" and "I" reversed.

C

Reported from Auburn, Ala., MS. of Alsobrook.

Same as stanzas 1 and 2 of *A*, with trifling verbal variations.

D

Reported from Auburn, Ala., 1915–1916, MS. of J. S. Burbage, as heard at a sawmill.

Same as stanza 1 of *A*, with trifling verbal variations.

E

Reported from Durham, N. C., 1919, MS. of J. G. Neal, as from Marion, western North Carolina.

Same as stanza 1 of *A*, with lines 3 and 4 omitted.

9

REPORTED from Greensboro, N. C., 1915–1916, MS. of Mr. and Mrs. J. J. W. Harriss, as heard in eastern North Carolina in the eighteen-eighties.

Line 2 completes many other stanzas that could not be recalled. Line 3 occurs in other spirituals as "Went down to the Valley."

See Psalm xl, 2: "He brought me up . . . out of the miry clay, and set my feet upon a rock."

Cf. Fenner, 1901, p. 25: "He pluck-a my feet out de miry clay"; also Ibid., p. 235 and Marsh, 1877.

The song appears to be derived from the revival song of the whites, "Oh, He's Taken my Feet (*The Revivalist*, 1868, p. 65) with its chorus:

Oh, he's taken my feet from the mire and clay
And he's placed them on the Rock of Ages.

O my li'l sistah; I'm so glad,
My feet been taken out de miry clay.

Went down to de low groun'; went dere to pray;
My feet been taken out de miry clay.

10

SHOW ME THE WAY [1]

A

REPORTED from Durham, N. C., 1925, MS. of N. I. White. Sung by Ed Lloyd, as from Creedmoor, N. C. The tune is given in Appendix I, p. 406.

With the last stanza, cf. Lazarus in Luke, xxiv, 39: "Behold my hands and my feet."

The third line of the last stanza occurs generally as: "I looked at my feet and dey looked so too."

This song is very similar to "The Good Old Way", Allen, 1867, p. 84, and Marsh, 1877, p. 156.

For the origin of stanza 2, see preceding note.

> I went down in the valley one day,
> Good Lord, show me the way.
> Talkin' about dat good old way,
> Good Lord, show me the way.

Chorus

> Tell me, who shall wear the starry crown,
> Good Lord, show me the way.
> Show me the way, Oh, show me the way,
> Way down in the valley to pray.

> My feets been taken out de miry clay,
> Good Lord, show me the way;
> Placed on the rock of eternal ages,
> Good Lord, show me the way.

> I looked at my hands and dey looked bran' new
> Good Lord, show me the way,
> I wondered to the Lord was my soul so too,
> Good Lord, show me the way.

B

Reported from Auburn, Ala., 1915–1916, MS. of R. Langdon.

Several printed songs contain this stanza (for example, Odum, 1925, p. 280). It occurs sometimes as

> I went down in the valley, did n't go for to stay
> My soul got happy and I stayed all day

(Kennedy, 1925, p. 161, as from Louisiana). This was parodied as early as the

---

[1] Local title in North Carolina.

eighteen-forties in stanza 6 of "Old Napper Rise" (*Negro Singer's Own Book*, 1846[?], p. 27):

> I went down to New Orleans
> Did n't go to stay
> Laid my head in yaller gal's lap
> Yaller gal fainted away.

"Down in the valley" is a favorite expression; cf. Kennedy, 1924, p. 122; Ludlow, 1884, p. 4; Marsh, 1877, p. 187; also the gospel hymn of white people, "Down in the valley with my Saviour I would go."

> I went down in the valley to pray
> My soul got happy and I stayed all day.

II

A

REPORTED from Auburn, Ala., 1915–1916, MS. of R. Langdon. "Sung at a religious meeting."

The chorus and each of the separate stanzas, except stanza 1, are found in most of the printed collections. Lines 3 and 8 are especially common, as are stanzas 3 and 4, with slight variations, such as "all my folks" for "Brother Peter," and "white horses" for gray.

"Walking and talking with Jesus" (stanza 2) occurs abundantly in the hymns of the whites.

Variations of the hypocrite couplet are common; see *B* version and no. 12 below.

> Hypocrity, hypocrity, dress so fine,
> You ain't got God Almighty on yo're min'.

Chorus

> I'm goin' to lay down my life for my Lawd,
> For my Lawdy, Lawdy, Lawdy,
> For my Lawdy, Lawdy, Lawdy;
> I'm goin' to lay down my life for my Lawd.

> In that graveyard I'm goin' to walk;
> Me and my Lawd's goin' to have a little talk.

> If you get there before I do,
> Tell brother Peter I'm comin' too.

> Two gray horses side by side,
> Me and my Lawd's goin' take a ride.

$\mathcal{B}$

Reported from Durham, N. C., 1925, MS. of John Bridgers, as from Lanark, Fla. Sung by white people on excursion parties.

Each of the stanzas occurs in printed versions of other spirituals. Cf. Kennedy, 1924, p. 154, and 1925, p. 132, both from Louisiana; Barton, 1899, p. 8.

The first couplet occurs in Odum, 1926, p. 194, in a spiritual used as a work song.

The second couplet occurs in Work, 1907, pp. 50, 53. Cf. no. 70 in this chapter.

Stanza 3, with a slight variation, occurs in a work song in Scarborough, 1925, p. 229, as from Virginia.

> Look out, sister Hannah, how you walk on the cross!
> Your foot might slip and your soul git los'.
>
> Gwina lay down my soul
>   For my Lord,
> Yes, for my Lord, yes, for my Lord.
> Gwina lay down my soul
>   For my Lord,
>   For my Lord.
>
> Look at the sun; see how she run;
> Don't let her ketch you wid yer work undone.
>
> Hypocrite, a-member, the Lord, he despise
> De tongues will slip, and dey will tell lies.

C

Reported from Durham, N. C., MS. of N. I. White. From Creedmoor, N. C., as sung by Ed Lloyd. As in A, with the added stanza:

> Look over yonder in the fields of green,
> Religion floatin' like a water screen.

12

$\mathcal{A}$

REPORTED from Auburn, Ala., 1915-1916, MS. of A. H. Williamson, as from Lowndes County, Ala. In the printed collections it occurs occasionally as a stanza:

> Hypocrite, hypocrite, de Lawd despise,
> Dey can't stop dere tongues from tellin' lies,

without the last line, which occurs in other combinations. The *Journal of American Folk Lore*, 1913, pp. 374-376 (as from Georgia) prints a twelve-stanza song beginning with this couplet, and using the "Ain't Gwine Grieve

My Lord No More," refrain, with footnote citations of parallel stanzas in other spirituals.

> De hippercrits, de hippercrits,
> De good Lawd despise,
> Dey tongue's so slick
> Till dey will tell lies,
>   Settin' down side ov de lam' and Father Abraham.

B

Reported from Durham, N. C., 1925, MS. of N. I. White, as from Creedmoor, N. C. Sung to me by Ed Lloyd.

The separate couplets, with or without interlines, are found in other printed songs. For a variation of the first couplet, see *A* version, and cf. Work, 1907, p. 3; *J. A. F. L.*, 1913, p. 374 (as from Georgia); Odum, 1925, p. 85.

> Hypocrite, hypocrite, God despise
>   Join in dis band,
> Tongue so supple an' dey will tell lies
>   Join in dis band.
>
> Never seen the like since I been born,
>   Join in dis band;
> People keep comin' and de train done gone,
>   Join in dis band.
>
> Come on sinner with your ups and downs,
>   Join in dis band;
> Lord's goin' to meet you on half way ground,
>   Join in dis band.

13

Reported from Auburn, Ala., 1915–1916, anonymously.

"Don't you want to go" and "I want to go" are common expressions in the Negro spirituals which find their analogies in various hymns sung by the white people. Songs of this type are commonly prolonged indefinitely, as long as there is a supply of relatives, backsliders, hypocrites, elders, deacons, preachers, etc., to be addressed. Cf. Barton, 1899, p. 31; Burlin (Hampton Series), 1918–1919, ii, 22; Fenner, 1901, p. 24; Marsh, 1877, pp. 202, 203.

> Oh brother! don't you want to go,
> Oh brother! don't you want to go,
> Oh brother! don't you want to go,
> Stepping down to Jordan to the sea.
>
> Oh mother! etc.
>
> Oh sister! etc.

14

REPORTED from Durham, N. C., 1925, as from Creedmoor, N. C., MS. of N. I. White, as sung to me by Ed Lloyd.

> O Brother, don't you want
>   Good news.
> O Brother, don't you want
>   Good news.
> I'll lay down my life,
>   Take up the cross,
> Carry it to Jesus,
>   Good news.
>
> O Auntie, etc.
>
> O Deacon, etc.
>
> O Preacher, etc.
>
> O Christian, etc.

15

REPORTED from Auburn, Ala., 1915–1916, MS. of A. H. Williamson, as from Lowndes County, Ala.

The only common elements in this song are the refrain and the brother in heaven. The refrain is the same as that of "Ain' da's good News," Kennedy, 1924, p. 14. A secular song in the *Negro Singers' Own Book*, 1846(?), p. 165, and *Christy's Nigga Songster*, n. d., p. 50, has for refrain, "Good news, hark, good news." Cf. also Edwards, 1895, p. 36, "Good News in the Kin'dom"; Fenner, 1901, p. 52. "Good news," originating probably from Luke xi, 10, is a common note in the gospel hymns of the whites; for example, the refrain, "Good news from Heaven."

With the refrain, cf. "Fo de Lawd," Hallowell, 1905, p. 42, as from Alabama. A variant of this refrain, "To lay this body down," is reported by W. H. Russell (*My Diary North and South*, Boston, 1863) as heard sung by slaves in South Carolina in 1861.

> I been 'buked and I been 'bused,
> I been 'buked and I been 'bused,
> I'm gwine ter lay down dis world
> An' shoulder up my cross,
> An' I'll take it home ter Je-sus,
> Ain't dat good news.

I got a brudder 'way in de glory,
Ain't dat good news,
I got a brudder 'way in de glory,
Ain't dat good news,
I'm gwine ter lay down dis world
An' shoulder up my cross,
An' I'll take it home ter Je-sus,
Ain't dat good news.

16

HOLD YOUR LIGHT [1]

BASED on Matthew v, 16, "Let your light so shine." A good example of how a spiritual may be developed to any desired length from a simple text. There are other spirituals about the shining light, some of which involve the parable of the Foolish Virgins; for example, "Keep Yo' Lamp Trimmed and A-Burning," and no. 37, in this chapter.

The refrain, "Hold your light," occurs in two songs quoted by T. W. Higginson (*Letters and Journals*, 1921, pp. 219–220), as sung by Negro Union troops during the Civil War; also in the first song in Higginson's article "Negro Spirituals," in *Atlantic Monthly*, June, 1867, p. 685. Cf. *New Republic*, 1917, p. 214, and Marsh, 1877, p. 190; also no. 37 below.

A

Reported from Auburn, Ala., 1915–1916, MS. of A. H. Williamson, as from Lowndes County, Ala.

Oh! Brudder, can't you hol' out yo' light,
Oh! Brudder, can't you hol' out yo' light,
Oh! Brudder, can't you hol' out yo' light,
An' let yo' light shine ober de world.

Oh! Elder, can't you hol' out yo' light,
Oh! Elder, can't you hol' out yo' light,
Oh! Elder, can't you hol' out yo' light,
An' let yo' light shine ober de world.

Oh! Sister, can't you hol' out yo' light,
Oh! Sister, can't you hol' out yo' light,
Oh! Sister, can't you hol' out yo' light,
An' let yo' light shine ober de world.

[1] No local title given.

B

Reported from Durham, N. C., 1925, MS. of N. I. White. Sung by Ed Lloyd,
as from Creedmoor, N. C.

Chorus

O Christian, hold up yo' light,
Hold yo' light till the heaven doors close.

When I was a mourner just like you,
   Hold yo' light till the heaven doors close,
I kep' on mournin' till I come through,
   Hold yo' light till the heaven doors close.

Wish that mohner would rise and tell,
   Hold yo' light till the heaven doors close,
How he shurned that dismus Hell,
   Hold yo' light till the heaven doors close.

Come on, seeker, now's yo' time,
   Hold yo' light till the heaven doors close,
While the Gawspel train is on de line,
   Hold yo' light till the heaven doors close.

17

REPORTED from Auburn, Ala., 1915–1916, MS. of A. H. Williamson, as from
Lowndes County, Ala.

Oh, crap-shooter, Oh, crap-shooter,
You can shoot all ober dis world,
You can shoot from de six, from de seven, to de 'leben,
But God knows you can't shoot er inter heben.

Oh, back-biter, Oh, back-biter,
You can bite all ober dis world,
You can bite from de six, to seben, to de 'leben,
But God knows you can't shoot er inter heben.

Oh, schemer, Oh, schemer,
You can scheme all ober dis world,
You can scheme from de six, to de seben, to de 'leben,
But God knows you can't scheme inter heben.

18

A

REPORTED from Durham, N. C., 1925, MS. of N. I. White. Sung by Ed Lloyd, as from Creedmoor, N. C.

You can play the ace and tray,
But it sho' will lead you astray.
It's awful sad when the Holy Ghost is gone.

You can weep and you can moan,
But hell goin' be yo' home.
It's awful sad when the Holy Ghost is gone.

You can play the ace and deuce,
But God 'll ketch you with no excuse.
It's awful sad when the Holy Ghost is gone.

You can pass the whiskey round,
But you must lay yo' body down.
It's awful sad when the Holy Ghost is gone.

B

Reported from Durham, N. C., 1919; MS. of W. B. Jeffrey, as from Clayton, N. C. "Sung by a cripple Negro on the street."

The same as the first two stanzas of *A*, except that each stanza is "given gravy" by the characteristic "um-m, um-m" at the end.

19

A

REPORTED from Durham, N. C., 1925, MS. of N. I. White. From Creedmoor, N. C., as sung to me by Ed Lloyd, who says there are many other verses which he cannot recall, and that "Hallelujahs" are sometimes inserted irregularly for emphasis.

"Run, sinner, run," may be connected with the old secular song, "Run, nigger, run" (IV, no. 23). The hunt for a hiding-place is common in the spirituals, and may be derived from the camp-meeting songs and sermons of the whites, often connected with Revelation vi, 16, and half-a-dozen references to hiding in Psalms and Isaiah.

Soon one mornin' Death come creepin' in de room,
Soon one mornin' Death come creepin' in de room,
Soon one mornin' Death come creepin' in de room, Hallelujah,
Lord, O Lord, what shall I do?

O Death done got my mother and gone,
O Death done got my mother and gone,
O Death done got my mother and gone, Hallelujah,
O my Lord, O my Lord, what shall I do?

Run, sinner, run, an' hunt you a hidin' place,
Run, sinner, run, an' hunt you a hidin' place,
Run, sinner, run, an' hunt you a hidin' place, Hallelujah,
O Lord, O Lord, what shall I do?

O sinner, what you gonna do that day,
O sinner, what you gonna do that day,
O sinner, what you gonna do that day, Hallelujah,
O Lord, what shall I do?

You go to God, be driven away, etc.
Read, read, see what de Bible say, etc.
Man, man, take up your bed and walk, etc.
The blind man stood on de way and cried, etc.
O Death done got my father and gone, etc.
O Church, get all yo' business right, etc.
I'm so glad — got my religion in time, etc.

ℬ

Reported from Auburn, Ala., 1915–1916, MS. of W. M. Little, as from north-eastern Georgia. "Sung by Negro washwoman." Cf. no. 21B, in this chapter.

One morning soon death come creepin' in the room,
O my Lord, O my Lawdy, what shall I do?
Run, sinner, run, hunt you er hidin' place,
Run, sinner, run, hunt you er hidin' place.

20

I'M GOIN' T' WEAR THAT STARRY CROWN
OVER THERE [1]

REPORTED from Durham, N. C., 1925, MS. of Austin L. Elliott.

"Over there" is the refrain of a gospel hymn of the white people that I can recall hearing in my childhood. The starry crown is common to religious songs of Negroes and white people alike.

Fix me, Jesus, fix me right,
Death come slippin' in the house at night.

[1] Local title.

I'm goin' to wear that starry crown over there.
Over there, I'm goin' t' wear
That starry crown, over there.
Fix me, Jesus, fix me right,
Death come slippin' in the house at night.
I'm goin' t' wear that starry crown over there.

21

WHERE SHALL I BE [1]

A

REPORTED from Durham, N. C., 1925, MS. of N. I. White. From Creedmoor, N. C., as sung by Ed Lloyd, who says there are many other stanzas. It was first sung in Creedmoor by a travelling revivalist, says Ed, and remained fixed in the community afterwards.

The refrain is the same as that of "Where Shall I be When de Firs' Trumpet Soun'" (from Lowndes County, Ala.), in Hallowell, 1905, p. 8. I have seen variants of it elsewhere. The first trumpet is a reminiscence of the successive trumpet calls of Judgment Day in Revelation, and there is an obvious connection with Revelation vi, 16: "And said to the mountains and rocks, Fall on us, and hide us from the face of Him that sitteth on the throne, and from the wrath of the Lamb."

In *George Christy and Wood's Melodies* (*New Song Book*), copyright 1854, p. 96, there is a minstrel song, "A Few Days," which deals with the end of the world and has all the characteristics of a spiritual.

In I. E. Keiser's *Baptist Evangelical Song Book and Working Guide* (Rankin, Pa., n. d.), p. 26, which is used in Negro Baptist churches in Durham, there is a version of this song which is evidently not an old spiritual, beginning:

> When Judgment Day is drawing nigh
>   Where shall I be?
> When God the works of men shall try
>   Where shall I be? etc.;

with the same chorus as the present version.

When the rocks and the mountains flee away,
    Where shall I be?
. . . . [2]
Where shall I be?

Chorus

O where shall I be when the first trumpet sounds,
    Tell me where shall I be when it sound so loud?
It will sound so loud it will wake up the dead,
    O where shall I be when it sounds?

---

[1] Local title.

[2] Ed could not recall this line, and his memory did not react spontaneously to my suggestion, based on variants of the stanza in other spirituals, that it might be something like: "And I shall find a new hidin' place that day."

From the east to the west the fire shall roll,
 Where shall I be?
Then what will become of my poor soul,
 Where shall I be?

𝓑

Reported from Greensboro, N. C., 1915–1916, MS. of Mrs. J. J. W. Harriss, as heard in eastern North Carolina in the eighteen-eighties.
 Stanza 1 occurs in Marsh, 1877, p. 141; and, without the last two words, in *J. A. F. L.*, v, 124 (1892).
 Evidently based on Revelation vi, 16.

O de rocks an' de mountains will all flee away,
An' you shall have a new hidin' place dat day.
Mo'ner, Mo'ner, give up yo' heart fo' God,
An' you shall have a new hidin' place dat day.

22

DEN MY LITTLE SOUL WILL SHINE [1]

RINGING bells play a considerable part in spirituals. They may take their origin from the religious songs of the whites (for example, the gospel hymns, "Ring the Bells of Heaven," and "The Gospel Bells are Ringing"), where the bells are almost certainly church bells or wedding bells, or they may come from the Negroes' own church bells, or from the bells commonly used on plantations to summon hands. They cannot have a Scriptural origin, as bells were unknown to the people of the Bible. "Shining souls" was and still is a part of the special vocabulary of the evangelical religions. It has a Scriptural basis in Isaiah, lx, 1 ("Arise, shine, for thy light has come"), Daniel, xii, 13 ("The wise shall shine as the brightness"), Matthew, xiii, 43 ("The righteous shine as the sun"), etc.

𝒜

Reported from Greensboro, N. C., MS. of Mrs. J. J. W. Harriss, as heard in eastern North Carolina in the eighteen-eighties. Incomplete.
 In 1918 a very old lady told me in Boston that she distinctly recalled the first line of this song as the basis of a song she had heard sung on a Tennessee plantation before the Civil War. The refrain, slightly varied, occurs in a secular Bre'r Rabbit song in Scarborough, 1925, p. 173, as from South Carolina. With the first line, cf. Johnson, 1926, p. 183.
 Line 4 reflects the interest in burying found in several other spirituals and secular songs (as well as in some traditional English songs), and much exploited by writers of fiction about Negroes. The same line occurs in Edwards (Bahama), 1895, p. 37; Marsh, 1877, p. 220; Fenner, 1901, p. 1, and in Armstrong and Ludlow, *Hampton and its Students*, 1874.

---

[1] No local title given.

With Isaiah, lx, 1, cf. "Rise, Shine," Murphy, 1904, p. 16; Marsh, 1877, p. 217; Fenner, 1901, p. 40.

> Sistah Mary, an' de bell done rung,
> Sistah Mary, an' de bell done rung;
> Den my little soul will shine.
>
> Don't care where you bury my body,
> Don't care where you bury my body;
> Den my little soul will shine.

B

Reported from Durham, N. C., 1925, MS. of N. I. White. From Creedmoor, N. C., as sung by Ed Lloyd. With stanza 1, cf. Johnson, 1926, p. 110.

> Run, sinner, run, yo' house on fire,
> Run, sinner, run, yo' house on fire,
> Den my little soul goin' to shine, home,
> Den my little soul goin' to shine, home,
>
> I'm goin' to join that big baptizin',
> I'm goin' to join that big baptizin',
> Den my little soul goin' to shine, home,
> Den my little soul goin' to shine, home.
>
> I'm goin' to shine to the throne of mercy,
> I'm goin' to shine to the throne of mercy,
> Den my little soul goin' to shine, home,
> Den my little soul goin' to shine, home.

23

REPORTED from Durham, N. C., 1919, MS. of D. B. Newton, as from Marlboro County, S. C. Sung also by Negroes around Durham, N. C.

Apparently related to the printed spiritual, "Peter, go ring-a dem bells," Marsh, 1877, p. 236, but contains no identical lines. Cf. "Clar de Track," in *Negro Singers' Own Book*, 1846(?), p. 111, also "Old Pee Dee" and "The Raccoon Hunt," pp. 173, 425.

> Ring dem bells and Jim Crack Corn,
> I never see de like since I been born.

Cf. also Kennedy, 1924, pp. 24, 152; Barton, 1899, p. 35; Edwards (Bahama) 1898, p. 44; Marsh, 1877, pp. 204, 236; Burleigh, 1917–1924; Fenner (reprint of 1924), p. 2; *Southern Workman*, xxix, 702; Fisher, 1926, p. 134. Cf. no. 22, above, note.

Go ring dem bells, bells, bells, at de Zion of Glory.
Go ring dem bells, bells, bells, at Hebren's door.
Oh! go today, day, day, and not tomorrow.
Go ring dem bells at Hebren's door.

24

CREATION [1]

A

REPORTED from Auburn, Ala., 1915–1916, MS. of Mrs. J. R. Rutland, as heard
sung in Pike County, Ala., and Tuscaloosa, Ala.

It is found in several printed collections of Negro songs, and is often sung by
white people as a picnic song. I have heard it sung by students, both of Randolph-Macon College for Women and Trinity College, but only once by Negroes. The refrain is apparently based on the resurrection of dry bones in
Ezekiel xxxvii. Sometimes the word "dry" is used instead of "dese."

On p. 11 of *Old Slack's Reminiscence and Pocket History of the Colored Profession from 1865 to 1891*, by Ike Simond, Chicago, 1891, I find that, about 1882,
"Taylor Green told everybody 'Dem bones Gwine Rise Again' and Billy Banks
said, if they did, he would 'meet 'em when the sun went down.'"

Cf. Barton, 1899, p. 32.

> Lord he thought he'd make a man,
>   Dese bones gwine rise ergain,
> Mixed a little bit o' dirt and san',
>   Dese bones gwine rise ergain.

> *Chorus:*
> I know it, indeed I know it, brother,
>   Dese bones gwine rise ergain.

> Thought he make er 'oman too,
>   Dese bones gwine rise ergain,
> Did n't know zactly what to do,
>   Dese bones gwine rise ergain.

> He took a rib from Adam's side,
>   Dese bones gwine rise ergain,
> An' made Miss Eve fo' to be his bride,
>   Dese bones gwine rise ergain.

> Put 'em in a garden rich and fair,
>   Dese bones gwine rise ergain.
> Tol' 'em to eat whatever was there,
>   Dese bones gwine rise ergain.

[1] Local title.

Of this tree you must not eat,
　　Dese bones gwine rise ergain,
If you do you 'll have to skeet,
　　Dese bones gwine rise ergain.

Sarpent wound aroun' the stump,
　　Dese bones gwine rise ergain,
At Miss Eve his eye he wunk,
　　Dese bones gwine rise ergain.

Lord he come wid monstrous voice,
　　Dese bones gwine rise ergain,
Shook dis ole earth to its very joists,
　　Dese bones gwine rise ergain.

Adam, Adam, where art thou,
　　Dese bones gwine rise ergain,
Here, Marse Lawd, I'm comin' right now,
　　Dese bones gwine rise ergain.

Et my apple I do believe,
　　Dese bones gwine rise ergain,
No, Marse Lawd, I spec' it was Eve,
　　Dese bones gwine rise ergain.

Out of this garden you must get,
　　Dese bones gwine rise ergain,
Earn yo' living by yo' sweat,
　　Dese bones gwine rise ergain.

Of this tale there is no more,
　　Dese bones gwine rise ergain.
Eve ate de apple, gave Adam de core,
　　Dese bones gwine rise ergain.

Cain thought Abel played a trick,
　　Dese bones gwine rise ergain.
Hit 'em in the head wid a piece of brick,
　　Dese bones gwine rise ergain.

B

Reported from Durham, N. C., 1925, MS. of N. I. White. From Creedmoor, N. C., as sung by Ed Lloyd, who says he has never heard the stanzas of *A* version. Sung to same tune as *A*.

　　Line 1 was originally probably "Matthew, Mark, Luke, and John," as in Perrow, 1913, p. 151. The couplet, "Matthew, Mark, Luke and John Bless the bed that I lie on" was quoted by Wordsworth in "The Redbreast" (composed 1834) and explained by him as part of a child's prayer in general use in the northern counties. Puckett (1926, p. 75) reports the couplet as found among Mississippi Negroes and cites R. Chambers, *Popular Rhymes of Scotland*, pp. 149–150.

> Mary, Martha, Luke, and John,
>   Dese bones gwine rise again.
> Take your little truth and munch along,
>   Dese bones gwine rise again.
>
> Way up yonder 'tween the earth and sky,
>   Dese bones gwine rise again.
> Dat's where King Jesus bled and died,
>   Dese bones gwine rise again.
>
> Dey nailed his hands and rivet his feet,
>   Dese bones gwine rise again,
> The hammers was heard in Jerusalem street,
>   Dese bones gwine rise again.
>
> Annanias and Sapphias,
>   Dese bones gwine rise again,
> Dey was struck dead for liars,
>   Dese bones gwine rise again.

C

Reported from Auburn, Ala., 1915–1916, MS. of G. E. Lumpkin, as from northern Alabama.

Lacks stanzas 10, 11, 12 of *A*, but otherwise the same, except for several slight verbal variations as "trunk" for "stump" (stanza 6) and "noise" for "voice" (stanza 7).

D

Reported from Greensboro, N. C., 1915–1916, anonymously. Stanza 12 of *A*.

E

Reported from Auburn, Ala., 1915–1916, MS. of R. R. Beard, as from Mobile County, Ala. "Sung by Negro preacher." The couplet occurs in other songs; cf. Kennedy, 1925, p. 38, as from Louisiana.

That this couplet was known to Jamaican Negroes is suggested by a somewhat sarcastic four-line song in Walter Jekyll's *Jamaican Song and Story*, 1907, ending:

> Some come with jackass, some come with bus,
> Dip them in the healing stream.

> Some come cripple an' some come lame,
> An' some come a-speakin' of Moses' name;
> Old dry bones gwine ter rise ergain.

25

REPORTED from New York City, 1923. Taught me by a Jewish graduate of the College of the City of New York. The minstrel books of the eighteen-forties contain so many references to the Millerites, who actually did purchase long white gowns and await the "great day," that I suspect this song may have had a minstrel origin, though its occurrence in Perrow, 1913, p. 160 (as from Virginia) seems to indicate that it was taken seriously by the Negroes.

> Well, de Good Book say dat Cain killed Abel,
> > Yes, Abel,
> Dat he hit him in de head wid de leg of a ta-able,
> > Yes, good Lord.
> Did n't Daniel in de lion's den
> Say unto dem collud men
> Git yo' long white gown an' pass 'em around,
> An' be ready when de great day comes.
> Yes, Lord, I'm ready; yes, Lord, I'm ready,
> I'll be ready when de great day comes.

26

ER CLIM'IN' UP THINE HILL [1]

A

REPORTED from Auburn, Ala., 1915–1916, MS. of Miss Alma Smith.

The two lines of the chorus occur independently in printed spirituals. Probable Scriptural origin for "climbing up thine hill" is found in Psalm xv, 1 ("Who shall dwell in thine holy hill?"), xxiv, 3 ("Who shall ascend the hill of the Lord?"), and xliii, 3 ("Bring me to thy holy hill").

Cf. Marsh, 1877, p. 200.

> I wore my knees up to the bone,
> I wore my knees up to the bone,
> I wore my knees up to the bone,
> > Er clim'in' up thine hill.

Chorus:

> Lord, I'm almos' surrounded,
> Lord, I'm almos' surrounded,
> Lord, I'm almos' surrounded,
> > Er clim'in' up thine hill.

[1] Local title.

Oh, mother, you don't know how good God is,
Oh, mother, you don't know how good God is,
Oh, mother, you don't know how good God is,
    Er clim'in' up thine hill.

ℬ

I'M CLIMBIN' [1]

Reported from Durham, N. C., 1925, MS. of N. I. White. From Creedmoor, N. C., as sung by Ed Lloyd, who says there are a number of stanzas which he cannot recall. Used most commonly in opening Sunday School.

I'm climbin', I'm climbin', I'm climbin', bless God,
    Climbin' up Zion's hill,
The more I shout the happier I am
    Climbin' up Zion's hill.

When I'm almost done I've just begun,
    Climbin' up Zion's hill,
I'm climbin', I'm climbin', I'm climbin', bless God,
    Climbin' up Zion's hill.

27

ROLL, JORDAN, ROLL [2]

It is probable that the songs about Jordan, which were common among the camp-meeting songs of the whites and are still to be found in any hymn-book, were among the first Negro spirituals developed. In "The Hireling and the Slave," a descriptive poem of John Russell (W. J. Grayson), Charleston, 1854, I find the following (p. 65):

> Lingering, they love to sing of Jordan's shore
> Where sorrows cease, and toil is heard no more,

and a note (p. 97) says that the favorite subjects of Negro hymns are "Jordan's banks and the happy land to which the singers are travelling."

W. H. Russell, in *My Diary North and South*, Boston, 1863, p. 126, mentions the fondness of slaves for singing about "the river Jawdam." See also Dwight's *Journal of Music*, 1862, xxii, 255.

Jordan songs occur in practically all the collections; for example, Allen, 1867; Marsh, 1877; Fenner (reprint of 1924) p. 165; Johnson, 1925, p. 105, Fisher; 1926, p. 88. Niles, 1927, p. 153, gives a parody of "Roll, Jordan Roll" as sung by Negro soldiers in France.

---

[1] Local title.   [2] No local title given.

A

REPORTED from Auburn, Ala., 1915–1916, MS. of Miss Helen Blasingame, as heard at a Negro revival meeting. Sung also by Negroes around Durham, N. C.

Roll, Jurding, roll, roll, Jurding, roll;
   You oughter been settin' in the Kingdom
    To hear sweet Jurding roll.

Oh! Mother, you oughter been there;
   Yes, my Lord, you oughter been settin' in the Kingdom
    To hear sweet Jurding roll.

Then roll, Jurding, roll, roll, Jurding, roll;
   You oughter been settin' in the Kingdom
    To hear sweet Jurding roll.

Oh! Sister, you oughter been there;
   Yes, my Lord, you oughter been settin' in the Kingdom,
    To hear sweet Jurding roll.

B

Reported from Durham, N. C., 1919, MS. of Eugene C. Crawford.

Roll on, Jordan, roll;
Roll on, Jordan, roll;
I want to be setting in the Kingdom
To hear old Jordan roll.

28

REPORTED from Auburn, Ala., 1915–1916, MS. of J. P. Creel, as from South Carolina. "Sung by Negroes at camp-meeting."
   Stanza 1 is a variation of the common,

        Two white horses side by side
        Me and my Jesus going to take a little ride,

of the printed collections. Stanza 2 must date from the eighteen-eighties and nineties when the cotton mill industry was developing in South Carolina.

Two big horses hitched to a slide,
Me and my Jesus am a gwine to take a ride.

Chorus
Hallelujah! I'se been under the water,
Hallelujah! Amen.

I'll pour oil of salvation on my spindles,
I'se gwine into heaven lickety brindle.

When you hear me pop my whip,
You may know I'se out on a heavenly trip.

When you hear massa Jesus talking to a coon,
You may know the great millennium am a coming mighty soon.

29

REPORTED from Auburn, Ala., 1915–1916, MS. of J. R. Jackson.
Stanza 1 I have heard sung with "Pharaoh's Army." The idea of stanza 2
is found in several songs.
The refrain occurs in a number of songs; for example, no. 70, in this chapter.

> One o' these days, 'bout twelve o'clock
> This old world's a gonna reel and rock,
> I ain't gonna grieve my Lord no more,
> I ain't gonna grieve my Lord no more.

> I'm goin' to heaven and I'm gonna ride
> Six white horses side by side,
> I ain't gonna grieve my Lord no more,
> I ain't gonna grieve my Lord no more.

30

A

REPORTED from Auburn, Ala., 1915–1916, MS. of A. L. Holloway, as from
Monroe County, southern Alabama.
Sung by Negroes around Durham, N. C.
Lines 3 and 4 are evidently from the hymn lines,

> Rock of ages, cleft for me,
> Let me hide myself in Thee,

which has always been popular in camp-meetings and revivals as well as in regular church services. For other adaptations of lines from "Rock of Ages" see
Edwards (Bahama), 1895, p. 40, and Kennedy (Louisiana) 1925, p. 90.

> O my brother, when de world's on fier
> Don't you want God's bosom to be yo' pillar,
> Hide me over in de rocks of ages,
> Rock of ages, pray for me.

> O my sister, etc.

> O my elder, etc.

𝐵

Reported from Auburn, Ala., 1915–1916, MS. of J. N. Dubberly.

> O my loving pastor,
> When the world talks about you
> Don't you want God's bosom
> To be your pillar,
> Hide me over in rocks of ages,
> Rocks of ages cleft for me.

> O my loving sister, etc.

> O my loving brother, etc.

31

CITY OF THE REFUGE [1]

REPORTED from Durham, N. C., 1925, MS. of N. I. White. From Creedmoor, N. C., as sung by Ed Lloyd.

The refrain is as in Scarborough, 1925, p. 208, with music, as from South Carolina.

With stanza 1, cf. nos. 42 and 43 in this chapter.

Variants of stanza 3 occur in many spirituals; for example, Scarborough, 1925, p. 256, as from South Carolina. A variant occurs in "Blow Your Trumpet, Gabriel" (Allen, 1867), with a note that the song was known in Charleston, S. C., twenty-five years before.

Stanza 4 is probably descended from the old camp-meeting song of the whites, "Where are Now the Hebrew Children" in E. W. Miller, *The Southern Harmony and Musical Companion*, Philadelphia, 1847 (first edition, 1835) p. 276; also in Theron Brown and Hezekiah Butterworth, *The Story of the Hymns and Their Tunes*, New York, 1906, p. 270. An ante-bellum novelist (Caroline Lee Hentz, *The Planter's Northern Bride*, Philadelphia, 1854, i, 59) describes a scene in which Negroes improvise a funeral hymn of their own from this song.

The tune is given in Appendix I, p. 407.

> Noah's hammer ring, Sinner, repent,
> Noah's saw ring Judgment,
> He had to run, he had to run, he had to run to the City of Refuge,
> He had to run.

> There was a man in Pharisee
> Whose name was Nicodemus [2] who wouldn't believe;
> The same came to Christ by night,
> Want to be taught out o' human sight,

---

[1] Local title.

[2] I have seen somewhere a spiritual stanza in which Nicodemus becomes Nigger Demus.

He had to run, he had to run, he had to run to the City of Refuge,
He had to run.

Paul and Silas was bound in jail,
One sang and the other one prayed;
Stayed in jail all night long,
But the angel came and unlocked the door.
They had to run, they had to run, they had to run, to the City of
    Refuge,
They had to run.

Hebrew children were cast in the fiery furnace,
They went in but they were not punished.
How many was there, do you know,
Wan't but three, but I saw fo',
They had to run, they had to run, they had to run to the City of
    Refuge,
They had to run.

I don't know, Oh my Lord,
But it looks like to me it's the son of God;
They had to run, they had to run, they had to run to the City of
    Refuge,
They had to run.

32
THAT OLD–TIME RELIGION [1]

A WELL-KNOWN camp-meeting song of both Negroes and white people. I can
recall hearing it in my boyhood as a camp-meeting song of the white people,
and my mother heard it sung regularly by white people at the Rock Springs
Camp Ground, Lincoln County, western North Carolina, about 1875. It is still
sung by both white people and Negroes and is of indefinite length.

Cf. Marsh, 1877, p. 158; Perrow, 1913, p. 148; H. D. Benedict, *Belair
Plantation Melodies*, 1924; Ernest Newton, *This Old-Time Religion*, 1925; Johnson, 1925, p. 76; Odum, 1925, p. 142; *Ham-Ramsay Revival Hymns*, no. 238.

At the Pleasant Valley Christian Church (Negro) in Durham it is sung from
a hymn-book called *Gems of Love*, and consists of ten stanzas, like those of the
present version, but includes only two of the present stanzas (3 and 8).

Perrow's version, as sung by mountain whites, contains lines which he saw
the singers improvise about a peculiar local circumstance. In the *Ham-Ramsay
Revival Hymns* (no. 191) a part of "The Old-Time Religion" forms the concluding portion of another hymn, copyrighted by Mr. Ramsay, and in *The Baptist
Evangelical Song Book and Working Guide* (n. d.), used in Durham Negro
churches, I find a part of it worked into the song, "I am Determined to
Hold Out."

Local title around Durham, N. C.

A

Reported from Durham, N. C., 1925, MS. of N. I. White, from Creedmoor, N. C., as sung by Ed Lloyd.

> Gimme that old-time religion,
> Gimme that old-time religion,
> Gimme that old-time religion,
>   It's good enough for me.
>
> It is good in time of trouble,
> It is good in time of trouble,
> It is good in time of trouble,
>   It's good enough for me.
>
> It was good for Paul and Silas, etc.
>
> It'll make you love your neighbor, etc.
>
> It'll make you love your brother, etc.
>
> It'll take you home to heaven, etc.
>
> It was good for the Hebrew children, etc.
>
> It'll be good when I am dying, etc.

B

Reported from Auburn, Ala., 1915–1916, MS. of W. E. Lasater. Evidently somewhat corrupted.

> Give me that good ole time religion,
> It's good enough for me,
> It's good enough in time of trouble,
> It's good enough when the world talks about you,
> It's good enough for me when the world is on fire.

33

Reported from Auburn, Ala., 1915–1916, MS. of W. E. Lasater. "Sung in Negro church."

Lines 3 and 4 are common in the uncorrupted form,

> The morning star was a witness, too;

as are lines 5, 6, 7, 8, 12, and 14. With lines 3 and 4, cf. Fenner, 1901, p. 146; Barton, 1899, pp. 14 and 45; Edwards (Bahama), 1895, p. 29. The witness occurs often in Negro spirituals, generally in the religious sense in which the word is used in hymns of white people, derived from numerous Biblical passages.

Parts of this song, and several songs with a refrain about joining the band, are sung by Negroes around Durham, N. C.

Joining the band (or the union band) is common to several printed spirituals. Such early religious song-books of the whites as *Zion Songster*, second edition, 1827, *The Southern Harmony and Musical Companion*, 1835, *The Christian's Companion*, 1836, *The Christian Lyre*, 1830, and books of early revival songs like *The Revivalist* (1868), abound in references to union, the union band, etc.

> Hallelujah, Hallelujah, we'll jine the union band,
> Make ole Satan leave me alone,
> Let me do my master's will,
> My head got wet with the morning dew,
> The morning star bow down with the wetness dew,
> I went down in the valley to pray,
> When I got there, ole Satan was there.
> My soul got happy and I stayed all day.
> There wasn't but one thing I done wrong,
> I stayed in my sins one day too long,
> One day, one day, walking along
> I heard a voice in the sky,
> It made me think my time was near,
> That must have been my Lord passing by.

34

THE OLD SHIP OF ZION

THIS song, which exists in at least two distinct versions, with numerous variants, has long been a popular revival song of both white people and Negroes. It was one of the favorite songs at the ante-bellum camp-meetings in which Negroes and whites participated together. The earliest mention of the song I have noticed is in Sarah Josepha Hale's *Liberia, or Mr. Peyton's Experiment*, New York, 1853, pp. 36, 41, where it is sung by both white people and Negroes as a familiar camp-meeting song.

The gospel ship, of which this song is the best-known exemplar, has been the subject of many religious songs of both whites and Negroes from the early nineteenth century to the present time. It is simply one of the common variations of the journey to Heaven, which involves the pedestrian pilgrimage (common in the early nineteenth century but now out of date), the heavenly chariot, the gospel ship, and the gospel train — all common to both white people and Negroes. In the irreligious "Shortnin' Bread" even the tail of a kite carries passengers. An ultra-modern variant of the tendency to modernize the means of communication is the telephone to Heaven, also used by both races.

I have found different gospel-ship songs in practically all the early religious song-books of the whites that I have examined, for example, *Zion Songster*, second edition, 1827; *The Christian Lyre*, 1830, etc. An especially interesting example is "The Heavenly Mariner," no. 34 in John C. Totten's *Selection of*

Hymns and Spiritual Songs, etc., 19th ed., New York, 1827. In an elaborate allegory of thirteen stanzes, Hope is the anchor, Faith the quadrant, Christ the sun, the Bible the chart, conscience the plummet line, the Holy Ghost the steersman, etc.

The gospel-ship songs, and notably "The Old Ship of Zion," have become entangled both in words and music with "Put John on the Island" (no. 35, below), and in the words of some stanzas with the gospel chariot and Christian warfare. There are also occasional verbal connections with the gospel-train songs. A common link is King Jesus, who is captain, driver, or conductor.

Among the religious song-books of the whites containing the gospel ship may be cited *The Southern Harmony and Musical Companion*, Philadelphia, 1835, "The Spiritual Sailor"; *The Sacred Harp*, Philadelphia, 1867, "The Gospel Voyage"; *The Revivalist*, Philadelphia, 1868, p. 185, "Old Ship Zion" (similar to both *A* and *C* versions following); the *Ham-Ramsay Revival Hymns*, Chattanooga, Tenn., 1917–1925 (?), no. 304, "The Old Ship of Zion" (*A* version below).

Among Negro song collections may be cited Marsh, 1877, p. 165, "My Ship is on the Ocean"; Fenner, 1901, p. 55, "Don't You View Dat Ship"; and "The Old Ship of Zion," Ibid., p. 85; Higginson, (*Atlantic Monthly*), 1867, p. 685, nos. 19–20, Barton, 1899, p. 44, Edwards (Bahama), 1895, p. 52; Murphy, 1904, p. 32; *New Republic*, 1917, p. 214; Kennedy, 1925, p. 41.

A

Reported from Durham, N. C., 1925, MS. of Mrs. O. B. Thompson. As sung around Columbia, Tenn. Mrs. Thompson remembers hearing it sung by her mother and grandmother before 1860.

The tune is quite distinct from that of the *C* version.

> What ship is that will take us all home?
>   O glory, hallelujah.
> 'T is the old ship of Zion, hallelujah.
>
> So you think she will be able to take us all home?
>   O glory, hallelujah.
> I know she will be able, hallelujah.
>
> Come along, come along, and let us go home,
>   O glory, hallelujah.
> Our home is over Jordan, hallelujah.
>
> What kind of freight have you on board?
>   O glory, hallelujah.
> Love to God and one another, hallelujah.
>
> We have some friends before us gone,
>   O glory, hallelujah.
> By and by we'll go and meet them, hallelujah.

ℬ

Reported from Durham, N. C., 1926, MS. of N. I. White, as sung by H. E. Spence.

"Sung in eastern North Carolina since the eighteen-eighties by both white people and Negroes."

The tune is the same as that of the *A* version, except for the chorus. Stanzas 1 and 2 belong to the *A* version, stanza 3 and chorus to the *C* version. The invocation to "go home," and "My home is over Jordan," are common both to the Negro spirituals and to the camp-meeting songs of the white people.

O what ship is this that will take us all home?
 O glory, hallelujah.
'T is the old ship of Zion, hallelujah.

Chorus
Come along, come along, let's all go home,
 O glory, hallelujah.
My home is over Jordan, hallelujah.

Do you think she will be able to take us all home?
 O glory, hallelujah.
No doubt she will be able, hallelujah.

She has landed many a thousand and can land as many more,
 O glory, hallelujah.
She has landed them in heaven, hallelujah.

C

Reported from Durham, N. C., 1925. Written down for Mrs. O. B. Thompson by her cook, as sung in the Negro Baptist churches of Durham. My mother remembers this version as sung at the Rock Springs Camp Ground, Lincoln County, western North Carolina, in 1875. I have heard one stanza not in this version: "She'll be coming round the mountain," and a parody on stanza 5, sung by students: "She'll be loaded with corn liquor."

The old ship of Zion when she comes, when she comes,
The old ship of Zion when she comes, when she comes,
'T is the old ship of Zion, the old ship of Zion,
The old ship of Zion when she comes.

She has landed many a thousand when she comes, when she comes.
She has landed many a thousand when she comes, when she comes,
She has landed many a thousand, landed many a thousand,
She's landed many a thousand when she comes.

She landed my dear mother when she comes, etc.

She landed my old father, etc.

She'll be loaded with bright angels, etc.

Oh, she runs so level and study, etc.

It will land you safe in glory, etc.

The old ship of Zion when she comes, etc.

35

REPORTED from Durham, N. C., 1926, MS. of N. I. White, as sung by H. E. Spence. He has heard it in eastern North Carolina, near the Dismal Swamp, as early as the eighteen-eighties, and since.

The basic lines of stanzas 6, 7, and 8 occur constantly in the "Ship of Zion" songs, and the tune is the same as that of the *B* version of the "Old Ship of Zion." Stanzas 7 and 8 also occur in some of the songs dealing with the chariot, "captain," being changed to "driver" (for example, Barton, 1899, p. 44). "King Jesus is the captain" also occurs in various songs of Christian warfare, both white and Negro.

John is evidently a composite of the Apostle John and John the Baptist.

Cf. *Southern Workman*, xxx, 590 and Fenner (reprint of 1924), p. 122.

The tune is given in Appendix I, p. 407.

> Oh, we'll put John on the island
>> When the bridegroom comes.
> Oh, we'll put John on the island
>> When he comes.
> We'll put John on the island,
> We'll put John on the island,
> We'll put John on the island,
>> When he comes.
>
> O we put him there to starve him
>> When the bridegroom comes,
> O we put him there to starve him
>> When he comes.
> We put him there to starve him,
> We put him there to starve him,
> We put him there to starve him,
>> When he comes.
>
> But you can't starve a Christian, etc.
>
> Fed him on milk and honey, etc.
>
> O look down Jordan's river, etc.
>
> O see that ship come sailin', etc.
>
> She's loaded with bright angels, etc.
>
> King Jesus is the captain, etc.

36

REPORTED from Durham, N. C., 1926, MS. of N. I. White, as sung by H. E. Spence. He has heard it sung in eastern North Carolina, near the Dismal Swamp, as early as the eighteen-nineties, and since, mainly by white people at corn-shuckings and log-rollings. In 1911 and 1912 students at Trinity College, N. C., used parts of it, to the same tune, as a "pep" song at baseball games, with "hang" for "drag" in the chorus, and the name of the opposing team for "devil" in the last stanza.

The tune is given in Appendix I, p. 408.

Chorus

We'll roll, we'll roll the chariot along,
We'll roll, we'll roll the chariot along,
We'll roll, we'll roll the chariot along,
And we won't drag on behind.

If the sinner's in the way, why we stop and take him on,
If the sinner's in the way, why we stop and take him on,
If the sinner's in the way, why we stop and take him on,
And we won't drag on behind.

If the drunkard's in the way, why we stop and take him on, etc.

If the gambler's in the way, etc.

If the harlot's in the way, etc.
     (and so on, *ad. lib.*, but the last stanza is always):

If the devil's in the way, why we will run it over him, etc.

37

REPORTED from Auburn, Ala., 1915–1916, MS. of W. E. Lasater. Sung by Negroes around Durham, N. C.

All the lines occur in other printed songs. Based on the parable of the Foolish Virgins, like several other Negro songs.

In J. Thornton, *The Cabin and the Parlor*, Philadelphia, 1852, p. 22, a bit of slave conversation based upon the text, "Keep your lamps trimmed and burning," suggests that the spiritual of that name, which is related to the present one, was in existence in 1852.

Cf. Marsh, 1877, p. 190; *Southern Workman*, xxix, 206, xxv, 528, xlv, 88; Johnson, 1925, p. 170; and no. 16A in this chapter.

Oh, brother, what are you going to do when your lamp goes out?
Come on, sister, with your ups and downs,
The Lord is gwine to meet you on half-way ground.
Oh, sinner, what are you going to do when your lamp goes out?

38

REPORTED from Auburn, Ala., 1915–1916, MS. of W. E. Lasater. Sung, with some differences, by Negroes around Durham, N. C.

Lines 3, 5, and 6 occur in several printed spirituals. The refrain "That suits me" occurs in Kennedy, 1924, p. 153, with a part of no. 57 in this chapter (slightly different in one line), making an independent spiritual.

I have heard the first line explained as an invitation to begin one of the marches around the room which sometimes occur in Negro worship.

The first six lines are as in "Dat Suits Me," Hallowell, 1905, p. 63, as from Alabama. Cf. also "Dat Suits Me," Kennedy, 1925, p. 132, as from Louisiana.

> Come on, brother, let's go around the wall,
>   That suits me,
> Come on, sister, let's go around the wall,
>   That suits me.
> I don't want to stumble and I don't want to fall,
>   That suits me.
> Come on, sister, with your ups and downs,
> The Lord is going to meet you on half-way ground.

39

REPORTED from Auburn, Ala., 1915–1916, MS. of D. Q. McCord. "Church song."

One of my colored friends says he thinks this is a "coon song," but not properly a church song. He says he has heard it sung near Durham, N. C.

> Come 'ere, chillun, an' listen to me;
> I'll tell you 'bout whale swallowin' Jonah,
> While sailin' on de sea,
> Yes, es-es, Yes, es-es, Yes, es-es.
>
> Three long days and three long nights,
> Jonah in de belly of de whale swelled,
> Yes, es-es, Yes, es-es, Yes, es-es.
>
> De whale 'gin to pinch an' ole Jonah 'gin to scratch,
> So de whale flung Jonah in a sweet 'tater patch.
> Yes, es-es, Yes, es-es, Yes, es-es.

40

REPORTED from Durham, N. C., 1925, MS. of N. I. White, as sung by Ed Lloyd, who says it is incomplete. From Creedmoor, N. C.

> The whale swallowed Brother Jonah,
>   Yes, he did, no, he did n't.

Puked him up on sandy land,
An' a goad vine growed around Brother Jonah's head.
The greatest prayer that ever I heard
Was the prayer that Jonah prayed,
When the worm came an' cut the goad vine down
From around Brother Jonah's head.

41

REPORTED from Durham, N. C., 1925, MS. of N. I. White. Used occasionally as a campus song by Trinity College students about 1910. Both stanzas are as in Barton, 1899, p. 40.

Another song suggesting the influence of the catechisms on which religious education of ante-bellum Negroes was largely based.

Who did, who did, who did swallow Jonah, Jonah,
Who did, who did, who did swallow Jonah, Jonah,
Who did, who did, who did swallow Jonah, Jonah,
Who did swallow Jonah, who did swallow Jonah — dow-own?

Whale did, whale did, whale did swallow Jonah, Jonah,
Whale did, whale did, whale did swallow Jonah, Jonah,
Whale did, whale did, whale did swallow Jonah, Jonah,
Whale did swallow Jonah, whale did swallow Jonah—dow-own!

42

REPORTED from Auburn, Ala., 1915–1916, MS. of W. E. Lasater.

Cf. "De Ole Ark's a-Moverin'" in the printed collections; for example, "Who Built de Ark," Fisher, 1926, p. 204, which was a popular song on the minstrel stage in the early eighteen-eighties, according to *Old Slack's Reminiscence and Pocket History of the Colored Profession from 1865 to 1891*, by Ike Simond (Chicago, 1891), p. 14.

The first two lines of this chorus are quoted as the title of a song sung by South Carolina Negroes, listed in *J. A. F. L.*, 1914, p. 249; a similar chorus also occurs in "Norah," a hammer song, in Scarborough, 1925, p. 223, with music. Noah occurs frequently in the various versions of the "Creation Song" in the old minstrel books; cf. III, no. 25, V, no. 26, XIII, no. 14.

Odum quotes a variant (Odum, 1926, p. 191) used as a work song.

The question-and-answer opening suggests the influence of the catechisms on which the early religious instruction of Negroes by Methodists and Baptists was mainly based. Cf. the similar opening of a Noah song in *J. A. F. L.*, 1910, p. 435.

Who built the ark? Noah built the ark;
Some say Noah was a foolish man,

But I says he's a wise man,
For he built his ark on hard ole ground,
He built his ark of gopher wood.
All beasts' kind went to his ark,
Noah came riding by,
And they poked a scorning finger at him,
Ole Noah tell the ark to move, move, move.

43

REPORTED from Durham, N. C., 1919, MS. of N. I. White, as heard in Statesville, N. C., about 1907 and Durham, N. C. about 1912. Popular at that period
as a picnic and campus song among white people.
    A slightly different version occurs in Edwards (Bahama) 1895, p. 27.

No-eh built de ark,
    Yes, he di-id,
No-eh, built de ark,
    Yes, he di-id,
No-eh built de ark,
    Yes, he di-id,
Ole man No-eh built de ark.

44

REPORTED from Auburn, Ala., 1915–1916, MS. of D. Q. McCord. "Church
song used when taking up collection. Sung over and over until all money is
given."
    The refrain has considerable Scriptural background: 2 Kings, xvii, 17 ("And
they caused their sons and daughters to pass through the fire"); 2 Kings, xxiii,
10 ("that no man might make his son and his daughter to pass through the
fire"); Deuteronomy, xviii, 10 (the same); Isaiah, xxiv, 15 ("glorify the Lord
in the fires"), and xliii, 12 ("when thou walkest through the fire").

O! who's gointa help dat missionary band,
Coming up through de fi-er,
O! who's gointa help dat missionary band,
Coming up through de fi-er.
If you ain't got a quarter, a dime'll do,
Coming up through de fi-er,
But we'd rather have de quarter and dime too,
Coming up through de fi-er.

45

A

REPORTED from Auburn, Ala., 1915–1916, MS. of D. Q. McCord. "Church song sung by cotton-field Negroes."
Although not identical with the printed versions of "Reign Marse Jesus, O Reign," (for example, Marsh, 1877, p. 189), there is not a line in it which is not found in that or other printed spirituals.

> Ef effer 'ligion wuz a thing dat money could buy,
> Oh, reign, Marse Jesus, oh reign,
> De rich would live an' de po' would die,
> Oh, reign, Marse Jesus, oh reign.
>
> Oh reign, reign, reign, oh, my Lord,
> Oh reign, Marse Jesus, oh reign.
> Oh reign, reign, reign, oh my Lord,
> Oh reign, Marse Jesus, oh reign.
>
> But de Lord, he 'lowed, dat he would n't have it so,
> Reign, Marse Jesus, oh reign,
> So de rich mus' die, jes same as de po',
> Oh reign, Marse Jesus, oh reign.

B

Reported from Durham, N. C., 1925, MS. of N. I. White. From Creedmoor, N. C., as sung by Ed Lloyd.
This is the same in structure as the *A* version and is based on the same two common couplets. In the *A* version a new song is made by taking well-known couplets and equipping them with interlines and chorus; in the *B* version still another song is produced by changing the interline and chorus.
Stanza 3 is from the chorus of the gospel hymn, "Happy Day," still sung at white revivals:

> Happy day, happy day,
> When Jesus washed my sins away.

I am practically certain that I have seen stanza 4 and stanza 8 in old revival hymns, but I can cite no particular passage.

> If-a 'ligion was a thing that money could buy,
> Good-bye, goin' to leave you behind,
> De rich would live and de po' would die,
> Good-bye, goin' to leave you behind.

Chorus

Farewell, mohner, goin' to leave you behind,
Farewell, mohner, good-bye, goin' to leave you behind.

But de Lord he wouldn't have it so,
Good-bye, goin' to leave you behind,
So de rich must die, just de same as de po',
Good-bye, goin' to leave you behind.

I never will forget that day,
Good-bye, goin' to leave you behind.
When Jesus washed my sins away,
Good-bye, goin' to leave you behind.

Shout away, I know you're free,
Good-bye, goin' to leave you behind,
Christ has bought your liberty.
Good-bye, goin' to leave you behind.

Can't you remember and remember well,
Good-bye, goin' to leave you behind,
The date you left the gates of hell,
Good-bye, goin' to leave you behind.

Hell is a dark and dismus place,
Good-bye, goin' to leave you behind,
If a sinner go there he don't deserve no grace,
Good-bye, goin' to leave you behind.

If this day was Judgment Day,
Good-bye, goin' to leave you behind,
Every soul would try to play,
Good-bye, goin' to leave you behind.

Want to go to heaven as I die,
Good-bye, goin' to leave you behind,
Shout salvation as I fly,
Good-bye, goin' to leave you behind.

When I get to heaven goin' to shout and sing,
Good-bye, goin' to leave you behind,
I'm goin' to drink water out de healin' spring,
Good-bye, goin' to leave you behind.

46

REPORTED from Auburn, Ala., 1915–1916, MS. of S. A. Allen. "Heard sung by Negroes in Shelby County (Ala.) jail, who would count as high as one hundred and fifty, using the last two lines as a refrain and singing the refrain on every number divisible by five."

With slight verbal variations, this is the same as in Perrow, 1913, p. 154, as from Alabama in 1908.

> There's one, there's two, there's three, there's four
> Little angels,
> There's five little angels,
> There's five little angels in the band,
> On a Sunday morning,
> On a Sunday morning soon.

47

REPORTED from Auburn, Ala., MS. of R. M. Beasly. One of my colored friends tells me that this is a "coon song." Also sung around Durham, N. C.

Here the spiritual is obviously based upon the counting-rhyming game common to Caucasian folk-lore. Cf. III, no. 24.

> The animals came in one by one
> Noah said go get yore gun,
> The animals came in two by two,
> Noah said take my axe and cut work in two,
> Animals came in three by three,
> Work's been waiting a thousand years for me,
> The animals came in four by four,
> Noah says go shut the door,
> Hallelu, hallelu, hallelujah to the Lawd,
> The animals came in five by five,
> Before I work I'll be buried alive,
> Animals came in six by six,
> The elephant laughed at the hyena's tricks,
> Hallelu, hallelu, hallelujah to the Lawd.

48

REPORTED from Durham, N. C., 1919, MS. of Walter J. Miller.

Based on the counting-rhyming game. The rhyming of dates in Negro songs is at least as old as the minstrel songs of the 1840's. Cf. IV, no. 27, and note.

> Eighteen hundred and forty-four,
> Christ done open dat Heavenly door,

Eighteen hundred and forty-five,
Christ done made dat dead man 'live.

Eighteen hundred and forty-six,
Christ done gut us a place done fix,
Eighteen hundred and forty-seven,
Christ done set dat Heavenly table.

Eighteen hundred and forty-eight,
Christ done made dat crooked way straight,
Eighteen hundred and forty-nine,
Christ done turned dat water to wine.

Eighteen hundred and forty-ten,
Christ done moan for his oldest friend.
Eighteen hundred and forty-eleven,
Christ be at de door when you gits to Heaven.

49

REPORTED from Auburn, Ala., 1915-1916, MS. of R. M. Beasly. Sung by
Negroes around Durham, N. C.
   The refrain is that of "Walk Jerusalem Just Like John" which is found in
several collections. The last three lines seem to be improvised.

I want to be ready,
I want to be ready,
I want to be ready,
Walking to Jerusalem just like John.
Oh Lord, won't you come by here,
Now is the needed time,
Lord, won't you hear my prayer.

50

REPORTED from Auburn, Ala., 1915-1916, MS. of R. M. Beasly.
   All except line 4 is direct from the gospel hymn, sung commonly in Methodist
churches of the whites in the nineteen hundreds, "There is rest for the weary."

There is rest for the weary,
There is rest for the weary,
There is rest for you.
Christian peoples has a home in glory,
There is rest for you.
On the other side of Jordan
There is rest for you.

51

A

REPORTED from Auburn, Ala., MS. of R. M. Beasly.

Except for the grammar of line 3 it is identical with stanza 1 of Thoma Haweis's hymn included in several hymn-books of the white churches from the early nineteenth century to the present time. It is also used as a stanza in "My Soul Wants Something That's New," Barton, 1899, p. 147, where it is followed by stanza 2 of Watts's "Alas and Did My Saviour Bleed?"; in Hallowell (Alabama), 1905, p. 31; and Odum, 1926, p. 195, as a religious work song.

> Dark was the night and cold was the ground
> In which the Lord was laid,
> Sweat like blood run down in drops
> And in agony he prayed.

B

Reported from Durham, N. C., 1925, MS. of N. I. White. From Creedmoor, N. C., as sung by Ed Lloyd.

Stanzas 1 and 2 occur as stanzas 1 and 2 of "Am I Born to Die?" with the refrain, "Am I born to die?" in Hallowell, 1905 (Lowndes County, Ala.), p. 31. The remaining stanzas in the Hallowell song are different, but seem similarly related to various regular hymns. For other appearances of stanza 1 in spirituals, see preceding note.

Practically all the rest of the song is from various hymns of the whites; the second stanza from John Newton's "Amazing Grace"; the fourth from Isaac Watts's "Am I a Soldier of the Cross?" and the chorus was found by Allen (*Slave Songs of the United States*, 1867, p. lx) "abundantly in Methodist hymn books."

> Dark was the night and cold was the ground
>   In which the Lord was laid.
> Sweat like blood run down in drops,
>   And in agony he prayed.

Chorus

> Remember me, remember me,
> O Lord, remember me.

> I once was lost but now I'm found,
>   Was blind but now I see.
> Remember me, remember me,
>   O Lord, remember me.

I heard the voice of Jesus say
I am this dark world's light,
Look unto me, the moon shall rise,
And all thy days be bright.

Must I be carried to the skies
On flowery beds of ease,
While others fought to win the prize
And sailed through bloody seas.

52

REPORTED from Auburn, Ala., 1915–1916, anonymously. It is still sung at the Pleasant Union Christian Church, Durham, N. C.

This whole song, with slight verbal variations, occurs in Scarborough, 1925, p. 172, as the chorus of "Raccoon Up de Simmon Tree." Cf. also "Some O' These Days," a spiritual used as a work song, Odum, 1925, p. 107.

Walking the golden streets is a phrase from the early- nineteenth-century religious song-books. Cf. *Zion Songster*, second edition, 1827, p. 169:

Great tribulation you shall meet,
But soon shall walk the golden street.

On p. 7 of *Old Slack's Reminiscence and Pocket History of the Colored Profession from 1865 to 1891*, by Ike Simond, Chicago, 1891, I find that in 1877 "Jim Bland's *Golden Slippers* was in the mouth of every man, woman and child in the land." Robert Russa Moton, in *Finding a Way Out: An Autobiography* (1921), p. 60, records his distress at hearing this song in his boyhood (the late eighteen-seventies) as a minstrel song, after he had long been accustomed to it as a hymn.

Oh, dem golden slippers,
Oh, dem golden slippers,
Dem's de slippers I'se a-gwine to wear,
Because dey looks so neat.

Oh, dem golden slippers,
Oh, dem golden slippers,
Dem's de slippers I'se a-gwine to wear,
When I walks on de golden street.

53

REPORTED from Durham, N. C., 1925, MS. of N. I. White. From memory as heard in Pine Street A. M. E. Church. The same as in Macy, 1887, p. 3. The differences are so very much slighter than is usually the case that I suspect it was learned from this book.

With this and the preceding song compare no. 298 in the *Ham-Ramsay Revival Hymns*, used extensively in Southern revivals to-day (Chattanooga, Tenn., n. d., but between 1917 and 1925).

> If you will come to Jesus you will outshine the sun,
> You will outshine the sun, you will outshine the sun,
> And walk the golden streets on high.

(The remaining six stanzas differ only in the *if* clauses.)

The first stanza is a descendant of the gospel shoes frequently mentioned in the religious songs of the whites in the early nineteenth century; for example, *Zion Songster*, second edition, 1827, p. 163:

> What kind of shoes are those you wear,
> On which you boldly stand.

What kind of shoes are you goin' to wear? Golden slippers.
What kind of shoes are you goin' to wear? Golden slippers.
Golden slippers I'm bound to wear,
Outshine the glittering sun.

Chorus

Yes, yes, yes, yes, yes, my Lord,
I'm goin' to join that heavenly choir.
Yes, yes, yes, yes, my Lord —
I'm a soldier of the cross.

What kind of crown you goin' to wear? Starry crown.
What kind of crown you goin' to wear? Starry crown.
Starry crown I'm bound to wear,
Outshine the glittering sun.

What kind of robe you goin' to wear? White robe.
What kind of robe you goin' to wear? White robe.
Long white robe I'm bound to wear,
Outshine the glittering sun.

What kind of harp you goin' to play? Golden harp.
What kind of harp you goin' to play? Golden harp.
Golden harp I'm bound to play,
Outshine the glittering sun.

54

REPORTED from Durham, N. C., 1919, MS. of J. P. Jones. "I have heard old Negro women singing this on washday at my home."

"Jacob and Joseph and Josiah and Noah" are an echo of the various "witnesses" mentioned in the early-nineteenth-century religious songs of the whites, and echoed in other Negro spirituals, for example, Work, 1907, p. 10; Johnson, 1925, p. 130; in which Methuselah, Samson, and Daniel are witnesses. Cf. *Zion Songster*, second edition, 1827, p. 82;

> There was Joshua and Joseph, Elias and Moses
> That prayed and God heard from his throne;
> There was Abraham and Isaac, and Jacob and David,
> And Solomon and Stephen and John.

For another "witness" passage, see *Ibid.*, p. 117.

> Lord, I wish I wus in heaven,
> Lord, I wish I wus there for I'd stay,
> Lord, I wish I wus in heaven this day,
> For I'd play on de golden harp, harp, harp,
> For I'd play on de golden harp, harp, harp,
> There'll be Jacob and Joseph, and Josiah and Noah
> And God knows how many more,
> And God knows how many more.
> There'll be Jacob and Joseph, and Josiah and Noah,
> There'll be Jacob and Joseph, and Josiah and Noah,
> Ain't that a heavenly crew, crew, crew,
> Ain't that a heavenly crew, crew, crew.

55

REPORTED from Auburn, Ala., 1918, MS. of W. S. Lindsay. Also sung by Negroes near Durham, N. C.

> Father gwine to miss me in my walk,
> Father gwine to miss me in my talk,
> Father I know you're gwine to miss me when I'm gone.

Chorus

> When I'm gone,
> When I'm gone,
> Father, I know you're gwine to miss me when I'm gone.

Mother, sister, and brother substituted for father in stanzas 2, 3, and 4.

56

DON'T YOU SEE? [1]

REPORTED from Auburn, Ala., 1917, MS. of F. W. Calhoun, as from Muscoda, Ala. "A camp-meeting song of Negroes heard at one of their revivals." Also sung by Negroes near Durham, N. C.

The last couplet appears in other spirituals.

"Don't You See?" is the title and refrain of a spiritual from Louisiana, Kennedy, 1925, p. 88.

> Go to bed, children, and don't you cry,
> Fer your dada and mammy have got to die.
> Don't you see? Don't you see?
>
> Father and mother how can you bear,
> To hear your children curse and swear?
> Don't you see? Don't you see?
>
> Come up brethern and sistern right now,
> Git your sins out, git down and bow,
> Don't you see? Don't you see?
>
> Call on de Lord if you hafto shout,
> Talk from your soul, git it stirring about.
> Don't you see? Don't you see?

57

REPORTED from Durham, N. C., 1919, MS. of French W. Graham, as heard in Grayson County, Va., 1914.

Also sung by Negroes around Durham, N. C.

The idea of "I want to go to Heaven" and "I long to be there" is common to many spirituals and old revival songs, and not entirely absent from hymns still in use by white people. White is the conventional color for all ascension clothing in both the Negro spirituals and the gospel songs and hymns of the white people. In the Millerite excitement of the early eighteen-forties, white robes somewhat resembling nightgowns were sold by the thousand. The convention has a Scriptural origin in Ecclesiastes, ix, 8 ("Let thy garments be always white"); Revelation, iii, 4 ("Walk with me in white"), iii, 5, etc.

Cf. Marsh, 1877, p. 202; Barton, 1899, p. 31; Fenner, 1901, p. 24; Burlin (Hampton Series) 1918–1919, i, 22; Kennedy (Louisiana) 1924, p. 154.

> I want to go to Heaven and I want to go right,
>   Oh, how I long to be there.
> I want to go to Heaven all dressed in white,
>   Oh, how I long to go there.

[1] Local title.

I want to go to Heaven at my own expense,
  Oh, how I long to be there.
If I can't get through the gate I'll jump the fence,
  Oh; how I long to be there.

58

A

REPORTED from Greensboro, N. C., 1919, MS. of N. I. White. I learned this song from Miss Guelda Elliott, who learned it in Lexington, N. C., in 1907, from a Negro washerwoman at her work.

Also sung by Negroes around Durham, N. C.

Cf. Burlin (Hampton Series), 1917–1918, i, 14; Burleigh, 1917–1924; Hugo Frey, *A Collection of Negro Spirituals*, 1924; Johnson, 1925, p. 94; Fisher, 1926, p. 168.

'T ain't my mother, 't ain't my sister, but it's me, O Lord,
  A-standin' in the need of prayer;
'T ain't my mother, 't ain't my sister, but it's me, O Lord,
  A-standin' in the need of prayer.

Hit's me, hit's me, hit's me, O Lord,
  A-standin' in the need of prayer;
Hit's me, hit's me, hit's me, O Lord,
  A-standin' in the need of prayer.

'T ain't my father, 't ain't my brother, etc.

'T ain't my uncle, 't ain't my cousin, etc.

'T ain't my preacher, 't ain't my deacon, etc.

B

Reported from Durham, N. C., 1919, MS. of W. Q. Grigg, as from western North Carolina. "Sung by Negroes at a big meeting."

It's me, it's me, it's me, O Lord,
Standing in the need of prayer.
It's not my deacon, it's not my elder,
  but it's me, O Lord,
Standing in the need of prayer.

59

A

REPORTED from Durham, N. C., 1919, MS. of R. B. Edwards.

Lines 1 and 3, with different refrains, are found in several other songs. Cf. *J. A. F. L.*, 1897, p. 264; practically all versions of "Swing Low, Sweet Chariot," etc. They constitute one of the commonest of all spiritual stanzas, and are found just as commonly in the early camp-meeting songs of the whites. In Theron Brown and Hezekiah Butterworth, *The Story of the Hymns and Their Tunes* (New York, 1906), p. 273, the stanza is given as an example of the tune-leader's improvisation in "Canaan, Bright Canaan." I find the stanza in a number of other camp-meeting songs; for example, *The Revivalist*, 1868, in three distinct songs: "Canaan," p. 207, "Roll Call," p. 176, and "To that Land," p. 36.

If you get there before I do, all right, all right,
Jesus will make it all right.
Just tell them that I am coming too, all right, all right,
If you get there before I do, all right,
Just scratch a hole and pull me through, all right, all right.

B

Reported from Durham, N. C., 1925, MS. of N. I. White. From Creedmoor, N. C., as sung by Ed Lloyd.

I have heard a modern revival hymn of the white people, with the chorus "Jesus will make it all right," but I have not found it in print.

If my mother wants to see me,
Jesus will make it all right,
I'm on my horse in the battle field,
Jesus will make it all right,
All right, all right,
Jesus will make it all right.

Stanzas 2–6, for "mother" substitute "friends," "deacons," "daddy," "brother," "sister," etc.

60

THE GOSPEL POOL [1]

A

REPORTED from Durham, N. C., 1919, MS. of W. A. Ellison, Jr.

This song parallels the custom I have seen practised in white revival meetings of the telling of religious "experiences" by recent converts, to encourage waverers. Lines 4, 5, and 8 are probably based on the pool of Bethesda,

[1] No local title given.

John, v, 3, 4 (the moving of the water) and numerous other Biblical passages less directly applicable. Cf. *Zion Songster*, second edition, 1827, p. 141, "The Gospel Pool."

Several printed spirituals contain the line "I looked at my hands; my hands looked new." Cf. Edwards (Bahama), 1895, p. 146; Fenner, 1901, p. 127; Work, 1907, p. 48.

> "Brother, how did you feel dat day
> When yo' los' yo' guilt and burden?"
> "I felt like de Lord God done freed my soul
> An' de holy water moved on,
> I run all about, brethren, I run all about,
> I felt brand new, brethren, I felt brand new,
> My hands looked new, brethren, dey looked new;
> And de green trees bowed, brethren,
> De green trees bowed."

ℬ

Reported from Durham, N. C., 1919, MS. of R. B. Edwards.

Same as *A*, with "healing waters" for "holy waters" in line 4 and with lines 1 and 2 repeated as 8 and 9.

61

MOST DONE SUFFERING [1]

𝒜

REPORTED from Durham, N. C., 1919, MS. of W. A. Ellison, Jr.

Every line of stanza 1 and line 1 of stanza 2 are common property to the spirituals and, with some differences of expression, to the gospel and camp-meeting songs of the white people. The latter part of stanza 2 seems related to such well-known old gospel hymns as "Tell it to Jesus" and "Take it to the Lord in Prayer."

Cf. Barton, 1899, p. 6, and VII, no. 33.

> Rough, rocky road, I'se most done suffering.
> Rough, rocky road, I'se most done suffering.
> Rough, rocky road, I'se most done suffering.
> I'm bound to carry my soul to de Lord.
> I'm bound to carry my soul to de Lord.
>
> My sister 's on de road,
> I'm most done suffering.
> My sister 's on de road,
> I'm most done suffering.

[1] No local title given.

My mother 's on de road,
I'm most done suffering.
My mother 's on de road,
I'm bound for to carry
My soul to de Lord.

I'm going to heaven to live with Jesus.
I'm going to heaven to live with Jesus.
I live on my Jesus while I suffer here,
I'm going to tell him how you 'buse me,
I'm going to tell him how you 'buse me,
I'm going to tell him how you 'buse me,
While I'm suffering here.
I'm going to tell him 'bout my troubles
While I'm suffering here.

B

Reported from Durham, N. C., 1919, MS. of R. B. Edwards. "This is an old slavery song, said to have been sung by slaves when they went to work."

Rough rock road,
I am most done suffering.
Rough rock road,
I am most done suffering,
Rough rock road.
I am bound to carry my soul to the Lord.
Put me on the road, most done suffering.
Put me on the road, I am most done suffering.
I am bound to carry my soul to the Lord.

My sister is on the road,
I'm most done suffering.
My sister is on the road,
I'm most done suffering.
I am bound to carry my soul to the Lord.
I am bound to carry my soul to the Lord,
I am bound to carry my soul to the Lord,
My mother is on the road, I'm most done suffering,
My mother is on the road, I am most done suffering.
I am bound to carry my soul to the Lord.

62

HOW IT TIS–A WITH ME [1]

A

REPORTED from Durham, N. C., 1919, MS. of James Cannon. "Heard probably in either Virginia or North Carolina."

> How it 'tis-a with me-a,
> How it 'tis-a with me and my Lord,
> Nobody knows but myself and my God
> How it 'tis-a with me.

B

Reported from Durham, N. C., 1925, MS. of N. I. White. From Creedmoor,
N. C., as sung by Ed Lloyd, who says it was a favorite about ten years ago.

The first couplet, with or without interlines, occurs in a number of other
spirituals.

> Sometimes up and sometimes down,
>   How it tis-a with me,
> Sometimes almost on the ground,
>   How it tis-a with me.
> Nobody knows but myself and my Lawd
>   How it tis-a with me.

63

I GOT A MOTHER [2]

REPORTED from Durham, N. C., 1919, MS. of Jay L. Jackson.

Relatives in the promised land are frequently encountered in the spirituals,
and in the gospel hymns and the old camp-meeting songs of the white people.
The journey to the promised land (heaven, Zion, etc.) is the basis of many spirituals and camp-meeting songs of white people. I find both the relatives and the
journey in practically all the early song-books of the whites.

In the *Ham-Ramsay Revival Hymns*, Chattanooga, Tenn., n. d., but published
between 1917 and 1925, and still in extensive use in Southern revivals (white),
I find (no. 143), "I Have a Mother in the Promised Land," copyright, 1915, by
W. J. Ramsay, beginning:

> I have a father in the promised land
> And I hope some day we'll all get there
>   Way over in the promised land.

No local title given.   [2] Local title.

The remaining four stanzas are the same, except for "father," read "mother,"
"brother," "sister," "saviour."

Cf. Work, 1907, pp. 27, 31, 76; Perrow, 1913, p. 148 (as by mountain whites);
Southern Workman, xxx, 510; Odum, 1925, pp. 110, 138; also no. 64 in this
chapter.

I'se got a mudder in the promised land,
I'se won't stop workin' till I'se shakes huh han'.
I'm on muh way, I'm on muh way
To the promise' land.

I'se gotter fatha' in the promised land,
I'se ask muh fatha, come and go wid me,
If yuh don't go, I'll journey on
To the promise' land.

I'se gotter brotha in the promised land,
I'se ask muh brotha does he wanta go long,
If he don't wanta go, I'll journey on
To the promise' land.

64

REPORTED from Durham, N. C., 1925, MS. of N. I. White. From Creedmoor,
N. C., as sung by Ed Lloyd, who says there are several other stanzas.

The first and last stanzas are common to a number of spirituals.

"Holy Ghost," in line 2, may be either a shout or a mere expletive, as "Mount
Zion" in Paul Robeson's singing of "On My Journey Now":

"Would n't take nothin' for my journey now (Mount Zion)," etc.

Cf. Burlin, *Poetry Magazine*, 1917, p. 151.

Keep yo' hand on the gospel plow,
Would n't take nothin' for my journey now, Holy Ghost.

Chorus

Keep yo' hand on the gospel plow,
    Hold on, hold on,
Keep yo' hand on the gospel plow,
    Hold on.

Did n't come here for to stay always,
Just come here to fill my place.

I got a mother in the promised land,
Never shall rest till I shake her hand.

65

WE GWINETER GIT DOWN AN' PRAY [1]

REPORTED from Columbia, Tenn., 1925, MS. of Mrs. O. B. Thompson.
Cf. the common stanza:

> I heard a mighty rustlin' up in the sky,
> Well it must a been my Lord a passin' by.

Brudder, brudder, whar was you,
Brudder, brudder, whar was you,
When my good Lord passed by?
My good Lord has been here, been here, been here,
And blessed my soul and gone.

Sister, sister, whar was you,
Sister, sister, whar was you,
When my good Lord passed by?
My good Lord has been here, been here, been here,
And blessed my soul and gone.

Art thou one little girl, one little boy?
We gwineter git down and pray,
Art thou one young lady, or one young gentl'man?
We gwineter git down an' pray!

66

REPORTED from Durham, N. C., 1925, MS. of N. I. White. From Creedmoor,
N. C., as sung by Ed Lloyd.
This spiritual, which contains no common spiritual lines, is an excellent ex-
ample of how a spiritual may be composed by any singer who knows the form.
It is capable of indefinite extension, and the first stanza is repeated irregularly
as chorus. Cf. no. 69 in this chapter.

Been a great change since I been born,
Been a great change since I been born,
Been a great change since I been born,
Been a great change since I been born.

The things I used to do I don't do now,
The things I used to do I don't do now,
The things I used to do I don't do now,
The things I used to do I don't do now.

[1] Local title.

Places I used to go I don't go there now,
Places I used to go I don't go there now,
Places I used to go I don't go there now.

Oh the people I used to see, I don't see 'em now,
Oh the people I used to see, I don't see 'em now,
Oh the people I used to see, I don't see 'em now.

67

THE WHEEL [1]

REPORTED from Durham, N. C., 1919, MS. of Jay L. Jackson.

The wheel is that of Ezekiel (Ezekiel, i, 15–26) whose imperfectly comprehended mysteries are here simplified. The refrain is found in other spirituals. Ezekiel's wheel, as the wheel of time, occurs in Fenner, 1901, p. 136 and as a wheel within a wheel (connected with chariot wheel), Ibid., p. 110. Cf. Murphy, 1904, p. 34, *Southern Workman*, xxviii, 464, xxix, 560, xxxvi, 207; Odum, 1925, p. 81; Johnson, 1926, p. 144.

> Zika made a wheel,
> Made it on the groun',
> Ever time the win' blow
> That wheel go roun',
> Let's take a ride on the chariot wheel,
> Let's take a ride on the chariot wheel.

68

REPORTED from Durham, N. C., 1919, MS. of Thomas T. Neal, as from Laurinburg, N. C. "Sung after recent 'conviction' at camp-meetings."

Line 3 is the title and refrain of a well-known printed spiritual; Work, 1907, p. 7 and Fenner (reprint of 1924) p. 166.

The couplet occurs as a stanza (generally with "mad" for "sad") in several printed spirituals. Cf. Perrow, 1913, p. 154, Edwards (Bahama) 1895, p. 58; Ludlow, 1884, p. 4, etc.

Also sung by Negroes around Durham, N. C.

Similar couplets occur in the early-nineteenth-century religious song-books of the whites.

Cf. also the teasing rhyme of white children:

> Tom is mad and I am glad
> And I know what will please him,
> A bottle of wine to make him shine
> And a little girl for to squeeze him.

For "Tom" is substituted the name of the one teased and for "little girl" the name of his supposed sweetheart.

---

[1] Local title.

Satan is mad and I am glad
'Cause he lost a soul he thought he had,
I know the Lord laid his hands on me.

69

REPORTED from Durham, N. C., 1925, MS. of N. I. White. From Creedmoor,
N. C., as sung by Ed Lloyd.

This is one of those songs, like many of the early camp-meeting songs of the
whites, that is capable of indefinite extempore expansion. Cf. no. 66 in this
chapter.

I'm on my way to the heavenly land,
I'm on my way to the heavenly land,
I'm on my way to the heavenly land,
I'm on my way, God knows I'm on my way.

If the seeker won't go, I'll journey on,
If the seeker won't go, I'll journey on,
If the seeker won't go, I'll journey on,
I'm on my way, God knows I'm on my way.

If my sister won't go, I'll journey on,
If my sister won't go, I'll journey on,
If my sister won't go, I'll journey on,
I'm on my way, God knows I'm on my way.

I'm on my way to the heavenly land,
I'm on my way to the heavenly land,
I'm on my way to the heavenly land,
I'm on my way, God knows I'm on my way.

70

AIN'T GONNA GRIEVE MY LORD NO MORE [1]

REPORTED from Durham, N. C., 1919, MS. of W. H. Lander, from Marlboro
County, S. C.

All except possibly the first couplet is found in different combinations of
other spirituals.

For the chorus, cf. *J. A. F. L.*, 1913, pp. 374–376, as from Georgia, and no. 29
in this chapter.

With stanza 1, cf. no. 10 in this chapter; and for parodies, III, no. 1, XII,
no. 40, IX, no. 55. In Sankey's *Gospel Hymns*, numbers 5 and 6 combined,

---

[1] Local title.

1892, every stanza of no. 148 begins, "Down in the valley with my Saviour I would go."

With stanza 2, cf. Work, 1907, pp. 50, 153, and no. 11 *B*, in this chapter; with stanza 4, cf. Marsh, 1877, p. 200; with stanza 5, cf. 11 *B*, in this chapter.

Oh! down in the valley where I was told
The grace of God is better than gold,
The grace of God is better than gold.

Chorus

Ain't gonna grieve my Lord no more,
Ain't gonna grieve my Lord no more.

Oh! watch the sun, see how it run,
Never let it catch you with your work undone,
Never let it catch you with your work undone.

Oh! down yonder in the harvest field,
The angels are working on the chariot wheel,
The angels are working on the chariot wheel.

Oh! Satan's like a snake in the grass,
Always in some Christian's path,
Always in some Christian's path.

Oh! mind, my sister, how you walk on the cross,
Your right foot'll slip and your soul'll get lost,
Your right foot'll slip and your soul'll get lost.

71

REPORTED from Durham, N. C., 1919, MS. of Edwin P. Gibson, as from Scotland County, N. C. "Sung in the cotton fields." Other stanzas could not be recalled.

Also sung by Negroes around Durham, N. C.

"All night long" is a common refrain in work songs. The other lines, with "glory" and "heaven" or "promised land" in line 1, are common to the spirituals. Cf. Fenner, 1901, p. 24; Burlin (Hampton Series), 1918–1919, i, 22; and no. 64 in this chapter. For a possible connection of the line with secular songs cf. VII, no. 80, IX, nos. 14 and 33, and X, no. 29.

I've got a brother in the snow-white fields,
Praying all night long.
I want to go to heaven when I die,
Oh, my Lawd!

72

A

REPORTED from Durham, N. C., 1919, MS. of Edwin P. Gibson, as from Scotland County, N. C. "Heard in the cotton fields."

Also sung by Negroes around Durham, N. C.

It has the common refrain of the printed versions of "Some of these days," but adds, "God knows." The first lines of stanzas 1, 2, 3, and 4 are found in several printed spirituals.

The first two stanzas appear to be based on the gospel hymn of the whites, "I Must Tell Jesus All of my Troubles."

Stanza 3 seems to be based on John, xxi, 12 ("Jesus said unto them, Come and dine"). In *Gems of Love*, one of the little manila-bound song-books used by the Pleasant Valley Christian Church (colored) of Durham, N. C., I find two songs based on this text, one a spiritual ("Welcome Table," no. 95) and one a regular gospel hymn ("Come and Dine," no. 61).

I'm gwine tell my loving Saviour,
I'm gwine tell my loving Saviour
Some of these days, God knows.

I'm gwine tell him all my troubles,
I'm gwine tell him all my troubles
Some of these days, God knows.

I'm gwine eat at the welcome table,
I'm gwine eat at the welcome table
Some of these days, God knows.

I'm gwine ride in the golden chariot,
I'm gwine ride in the golden chariot
Some of these days, God knows.

I'm gwine whip the golden horses,
I'm gwine whip the golden horses
Some of these days, God knows.

B

Reported from Durham, N. C., 1919, MS. of W. L. Hampton, as from Durham County in 1909. "Heard from a Negro cook."

All of the lines occur in various other spirituals. The *Methodist Hymnal* of 1854 contains three hymns dealing with walking with Christ and five with walking with God — nos. 176, 225, 351, 628, 720, 869, 934.

Cf. Marsh, 1877, p. 138; Edwards (Bahama) 1895, p. 43; Barton, 1899, p. 30; Kennedy (Louisiana) 1925, p. 39.

I'm going to walk and talk wid my Jesus
Some of these days;
I tell you that I'm going to walk wid my Jesus
Some of these days;
I'm going to walk and talk wid my Jesus
Some of these days.

73

REPORTED from Durham, N. C., 1919, MS. of E. C. Lovell, as from King's Mountain, N. C. "Sung by Negroes at revival at Cleveland, N. C., 1916."

Also sung by Negroes around Durham, N. C.

In Sankey's *Gospel Hymns*, numbers 5 and 6 combined, 1892, no. 138 is based largely on a repetition of the line, "Just over in the morning land."

There's a place prepared by my Savior's side,
Just over in the glory land;
There's a place prepared by my Savior's side,
Just over in the glory land.

Chorus

Just over in the glory land,
I'll jine the happy angel band;
Just over in the glory land.

74

REPORTED from South Casco, Me., 1918, MS. of Lucius Chapin, as from Richmond, Va., 1918.

Also sung by Negroes around Durham, N. C.

Stanza 3 is an importation from "Sister Mary," no. 3 in this chapter. Most of the stanzas to the same tune were sung to me by a friend in St. Louis, Mo., whose mother learned them in Alabama.

The last stanza occurs in Murphy, 1904, p. 35; cf. *J. A. F. L.*, 1910, p. 436, where stanza 1 of my version serves as refrain for eight stanzas, beginning with stanza 4, below.

Cf. also Perrow, 1913, pp. 123, 162; Johnson, 1925, p. 74; and nos. 19 *B* and 21 *A* above.

The hiding-place is Scriptural and occurs in a number of well-known hymns of the whites; for example, "Rock of Ages" and Newton's "Be Thou my Shield and Hiding-place" (stanza 4 of Hymn 92 in the *Christian Psalmist*).

Went down to the rocks to hide my face,
Went down to the rocks to hide my face,
Went down to the rocks to hide my face,
The rocks cried out no hiding-place,
No hiding-place down there.

Pharaoh's daughter lookin' for roses,
Pharaoh's daughter lookin' for roses,
Pharaoh's daughter lookin' for roses,
Stumped her toe and fell over Moses,
No hiding-place down there.

Sister Mary wears a golden chain,
Sister Mary wears a golden chain,
Sister Mary wears a golden chain,
And every link's in Jesus name,
No hiding-place down there.

Sinnaman sitting on the gates of hell,
Sinnaman sitting on the gates of hell,
Sinnaman sitting on the gates of hell,
The gates flew open and in he fell,
No hiding-place down there.

Sinnaman row your boat one side,
Sinnaman row your boat one side,
Sinnaman row your boat one side,
Cause you can't get to heaven on the ebbing tide,
No hiding-place down there.

Cause hell is deep and hell is wide,
Cause hell is deep and hell is wide,
Cause hell is deep and hell is wide,
You can't touch the bottom and you can't touch the side,
No hiding-place down there.

75

A

REPORTED from Durham, N. C., 1925, MS. of N. I. White. From Creedmoor, N. C., as sung by Ed Lloyd.

With a different sequence of stanzas and with "So glad" for "Holy Ghost" in line 1, this is the same as "I Done Done" from Lowndes County, Ala., in Hallowell, 1905, p. 21. Cf. also Work, 1907, p. 69; Johnson, 1925, p. 180; Fisher, 1926, p. 130.

Holy Ghost, I done done,
Holy Ghost, I done done,
Holy Ghost, I done done,
I done done what you told me to do.

You told me to pray an' I done dat too,
Now I done done what you told me to do.

Holy Ghost, I done done,
Holy Ghost, I done done,
Holy Ghost, I done done,
I done done what you told me to do.

You told me to pray an' I done dat too,
Now I done done what you told me to do.

Holy Ghost, etc.

You told me to sing, an' I done dat too,
Now I done done what you told me to do.

Holy Ghost, etc.

You told me to moan, an' I done dat too,
Now I done done what you told me to do.

Holy Ghost, etc.

You told me to weep, an' I done dat too,
Now I done done what you told me to do.

B

Reported from Durham, N. C., 1919, MS. of K. W. Litaker, as from Cabarrus County, N. C. "Sung by an old Negro when he was going to preaching."
This seems to be based on the first line of "I've Done What You Told Me to Do," as in Work, 1907, p. 69.

Lord, this old nega done done what you told me to do,
This old nega done done what you told me to do,
Lord, this old nega done done what you told me to do,
This old nega done done what you told me to do,
This old nega done done what you told me to do.
        O---h!------L-o-r-d.
        O---h!------L-o-r-d.

76

REDEEMED [1]

REPORTED from Durham, N. C., 1925, MS. of N. I. White. From Creedmoor, N. C., as sung by Ed Lloyd.
Part of the first stanza seems to have been lost and compensated for by introducing a modification of the chorus.

---

[1] Local title.

The chorus is as in the spiritual, "Joshuway," *J. A. F. L.*, 1921, p. 121, as from Georgia.

The whole song is probably from one or more early-nineteenth-century hymns, but I cannot locate any of the stanzas.

Chorus

Redeemed, redeemed, redeemed, redeemed,
I been washed in the blood of the Lamb,
Redeemed.

'T is Jesus Christ that I long to find,
Pray tell me where he is,
Redeemed,
Redeemed, I 'm washed in the blood of the Lamb,
Redeemed.

If you go down in yonder fold
And search among those sheep
That 's where you would find, so I been told
With those he loved to keep.

What signal shall I tell him by,
From any other man?
He wears salvation on his brow
And in his arms a lamb.

I 'll thank you friends for yo' advice,
I 'll find him if I can,
And if I do I will rejoice,
Christ is a friend to man.

77

A

REPORTED from Durham, N. C., 1919, MS. of K. W. Litaker, as from Cabarrus County, N. C. "Sung by an old Negro when he was going to preaching."

"I 'm on my way to Heaven" is a line found in the early gospel song-books, the revivalist songs, and regular hymns of the white people, as well as in Negro spirituals; for example, *Zion Songster*, second edition, 1827, p. 150, and Kennedy (Louisiana), 1924, p. 14.

Lord I 'm on my way,
Lord I 'm on my way,
Lord I 'm on my way,
Lord I 'm on my way.

ℬ

Reported from Durham, N. C., 1925, MS. of N. I. White. From Creedmoor, N. C., as sung by Ed Lloyd, who says there is no definite limit for the repetitions of the first line.

> I'm on my way and I can't turn back,
> I'm on my way and I can't turn back,
> I'm on my way and I can't turn back,
> I'm on my way and I can't turn back,
> I'm on my way and I can't turn back,
> I'm on my way.

78

REPORTED from Durham, N. C., 1919, MS. of K. W. Litaker, as from Cabarrus County, N. C., between 1917 and 1919. "Sung by an old Negro when he was going to preaching."

> Going up, going up, going up, going up,
> To the good Lord!
> Going up, going up, going up, going up,
> To the good Lord!

79

REPORTED from Durham, N. C., 1919, MS. of Thomas Litaker, as from Cabarrus County, N. C. "Sung on the farm by Negro tenant."
This is a line from a hymn sung by white people.

> O bear me away on your snow-white wings
>   To my eternal home.
>
> O bear me away on your snowy-white wing,
> O bear me away on your snowy-white wing.

80

REPORTED from Durham, N. C., 1919, MS. of J. P. Jones, as from Durham County, N. C.

The Lord said to his crowd —
All you people are mine, mine.
All you people are mine, mine.
The Devil come along with the Bible under his arm and said,
If I had my justice here half these people would be mine, mine,
If I had my justice here half these people would be mine, mine.

81

AN ANTE-BELLUM CHANTED PRAYER [1]

REPORTED from Auburn, Ala., 1915–1916, MS. of J. H. Drake, as recollected by his father. "Remnant of prayer by a seven-foot slave named Battle."

Oh, Marster Jesus! Git on the swift flying horse of Zion,
And ride around Dr. Drake's plantation one more time
Oh! Lord.

(Negro women would join with their mournful chant):

Yes, Lord! Yes, Lord!

82

FRAGMENT OF A CHANTED NEGRO SERMON [2]

REPORTED from Saratoga Springs, N. Y., 1926, MS. of George Foster Peabody. As given to Mr. Peabody in 1925 by Dr. E. C. L. Adams, of Columbia, S. C.
Cf. James Weldon Johnson's volume of chanted Negro sermons, *God's Trombone*, New York, 1927.

Our Brother is dead,
He rests from he labor,
An' he sleeps, —
(Shrill voice of Sister: He sleeps, Oh, he sleeps!)
Wey de tall pines grow,
(Another voice: On the banks of a river.)
On the banks of a river.
(Several voices: On the banks of a river.)
He trouble is done
He's left dis world
On the wings of glory.
(Voice: On the wings of glory!)
Out of life's storm,
(Another voice: On the wings of glory!)
Out of life's darkness,
(Several voices: On the wings of glory!)
He sails in the light of the lamb.

---

[1] No local title given.
[2] No local title given. This song has since been printed as sketch no. 20 of Dr. Adams's *Congaree Sketches*, University of North Carolina Press, Chapel Hill, 1927. It is here used by the kind permission of the author and publishers.

Away from his troubles,
Away from the night.
(*Congregation :* In the light!
              ln the light!
              Of the lamb.)

He's gone to the kingdom above,
In the raiment of angels,
(*Voice of Sister :* In the raiment!
                 In the raiment of angels.)

To the region above,
An' he sleeps, —
(*Voices chanting throughout the congregation :*
Oh, he sleeps. —
Oh, he sleeps!
On the banks of a river.)
Wey de tall pines grow,
On the banks of a river.

An' he soul's in flight,
With a starry-crowned angel, —
To the golden height.
(*Sister :* Oh, yes, my Jesus, Jesus! with a starry-crowned angel.)
An' he sleeps,
Wey de tall pines grow,
On the banks of a river.
(*Congregation :* With the starry-crowned angels,
On the banks of a river.)

An' the flowers is bloomin'
In the blood of the lamb.
(*Shrill voice of Sister and taken up by congregation chanting and
    swaying :*
        The blood of the lamb!
        In the blood of the lamb.)
An' the birds is singin'
Wey the wind blows soft,
As the breath of an angel,
An' he sleeps!
Wey de tall pines grow,
On the banks of a river.
(*Voice :* An' he sleeps!)

(*Another voice:* Wey de tall pines grow.)
(*Several voices:* On the banks of a river.)
An' his sperrit is guarded
By a flaming-faced angel.
(*Sister:* Yes, Jesus, of a flaming-faced angel!
      On the banks of a river.)
Standing on mountains of rest.

An' he sleeps wey de tall pines grow
On the banks of a river.
(*Congregation:* Oh, he sleeps!
           He sleeps!)

83

REPORTED from Greensboro, N. C., 1915–1916, MS. of Mr. and Mrs. J. J. W. Harriss, as heard in eastern North Carolina in the eighteen-eighties. Constantly repeated "to work up the shouting."

O John, Jesus comin',
O John, Jesus comin',
O John, Jesus comin'.

84

A

REPORTED from Greensboro, N. C., 1915–1916, MS. of Mr. and Mrs. J. J. W. Harriss, as heard in eastern North Carolina in the eighteen-eighties.

Hol' my shaker an' hol' my shawl,
An' tell Bob Jones I'm shoutin' in de cool.

B

Reported from Durham, N. C., 1925, MS. of Miss Ethel Davis. "Heard at Negro church in Salisbury, N. C., by Claude and Norman Davis, about 1905. Used to initiate the shouting."

Hold my bonnet and hold my shawl
While I shout in the cool, good Lawd.

85

REPORTED from Durham, N. C., 1921, MS. of N. I. White, as heard sung by one of the Negro janitors at Duke University.

John Jasper was a Negro minister in Richmond, Va., who died several years ago. He was famous throughout Virginia and North Carolina for his sermon on the text, "The sun do move," which many white people heard with great interest. He is briefly discussed in Carter G. Woodson's *History of the Negro Church*, which includes his unusually impressive portrait.

> John Jasper was a man
> And he preached it in the land,
> And he told it to the people that the sun do move.
> Well the sun do move; well the sun do move,
> He told it to the people that the sun do move.

86

TIM OF THIS [1]

REPORTED from Durham, N. C., 1919, MS. of W. A. Ellison, Jr. "Heard from a colored preacher."

A curious mixture of secular and religious song traits. Lines 5, 6, 7, and 8 are stanza 7 of "Jerusalem, My Happy Home" as printed in *Zion Songster*, second edition, 1827, but omitted from the hymn as printed in the *Christian Psalmist*, tenth edition (1856), and *Methodist Hymnal*, 1854 and 1905. The same lines occur as stanza 7 of another hymn in John C. Totten's *Selection of Hymns and Spiritual Songs as Usually Sung at Camp Meetings*, etc. (19th edition, New York 1827), p. 83.

Lines 11, 12, and 13 occur in many spirituals as a stanza, and the last two lines as refrains.

The connection with "Home, Sweet Home" is obvious.

> There is no place in the height of Heaven,
> There is no place like home,
> Home, home sweet home,
> There's no place like home,
> Kind friends, I bid you all farewell.
> I leave you in God's care,
> And if I never more see you
> Go on, I'll meet you there.
> Home, home, sweet home,
> There's no place like home.
> Sometimes I'se up,
> Sometimes I'se down,
> Sometimes I'se almost on de ground,
> Glory to his name,
> Oh! glory hallelujah.

[1] Local title.

III

UPSTART CROWS — THE REACTION FROM RELIGION

IT would be too much to expect the Negro, or any other race, to live and sing constantly on the high plane of the spirituals. The spirituals are naïve, earnest. But the Negro is neither always naïve nor always earnest. He has at times a spirit of mockery that must come to the surface; he must follow the universal trivial practice of sometimes making light of the things he reveres. Thus he sings a considerable number of songs in which the spirituals are openly flaunted, or in which matter that is seriously treated in the spirituals is regarded as humorous.

This is the more remarkable from the fact that, when the Negro is singing spirituals in a spiritual mood, nothing is humorous or incongruous. Otherwise he would be compelled to smile with the thoughtless white man at certain things in the spirituals. He does smile, sometimes, but only because the white man does. The spiritual may even include parts of secular songs like "Settin' on a log," which Clarence Deming[1] heard in church in Mississippi in the eighteen-eighties, and be felt to be perfectly proper. And since the Negro may use the spiritual as a work song without any sense of impairing its dignity (just as white people use hymns similarly), it is difficult in particular cases always to be sure whether the singer is using sacred material lightly or light material sacredly.

There can be no doubt, however, that in moods of cynical flippancy and in moods of reaction the same Negro who has sung spirituals religiously may indulge in songs which make a mockery of them. The majority of such singing, however, is by a class of singers who are not in such good grace with the church as the typical singer of spirituals.

Not all of the songs of this sort are based upon spirituals. In the present group ten songs[2] seem to be based directly on the spirituals, while four[3] are based upon regular hymns, and are sung no more by

[1] See note to no. 21 in this chapter.
[2] Nos. 1, 2, 11, 12, 13, 18, 28, 29, 30, 35.
[3] Nos. 3, 4, 6, 24 *E*.

Negroes than by the white people with whom they probably originated. Most of the other songs in the group are mildly sacrilegious without definite connections with hymns or spirituals.

Since most of the songs in this group are social songs, many of them bear the mark of the old minstrel songs which have so profoundly influenced the older social songs of the Negro. Of the present group, eight[4] show more or less derivation from the ante-bellum minstrel songs.

The influence of the modern vaudeville stage is also to be seen. It is the home of flippant parody from which some of the cheap smartness of the present songs must almost inevitably have been drawn. It is also the chief conservator of the type of Negro humor herein preserved — the humor of drunkenness, appetite, and chicken-stealing, accentuated by contrast with religious expressions. These moods find a ready echo with the Negro as with the white man.

The most genuinely Negro of these songs are those in which the singer reacts directly to the mood of his own spirituals and prefers the present life to the life to come.[5] If he gets to the promised land, he will "slide right over" by greasing his hand with mutton suet, but he does n't care particularly to get there. He "don't want no golden chariot." "I'm going to live anyhow until I die," he sings; and he is going to live "on the high." When he sings his "you shall be free" refrain to all sorts of nonsense stanzas[6] and proclaims freedom to elephants, chickens, and spare-ribs in the same measure as to mourners, the refrain has long lost its original camp-meeting meaning of freedom from sin, and it is surely very far indeed from any connection with the Negro's hope for freedom such as most writers about the spiritual have been fond of ascribing to this and similar spiritual lines.

Though the mood of reaction expressed in these songs is genuine, it is only a minor phase compared with the much greater weight of the religious mood. Religion and high social spirits are two dominating elements in Negro folk-song. They are the elements in his racial character to which he owes most of the ability with which he has hitherto outfaced the calamity of a difficult situation. Generally they are not incongruous; they mix well in Negro practice. But occasionally they clash, or come into contact with brief moods of cynical depression, producing such songs as those here presented.

[4] Nos. 7, 8, 18, 19, 20, 21, 24 (A, B, C, D), and 25.
[5] Nos. 1, 2, 5, 26, 28, 32, 33, 34, 35.
[6] Nos. 8–23.

SONGS WITH ANNOTATIONS

The following songs classified in other groups might also be included in this class: V, 15, 26; VI, 34; VII, 82; VIII, 2, 20; IX, 18, 19, 29, 37, 55; XII, 15, 17, 32, 33; XIII, 14, 17*B*.

1

A

REPORTED from Durham, N. C., 1919, with no note as to where heard; MS. of Blake B. Harrison.

The last line is a parody on the regular line as included in most of the collections, "My soul got happy an' I stayed all day." Cf. II, no. 10.

> I went down in the valley to pray,
> I went down in the valley to pray,
> I went down in the valley to pray.
> I got drunk and stayed all day.

B

Reported from Auburn, Ala., 1915–1916, MS. of W. D. Kimbrough, as heard in Camden, Ala.

The first two lines are evidently a parody on the common spiritual couplet:

> I went down to the valley, I did n't go to stay,
> My soul got happy and I stayed all day.

> I went to the ribber but I did n't go to stay,
> But I got so drunk I could n't get away,
> My marster axed me whar I'd been,
> And the way he hit me was a sin.

2

REPORTED from Auburn, Ala., 1915–1916, MS. of T. M. Brannon, as from Barbour County, Ala. "Sung by Negro comedian."

> So low you can't crawl under,
> So high you can't climb over,
> You got to go through
> By the wool of the Lamb.

> Swing low, sweet chariot,
> Swing low, sweet chariot,
> Swing low, sweet chariot,
> Come for to take me home.

3

REPORTED from Durham, N. C., 1919, MS. of Thomas Litaker, as from Cabarrus County, N. C. Twenty years ago I heard this often sung by white people in Statesville, N. C.

Jesus lover of my soul,
Set me on top of telegram pole,
When the pole begins to break
Take me down for Jesus' sake.

4

A

REPORTED from Auburn, Ala., 1915–1916, MS. of B. H. Haynes, as from Clay County, Ala. Twenty years ago I heard this sung by white people in Statesville, N. C.

Jesus, lover of my soul,
How many chickens have I stole?
One last night, two night before,
Going back to-night to get two more.

B

Reported from Durham, N. C., 1919, MS. of Austin L. Elliott. Same as *A* with "two" for "one" in line 3.

5

REPORTED from Auburn, Ala., 1915–1916, MS. of C. C. Certain, as heard in Jackson, Miss. "Sung by construction gang, 1906."

Lor', Lor', if you're looking for Jesus, you can rise and fly;
If you're looking for de debil, you can stop and try.

6

REPORTED from Durham, N. C., 1919, MS. of Austin L. Elliott, who writes:
"The last one . . . I have not heard for more than ten years, although it was once very popular among the young Negroes. These Negroes delighted in laying great stress on this last song when they got together at a corn husking."
I can recollect lines 4 and 5 as very similar to a popular song sung in Statesville, N. C., about 1905. Cf. V, no. 9, XII, nos. 40–44.

Near my God to the chicken in a cedar tree,
Forty thousand dollar reward for me.

Chicken in a cedar tree.
Come down from behind that moon,
For I'se comin' up and git you soon.
Chicken you can't roost too high for me,
Chicken in a cedar tree.

7

REPORTED from Durham, N. C., 1919, MS. of Blake B. Harrison.

Lines 1 and 2 parody a popular church song of the white people of twenty years ago: "You must be a lover of the Lord, If you want to go to Heaven when you die." I have been familiar with the parody for years. The refrain is similar to that of a number of dance songs included in old minstrel books.

You'll have to be de lover of an undertaker's daughter
If you want to get a coffin when you die.

> *Refrain:* Hop along, sister Molly, hop along,
> Hop along, sister Molly, hop along.

8

REPORTED from Auburn, Ala., 1915–1916, MS. of S. A. Allen, as from Shelby County, Ala. "Sung by old Negroes on the farm."

The promise in this song was often made to faithful slaves. In one of her travel books Harriet Martineau tells of a mistress who was poisoned by a slave to hasten the day of liberation. These or closely similar stanzas occur separately several times in the early minstrel songs.

Cf. "Old King Crow" ("the words by Henry H. Paul") in *Negro Singers' Own Book*, p. 112; "Jenny Git your Hoe-Cake Done," *Ibid.*, pp. 359 and 408; and IV, no. 2.

Old massa he done promised me
When he died he gwine to set me free.
He lived so long his head grow ball,
Now he's decided not to live at all.

> *Chorus:* Oh, mourner, you shall be free
> When the good Lord set you free.

My old missus she promised me
When she died she'd set me free.
Now the devil done dead and gone
Left this nigger a hilling up corn.

> *Chorus:* Oh, mourner, you shall be free
> When the good Lord set you free.

9

REPORTED from Auburn, Ala., 1915–1916, MS. of W. R. Taylor, as from Louis-
burg, N. C.

Heard at a Negro minstrel show.

There are a number of secular songs on eating chittelings. The first five lines
are almost identical with stanzas in Perrow, 1913, p. 158 (as from South Carolina in 1909), and Scarborough, 1925, p. 225, both with the "You shall be free"
refrain.

> If you want to go to Heaven
> I'll tell you what to do;
> Just grease all over in Brunswick stew;
> The devil will grab at you and miss his man,
> Then you slip right over into the promised land.
> > Eat chittlings.

> *Chorus:* Oh, mourner, you shall be free.
> > When the good Lord sets you free.

10

REPORTED from Auburn, Ala., 1915–1916, anonymously.

> I have chiblings,
> You shall be free,
> Backbone, you shall be free,
> Spare ribs, you shall be free
> When de good Lord calls me home.

11

REPORTED from Durham, N. C., 1919, MS. of R. B. Edwards.

There are several printed spirituals with a stanza:

> Who dat comin' dressed in white?
> Must be de children of de Israelite;

sometimes followed by

> Who dat comin' dressed in black?
> Must be de mohners turnin' back.

Cf. Perrow, 1913, p. 156.

> What's that yonder looks so black?
> Has a head like a carpet-tack.
> Must be Aunt Dinah, you shall be free,
> You shall be free.

12

REPORTED from Auburn, Ala., 1915–1916, MS. of H. C. Abbot, as from Florida.
Cf. Perrow, 1913, p. 160.

The Lord made an elephant,
He made him stout;
The first thing he made
Was the elephant's snout.

He made his snout nigh long as a rail,
The next thing he made was the elephant's tail;
He made his tail to fan the flies,
The next thing he made was the elephant's eyes.

He made his eyes to see green trees,
The next thing he made was the elephant's knees.
Oh, elephant, you shall be free,
Oh, elephant, you shall be free,
When the good Lord sets you free.

13

REPORTED from Auburn, Ala., 1915–1916, MS. of J. H. Reynolds, as from
Macon County, Ga. "Sung on the farm."
    I have the same, with very slight verbal differences, from Albermarle County,
N. C., 1919, and, without the refrain, from Auburn, Ala., 1915–1916, MS. of
R. R. McAdory, as heard in Jefferson County, Ala.

Yonder comes Noah stumbling in the dark
With his hammer and nails for to build the ark.
Yonder comes the animals two by two
The hippopotamus and the kangaroo.
Shout, mourners, you shall be free
When the good Lord sets you free.

14

REPORTED from Auburn, Ala., 1915–1916, MS. of R. Chambers, as from Giles
County, Tenn. "Sung by old blacksmith and farm hands."

I love my wife, I love my baby,
I love dem flapjacks flopped in gravy.
Mourner, you shall be free, you shall be free,
When de good Lord set you free.

15

REPORTED from Auburn, Ala., 1915–1916, MS. of L. A. Nall, as from New Orleans. "Sung by track-layers."
    Cf. IX, no. 25; XI, no. 14; XII, nos. 30, 31.

My old lady done gone an' lef me here,
An' she did n't even leave me a dime for beer.
Po' mourner, we shall be free.
Po' mourner, we shall be free.

16

REPORTED from Auburn, Ala., 1915–1916, MS. of J. H. Owens.

Me and my wife had a fallin' out.
Listen and I'll tell you what it's all about.
It ain't no lie, it's a natural born fact,
She wanted me to work on the railroad track.

Chorus

Po' mourner, you shall be free,
Oh mourner, you shall be free,
You shall be free
When the good Lord set you free.

17

REPORTED from Auburn, Ala., 1915–1916, MS. of L. A. Nall, as from New Orleans.

Po' moner, in de morn we shall be free,
When de good Lord will make a li'l angel of me.

18

REPORTED from Auburn, Ala., 1915–1916, MS. of M. S. Perdue, as from southern Alabama. "Heard sung by Negro minstrel."
    Lines 3 and 4 of stanza 1, and all the succeeding stanzas, exist, independently or in combination, in various other songs, without the refrain. Cf. stanza 1 with III, 19, 20, IV, 11, VI, 9, 10, 34, 40 A and D, etc.; stanza 2 with XII, 39 (A–D), XIV, 5 B–7; stanza 3 with XII, 12; stanza 4 with VI, 26 C, 27 A and B.

Mourner, mourner, you shall be free
When the good Lord sets you free.
Way down yonder where I came from,
Big black nigger with a derby on.

Beef steaks, poke chop,
Gimme a little sop,
Make a nigger's mouth go flippity flop.
Mourner, you shall be free,
When the good Lord sets you free.

Some folks say preachers won't steal,
But I caught two in my corn field.
One had a bushel, one had a peck,
One had a roastin' ear hung round his neck,
Mourner, you shall be free when the good Lord sets you free.

Honey babe, you better turn me loose,
I'm going back to the buzzard roost.
Mourner, you shall be free,
When the good Lord sets you free.

Possum up the simmon tree, coon on the ground,
Coon say you sun of a gun, you better shake dem possum down.
Mourner, you shall be free when the good Lord sets you free.

19

REPORTED from Durham, N. C., 1919, MS. of Thomas Litaker, as from Cabarrus County, N. C. With slight variations, such as "Punkin Creek," "Still Water Creek," and "de beever creek," the stanza occurs (without the refrain) in Perrow, 1915, p. 135; Talley, 1922, p. 2; Christy's *Nigga Songster*, n. d., pp. 69, 239. Cf. also III, no. 20, IV, no. 11, VI, nos. 9, 10, 40 *A* and *D*, IX, no. 3.

Way down yonder on Cedar street
Where all dem niggers grow eleben feet,
Go to bed when it ain't no use,
Feet stick out like a chicken roost,
Shout to the Lord shamonyah,[1]
He will set you free.

20

REPORTED from Auburn, Ala., 1915–1916, MS. of M. G. Croswaithe.

Way down yonder on Eagle Creek,
Niggers don't grow but eleben feet;
When they're out it ain't no use
To build a ten-foot chicken roost.

[1] For "oh, mohner"?

Chorus

Alla Mohner, we shall be free,
We shall be free,
We shall be free,
For the good Lord sets us free.

21

REPORTED from Auburn, Ala., 1915–1916, MS. of E. L. Harper, as from Reform, Ala. "Heard sung by both whites and Negroes."
  Stanza 1 is sometimes sung as a part of "Shortnin' Bread"; cf. V, nos. 5 and 6. Stanza 3 has close analogies in *Negro Singers' Own Book*, "I Wonder Where He Went To," p. 246; "Where Did You Come From," p. 317; and "Jim Along, Josey," p. 410. Cf. Perrow, 1913, p. 158, and VI, nos. 47, 49. Stanza 2 occurs in several printed collections as an independent song.   Cf. Clarence Deming, *By Ways of Nature and Life*, p. 373 (from the Mississippi Bends, in 1884, heard in church):

> Big ole black man hidin' 'hind de log,
> Finger on de trigger, eye upon de hog.
>   Shiloh! Shiloh!

and see V, no. 4.

Great big negro black as tar,
Trying to go to heaven on a electric car,
Negro! You'll never get thar.

Chorus

You shall be free,
Just when the good Lord sets you free.

Great big Negro settin' on a log,
Finger on the trigger and eye on the hog,
Gun went bang! bullet went zip,
Jumped on dat hog with all his grip.

Fresh meat!

Well as I was going across the field
Great big black snake took and bit me on the heel.
Turned around and give him a grin.
Son-of-a-gun took and bit me again.

Great God! You shall be free, etc.

22

REPORTED from Auburn, Ala., 1915–1916, MS. of A. M. Kearly. See note to no. 21 in this chapter.

> Nigger in de wild woods settin' on a log,
> Finger on the trigger and eye on de hog;
> Gun said bum, the hog said bap,
> He jumped on the hog wid all his grap.
> Hunting spare ribs, don't forget the back bone
> And you shall be free.

23

REPORTED from Auburn, Ala., 1915–1916, MS. of A. M. Kearly. "Sung by deck hands."
    The first two lines, with slight verbal variations, occur in "Raise a Rucus Tonight," Talley, 1922, p. 91.

> It ain't no lie, it's a natural fact,
> You could have been colored without being so black,
> But you shall be free,
> When the good Lord sets you free.

24

A

BECAUSE of the fact that many spirituals contain unconscious humor and incongruity, it is hard to say whether this and the succeeding four songs are seriously or humorously intended. Since the reporters of them have indicated no religious connections, since they show some connections with the old minstrel books, and since Noah appears to be a humorous figure to the Negroes as well as to the old miracle-play writers, it seems most likely that they are really social songs.
    Reported from Auburn, Ala., 1915–1916, MS. of B. H. Haynes, as from Clay County, Ala.
    "Forty days and forty nights" is the last line of eight successive stanzas in Odum, 1925, p. 127. Cf. Ibid., p. 129.

> Forty days and forty nights the rain kept droppin',
> Forty days and forty nights it rained without stoppin',
> Forty days and forty nights the animals
> Kept a comin' two by two,
> All except the hippopotamus and the kangaroo.

B

Reported from Durham, N. C., 1919, MS. of Thomas Litaker, as from Cabarrus
County, N. C. "Heard sung by negro on father's place."
"Did n't it rain" occurs in Negro work songs. Cf. Odum, 1925, p. 129.

> Old Jonah got mad cause de rain kept a droppin',
> Did n't it rain,
> O did n't it rain!
> It rained forty days; forty nights without stoppin',
> O did n't it rain,
> Did n't it rain!

C

Reported from Auburn, Ala., 1915–1916, MS. of R. R. McAdory, as from Jef-
ferson County, Ala.
As a boy I was familiar with the second stanza as a vaudeville song without
Negro associations.

> Long come Noah
> Stumbling in the dark,
> Found himself a hammer, nail
> Built himself an ark.
>
> Long come the ani-mules!
> Er two by two,
> Hip-on-the-potamous
> And the kick-kanga-roo.

D

Reported from Durham, N. C., 1919, MS. of W. T. Huckabee, Jr., as from
Albermarle, N. C. "Heard sung by negro dray boy."
Combines C in one stanza, with slight verbal differences, followed by,
"Mohner, you shall be free," etc.

E

Reported from Durham, N. C., 1919, MS. of J. G. Neal, as from Marion,
western North Carolina.
This is a parody of the old camp-meeting hymn, "There's one wide river to
cross," retaining the refrain slightly altered.

> Animals came two by two,
>   There's one bright river to cross.
> The hippopotamous and the kangaroo
>   There's one bright river to cross.

Chorus

One bright river,
There's one bright river of Jordan.
  One bright river.
Good Lord the world is growing better,
Better every day.

F

Reported from Auburn, Ala., 1915–1916, MS. of B. Coplan, as heard in Birmingham, Ala. "Sung by whites."

This seems to be a modern vaudeville song, somewhat related to the various songs about Noah. The refrain is borrowed from the modern "Creation Song," II, no. 24.

Scarborough, 1925, p. 181, contains an interesting variant which employs a regular spiritual refrain ("Hallelu, hallelu, Halleluyah to de Lamb," etc.) and deals successively with the various passengers up to "nine by nine," in lines practically the same as the first lines of the stanzas here given; but in every case the following line is different from those in the present version.

Cf. II, no. 47.

In come de animuls two by two,
Hippopotamus and a kangaroo;
Dem bones gona rise agin.

In come de animuls three by three,
Two big cats and a bumble bee;
Dem bones gona rise agin.

In come de animuls fo' by fo',
Two thru de winder and two thru de do';
Dem bones gona rise agin.

In come de animuls five by five,
Almost dead and hardly alive;
Dem bones gona rise agin.

In come de animuls six by six,
Three wid clubs and three wid sticks;
Dem bones gona rise agin.

In come de animuls seben by seben,
Fo' from Hell and de others from Heaven;
Dem bones gona rise agin.

In come de animuls eight by eight,
Four on time and de others late;
Dem bones gona rise agin.

In come de animuls nine by nine,
Four in front and five behind;
Dem bones gona rise agin.

In come de animuls ten by ten,
Five big roosters and five big hens;
Dem bones gona rise agin.

Refrain

Dem bones gona rise agin,
I knows it, indeed I knows it, brother,
I knows it, dem bones gona rise agin.

25

REPORTED from Auburn, Ala., 1915–1916, MS. of M. L. Batson. Sung to the contributor, while a lad, by his uncle.

The first stanza is the first stanza of "Walk in the Parlor," published in the *Ethiopian Serenaders' Own Book* (n. d., but dated conjecturally 1857 by Library of Congress), p. 66 and in *Negro Singers' Own Book*, (n. d., but dated conjecturally 1846 by Library of Congress), as the first stanza of "Walk In" (p. 73), which continues with a burlesque account of the Creation, the flood, and various Biblical characters, the first two lines of stanza 4 being identical with the first two lines of stanza 2 below, and the last two lines of stanza 7 being the same as the last two lines below. The original refrain of "Walk In" (Walk In, Walk In, I Say," etc.) has been lost in the song below, and a genuine spiritual refrain, found in most printed collections as "Live-a-humble," has been parodied or misunderstood. All three of the following stanzas occur, with some variations, in Gumbo Chaff's *Ethiopian Glee Book*, 1848, p. 126, and in Christy's *Nigga Songster*, n. d., p. 131. For a variant of stanza 2 see White's *New Book of Plantation Melodies*, n. d., p. 23. Cox, 1925, lists twenty-three different publications of the song, in eight distinct versions, between 1847 and 1861.

Cf. V, no. 26, XIII, no. 14, and notes.

I'm from old Virginia wid a haid full o' knowledge,
And I nebber ben to free school or any odder college,
But I'll tell yo' a story what's a mighty simple fact;
The world was n't build in de twinkle ob a crack.

Refrain

Lib-a-hum-bug, lib-a-hum-bug, till
De good Lord comes again.

Adam was the first man, Eve was the tother,
Cain walked a tread-mill case he killed his brudder.
Old mudder Eve would n't sleep wid out a fedder;
Lawd bless you, honey, old Adam oughter killer.

Refrain

De clouds commence to rain, an' de rain commence to fall;
De water got so deep dat it drowned de niggers all;
It rained forty days jes' exactly by de count,
An' landed Noah's ark on de Allegainy mount.

Refrain

26

REPORTED from Auburn, Ala., 1915–1916, MS. of A. H. Childree, as from southern Alabama.
   Perrow, 1913, p. 58, gives the same song as from Mississippi in 1909.
   This is a slight variant of no. 9, in this chapter.

If you want to go to heben,
Let me tell you what to do:
Grease you hand with de muttin sue,
Take Saint Peter by de hand
Slide right over in de Promise Land.

27

REPORTED from Durham, N. C., 1919, MS. of D. B. Newton, as heard in Marlboro County, S. C.

Oh! I 'm going on to Hebun anyhow,
Oh! Yes, I 'm going on to Hebun anyhow.

28

REPORTED from Auburn, Ala., 1915–1916, anonymously.

I don't want to ride in no golden chariot,
I don't want to wear no golden crown,
I want to stay down here and be
Just like I am.

29

A

REPORTED from Auburn, Ala., 1915–1916, MS. of A. H. Williamson, as from
Lowndes County, Ala. Lines 2, 4, 5, 6 occur in various spirituals.

> I'm goin' ter live on de high till I die;
> Livin' does seem to be very high;
> Brick and stones goin' ter break my bones.
> I know yo' goin' ter talk about me
> When I'm gone,
> But I'm goin' ter live on de high till I die.

B

Reported from Durham, N. C., 1919, MS. of W. L. Hampton. "Heard from
Negro near Bahama, N. C., 1914."

> I'm going to live anyhow till I die;
> I'm going to live anyhow till I die;
> Sticks and stones may break my bones;
> 'Cause I talk about a body when they are dead and gone.
> I'm going to live anyhow till I die;
> I'm going to live anyhow till I die;
> Sticks and stones may break my bones;
> I'm going to start a graveyard of my own;
> I'm going to live anyhow till I die.

30

REPORTED from Durham, N. C., 1919, MS. of J. G. Neal, as from Marion,
western North Carolina.
The refrain has a long history. See note to IV, no. 29 *A*.

> Whale swallowed Jonah
> Head and tail.
>   Sing song kitty
>   Won't you *ki meo*.

31

REPORTED from Auburn, Ala., 1915–1916, MS. of J. C. Lawton, as from Seminole, Fla. "Heard in surveying camp, sung to guitar."
        Cf. *J. A. F. L.*, xxvi, 190 (Maryland). Perrow, 1913, p. 160, gives a curiously similar song from East Tennessee, as heard about 1897.

I was born about four thousand years ago,
Ain't nothin' ever happened that I don't know,
I seen King Pharoe's daughter seeking Moses on the water,
I can lick the man that says that that ain't so.

Chorus

For I'm a highly educated man,
Keep my brains within my head to plan;
I've lived on earth so long that I've learned to sing this song,
Abraham and Isaac rushed a king.

Seen old Satan, when he cussed old Adam sore,
And old Adam jes' hollered for more.
I was peepin' through the bushes at the apple they were eating,
I can prove that I was the man that et the core.

Chorus

Seen ole Noah when he built that famous ark,
For I was creeping near there in the dark.
Seen ole Jonah swallowin' de whale, and I pulled de lion's tail;
I've sailed all over Canaan on a log.

Chorus

32

REPORTED from Auburn, Ala., 1915–1916, MS. of E. Oliveira, as from New Orleans.

It takes a rubber ball to bounce,
It takes a baseball to roll,
But it takes a mighty good preacher
To send salvation to my soul.

33

REPORTED from Auburn, Ala., 1915–1916, anonymously.

> Born all the way from Atlanta,
> Be baptized all the way from Atlanta, buddy,
> For to be baptized.

34

REPORTED from Auburn, Ala., 1915–1916, MS. of L. A. Nall, as from New Orleans.

> Niggers in de corn field, and li'l hogs in de yard,
> Old mammies in de church a prayin' to de Gawd.

35

REPORTED from Auburn, Ala., 1915–1916, MS. of B. A. Wooten, as from Marengo County, Ala.

> Sometimes I feel like a feather in the air,
> Sometimes I feel like I never prayed a prayer.

IV

SOCIAL SONGS — DANCE AND BANJO

THE social folk-songs of the Negro, as distinguished from religious songs and work songs, are to be found mainly in the groups devoted to animals, narrative songs and ballads, parodies of religious songs, and recent events, in addition to the present group. They are so interwoven with the work songs that a hard-and-fast division is not always possible. They are used by the Negro, as most songs are used by the white people, simply for entertainment and enjoyment, with no particular function to be served except occasionally the rhythm of a dance, the speeding-up of a corn-shucking, the encouragement of a hunt, or the lulling of an infant.

They are among the songs first encouraged by the planters in order to keep up the spirits of the slaves. Dance songs, as I have shown in Chapter I, were encouraged from the very first. They are the songs of which the early black-face minstrels, led by "Jim Crow" Rice, first saw the stage value, ignoring the work songs and religious songs that must have been in existence at the time.

It is doubtful if any of the very earliest of these songs are still in tradition. They were probably too simple and incoherent to be thought worthy of notice by any white person who encountered them; and they were probably supplanted in Negro tradition by imitations of the early minstrel imitations, which were very far-fetched and badly mixed imitations indeed, but which gave the Negro song a value and a currency far beyond anything it had previously enjoyed. The songs which the minstrels imitated must have been a second stage in Negro folk-song, after the Negro had become much more adept in the white man's language and ways than he had been throughout the eighteenth century. Something of what these songs were may be imagined from a few scraps preserved by early travellers, novelists, and other observers. I have reprinted a few of these in Appendix V.

Upon the social songs of the present group, as upon the songs about animals, the black-face minstrel has written large the impress of the times when "Jump Jim Crow" received twenty enthusiastic encores on its first appearance in New York, became London's most popular song, and was heard by Bayard Taylor even among the Hindoo minstrels in Delhi. I am inclined to think, however, that the animal songs are older than those about plantation life. I do not believe that slaves, even with the freedom of speech sometimes allowed them, would have ventured to compose and sing openly many of the songs about ole massa's stinginess or ole missis' promises of freedom, before the black-face minstrel had made them harmless commonplaces. Originating such songs would be a rather heavy presumption on ole massa's tolerance.[1]

Nearly half of the songs in this group are either wholly or in part the same as songs found in the early minstrel books.[2] Often one current Negro song will show different passages from several different minstrel songs. The same passage, in fact, may often be found in several minstrel songs, for the old minstrel songs, like the Negro songs of to-day, were frequently conglomerate. Both these phenomena are revealed by so many annotations throughout this book that citations at this point would be superfluous. There is another phenomenon, however, not so clearly revealed by the annotations: namely, that one of the minstrel songs may diffuse itself throughout a number of widely different traditional songs. Of this I will cite only one example, a jig song called "What's de Matter, Susey," composed and sung with unbounded applause, at White's Melodeon, by the original "Old Dan Emmett."

Sambo had a son born, he thought it was a daughter,
Yaller Sal de Georgia Stag, de big buck in de water.

Chorus
What's de matter, Susey?
What's de matter, my dear?
What's de matter, Susey?
I'm gwine away to leab you.

I floated down de ribber, I landed in Orleans,
I saw whar Massa Jackson killed de Packenheens.

What's de matter, etc.

Nigger on de woodpile, could'nt count eleben,
Put 'im in de fedder bed, he tink he gwine to heaben.

What's de matter, etc.

[1] That it was occasionally done, however, perhaps with a little sly ambiguity, is indicated by the Christmas gift song in Appendix V, p. 455.
[2] Nos. 1, 2, 3 *A–G*, 4, 5, 8, 9, 11, 13, 17, 18, 21, 23, 27, 29, 31, 33, 34, 35, 36, 40, 47.

Betwixt de white and brack folks, I'm sure dar is no kin;
De whites has got de softest head, de niggers de softest skin.

What's de matter, etc.

Massa on de cellar door, a mendin' ob his shoes;
De nigger on de telumgraph a readin' ob de news.

What's de matter, etc.

Old folks an' young folks, you'd better go to bed;
You only put de debble in de little nigger's head.

What's de matter, etc.[3]

The last line of the chorus is a common sentiment in traditional Negro songs, but may of course be independent of the minstrel stage in origin. The first two stanzas, so far as I know, are not preserved in Negro songs of to-day. The third stanza is apparently related to some of the modern "shortnin' bread" stanzas wherein little niggers are "layin' in the bed" and "tryin' to get to heab'n." Stanza 4 is the same kind of trivial comparison of white folks and Negroes found in many modern songs. Stanzas 5 and 6 have both descended, very little changed, in XIII, no. 8 *C* and IX, no. 6. Other minstrel songs that have contributed a number of stanzas each to different songs in this collection are the "Creation" songs and "De Original Ole Jim Crow."

Nine of the songs in this group [4] show the influence of traditional songs of the white people, while nine [5] others without being definitely referable to either of the two influences just mentioned, show evidence of somewhat greater age than most of the Negro work songs. Taken together with the songs related to the early minstrels and those showing connections with the older songs of the white people, these show that the great majority of the songs in this group are old. They testify to the conservatism which is one of the chief traits of the folk-Negro. Ole massa and ole missis have been a long time dead; hunting parties and corn-shuckings are not so common as they once were, but they live tenaciously in song. Such songs are doubtless already on the wane; it will be noted that many of those in this collection are from older people. They are becoming probably a little strange to the urbanized and semi-sophisticated singer, but their waning, while certain, will be slow. I, for one, hope so. They

[3] Page 38 in White's *New Illustrated Ethiopian;* n. d., but probably belonging to the early eighteen-fifties.
[4] Nos. 9, 10, 12, 14, 15, 29, 31, 32, 42.
[5] Nos. 7, 15, 16, 19, 20, 24, 25, 30, 41.

epitomize the good feeling and the jollity of a race distinguished for these qualities and are vastly superior to the "blues," which now seem to be capturing the field.

The type of song which they represent will go on, is already going on, under the same conditions that produced most of the older songs in this group. The old minstrels, with their bones and tambourines and "monstrous applause," are as dead as ole massa and Uncle Ned, but the modern coon song writer, the vaudeville stage, and the popular song hit are still with us and are supplying the songs which the folk-Negro takes up, half forgets, garbles, adds to, and finally makes his own. In the present group there are four songs [6] which show the influence of the coon song writer. Other groups of social songs in this collection show all the more modern influences much more clearly.

SONGS, WITH ANNOTATIONS

The following songs classified in other groups might also be included in the present class: II, 5, 7 *C*, 10 *B*, 24 *A*, 25, 47; III, 1 *B*, 7–11, 18–22, 24 *F*, 25; V, 1–37; VI, 1, 3–9, 12, 19, 29, 47, 52; VII, 24, 44, 57, 60, 71, 72; VIII, 1, 3, 17, 22; IX, 7; X, 1–27, 31–38, 50, 59, 61, 65–67, 69, 75, 78, 79, 80, 81, 84, 85; XI, 18; XII, 9, 10, 12, 14, 17, 18, 22, 28, 33, 39, 40, 43, 44, 46, 48; XIII, 1–6, 8, 10, 11, 13, 15–17; XIV, 1–16, 25.

I

REPORTED from Greensboro, N. C., 1915–1916, MS. of Mr. and Mrs. J. J. W. Harriss, as heard in eastern North Carolina.

The first two lines are really a variant of

> My ole missus promised me
> When she died she'd set me free;
> Now ole missus dead and gone
> Left this nigger hoein' up corn.

This stanza, with either "massa" or "missus" in the first line, and with a variety of conclusions and combinations with other songs is still widely current and occurs in *Uncle Remus and His Friends*, 1892, p. 200 (cited by Perrow); Perrow, 1915, p. 138; Talley, 1922, p. 25; Scarborough, 1925, pp. 106, 165, 179, 194, 223, 224 (five times), 225; Odum, 1926, pp. 173, 176. These citations attest the contemporary existence of the stanza in practically every section of the South. The most interesting variations are that

> Old Missus lived till her head got bald,
> She got out of de notion of dyin' at all;

or,

> A dose of poison helped her on.

---

[6] Nos. 28, 43, 44, 50.

The stanza occurs commonly in the old minstrel books, with the usual number of variations and combinations; for example, in *Negro Singers' Own Book*, 1846(?), p. 112 ("the words by Henry H. Paul"), and pp. 359, 408; Gumbo Chaff's *Ethiopian Glee Book No .4*, 1850, p. 218; Christy's *Nigga Songster*, n. d., p. 121; White's *New Book of Plantation Melodies*, n. d., p. 44.

Lines 3 and 4 belong originally to a stanza commonly found in "De Blue Tail Fly," as in Scarborough, 1925, p. 203; *Negro Singers' Own Book*, 1846(?), p. 49; "De New Blue Tail Fly" ("by a U. S. N. officer"), *Ibid.*, p. 413; Gumbo Chaff's *Ethiopian Glee Book*, 1848, p. 64. As a stanza in "Jim Crack Corn," it occurs in *Negro Singers' Own Book*, pp. 58, 140; Gumbo Chaff's *Ethiopian Glee Book*, 1848, p. 64; Christy's *Nigga Songster*, n. d., p. 109.

The promise of freedom on which the first of these stanzas is based was made not uncommonly and was sometimes carried out. Harriet Martineau in *Society in America* (London, 1837) discusses this practice in her chapter on "The Morals of Slavery," and cites a case in which a mistress was poisoned to hasten the promised emancipation.

> My ole missus dead an' gone
> Lef' dis niggah to blow his horn.
>
> Ole massa dead now, let him res';
> Say all things is for de bes'.

2

REPORTED from Auburn, Ala., 1915–1916, anonymously.

Practically the same as in Talley, 1922, p. 25. Cf. also Perrow, 1915, p. 138; Scarborough, 1925, pp. 194, 224; Odum, 1926, pp. 173, 176; also preceding note.

The tune is given in Appendix I, p. 408.

> My ole mistis promised me
> When she died she'd set me free.
> She lived so long
> That her head got ball,
> And the Lord could n't kill her with a hickory maul.

3

MASSA HAD A YALLER GAL [1]

VARIOUS stanzas of this song are still widely current in the South. Variants appear in *Literary Digest*, May 27, 1916, p. 1558, as from northern South Carolina, 1876–1886; Talley, 1922, p. 62 (in a somewhat mixed condition); Odum, 1925, p. 236, and 1926, p. 179; Scarborough, 1925, pp. 66–68, 102. Some of its descriptive details are frequently carried over into the "I wouldn't marry a yaller gal" song (X, no. 31), as in Talley, p. 63.

---

[1] No local title given.

In the old minstrel books the song was known as "The Gal from the South,"
and generally consisted of three eight-line stanzas dealing with her hair and
eyes, her nose, and the tailor-shop experience, with a chorus repeating the lines
from stanza 1 about her hair. See *Ethiopian Serenaders' Own Book*, 1857(?),
p. 147; *George Christy and White's Melodies (New Song Book*, copyright, 1854)
p. 85 ("as sung by George Christy with tremendous applause"); White's *New
Book of Plantation Melodies*, n. d., p. 77.

A

Reported from Auburn, Ala., 1915–1916, MS. of J. E. Hillhouse. "A Mississippi
song."
　　Stanzas 1 and 2, with slight verbal variations, occur in Odum, 1925, p. 236,
and 1926, p. 179; Scarborough, 1925, pp. 66, 68; and in all the minstrel versions
cited above. Stanza 1 without stanza 2 occurs in Scarborough, 1925, pp. 67,
102. Stanza 3 occurs in Talley, 1922, p. 62, and Puckett, 1926, p. 76.

> Old master had a yellow gal,
> He brought her from the south;
> Her hair was wropped so close an' tight,
> She could n't shet her mouf.
>
> He carried her into the barber shop
> To have her mouf cut small;
> She backed her years all at once
> And swallowed shop and all.
>
> Her head looked like a coffee pot,
> Her nose looked like the spout,
> Her mouf looked like the fireplace
> With the ashes taken out.

B

Reported from Auburn, Ala., 1915–1916, MS. of A. H. Williamson, as heard in
Lowndes County, Ala.
　　See note to *A*, above.

> Massa bought a yaller gal,
> He bought er frum de south;
> Her head look like de coffee pot
> An' er nose look like de spout.
>
> Massa bought a yaller gal,
> He bought er frum de south;
> Her mouth look like de fireplace
> Wid de ashes taken out.

Massa bought a yaller gal,
He bought er frum de south;
She wrapped er hair so dad-blamed tight
Till she could n't shut er mouth.

C

Reported from Auburn, Ala., 1915–1916, MS. of G. E. Bargin, as heard near Birmingham, Ala. "Another verse of Yaller Gal."

Massa had a yaller gal,
She came from de south;
She had a head like a coffee pot
An' a nose jes' like de spout,
An' eber time she turn her head
She pour dat coffee out.

D

Reported from Greensboro, N. C., 1915–1916, MS. of J. J. W. Harriss, as heard in eastern or central North Carolina.

Massa owned a yaller gal,
Kept her in de kitchen,
Ev'ry time she combed her haid
She cotched de li'l fishes.

Massa owned a yaller gal,
Use to wash de platters,
Ev'ry time she combed her haid
She cotched de alligators.

E

Reported from Auburn, Ala., 1915–1916, MS. of L. N. Rivais.
Stanza 1 is the same as stanza 1 of A, above.
In the modern versions the combination of "The Gal from the South," with stanzas from other songs, is by no means uncommon. Both the Odum versions cited in the note to A, above, occur with stanzas and refrains from other songs; two of Miss Scarborough's versions (p. 67) are with choruses not a part of the song, and one of her versions (p. 102) contains both stanzas and chorus from other songs.

Ole marster had a yaller gal,
He brought her from the south,
She combed her hair so doggone tight,
She could n't shut her mouth.

Ole marster had a big black dog,
Blind as he could be,
He treed a nigger through a crack;
I believe dat dog could see.

F

Reported from Auburn, Ala., 1915–1916, MS. of S. A. Allen.
   Stanzas 1 and 2 are practically as in *A*, above. See also note to *E*.
   Stanza 3 is practically as in Scarborough, 1925, p. 102, with stanza 1, as from
Virginia. Stanza 4 is a variant of VIII, no. 22, *q. v.*
   Stanzas 5 is a variant of two successive stanzas in Odum, 1925, p. 237; also
with stanzas 1 and 2, as in the present song. Cf. also VIII, no. 23.

Old massa had a yaller gal,
He brung her from the south,
She curled her hair so doggone tight
She could not shut her mouth.

He carried her down to the blacksmith shop
To get her mouth cut small;
She turned around, backed her years,
And swallowed blacksmith shop and all.

Old massa had a banjo,
Its strings were made of twine;
The only tune that I could play
Was "I wish that gal was mine."

Old massa had a great big house,
It was sixteen stories high,
And every story in that house
Was filled with chicken pie.

Massa had an old grey mule,
His name was E'phram Jones,
And every tooth in his head
Held a barrel and half of corn.

G

Reported from Auburn, Ala., 1915–1916, MS. of B. A. Wooten, as heard in
Marengo County, Ala.
   Cf. the preceding songs, with notes.
   Stanza 1 is a variant of no. 24, in this chapter; stanza 3 is a variant of VIII,
no. 15; stanza 4 is a variant of VI, no. 31.

Ole marster bought a black man,
He bought him in de north;
The only fault I find with him
He cut his moustache off.

Ole marster bought a yaller gal,
He bought her from the south,
She wrapped her hair so hellish tight,
She could n't shut her mouth.

Times gittin' hard, money gittin' scarce,
Time I make my cotton and cohn, I'm gwine to leave this place.

Of all the beasts that roam the woods
I'd rather be a squir'l,
Curl my tail upon my back
And travel all over this worl'.

Wish I was a Jersey bull
In some shady place,
Every time I'd smell a cow
I'd wrinkle up my face.

If I had ten thousand bricks I'd build my chimney higher,
I'd take li'l Sally by the hand and sit down by the fire.

4

REPORTED from Auburn, Ala., 1915–1916, MS. of Hammond, as heard in south-eastern Alabama. "Was evidently a slave song. Was accompanied with a banjo."
    The last four lines go back to the old minstrels. Cf. "De Bran New Old Dan Tucker," p. 214 in *Negro Singers' Own Book:*

De toads dey jumped and de tadpoles danced,
De hogs dey squealed and de possums pranced.

Ole master had a fine buggy,
He filled it up wid peaches,
He run against a sign board,
And busted it all ter pieces.
De hoss begun ter kick up,
De mule begun ter prance,
De ole sow whistled
And de pigs all danced.

5

OLE MASSA WAS A STINGY MAN [1]

REPORTED from Auburn, Ala., 1915–1916, MS. of R. Allen, as heard in Jackson County, Ala.

This is practically the same as stanza 1 of "Come Day, Go Day, or Massa is a Stingy Man," *Negro Singers' Own Book*, 1846(?), p. 301 (as "sung with ever-lasting shouts of applause by the renowned old Dan Emmet"). A variant of the stanza occurs in "De Ole Stingy Man," Christy's *Nigga Songster*, n. d., p. 59.

> Ole marster was a stingy man
> And everybody know'd it;
> Kept good likker in his house
> And never said here goes it.

6

SIMON SLICK [1]

REPORTED from Auburn, Ala., 1915–1916, MS. of L. Brown, as heard in Choctow County, Ala. "Sung by Negro guitar picker."

Cf. no. 3 *F*, in this chapter, and VI, nos. 1 and 3, and Odum, 1925, p. 237.

> Massah had an old black mule,
> His name was Simon Slick,
> The only mule with screamin' eyes,
> An' how that mule could kick.

> #### *Chorus*
> Hi yi for your greenback,
> Hi yi for your change,
> Hi yi for your money, good Lord,
> An' don't you differ with me.

> He kicked the feathers from the goose,
> He broke the elephant's back,
> He stopped the Texas railroad train
> An' he kicked it off the track.

7

REPORTED from Auburn, Ala., 1915–1916, MS. of J. H. Drake, as heard in Auburn, Ala. "From father. Jig song."

I do not think I have seen this song or anything closely resembling it in the minstrel books, but it has a convincing ante-bellum flavor. The last two lines

---

[1] No local title given.

seem to be related to lines 9 and 10 of V, no. 12, which are a variation from the chorus of *Wake Nicodemus*, written by Henry Clay Work and copyrighted in 1864. "A good time" in *Wake Nicodemus* has become "hard times" in my two variants probably because the phrase is a common one in the old minstrel songs.

> Coming from my wife's house t'other Monday morning,
> I met the overseer and he looked so severe,
> With a bull whip in one hand and a cow whip in the other
> And a little strop of leather for to tie my hands together.
> Lookout for hard times for the cold is coming,
> Way down in the cane-brake a negro got to go.

8

REPORTED from St. Louis, Mo., 1926, MS. of Elizabeth White. "Sung by Mr. Randolph Harrison to his daughter about 1810–1812 and given to E. White by his grand-daughter, Miss Mary R. Blaine, of Louisville, Ky., in August, 1917."

With stanza 1, cf. the following, which occurs in "De Ole Virginny Break Down" and also in "Juba," pp. 130 and 223 of Christy's *Nigga Songster*, n. d.:

> I got up in the mornin' 'bout broke ob day,
> I went to de ribber, my canoe gone away.
> When I got to de ribber rader wide
> I look ober yonder, my canoe on toder side.

The last stanza is the same as VI, no. 48, *q. v.*, and note.

> I peeped through de crack,
> I seed de break uh day.
> I went down de landin';
> My cunnoo [1] gone away.
> I put muh foot in de water.
> De water so cold I cyan't go through.
>
> I went down de stable
> Tuh catch Marsteh's bay horse.
> I put de saddle on him,
> He trot like I don't keer.
>
> Aw pore niggah! He walk, he rode,
> He stump he toe an' he broke he gou'd.
> Muh Massah no good an' muh Missis no finny.
> I ain't eat no meat since I come from Guinea.

[1] Canoe. Cun'noo is the pronunciation required by the scansion in most cases in which the word occurs in the older ante-bellum minstrel songs.

Snake bake de hoecake,
Set de frog tuh mind it;
De frog went tuh noddin'
An' de lizard stole muh hoecake.

Bring back muh hoecake,
You long-tailed Nanny!

9

REPORTED from Auburn, Ala., 1915–1916, MS. of R. R. Beard, as heard in Mobile County, Ala. "Sung by grandfather."

This stanza occurs, with a refrain, in "Charleston Gals," Scarborough, 1925, p. 163, with music, where it is quoted from Allen's *Slave Songs*, 1867. "Charleston Gals" occurs in many of the ante-bellum minstrel books.

The song is of English origin. It was originally part of a sailor's ceremony and is found in a number of collections of sailors' songs. It is fully annotated in Roland Palmer Gray's *Songs and Ballads of the Maine Lumberjacks*, 1924, p. 104, to which Professor Kittredge cites me.

A number of variants of the stanza occur in sailor chanteys as quoted by Captain Dingle in various sea-stories that appeared in the *Saturday Evening Post* three or four years ago.

An interesting variant of twelve lines, containing all of the present song, occurs in Talley, 1922, p. 16.

Hey! My little man come a-ridin' by,
Ef you don't mind my little man, yo' hoss will die;
Well, ef he dies, I'll tan his skin,
An' ef he lives I'll ride him ergin.

10

REPORTED from Auburn, Ala., 1915–1916, anonymously.

Cf. Perrow, 1915, p. 133 (as from Mississippi country whites in 1909). If my memory does not trick me, Perrow's stanza, which follows, is a part of a ballad of considerable length which I have heard as "The Soldier From Over the Rhine":

There was an old man from over the Rhine,
    Snappoo! Snappoo!
There was an old man from over the Rhine,
Who came for some beer and who came for some wine,
    Snap-peter, snap-pider, fi-nan-ago-neda-snappoo!

Snappo-snap-peter, snap-nanny goat eater, snap-po,
I'm gwine away and never come back no more.

11

REPORTED from Auburn, Ala., 1915–1916, anonymously.

Cf. stanza 7 of "Going ober de Mountain," *Negro Singers' Own Book*, 1846(?), p. 250:

> In ole Virginny whar I was born,
> Dey feed us niggers on possum corn,
> And den dey git so debilish fat,
> Dere heads swells up, dey can't wear a hat.

A variant of the first two lines occurs in "Picayune Butler," Gumbo Chaff's *Ethiopian Glee Book*, 1848, p. 117.

Related stanzas occur in *Negro Singers' Own Book*, p. 312, Christy's *Nigga Songster*, n. d., pp. 69, 239, and Talley, 1922, p. 2.

On the first line, cf. III, nos. 19 and 20, VI, nos. 9, 40, IX, no. 3.

> 'Way down yonder where I was born,
> Dey feed us niggers on beef and corn;
> All us coons, we grow so fat,
> We can't wear no Stetson hat.

12

REPORTED from Auburn, Ala., 1915–1916, MS. of F. W. McMeans, as heard at Wolf Creek, Tenn. "Banjo Song."

Professor Kittredge cites me to Loraine Wyman and Howard Brockway: *Lonesome Tunes*, 1916, p. 33, where this couplet occurs as the last stanza of "The Ground Hog," as sung by Kentucky mountain whites; and to the bibliography in Cox, 1925, p. 498, where two versions are listed from Kentucky and one from North Carolina.

> Here comes Sal with a snicker and a grin,
> Ground hog gravy all over her chin.

13

REPORTED from Durham, N. C., 1919, MS. of David T. House, Jr.

This is practically the same as "Old Dan Tucker," sung all over the South by Polk Miller's quartet for years:

> Old Dan Tucker was a fine old man,
> Washed his face in a frying pan,
> Combed his hair with a wagon wheel,
> Died with the toothache in his heel.

> *Chorus:* Git out de way, old Dan Tucker,
>   You too late to git yo' supper.

Cf. also "Captain Dime," Talley, 1922, p. 5; Perrow, p. 131. Several of the ante-bellum minstrel books contain "Old Dan Tucker." There were also "De

Brand New Old Dan Tucker" (*Negro Singers' Own Book*, 1846 [?], p. 214), and occasional references to him in other songs. According to the author of "Negro Minstrelsy — Ancient and Modern" (*Putnam's Monthly*, v, 72–79, Jan., 1855), the song first appeared "in or about the year 1841."

> Old man Baker was a good old man,
> Beat his wife with a frying pan,
> Combed his head with a wagon wheel,
> And died with the toothache in his heel.

14

REPORTED from Auburn, Ala., 1915–1916, MS. of F. W. McMeans, as heard at Wolf Creek, Tenn. "Banjo Song."

Without definite evidence, I am of the opinion that this is an old banjo song of the whites. With stanza 2 cf. the Eliza Jane songs, no. 28, in this chapter.

> Cindy went to meetin',
> She shouted and she squeeled;
> She got so much religion
> She broke her stockin' heel.

> *Chorus*
> Get along home, Cindy, Cindy,
> Get along home, Cindy, Cindy,
> Fare you well.

> I went up to the mountain
> For to get a load of cane
> To make a jug of 'lasses
> Sweeter 'n Liza Jane.

15

REPORTED from Auburn, Ala., 1915–1916, MS. of J. H. Drake, as heard in Auburn, Ala. "From father. Jig song."

A variant of stanza 1, with music, occurs as "Ole Aunt Kate," in Scarborough, 1925, p. 99, where it is said to be an elaboration from "Juba," no. 18, in this chapter, *q. v.*

The first stanza bears an interesting similarity to a song quoted by Frederick Douglass in 1855. See Appendix V, pp. 455–456.

> Old Kate, the garden gate,
> She sifted meal, she give me the husk,
> She baked the bread, she give me the crust,
> She biled the meat, she give me the skin,
> That's the way she took me in.

She asked me if I could n't come again,
I told her "Yes, I reckon I kin."
Old Kate git over, old Kate git over.

Went down to Rocky Pint,
And I went down to see the Pint.
I asked for the needle case
To unlock the bolt in the chist,
To git a piece of stinking beef
To eat along with ginger cake.
Old Kate git over, old Kate git over.

16

REPORTED from Greensboro, N. C., 1915–1916, MS. of J. J. W. Harriss, as heard in eastern or central North Carolina.

Chorus

Rock candy, my ladies,
Rock candy, my love,
Learn how to rock candy.

Ole massa sol' me,
Speculator bought me,
Took me to Raleigh [1]
To learn how to rock candy.

17

REPORTED from Greensboro, N. C., 1915–1916, MS. of Mr. and Mrs. J. J. W. Harriss, as heard in eastern or central North Carolina. "Corn-shucking song. Patted and sung."

The "Jim Crow" song was one of the earliest of the Negro minstrel songs. It was introduced upon the stage between 1833–1835 by Thomas D. Rice, known thereafter as "Jim Crow" Rice. Rice got it from Jim Crow, an old slave in Louisville, who used to execute a queer dance to the refrain:

Wheel about, turn about, do jus' so,
And ebery time I wheel about, I jump Jim Crow.

Probably this refrain is the only part of the original version that has been preserved. The stanzas in the extant versions seem, for the most part, to be improvised chatter, but the refrain was held fairly stable by virtue of the fact that it both described the dance (which was the real cause and centre of the song)

---

[1] Sometimes it is Richmond, Mr. Harriss tells me. "Rock candy," like "jump Jim Crow" and, later, "Ball the Jack," was a dance step. Mr. Harriss has heard another stanza which he considers a little too risqué for print.

and accompanied it. See Chapter I, p. 8. As early as 1855 the author of the article, "Negro Minstrelsy — Ancient and Modern" (*Putnam's Monthly*, v, 72-79) was unable to find the original "Jim Crow," though imitations flourished. Among the imitations in the *Negro Singers' Own Book*, 1846(?), are "De Original Jim Crow," p. 329; "Jim Crow's Ramble," p. 290; "De Latest Jim Crow," p. 253. Jim Crow is also mentioned in other songs, for example, "The Departed Niggas," p. 204. Scarborough, 1925, p. 126, quotes another minstrel version attributed to Rice; also, p. 217, two traditional variants, the first of which (from New Orleans) is practically the same as the lines here given, and the second a slight variation of Jim Crow's original refrain as quoted above. Cf. also Talley, 1922, p. 13.

> Whar you goin', buzzard;
> Whar you goin', crow?
> Gwine down to de low groun'
> To git mah grubbin' hoe.
>
> Fust upon yo' heel-top,
> Den upon yo' toe,
> Ev'ry time I turn aroun'
> I jump Jim Crow.

18

REPORTED from Durham, N. C., 1919, MS. of David T. House, Jr.

For a very similar variant, cf. Scarborough, 1925, p. 98 (with music, as "one of the best known jig tunes of the old South"); also Talley, 1922, p. 9.

"Juba," like "Jump Jim Crow," is a dance which the song both describes and accompanies. See Talley, p. 233, for the "Juba" dance.

I find the following:

> Ruberii, de cimmon seed, seed de Billy hop in jist in time
> Juba dis, Juba dat, round de kettle ob possum fat,
> Juba,

in *George Christy and Wood's Melodies* (*New Song Book*, copyright, 1854) p. 72, and also in "Juba," White's *New Illustrated Melodeon*, n. d., p. 50, as "sung by the great banjo player, R. F. Stanton, with deafening shouts of applause."

Dr. Wyeth, who supplied Miss Scarborough's version, told her that the music was an old African melody and that the Negroes said Juba was an old African ghost. There is a Fiote (Lower Congo) word, *nguba*, meaning ground-nut, from which, according to A. Werner (Walter Jekyll, *Jamaican Song and Story*, 1904, Introduction, p. x) the word *goober*, for peanut, is derived. Perhaps the word is connected with Juba.

> Juba dis and Juba dat,
> Juba shoot and kill a yellow cat,
> Juba up and Juba down,
> Juba shoot and missed the ground.

19

REPORTED from Greensboro, N. C., 1915–1916, MS. of Mr. and Mrs. J. J. W. Harriss, as heard in eastern North Carolina. "Dance song — complete."

Set to yo' pa'tner, dah, dah,
Set to yo' pa'tner, dah, dah.

20

REPORTED from Auburn, Ala., 1915–1916, MS. of Mrs. Frazier.
Mrs. Frazier told me that this was a dancing song among Negroes near Auburn, Ala., in her childhood before the Civil War. She illustrated how a "buck" would dance up to his partner to this tune.

If I had a jug of rum
An' sugar by de pound,
An' a silver spoon to stir it with,
I'd treat dem ladies round.

21

UNCLE NED [1]

"UNCLE NED" is not originally a Negro song, but belongs to the group of songs including "Old Black Joe," "Nellie Gray," "Swanee River," "Massa's in de Cold, Cold Ground," "Old Kentucky Home," etc., written shortly before and during the rise of Negro minstrelsy, most of them by Stephen Foster, by whom "Uncle Ned" was copyrighted in 1848. It is included in many of the ante-bellum minstrel books, substantially in its present form and also with a paraphrase, as in *D* following. See Gumbo Chaff's *Ethiopian Glee Book*, 1848, p. 116; White's *New Illustrated Melodeon*, n. d., p. 24; also, with the paraphrase (cf. note to *D*) in White's *Serenaders' Song Book* (copyright, 1851), p. 61; and *Ethiopian Serenaders' Own Book*, 1857, pp. 41–42.

The song passed into oral tradition among the Negroes, sometimes absorbing stanzas from other songs, and came even to being sung in churches (see note to *C*). For traditional versions, see Perrow, 1913, p. 125 (as from Mississippi, in 1909), where it has become somewhat mixed with the old college song of "Josephus and Bohunkus"; also Talley, 1922, p. 61, where it is somewhat mixed within itself.

A

Reported from Auburn, Ala., 1915–1916, MS. of W. N. Blakenship, as heard in Atlanta, Ga. "Sung by Negro who fought in Civil War."
"Digits," in line 5, is from the paraphrase.

---

[1] Local title.

Dere was an old nigger by de name of Uncle Ned
And he died long years ago,
He had no hair on de top of his head,
But a place where de wool ought to grow.

Chorus

Den lay down de shovel and de hoe,
And hang up de fiddle and de bow;
Dere's no more work for poor Uncle Ned
He's gone where de good old niggers go.

His digits were as long as de cane in de brake,
And he had no eyes for to see;
He had no teeth for to crack corn bread,
So he had to let de hoecake be.

One day old Ned was working in de field
Wid his fiddle hanging on a tree,
When up come death and cotch 'im by de heel
Says Ned come go wid me.

B

Reported from Auburn, Ala., 1915–1916, MS. of L. M. Hall, as heard in Memphis, Tenn. "Sung around cotton shed."
The same as stanza 1 and chorus of *A*, with slight verbal variations.

C

Reported from Auburn, Ala., 1915–1916, MS. of H. M. Kilpatrick, as heard in Pickens County, Ala. "Heard in a Negro church."
One of my colored friends tells me that he has known this song to be used sometimes in opening schools, and sometimes in church, but not in a religious sense.
Stanza 2 occurs commonly in "The Gal from the South," both anté-bellum and modern versions. See no. 3 *A–E*, in this chapter.

There was an old negro and his name was Ned,
He lived long years ago,
He had no hair on the top of his head,
Right where the wool ought to grow.

Chorus

Hang up the fiddle and bow
Lay down the shovel and hoe,
For there's no more work for poor old Ned,
He's gone where the good negroes go.

His head was like a coffee pot,
His nose was like the spout,
His mouth was like the fireplace
With the ashes taken out.

His neck was so crooked he could n't take a pill,
Had to take it through his nose,
His legs was so crooked he could n't walk
And he had no toes at all.

D

Reported from Auburn, Ala., 1915–1916, MS. of J. H. Drake, as heard in Auburn, Ala. "From father. Sung by slave Negroes."

The paraphrase looked so suspicious that at first I decided to throw it out as obviously having no place in a collection of Negro songs. Luckily a study of the old minstrel books revealed it as a surprising case of oral tradition. "Uncle Ned," with the paraphrase, occurs in *Ethiopian Serenaders' Own Book*, 1857, pp. 41–42, also in White's *Serenaders' Song Book* (copyright 1851), p. 61. I quote the paraphrase from the former:

OLD UNCLE EDWARD

There formerly might have been seen an aged individual,
Whose cognomen was Uncle Edward;
He departed this life some time since, some time since;
And he had no capillary substance, on the summit of his cranium,
On the place designed by nature for the capillary to vegetate.

Chorus

Then lay down the agricultural implements,
    Allow the violin and the bow to be pendent on the wall, —
For there is no more physical energy to be displayed,
    By indigent aged Edward,
For he has departed to the abode designated by a kind
    Providence for all pious, humane, and benevolent colored individuals.

Uncle Edward had digits equal in longitude to the
    Banboo formation which springs so spontaneously on the bank of the southern
        Mississippi,
And he had no oculars with which to observe
    The beauties of nature;
And he had no dental formations with which to
    Masticate the Indian meal-cake,
Consequently he was forced to permit the
    Indian meal-cake to pass by with impunity.

When Uncle Ned relinquished his hold on vitality,
    His master was exceedingly grieved,

And the lachrymal poured down his cheeks similar to the rain from Heaven,
    For he knew that the old man was laid beneath terra firma, terra firma,
He would never have the pleasure of beholding the physiognomy of the aged
    Edward any more.

There was an old nigger whose name was Uncle Ned
He died long ago, long ago;
He had no hair on the top of his head,
The place where the wool oughter grow.
Put away the shovel and the hoe
And hang up the fiddle and the bow
For there's no more work for poor old Uncle Ned
For he's gone where the good darkies go.

(Same song revised by Negro's educated son.)

There was an old colored individual
Whose cognomen was "Uncle Edwin,"
He departed this life long since, long since,
He had no capillary substance on the top of his cranium
The place where the capillary substance ought to vegetate.
Put away the agricultural implements
Let the violin and the bow hang suspended on the wall,
For there's no more manual labor to be performed by Uncle Edwin,
For he's gone where good colored individuals go.

22

REPORTED from Auburn, Ala., 1915–1916, MS. of R. M. Beasly. "Sung by the Negroes in family before dinner and at night."
    The same, with slight verbal variations, as stanza 1 of "There Was an Old Nigger, His Name Was Dr. Peck," Scarborough, 1925, p. 197 (as from Alabama), which has the "You shall be free" chorus and the well-known rattlesnake (or blacksnake) quatrain for stanza 2.

There was a Doctor by the name Peck, Peck,
He fell in a well and broke his neck,
His wife did n't weep and his sister did n't moan,
He order taken sick and let the well alone.

23

RUN NIGGER RUN [1]

THIS song, which is still remembered by most Southern people whose memories go back of the eighteen-sixties, is based on the ante-bellum patrol. After it was too late to work in the fields, the slave's time was his own. He could, and frequently did, visit friends or relatives on neighboring plantations. Although some planters tried to curb this practice as likely to lead to discontent, it was pretty generally tolerated until the slave insurrections of the eighteen-twenties and thirties led to strict measures against Negro education, and Negro meetings without the presence of white witnesses. In practically all counties patrols were formed which arrested and whipped all Negroes found off their plantations after dark without written passes. These patrols, or "patterolers," figure in several of the ante-bellum novels of Southern life. Of course, they failed to break up the practice of slipping off at nights, but they impressed themselves mightily on the errant Negro's sensibilities, as the song shows. Running was much better than explaining. I think there is a psychological connection between this song and the whole-hearted refrain of the spiritual, generally called "City of Refuge" (II, no. 21), wherein it is said of Paul and Silas and various others that

> They had to run, they had to run,
> They had to run to the City of Refuge,
> They had to run.

Traditional variants occur in *Uncle Remus and His Friends*, p. 200, Perrow, 1915, p. 138 (as from Virginia in 1909), Scarborough, 1925, p. 12, with music (as from Kentucky), p. 24, with music (as from Louisiana), p. 25, with music. The first and last are used as refrains to stanzas from different spirituals.

The only version I have seen in ante-bellum song-books is "Run, Nigger, Run," in White's *Serenaders' Song Book* (copyright, 1851), p. 66, graced with a lively illustration and interspersed passages of prose dialogue:

> De sun am set — dis nigger am free,
> De colored gals he goes to see.
> I heard a voice cry, "Run, dad, fetch you!
> Run, nigger, run or de M. P.'ll catch you!"

> *Chorus and Repeat*
> Run, nigger, run, de M. P.'ll catch you!
> Run, nigger, run, tum a du daddle da!

Three other stanzas describe mainly the manner of the running.

A

Reported from Auburn, Ala., 1915–1916, MS. of J. R. Rutland.

As in *Uncle Remus and His Friends*, p. 200; Perrow, 1915, p. 138; Scarborough, 1925, pp. 12, 24.

> Run, nigger, run, paderow catch you;
> Run, nigger, run, it's almost day.

[1] No local title given.

ℬ

Reported from Auburn, Ala., 1915–1916, MS. of Jas. O. Avery, as heard in Guin, Ala.

Practically the same as in Scarborough, 1925, pp. 12, 25.

> Run nigger run, padarow catch you,
> Run nigger run, padarow catch you.
> Nigger run and nigger flew,
> Nigger tore his shirt tail in two.

C

Reported from Auburn, Ala., 1915–1916, MS. of M. S. Purdue.

> Negro run, negro blew,
> Negro tore himself half in two.

D

Reported from Durham, N. C., 1919, MS. of Walter J. Miller. "Heard sung by father. Favorite slave song."

Evidently a condensation of stanza 2 of the Wyeth (ante-bellum) version, given in Scarborough, 1925, p. 24. Cf. VI, no. 47, and note.

> Run, nigga, run, or patrol will ketch you.
> Run so fast — stuck his head in a hornet's nest.

24

Reported from Auburn, Ala., 1915–1916, MS. of S. A. Allen, as heard in Shelby County, Ala.

This song is evidently a humorous reply to the propaganda spread among the Negroes during the Civil War about the treatment to be expected from Yankees. Somewhat the same propaganda occurs in the pro-slavery novels which dwelt upon the miserable treatment accorded Negroes in the North.

Cf. no. 3 G in this chapter.

> The Yankees they caught me
> And tuck me to de nauth;
> The only harm they done to me,
> They cut my mustash off.

25

REPORTED from Greensboro, N. C., 1915–1916, MS. of J. J. W. Harriss. "Incompletely recalled."

Perhaps this song refers to the burning of Richmond after Lee's retreat from the city.

> Richmond is no mo',
> Heah my banjo moan.

26

REPORTED from Greensboro, N. C., 1915–1916, MS. of J. J. W. Harriss, as heard in east central North Carolina. "Sung by Negro at Reconstruction political meeting."

The first two lines are as in "I'm Going Back," Odum, 1925, p. 217 (repeated from Odum, *J. A. F. L.*, 1911). The last line, with a variant for the preceding lines, occurs in "I Would Rather Be a Negro than a Poor White Man," Talley, 1922, p. 42.

Cf. V, no. 8 *C*.

> My name is Sam,
> I don't give a damn,
> I'd rather be a nigger'n a po' white man.

27

KINGDOM COMING

REPORTED from Auburn, Ala., 1915–1916, MS. of J. P. Creel. "Negro war song during Civil War. Called 'Savannah River.'"

This is another case (cf. "Uncle Ned," "Camptown Races," "Skewbald," etc.) of the way in which oral tradition may transform a song of individual authorship into a folk-song. The song occurs in Frank Moore's *Songs of the Soldiers*, 1864, p. 189, without the author's name. I am indebted to Professor Kittredge for informing me that it was written by Henry Clay Work, the author of "Marching Through Georgia," "Babylon is Fallen," and "Wake Nicodemus" (V, no. 12). Professor Kittredge cites later appearances of the song as follows: *The Shilling Song Book No. 2*, Boston, copyright 1862, p. 14; *Bryant's Cane Break Refrains*, New York, copyright 1863, p. 58 ("as sung by Bryant's Minstrels"); H. T. Burleigh, *Negro Minstrel Melodies*, New York, copyright 1908 (words and music).

Work's songs have been reproduced in their original sheet-music form in *Songs of Henry Clay Work (1832–1884)*, "Compiled by Bertram G. Work, nephew of the author, and Presented with his Compliments," New York, n. d. According to the compiler's preface, "Kingdom Coming" was composed at the

outbreak of the Civil War; it was copyrighted and published in 1861. Stanza 1
and chorus are as follows:

> Say, darkies, hab you see de massa
> Wid de muffstash on his face;
> Go long de road some time dis mornin',
> Like he goin' to leave de place?
> He seen de smoke way up de ribber
> Where de Lincum gunboats lay,
> He took his hat and left berry sudden,
> An' I suppose he's runned away.
>
> De massa run, ha! ha!
> De darky stay, ho! ho!
> It must be now de kingdom's comin',
> In de year ob Jubilo.

The first two lines of the present version appear to be either imported from
another song or improvised upon an old model; e. g.,

> Seventeen hundred and sebenty six,
> De year I got my jawbone fixed,

which Miss Scarborough (1925, p. 125) prints as part of an ante-bellum dance
song from Virginia, and which I have seen in the old minstrel books. The re-
mainder of the present song is made over or imperfectly recalled from the older
version.

The last three lines below represent a badly confused memory of stanzas 3
and 4 of the original version.

For another traditional version showing considerably more variation from
the original, see Talley, 1922, p. 58, "Year of Jubilee."

For the singing of Negro Union soldiers in the South, from which the traditional versions probably arose, see Thomas Wentworth Higginson's *Army Life
in a Black Regiment*, Boston, 1870; and *Letters and Journals of Thomas Wentworth Higginson*, edited by Mary Thatcher Higginson, Boston, 1921.

> In eighteen hundred and sixty-one
> Dem dar Yankees fired dat great big gun;
> It looked mighty sispicious; somethin's gwine ter happen
> Fer de way dem white folks done.
>
> Old massa he runned away
> When he looked up de ribber where dem gun boats lay.
> It must be now dat de kingdom am a coming
> In de year of jubilee.
>
> De cider's in de cellar and de key's not throwed away;
> De darky am a gwine to hab some fun,
> For it'll all be confiscated when de Lincoln soldiers come.

28

ELIZA JANE

VARIOUS songs about Eliza Jane are sung by both whites and Negroes, in addition to other songs into which a stanza, or a line, or a part of the chorus, has been attracted from the Eliza Jane songs. Probably they go back to one or more common originals, but I have seen no printed version older than several here given. A comparison with other published versions shows that they all depend on five episodes, generally treated in distinct songs; a proposal, a sleigh-ride, a visit to Eliza Jane, goodbye, and Eliza's death on the train.

"Goodbye, Eliza Jane" was copyrighted in 1903 by Harry Von Tilzer, author of several other ragtime or "coon" songs which have found their way into popular tradition; for example, "Alexander," "Please Go Way and Let Me Sleep" (cf. XIV, no. 32), and "What You Goin' to Do When the Rent Comes Round?" (cf. no. 43, in this chapter).

Intrusions from other songs are common. In particular the sleigh-ride, which looks suspicious in a Negro song, has become very much mixed with a mule song.

I find the following Eliza Jane variants: *J. A. F. L.*, 1890, p. 290 (from Virginia); *Ibid.*, 1893, p. 131 (from North Carolina mountain whites); Perrow, 1915, pp. 178–180 (eight variants, from Tennessee, Mississippi, Indiana, and Kentucky, all but two from whites); Burlin (Hampton Series), 1919, iv, 41; Talley, 1922, p. 134; Odum, 1925, pp. 235, 237 (republished from *J. A. F. L.*, 1911), 1926, p. 180; Scarborough, 1925, pp. 8, 169, 192, 227.

A

GIT ALONG LIZA JANE [1]

Reported from Greensboro, N. C., 1915–1916, MS. of Mrs. J. J. W. Harriss, as heard in eastern or central North Carolina.

Variants of stanza 1 occur in Perrow, 1915, p. 180, and Talley, 1922, p. 134.
Variants of the refrain occur in Talley, p. 134 and Scarborough, 1925, p. 134.

> Ask Miss Liza to hab me,
> Says, "Law, ain't you shame?"
> Ask Miss Liza to hab me,
> Says, "Git along, Liza Jane."

Refrain

> Git along, Liza Jane,
> Git along, Liza Jane,
> Git along, Liza, my true love,
> Git along, Liza Jane.

[1] Local title.

Dis here world an' one more,
An' where will I be?
Sittin' by de side ob my true love,
An' she by me.

B

Reported from Greensboro, N. C., 1915–1916, MS. of Mrs. J. J. W. Harriss, as heard in eastern North Carolina. "Imperfectly recalled."

A variant of stanza 1 occurs in Perrow, 1915, p. 179 (as from Tennessee mountain whites in 1905) and in Scarborough, 1925, p. 8. With the second stanza, cf. *J. A. F. L.*, 1890, p. 290, from Virginia.

Little ole Liza Jane,
Little ole Liza Jane,
Little ole Liza Jane,
She died on de train.

Go long, go long, go long, Liza Jane,
Go long, go long, go long, Liza Jane,
Go long, go long, go long, Liza Jane,
She died on de train.

C

Reported from Auburn, Ala., 1915–1916, MS. of R. Chambers, as heard in Giles County, Tenn. "Brought from mountains of Virginia and Tennessee in 1868."

Variants of this stanza are among the most common of the Eliza Jane stanzas. Cf. *J. A. F. L.*, 1893, p. 132 (as from North Carolina mountain whites); Perrow, 1915, p. 179–180 (three variants from Mississippi country whites in 1909); Talley, 1922, p. 134; Scarborough, 1925, p. 8.

She went up the new cut road,
I went down the lane,
Threw my hat in the corner of the fence,
Good-by, Liza Jane.

D

Reported from Durham, N. C., 1926, MS. of N. I. White, as heard in Statesville, N. C., about 1904, sung by travelling Negro minstrels.

This seems to be slightly related to Scarborough, 1925, p. 227.

Good-bye, Miss Eliza Jane,
I'm gwine to leab you;
Don't care, Miss Eliza Jane,
If it do grieb you.
Good-bye, Miss Eliza Jane, good-bye, Miss Eliza Jane,
Good-bye, Miss Eliza Jane.

ε

Reported from Auburn, Ala., 1915–1916, MS. of L. N. Rivais.

For variants of stanza 1, see Perrow, 1915, p. 180 (from Mississippi in 1909); Odum, 1925, p. 236 (reprinted from Odum, *J. A. F. L.*, 1911); Ibid., 1926, p. 180.

For the chorus, cf. Odum, as above.

> Gwine down by de pars'nage,
> Now Liza you keep cool;
> I has n't got time to squeeze you,
> I'se busy wid dis mule.

Chorus

> Whoa, mule, whoa,
> Whoa, mule, I say;
> Keep your seat, Miss Liza Jane,
> An' hang to dat sleigh.

> De mule he jumped to one side,
> De sleigh she went kerflap,
> Broke my new suspenders,
> Sal fell on my lap.

F

Reported from Auburn, Ala., 1915–1916, MS. of F. W. McMeans, as heard at Wolf Creek, Tenn. "Banjo song."

I do not find this stanza in any of the published Eliza Jane variants. It is practically the same as X, no. 66, and is probably an entirely independent stanza attracted into the Eliza Jane songs.

For the refrain, cf. VI, no. 4.

> When I went to see Miss Liza Jane,
> She was standin' in the door,
> With shoes and stockin's in her hands
> And feet all over the floor.

> Whoa! mule.

G

MY LIZA JANE [1]

Reported from Auburn, Ala., 1916, MS. of F. W. Calhoun. "This was heard by my grandfather, Mr. C. S. Kearley, and was sung by a farm hand in the corn field, accompanied with banjo."

---

[1] Local title.

Only the last stanza belongs properly to Eliza Jane. With it, cf. Scarborough, 1925, p. 8; also the *B* and *C* variants, above.

Stanzas 1 and 2 occur independently and in various combinations. Cf. X, nos. 65, 67, 75.

Saturday night and Sunday too, pretty gals on my mind;
Monday morning just 'fore day, white folks got me gwine,
White folks got me gwine, white folks got me gwine.

When I go to my gal's house and she is at home,
I lays myself back in de big arm cheer and picks on de old banjo,
And picks on de old banjo, and picks on de old banjo.

As I went down de new cut road, she went down de lane.
Was de last time I saw my true love, so go 'long, Liza Jane.
Go long, Liza Jane, go long, Liza Jane.

29

KEEMO KIMO [1]

VARIANTS of this song occur both with and without the nonsense lines, in various combinations with stanzas originally from other songs. In Scarborough, 1925, p. 201 (as from Virginia), the song is composed of the first two lines of *A*, slightly varied, followed by all of *B*, without the nonsense lines. This is practically the same as stanza 6 of "Git Along John," *Negro Singers' Own Book*, 1846(?), p. 312, also without the nonsense lines. In Odum, 1926, p. 187, the four lines occur under the title "Kitty Kimo," with a variant of the nonsense lines as a chorus and with three other old stanzas, all from different ante-bellum minstrel songs. In *George Christy and Wood's Melodies (New Song Book*, copyright, 1854), p. 1, the lines occur with an interline refrain, "Sing song Kitty cant you Ki me O," and a nonsense chorus similar to the last four lines of *A*. Cf. also Christy's *Nigga Songster*, n. d., stanza 3 of "Cum Along, John the Piper's Son," p. 68, and stanza 3 of "Git Along John," p. 239.

The nonsense chorus is considerably varied in different versions. It occurs in part in the "The Frog in the Well" (Campbell and Sharp, 1917, p. 319); also as from Virginia (with music), without other stanzas, in Scarborough, 1925, p. 156. In Scarborough, 1925, p. 157 (as from Texas) the chorus occurs with two stanzas of the "Way down South" variety, as in Odum and *Negro Singers' Own Book*, and with the same interline refrain as in *George Christy and Wood's New Song Book*.

The refrain is not originally Negro, but is an old English nonsense rhyme. See Professor Kittredge's note on it in *J. A. F. L.*, xxxv, 396.

Professor A. L. Hench of the University of Virginia told me several years ago that a variant of the refrain was used in a yell at the preparatory school which he attended, and Mr. John Bridgers, of Duke University, has furnished me with

---

[1] No local title given.

a printed sheet of yells used at Trinity College, N. C., in 1921, in which the following variant is given:

> Kemo, Kimo, daro, Wah!
> Me my rumstickapumpadoodle,
> Sit back Pollywinkle
> In came an old cat
> Old silly, sally billy
> Hebo, Hibo, Dishcake, Gingercake,
> Trinity, Trinity, Trinity!

A

Reported from Auburn, Ala., 1915–1916, MS. of J. H. Drake, as heard in Auburn, Ala. "Slavery-time song."
    Cf. IX, no. 28.

> Milk in the dairy getting mighty old,
> Skippers and the mice working mighty bold,
> Sing song Kitty can't yer kinny meo
> Keymo ki mo doro hi me hi me ho.
> In come Sally singing, sometimes
> Penny with a wink turnings cat
> Sing song Kitty can't yer ki meo
> Key mo ki mo doro hi, me hi me ho.

B

Reported from Auburn, Ala., 1915–1916, MS. of R. R. Beard, as heard in Mobile County, Ala. "Sung by an ex-slave."

> A long-tailed rat an' a bole er souse,
> Jes' come down from de white folk's house.

C

Reported from Auburn, Ala., 1915–1916, MS. of J. E. Hillhouse, as heard in southern Alabama.
    The first and third lines do not occur in any of the variants I have seen.

> I went up to town to get a cake of cheese,
> The skippers and the maggets and a long-tailed mouse,
> Yonder come a nigger with a bucket full o' souse;
> Just come down from the white folk's house.

30

REPORTED from Auburn, Ala., 1915–1916, MS. of J. O. Lizenby, as heard in Houston County, Ala. "Sung by old Negro to the fiddle."

Oh! Once I wuz a rich man and wore silks and satins,
But now I am a poor man and wear my cotton battin'.

31

REPORTED from Durham, N. C., 1925, MS. of John Bridgers. "Sung by an old Negro mammy, an ex-slave, from Georgia, to children in the hearing of Mrs. A. K. Powers, in Wallace, N. C., about 1915."
   This is a corrupt tradition of part of "The Old Fox Song," an English nursery rhyme. Cf. the following stanza of the version in Halliwell's *Nursery Rhymes*, 1842, p. 30, for which I am indebted to Professor Kittredge:

> The farmer's wife she jumped out of bed,
> And out of the window she popped her head!
> Oh, husband! oh husband! the geese are all dead,
> For the fox has been through the town, o-oh!

Professor Kittredge also cites me to the version in Cox, 1925, p. 474, which contains most of the second stanza of the version below. Cox's bibliography for the song lists thirteen versions, English and American, including an eighteenth-century broadside.
   The last two lines below are modified from the old minstrel song, "Dandy Jim of Caroline", VIII, no. 17.

Old Mother Pickapot, lying in the bed,
Out of the window she poked her head,
   Saying, "Husband, husband, the gray goose is gone;
   Don't you hear her hollow, 'quincquanceed!'
   Don't you hear her hollow, 'quincquanceed'?"

The old fox went out one moonshiney night:
"Some meat, some meat we must have this night
Some meat, some meat we must have this night."
   The funniest old fellow in the county-O
   The funniest old fellow in the county-O.

32

REPORTED from Greensboro, N. C., 1915–1916, MS. of Mrs. J. J. W. Harriss, as "heard in N. C. about 1880."
   Professor Kittredge cites me to "The Silver Dagger," Cox, 1925, p. 343, which begins,

> O Mary, go and ask your mother
> If you my wedded bride may be

It is really a variant of the old English and Scottish ballad, "The Drowsy Lover," for which Cox lists numerous publications and discussions.

> Mary Bell, Go ask yo' mama,
> If you an' I be bride alone;
> If she say no, come back an' tell me
> An' Mary Bell will run away.

33

LYNCHBURG TOWN [1]

REPORTED from Greensboro, N. C., 1915–1916, MS. of Mrs. J. J. W. Harriss, as heard in eastern or central North Carolina.

For a variant with "Lynchburg" for "Richmond," see Perrow, 1915, p. 139. as from Virginia in 1909; with "Vicksburg" for "Richmond," see Scarborough, 1925, p. 192, used as chorus for "Hawkie Is a Schemin' Bird," as from Mississippi.

With the usual slight variations, the lines occur constantly in the ante-bellum minstrel books, where the town is almost always Lynchburg. Cf. *Negro Singers' Own Book*, 1846(?), in "A Going Along Down," p. 56, and "Lynchburg Town," p. 157; *Ethiopian Serenaders' Own Book*, 1857(?), in "Lynchburg Town," p. 80; Christy's *Nigga Songster*, n. d., in "Lynchburg Town" p. 113, and "Walk Along, Jumbo," p. 136. In all these instances the lines are used as a chorus to varying stanzas.

> I'm gwine down town,
> I'm gwine down town,
> I'm gwine down to Richmond town,
> To sell my 'baca down.

34

OH, SUZANNA [1]

REPORTED from Auburn, Ala., 1915–1916, MS. of H. C. Kilpatrick. "Heard from father. Old slave song."

This song, which was copyrighted in 1848 by Stephen Foster, has always been sung by white people more than by Negroes. It was a favorite with the ante-bellum minstrels. Cf. "Oh Susanna," in Gumbo Chaff's *Ethiopian Glee Book*, 1848, p. 88; Christy's *Nigga Songster*, n. d., p. 247; White's *New Illustrated Melodeon*, n. d., p. 11; and ("New Version"), *George Christy and Wood's Melodies* (*New Song Book*, copyright, 1854), p. 45.

> Oh, don't you cry, Suzanna,
> Now don't you cry for me,
> I'm here from Alabama
> Wid my banjo on my knee.

[1] No local title given.

It rained all day de day I left,
De weader it was dry,
De sun shone so hot I froze to death,
Suzanna, don't you cry!

35

REPORTED from Auburn, Ala., 1915–1916, MS. of J. W. McKinstry. "Sung by slavery time Negroes."

This song has all the earmarks of an old minstrel song, but I can cite no antebellum originals for any of the lines. The refrain is probably one of the many variants of the "Walk in de Parlor" refrain found in many of the old minstrel songs.

Old Dan Cox rides a gray horse,
Old Dan Cox rides a gray horse,
Old Dan Cox rides a gray horse,
His knees sticks out for a telegraph pole,
But that don't amount to anything at all.
Walk in Joe along with the girls, not a picky ninny to spend.

We ate four kinds of meat for breakfast,
We ate four kinds of meat for breakfast,
We ate four kinds of meat for breakfast,
Sheep, ram, mutton, and goat, old Dan Dutton
Ate a whole leg of mutton walked off and said nothing,
Walk in Joe with the girls, not a picky ninny to spend.

36

REPORTED from Auburn, Ala., 1915–1916, MS. of A. M. Kearly. "Heard in commencement speeches."

Practically the same as in Talley, 1922, p. 153, and Scarborough, 1925 (from Texas as a children's game song).

It comes from the old minstrel rhyme:

Possum up a gum tree, saucy, fat and dirty,
Come kiss me, gals, or I'll run like a turkey.

In "Neber Do to Gib it Up," p. 227, *Negro Singers' Own Book*, 1846(?), and p. 152 in Christy's *Nigga Songster*, n. d.

Here I stand black and dirty,
If you don't come and kiss me, I will run like a turkey.

37

REPORTED from Auburn, Ala., 1915–1916, MS. of R. R. Beard, as heard in Mobile County, Ala. "Sung by grandfather."

> I'm des a little nigger,
> De white folks call me Mose,
> An' what I don't know about myself
> I nebber wants to knows.

38

REPORTED from Durham, N. C., 1919, MS. of Charlie E. Jordan. "The following sketch seems to be a holiday song and expressed the joyous feelings of a Negro on a holiday."

With slight verbal variations, all except the first two lines occur in "Raise a Rucus Tonight," Talley, 1922, p. 90, and Odum, 1926 (three variants) pp. 173–175. Also these variants consist of stanzas from various other songs, with the refrain, "Raise a rucus tonight," and all include stanza 2 below, with the usual slight verbal variations.

The tune is given in Appendix I, p. 409.

> My ole banjo hangin' on de wall,
> Ain't been tuned since a way last fall;
> Goin' to raise up a rucus tonight,
> Come along, my children, come along!

> Come while der moon am shinin' bright,
> Take a boat an' we'll go down de ribber afloat;
> We're gwine to raise up a rucus tonight.

39

REPORTED from Auburn, Ala., 1915–1916, MS. of R. Allen, as heard in Jackson County, Ala. "Market Street is probably the street by same name in Chattanooga."

For a classic description of the cake-walk, with which this song deals, see Mark Twain's *Defense of Harriet Shelley*.

> Oh, the fat one and the lean one
> Went walking for the cake,
> The fat one beat the lean one
> But the lean one swallowed the plate.
> If it had been mince pie
> Would ever bite been gone,
> That's the song of little nigger babe
> Down on Market Street.

40

REPORTED from Auburn, Ala., 1915–1916, MS. of H. I. Killingsworth, as heard in southwestern Georgia.

This song is an interesting descendant of Stephen Foster's "Camptown Races." The song was given to me as "complete," and is really a description of the original song rather than an account of the events with which it deals. The original was composed in 1851 and was commonly included in the early minstrel books without credit to Foster; for example, *Ethiopian Serenaders' Own Book*, 1857(?), p. 15; Christy's *Plantation Melodies* (dated by Library of Congress, 1851) p. 15, etc. In the minstrel books the versions are by no means uniform. Perrow, 1915, p. 134, quotes two stanzas as from Mississippi in 1909, which are close to the original and which preserve the "Do-da" refrain, but which do not occur in the Christy version cited above.

Uster be er song er long time ago,
"Camptown Races" dat we all know;
All about de bay an' de bob-tail nag,
And de saw-bone jinny wid de moneybag.

41

REPORTED from Durham, N. C., 1919, MS. of Thomas Litaker, as heard in Cabarrus County, N. C.

This song is related to a song of the white people, the tune and a few words of which I can remember from my childhood, but whether it is a part of the original, or a parody, I cannot recall enough to say. In the fragment I recall, "Mama won't 'low me to spit on the floor" and "Papa won't 'low me to dance."

Coon shine, ladies, coon shine.
Coon shine on the floor.
O my pa don't 'low me to coonshine
And my ma don't 'low me to try.
Git up in de morning 'fore day,
Coon shine on de sly.

42

REPORTED from Auburn, Ala., 1915–1916, MS. of J. H. Drake, as heard in Auburn, Ala. "Heard from father."

Line 6 occurs as a refrain in a spiritual I have heard sung by the Tuskegee singers. The last line is from "The Little Old Log Cabin in the Lane," which is not a Negro song at all.

The song is probably either a descendant of an old minstrel song, in which the Negro is made to sentimentalize as the white author would like to imagine him, or it comes from a later song of the same stripe.

I'm growing old and feeble now,
I cannot work no more;
I've laid the rusty blade away to rest.
Old marster and old mistress they are sleeping side by side
And their spirits they are roaming with the blest.
I ain't got long to stay here,
What little time I've got
I'll try to be contented and remain,
Till death shall finally call for me
And that good old dog of mine
In the little log cabin in the lane.

43

WHAT YOU GOIN' TO DO WHEN THE RENT COMES ROUND [1]

REPORTED from Auburn, Ala., 1915–1916, MS. of Alsobrook.
This is a modern minstrel song. I heard it at a Negro minstrel show in Statesville, N. C., about 1905. It was written by Harry Von Tilzer, probably about 1900. See note to no. 28, in this chapter.

Rufus Rastus Johnson Brown,
What you goner do when the rent comes round?
What you goner say? How you goner pay?
Never have a bit er expense till judgment day.
You know, I know rent means dough,
The landlord goner put us out in the snow;
Rufus Rastus Johnson Brown,
What you goner do when the rent comes around?

44

REPORTED from Auburn, Ala., 1915–1916, anonymously, as heard in Marshall County, Ala.
Practically the same as in Kennedy, 1925, p. 43 (from Louisiana).

What you goin' to do when the meat gibs out?
Set in the corner with lips poked out.

[1] No local title given.

45

REPORTED from Durham, N. C., 1919, MS. of Thomas Litaker, as heard in Cabarrus County, N. C.

Cf. "Karo Song," Scarborough, 1925, p. 170. The songs are not alike except in name, but the fact that the present song undoubtedly refers to a dance known as the Cairo makes me suspect that Miss Scarborough's song (most of the stanzas of which occur commonly in ante-bellum jig songs) is also a dance song and does not refer to the town of Cuero, as she supposes.

> Stick my head in a paper sack,
> Show dem niggers how to Cairo back.
> Shake dat flat foot,
> Shake dat flat foot.

46

REPORTED from Auburn, Ala., 1915–1916, MS. of J. R. Rutland, as heard in Auburn, Ala. "Sung by Negro minstrels."

> Come here, Jill, wid yo' key,
> Ole trouble is a huntin' after me.

47

REPORTED from Auburn, Ala., 1915–1916, MS. of W. D. Kimbrough, as heard in Camden, Ala.

This song represents a combination, which probably exists in some early minstrel stanzas I have not seen, of the first two lines of "Reel O'er the Mountain," Christy's *Nigga Songster*, n. d., p. 63, and stanza 3 of "Sound Your Horn," *Ibid.*, n. d., p. 161, as follows:

> A nigger come from Arkansas,
> De biggest fool I ever saw,

and

> De nigga's head so large
> It measures half a peck,
> He pulls his coat over his legs
> And buttons his trousers round his neck.

A variant of the first in "Over the Mountain" (Gumbo Chaff's *Ethiopian Glee Book*, 1848, p. 31) transfers the honor to Tennessee:

> De biggest fool I ever see
> Was nigger come from Tennessee.

Cf. VII, no. 85.

The biggest fool I ever saw
Came from the state of Arkansaw,
He put his shirt all over his coat
And buttoned his breeches around his throat.

48

REPORTED from Auburn, Ala., 1915-1916, MS. of James O. Avery, as heard in
Auburn, Ala.
    Cf. VII, nos. 50, 51.

I rose early one morning,
Just about half past fo',
I heard somebody knockin'
On my kitchen door,
On my kitchen door.

49

REPORTED from Auburn, Ala., 1915-1916, MS. of A. H. Williamson, as heard in
Lowndes County, Ala.

Three weeks my head's been nappy,
Three weeks since I seen my pappy.
I'm gwine ter marry as dey say,
I'm gwine ter marry Christmas Day.

50

REPORTED from Auburn, Ala., 1915-1916, anonymously.
    Cf. "Traveling Coon," XI, no. 5, and V, no. 14.
    Bob Cole's coon song, "Oh Didn't He Ramble," was copyrighted in 1921.

He rambled and he rambled till the butchers cut him down,
He came up to a farmer's house, and asked the price of geese,
You son-of-a-gun, you'd better run,
'Cause they're fifty cents apiece.

V

SOCIAL SONGS: NARRATIVE SONGS
AND BALLADS

THE songs in this group constitute a rather curious and decidedly mixed exhibit. Any reader only casually acquainted
with Negro songs might say of many of them that they are not Negro
songs at all. In a sense he would be right; there are hardly ten songs
out of the thirty-seven that I should venture to pronounce genuine
Negro folk-songs in both their origin and their present nature.
Seventeen of these songs[1] I feel sure are, either mainly or in part,
of "ballet"[2] or vaudeville origin; it is often impossible to say which.
Six of them[3] are at least partly derived from the ante-bellum minstrel songs. Six[4] are partly based on early songs of the white people;
the first on "Mary had a Little Lamb," the second on the "Derby
Ram," the third on two lines common in white folk-songs, the fourth
on "The Fifty Cents," the fifth on an old jig song of the white
people, and the sixth on a folk-song of the whites in print as early
as 1580. Numbers 30 and 32 are apparently nothing more than inaccurate versions of poems that had appeared in print some years
before the songs were reported.

Yet these songs are almost all in common circulation among the
Negroes. Many of them have been printed in other collections,
either entire or in part, as heard sung by Negroes; and many that
have not are so much like others that have, that it would seem un-
wise to exclude them from the collection. Of course, the Negroes
sing many of the same songs that white people sing, from regular
hymns to the latest musical comedy hits, without anyone venturing
to call such songs Negro folk-songs; but when they preserve songs

---

[1] Nos. 2 *A*, 8 *A* – *F*, 9, 11, 13, 14, 15, 17, 18, 19, 20, 22, 23, 24, 33, 35, 36.

[2] The term "ballet" as used by both white and Negro folk-singers is a corruption
of "ballad." In the usage of mountain whites it often applies to traditional English
popular ballads, but in Negro usage it signifies songs of individual authorship printed
on single sheets, like the English broadside ballads, and hawked about by the
composer.

[3] Nos. 4, 7, 12, 20, 21, 26.

[4] Nos. 13, 14, 20, 27, 28, 31.

that the white people have ceased to sing, with omissions, additions, and alterations, and seem to think of them as belonging primarily to the Negro, such songs do become, in a somewhat loose way, a part of the body of Negro folk-song. Let the process continue a few years longer till they have been more fully moulded by the general characteristics of Negro folk-song, and there will be no question. Reverse the process, and throw out of account all the older Negro songs that have their principal basis in "ballets," old folk-songs or hymns of the whites, or songs of the black-face minstrels of the middle of the nineteenth century, and a large proportion of those songs which the Negro has made indisputably his own would have to be discarded. The notes to the songs in my whole collection show nothing so clearly as the tendency of Negro folk-song to pick up material from any source and, by changing it or using it in all sorts of combinations, to make it definitely its own. Thus it does not seem wise to say that most of the songs in the present group are not really Negro at all; though it is well to point out that many of them are not so fully and typically Negro as most of the work songs and religious songs.

More than any other group of Negro songs, these songs show the influence of the modern vaudeville stage, of the popular song of the white people, which has had its day; and of the printed songs of those half-folk composers, the "ballet" writers, who come into printing offices with doggerel verses pencilled on ruled tablet paper and, paying cash and often giving no name, order printed broadsides, which are sung and sold wherever there is a gathering of Negroes.

The trail here becomes often too difficult to follow. A "ballet" writer might take for his starting point a well-known folk-song, like a John Henry hammer song, and elaborate it into a ballad. On the other hand, he might write the ballad when its incidents were fresh in the popular mind, and a number of short, genuinely popular songs might develop as off-shoots of the ballad. His most characteristic procedure, like that of broadside writers in all ages, would be to capitalize the group interest in some matter of sudden overwhelming folk-interest — a murder, a train-wreck, a war, a Titanic, or a Lindbergh. He would not be incapable of doing over a vaudeville song, or even a well-known recitation piece, like "Theology in the Quarters" (no. 30), or "Pomp's Soliloquy" (no. 32). Neither would the folk Negro be incapable of all these methods, without the presence of the "ballet" as a connecting link. Moreover, a reverse process is always in operation, in which professional song-writers, always on the lookout for material, adopt folk material, work it over into something partly their own, and hand it back to the folk to go through the familiar process once more.

This is what has happened with the blues; it is what happened, I strongly suspect, with such a song as "He Rambled," no. 14, in this group. This song was reported in 1915–1916 from Auburn, Alabama. Fragments of the same song occur in IV, no. 51, reported from Auburn, Alabama, in the same year, and in XI, no. 5, reported from Durham, North Carolina, in 1919. All three songs bear evidence of individual rather than folk origin. Twenty years ago I knew a song practically the same as the first stanza of no. 14. And yet Bob Cole, who copyrighted "Oh Did n't He Ramble," in 1921, would seem to be the author, but for the dates. What happened was that there was an earlier author, who probably did not copyright his song, from whom the songs in this collection took their rise; that Bob Cole founded his song on the imperfect folk memories of the original song preserved by such songs as those in this collection, and that later versions of the folk-songs show, or will show, indebtedness to Cole's song. Something very similar happened in the case of Stephen Foster's "Uncle Ned," a Negro folk version of which is to be found in this collection (IV, no. 22). Foster wrote this song in 1845 and copyrighted it in 1848, but in the short time elapsing between his first giving it to the Sable Harmonists and copyrighting it, two versions of it were copyrighted by other "authors." The early minstrel books are full of songs, each of which several famous performers claimed to have written.

In my notes I have tried to clarify the sources of a number of these songs for which printed sources or analogies exist. The songs of "ballet" origin, however, are fairly immune to the source-hunter because of the very fugitive and ephemeral nature of the "ballets" themselves. Such sources as I have found are mostly comparatively recent. This fact probably accounts for some of the differences between these and older songs which are felt to be more genuine folk-songs. After all, as other sections of this book show, many of the older songs went through a similar process, the only difference being that the signs of the process are more evident when the process is more recent.

The quality of humor found in these songs is quite commonly that of the vaudeville stage. In none of his folk-songs does the Negro hesitate to accept the white man's notion of Negro humor at face value. The tradition of buffoonery and humorous rascality, begun by the first minstrels in the late eighteen-twenties, is still alive. Ephraim Ham Johnson Brown, the haunted mansion, the voodoo man, Mr. Johnson's cat, the swain and his greedy girl, the gambling and stealing escapades, are all typical of the modern minstrel and vaudeville idea of Negro humor. "Willie the Weeper" (no. 17) and the preacher whose hunting on Sunday proved so calamitous (no. 23), are not even Negro characters, but both songs possess an extravagance dear to the Negro sense of humor.

The John Henry songs and the Frankie and Albert songs are by far the most widely known of the Negro ballads. Both songs have developed little cycles of their own. Various songs tell of John Henry's boyhood and his premonition that the mountains (variously located) would be his death; of his steel-driving ability, the contest with the steam drill, his death, and the valiant effort of his wife, Polly Ann, to keep up the family tradition by driving steel like a man. Their origin and connection with John Hardy are matters of some obscurity; they have been sung by white people as well as by Negroes; but in their present state they seem to be thoroughly Negro songs. The Frankie and Albert songs are said by Mr. Spaeth to have originated between 1850 and 1860, probably in St. Louis.[5] If they did originate in a slave state before the Civil War, they must have been started by white people. For that matter, they have always been sung by both white people and Negroes. The story of underworld faithlessness and retribution which they tell, embellished in many of the variants with unprintable details, is one that might easily belong either to the white or black race, or to both. Both have adopted it.

There are a few notes of pathos, such as no. 12 (evidently of a similar vintage to "Uncle Ned") and no. 20, the genuinely pathetic lament for "My old blue dog." Humor dominates, however, even when the singer's situation is one of danger or difficulty. It is the same humor found most commonly in other types of the Negro secular song, the boisterous humor of high animal spirits, without much of the sly quality which crops up occasionally in the work songs.

SONGS, WITH ANNOTATIONS

The following songs classified in other groups might also be included in the present class: II, 85; III, 21, 25, 31; IV, 3, 4, 6–8, 13–15, 21–24, 27, 28 E, 30, 40, 50; VI, 1, 3, 13, 21, 34, 50; XI, 1, 5; XII, 46, 48; XIII, 13.

---

[5] Sigmund Spaeth: *Read 'Em and Weep* (New York, 1927), p. 34.

I

JOHN HENRY [1]

JOHN HENRY ballads are known all over the country, as well as the work songs which grew out of them. For specimens of the latter, see VII, nos. 23 ff. Professor Cox (1925, pp. 175–177) gives the complete story of John Hardy, a West Virginia Negro steel-driver whom he identifies with John Henry. He also gives nine variants of the song, of from five to thirteen stanzas, in some of which John Henry and John Hardy are named interchangeably. Odum and Johnson (1926, p. 222) think the John Henry songs of separate origin, which became mixed with the John Hardy story in West Virginia. "We have never found a Negro who knew the song as John Hardy, and we have no versions which mention the circumstance of the murder and execution." The quoted sentence is true also of the present collection. Miss Scarborough (1926, p. 218) accepts Cox's opinion without discussion, but the songs she quotes mention John Hardy only. Short of identifying John Hardy with John Henry, Cox's opinion is supported by the belief of W. C. Handy, author of the "John Henry Blues" (1926, p. 37) that John Henry worked in West Virginia, and by the statement given me in 1919, by Harvey Harward, with VII, no. 23 B, that John Henry was a worker in the "Big Ben" tunnel of West Virginia and was famous for his steel-driving ability. According to this note, however, he died of overwork, as John Hardy did in the account given Cox by Mr. H. S. Walker. Mr. Harward's account is the same as that given me by several Negro singers.

For Professor Cox's full treatment of John Hardy and the development of the ballad, see Cox, *J. A. F. L.*, xxxii, (1919) 505.

Professor Cox (1925) cites fourteen other published variants. Add Scarborough (1925, pp. 219–221), seven shorter variants, from different localities; Odum (1926, pp. 221–240), eleven variants, and Handy (1926, p. 135), the "John Henry Blues."

Of the variants listed by Cox, two (Shearin' and Combs: Syllabus of Kentucky Folk-Song, p. 19, and Campbell and Sharp, *English Folk-Song from the Southern Appalachians*, pp. 257–258, from North Carolina in 1916) are similar to Cox's ballad of John Hardy the murderer. Two (*J. A. F. L.*, xxii, [1909] 247, from North Carolina, and *Berea Quarterly*, xiv, 26 [1910], from Kentucky), are more related to the ballads of John Hardy the steel-driving man, though not belonging absolutely to either group. The other ten, except for one of Mr. Cox's variants previously published by him in *J. A. F. L.*, xxvi, (1913) 180, from West Virginia, belong to the John Henry group. They were found in East Tennessee, 1905; Mississippi, 1909; Kentucky, 1912, South Carolina, 1914 (listed by title "That's the Hammer Killed John Henry"), Kentucky and West Virginia, 1915. To the same group belong all the variants I have added to Cox's citations. The John Henry songs quoted by Lomax in *J. A. F. L.*, xxviii (1915) 14, are from the same region (Kentucky and West Virginia) as Cox's John Hardy ballads and present a story practically as full and consecutive as the John Hardy story, but agree with that story only in the circumstances that John Henry and John Hardy were both steel-drivers in West Virginia. Mr. Guy B. Johnson tells me

---

[1] No local title given.

that since the publication of *Negro Workaday Songs* (1926) he has found nine John Henry narrative songs among the Negroes; specifically Jacksonville, Fla., 1920, Chapel Hill, N. C. (2), 1926; Covington, Ga. (2), 1926; Bolton, S. C., 1927; Carthage, N. C., 1927; Franklin County, Va., 1927; and "Jackson Hollow," 1912.

The following facts seem to be fairly clear:

(1) John Hardy and John Henry were both steel-driving men, probably Negroes, in West Virginia.

(2) John Hardy was a gambler, roué, and murderer, and was executed for murder.

(3) John Henry had no vicious traits, and died as a result of trying to beat a steam drill.

(4) John Henry songs are more commonly sung and have spread farther from West Virginia.

From these facts I draw the tentative conclusions that the John Henry and John Hardy songs both arose in West Virginia; that they have somewhat coalesced in that state, but are distinctly different songs, and that John Henry is probably the older of the two. The partial coalescence of the two in Cox's versions seems to be due to the fact that apparently both men were steel-drivers from the same locality, and that the steel-driving exploits of John Henry were probably already known in song when another steel-driver of similar name came to be celebrated in song for murder.

Among the Negroes John Hardy does not seem to be known, but John Henry seems to have given rise to two types of song, closely related, but fairly distinct. Both are work songs, but the first is purely narrative, while the second is a hammer song, the most widely distributed of all the John Henry or John Hardy songs, and possibly the original of the John Henry story. Such short songs as

> Chattanooga, Chickamauga,
> Tobe Domingus,
> Kill a nigger
> I'm Alabama bound,   (V, no. 3)

and

> Railroad Bill did not know
> That Jim McMillan had a forty-fo',   (XII, no. 1)

both based on known facts, show how this might happen.

For the John Henry hammer songs, see VII, nos. 23 ff.

A

Reported from Auburn, Ala., 1915–1916, MS. of B. A. Wooten, as heard in Marengo County, Ala.

For variant passages on John Henry as a baby, cf. Cox, 1925, p. 184 (West Virginia), Odum, 1926, pp. 222, 223, 225, 234.

> When John Henry was a baby
> Sittin' on 'is mother's knee,
> He said, O the Colorado Mountains
> Will be the death of me.

B

Reported from Auburn, Ala., 1915–1916, MS. of W. M. Little, as heard in Franklin County, northeastern Georgia. "Sung in mines by Negroes."
With the lines dealing with Polly Ann, cf. Odum, 1926, pp. 226, 227, 228, 232.

> When John Henry wuz er baby,
> You could hold him in de palm of yer hand.
> All de neighbors said John Henry would neber be er man.
> His father took him on his knee and said:
> "John Henry you goin' to be er steel-drivin' man."
> When John Henry got to be er man
> He married little woman, her name wuz Polly Ann.
> John Henry he got sick and had to go home,
> Polly Ann drove steel like er steel-drivin' man.

C

Reported from Auburn, Ala., 1915–1916, MS. of J. C. Hay, as heard in Huntsville, Ala. "Sung by young Negro while cutting buds in a tree nursery."

> John Henry had a little woman,
> And her name was Polly Ann;
> John Henry took sick and had to go to bed,
> And Polly drove steel like a man.

2

A

REPORTED from Auburn, Ala., 1915–1916, MS. of L. E. Jenkins, as heard in Auburn, Ala. "Sung among rowstabouts on the levee at New Orleans."
This song smacks very strongly of the modern vaudeville stage.

> The other night down in the Lice Kill Club,
> Old Ephraim Ham Johnson Brown
> Got to arguing about being so smart
> As any other man in town.
> "Well, you so smart, Ephraim Brown,
> Lemme hear you spell this name for me;
> Out of all the words I ever heard
> That word certainly did puzzle about me,
> Trans-mass-if I began — bam-dam-urailty.
> I ain't as ignorant as I look to be."

ℬ

Reported in Auburn, Ala., 1915–1916, MS. of R. M. Beasly, with no note as to where heard. Same as *A*, except the penultimate line, which reads:

> Spell me Trans-mans-ef I began bam dam yer aller T.

3

REPORTED from Auburn, Ala., 1915–1916, MS. of J. C. Lisenby, as heard in Dothan, Ala. "Tune: 'I'm Alabama Bound.'"

Mr. Lisenby told me that Tobe Domingers was the name of a Dothan policeman who killed a Negro. With the last line, cf. XI, no. 14. For a similar brief treatment of tragic themes, cf. XII, nos. 1, 2, 3, 4.

> Chattanooga, Chickamauga,
> Tobe Domingus,
> Kill a nigger;
> I'm Alabama bound.

4

REPORTED from Auburn, Ala., 1915–1916, MS. of B. H. Haynes, as heard in Clay County, Ala.

Cf. Perrow, 1915, p. 136 (as from Mississippi in 1909), Scarborough, 1925, p. 176 (from Texas); Odum, 1925, p. 234. In Odum and Scarborough it occurs with other stanzas and the "You shall be free" refrain. In Perrow it is a part of a mélange starting with "Way down Yonder in de Cornfield," and also employs the "You shall be free" refrain, but with a spoken line, "Gittin' the chiddlings."

Cf. in this collection III, nos. 21, 22; VI, no. 13; XIII, nos. 13, 14.

The song is probably descended from the ante-bellum minstrels. In stanza 4 of "History of Old Varginia" (*Negro Singers' Own Book*, 1846[?], p. 29), the following lines suggest the present song:

> Den I cocked de gun, my finger on de trigger;
> Slam, bang, went de gun, down fall de nigger.

> Big black nigger settin' on a log,
> Finger on the trigger, eye on a hog;
> Bang went the gun! The hog yell hip,
> The Negro jumped on the hog with all his grip,
> Oh! eatin' those chitlugs,[1]
> Oh! eatin' those chitlugs.

---

[1] Chittlings, or chitterlings, a Negro delicacy mentioned in several popular songs, and in W. C. Handy's "The Chicago Gowge," Handy, 1926, p. 142.

5

SHORTNIN' BREAD [1]

A

REPORTED from Auburn, Ala., 1915–1916, MS. of H. I. Killingsworth, as heard in southwestern Georgia. "Sung by oil-mill Negroes."

I have the second stanza from Durham, N. C., 1919, MS. of Harvey Harward, as "supposedly from southern Tennessee; sung by Negro mammy." *

Cf. Perrow, 1915, p. 142, nine stanzas, with music, as from East Tennessee mountain whites in 1912, with a slightly different refrain. Perrow's stanza 4 is a variant of my stanza 1. Scarborough (1925, pp. 149–153) gives four variants from West Virginia, Mississippi, Louisiana, and North Carolina, the first two with music. The West Virginia and North Carolina versions both contain variants of stanza 2, and the West Virginia version contains a variant of stanza 1.

I suspect that the "Shortnin' Bread" song originated with the whites.

> Two little niggers lyin' in de bed;
> One was sick and tuther dead.
> Sent fur de docter and docter said
> Dey eat too much of dat shortnin' bread.

Chorus

> My babe loves shortnin' bread,
> My babe loves shortnin' bread.

> Put on de spider,
> Put on de lid,
> Ma's gwine cook some
> Shortnin' bread.

* Mr. Harward's MS. deserves further quotation, in that it involves an anecdote about a Virginia justice of the peace famous for his dealings with Negroes, especially those from North Carolina.

"A few years ago a Negress was tried before Judge Crutchfield in Richmond, Virginia, charged with being intoxicated. The Judge asked her what she did while intoxicated; she replied that she sung 'Shortening Bread.' He ordered her to sing it which she did:

"'Put on the skillet,' etc. (as in stanza 2 above).

"Whereupon the Judge sang:

> "'$5.00 for the skillet,
> $5.00 for the lid,
> $10.00 fine for the shortening bread.'"

---

[1] Local title.

B

Reported from Auburn, Ala., 1915–1916, MS. of E. A. Caldwell, as heard in Jackson County, Ala.

Lines 1 and 3 are as in Perrow, 1915, p. 142; stanza 3, as sung by East Tennessee mountain whites in 1912; and in Scarborough, 1925, p. 152, as from North Carolina.

> Two little niggers lay in the bed,
> Heels cracked open like shorten' bread;
> One turned over and the other said,
>
> . . . .

C

Reported from Durham, N. C., 1919, MS. of W. T. Huckabee, Jr. "Heard sung by Negroes working in the street, eastern part of North Carolina."

The first two lines are as in Perrow, 1915, p. 142, stanza 6, as sung by East Tennessee mountain whites in 1912.

> Two little niggers black as tar,
> Tryin' to get to heaven on a 'lectric car.
> De street car broke, down dey fell,
> 'Stead a goin' to heaven they went to hell.

6

REPORTED from Auburn, Ala., 1915–1916, MS. of W. S. Black.

The first two lines represent a synthesis of stanzas 7 and 8 in Perrow, 1915, p. 142, as sung by East Tennessee mountain whites in 1912. A variant of the whole stanza occurs in Perrow, 1913, p. 171, as stanza 2 of the "Dummy Train" song, from Alabama in 1908; and another variant in Talley, 1922, p. 173.

> Great big nigger black as night
> Tried to get to Heaben on tail of a kite.
> Kite tail broke and nigger fell;
> Believe to my soul he went straight to hell.

7

REPORTED from Auburn, Ala., 1915–1916, MS. of H. Carder.

From childhood I have known this song as a song of the whites, with "blind" for "gray" in line 4. In this form, the stanza occurs in Scarborough, 1925, p. 185, as from New Orleans. For more widely differing variants, cf. Perrow, 1913, p. 127 (as from Kentucky mountain whites in 1905); Talley, 1922, p. 6; Scarborough, 1925, p. 110 (in a stanza of "Ole Virginny Neber Tire," attributed to Thomas D. Rice, of Jim Crow fame); Ibid., p. 184 (as from South Carolina), p. 185 (as from Louisiana). The following slight variant of the first stanza occurs in "De Original Jim Crow," *Negro Singers' Own Book*, 1846(?), p. 329, also as "sung by the celebrated Tom Rice," but different from the lines in "Ole Virginny Neber Tire":

> I cum to a ribber, and could n't get across
> So I gib half a dolla for an old blind horse.
> So I wheel about, etc.

In Gumbo Chaff's *Ethiopian Glee Book*, 1848, p. 124, the lines are the same as in "Ole Virginny Neber Tire," cited above.

The song was even carried to Jamaica, one of the variants of stanza 1 below occurring in Walter Jekyll's *Jamaican Song and Story*, London, 1907, p. 227. Cf. in this collection, VI, no. 7.

> Come to the river
> And could n't get across;
> Paid five dollars
> For an old gray horse.
>
> Horse would n't pull
> So I swapped him for a bull;
> Bull would n't bellow
> So I swapped him for a dollar.
>
> Dollar would n't pass
> So I bought me some grass;
> Grass would n't grow
> So I swapped it for a hoe.
>
> Hoe would n't dig
> So I swapped him for a pig;
> Pig would n't root
> So I swapped him for a boot.

8

A

REPORTED from Auburn, Ala., 1915–1916, MS. of A. H. Williamson, as heard in Lowndes County, Ala.

The "I got Mine" song was a popular vaudeville song about twenty years ago, presumably not a Negro song at all. But the Negroes have taken it up extensively, as the number and range of the following variants show. For another variant rather closely related to *A*, see Odum, 1925, p. 232.

The "I got Mine" refrain has become attached to many other songs.

> I went down to a coon crap game
> An' dat wuz against my will.
> De coons won every cent I had
> But a greenback dollar bill,

Er hundred dollar bet was on de table
An' de nigger's p'int wuz nine;
He turned dem dice roun' two er three times
An' he got mine.

Just about dat time de light went out
An' de coons had a scuffly time.
I grabbed dat hundred dollar bill
An' I got mine.
A coon reached for his forty-four
But he did n't reach for it in time;
For I reached up on de mantelpiece,
An' I got mine.

Chorus

I got mine, boys! I got mine,
Gimme a piece of dat chicken, babe,
An' less have er time,
A coon reached for his forty-four
But he did n't reach for it in time,
For I reached up on de mantelpiece,
An' I got mine.

B

Reported from Auburn, Ala., 1915–1916, MS. of R. A. Chambers.

I went to a nigger crap game
Although it was against my will.
Them coons won all the money I had
'Cept a greenback dollar bill.
Dat nigger's p'int was nine,
About de time de cops stepped in;
Den I got mine.

Chorus

Oh yes, I got mine, babe,
Oh yes, I got mine,
A hundred dollar bill on de table lay,
Dat nigger's p'int was nine;
About de time de cops stepped in,
And I got mine.

C

Reported from Auburn, Ala., 1915–1916, MS. of L. Brown, as heard in Choctaw County, Ala. "Sung by Negro guitar picker."
  Lines 7 and 14 probably come from the song of the Reconstruction years:

> My name is Sam and I don't give a damn,
> I'd rather be a nigger than a poor white man,

IV, no. 26 in this collection, of which variants occur in Talley, 1922, p. 42, and in Odum, 1925, p. 217.

> I went to the crap game the other night,
> Which was against my will.
> I bet the last hundred that I had
> On the whip-po-will,
> Every since then I've been wearing good clothes,
> Living on chicken an' wine,
> I'd rather be a nigger than a poor white man —
> Since I got mine.

Chorus

> I got mine, boys, I got mine;
> I grabbed that hundred-dollar bill
> An' to the window I did climb.
> Every since then I've been wearing good clothes,
> Living on chicken an' wine;
> I'd rather be a nigger than a poor white man —
> Since I got mine.

D

Reported from Auburn, Ala., 1915–1916, MS. of F. L. Brittain, as heard in Campbell County, Georgia. "Sung by an old Negro cook (male)."

> I went to a Negro crap game
> Which wuz against my will.
> Jest as I stepped in de door
> Dem niggers stood mighty still.
> Jest about den a cop stepped in,
> But you can bet I got mine,
> Reached up and grabbed me a hundred-dollar bill
> Through de window I went flyin'.

Chorus

> I got mine, boys, I got mine,
> Reached up and grabbed that hundred-dollar bill
> Through de window I went flyin'.

Ever since then I been in de 'sylum
Feedin' on chicken and wine;
But my boy you sho' can bet
Dat I got mine.

$\mathcal{E}$

Reported from Auburn, Ala., 1915–1916, MS. of W. S. Black, as heard in northern Alabama. "Sung on a road working camp."

I went down to a big crap game, went against my will;
Lost all the money that I had, but a greenback dollar bill,
Bet upon the table was a hundred against ninety-nine,
Police opened the door,
I grabbed that hundred dollars,
And to the window I did climb.
Some of the boys got six months, some got ninety-nine.
I did n't get no months at all, but I got mine.
Boys, I got mine.

F

Reported from Durham, N. C., 1919, MS. of H. O. Waltz. "Heard in a Negro minstrel show."

I went down that chicken roost
Chicken was on my mind;
I was so ragged,
Could n't keep from crying.
Soon as the watchman turned his back,
I got mine.
Got that chicken by the leg,
Thru the window I went flying.
Ever since then I been wearing good clothes,
Living on chicken and wine.
I am a leader of society,
Since I got mine.

I went down to a negro "crap" game,
Money was on my mind.
One hundred dollar bill laying on the table,
And the negro's point was nine.
Just then the coppers stepped in the door,
And said, "Here, boys, you're mine."
I grabbed that hundred dollar bill,
And Lord I got mine.

Some got six months, and some got nine,
And one guy sang Sweet Caroline;
And judge said, "Here — hundred dollar fine."
But the ball and chain went round my leg,
Since I got mine.

9

REPORTED from Durham, N. C., 1919, MS. of W. B. Jeffrey, as "heard sung in Selma, N. C."
Evidently of vaudeville or professional minstrel origin.

'T was in a hencoop one dark stormy night
I stopped to rest my weary self.
And to my great surprise
I spied some pullets sitting up on the shelf.
I started to shake hands with one nice old pullet,
When some buck shots passed my head.
I dropped my bag and I turned around
And to that gentleman said:
"Oh, mister, oh, mister, won't you listen like a friend?
Well there ain't no use to argue, just let this matter end.
Excuse me, Sir, for the wrong I've done.
O well there ain't no use to shoot that gun.
Just move one inch so I can run.
Thank you, that's a plenty."

10

REPORTED from Durham, N. C., 1919, MS. of French W. Graham, as heard in Grayson County, Va., 1908.
With lines 5 and 6, cf. X, no. 55.

Went to de chicken coop — chicken coop wuz locked;
'Nuf to make a nigger's mouth go flippety flop.
Retch my hand right thru de crack,
Kotch that chicken right by de back.
Took my gal to de milk-shake stand
She got struck on de milk-shake man.
Out with my razer and I cut 'im in de back,
Says "See here, nigger, don't none of your slack."

I I

REPORTED from Auburn, Ala., 1915–1916, MS. of W. E. Lasater.

Ole Mister beat me to the henhouse,
I caught them hens a-flying;
Ole Mister thought I had them all,
But I got mine.

Ever since I been wearing them good clothes,
1 been living on chicken and wine;
I am a gentleman of this society,
But I got mine.

Ole Mister beat me to the garden,
I caught them greens a-flying;
But he thought I had them all,
But I got mine.

I2

WAKE NICODEMUS [1]

REPORTED from Auburn, Ala., 1915–1916, MS. of R. Chambers, as heard in Giles County, Tenn. "Used by Senator Bob Taylor in his speeches and was probably printed after his death."
    I am indebted to Professor Kittredge for recognizing this song as "Wake Nicodemus," the words and music by Henry C. Work. See note to IV, no. 7. The original song consists of four eight-line stanzas and chorus. The present version is composed of stanza 1 and the chorus of the original, with lines 2 and 4 as 4 and 2 and with "good time" and "Uncle Lijah" in the original changed to "hard times" and "Uncle Lizah."

Nickodemus de slave was of African birth,
He libed long ergo very old,
He was reckoned as part ob de salts ob de earth,
He was sold for a bag full ob gold.

Oh! This last sad request as we laid him to rest
On de trunk ob an old hollow tree:
Wake me up in de morn at de break ob de day,
Wake me up for de grand jubilee.

[1] No local title given.

Oh! dere's hard times comin' and dey ain't far off,
Dere's hard times comin' on de way.
Oh, tell Uncle 'Lizah for to tell Uncle Pomp
For to meet me by de gum tree down in de swamp
And wake Uncle Nickodemus up today.

13

Reported from Auburn, Ala., 1915–1916, anonymously.

In the main this song is simply another of the numerous parodies of Mary's Lamb, that have been sung in minstrel shows and on vaudeville stages for years. The last line, however, is almost certainly a Negro touch. References to balling the jack (a Negro dance-step) are common in Negro songs of various types.

Mary had a little lamb,
His fleece was black as jet;
I went to school with Mary one day,
And have n't quit scratching yet.

Mary had a little lamb,
She tied him to de track,
Every time de train whistled
De lamb would ball de jack.

14

Reported from Auburn, Ala., 1915–1916, anonymously.

The first stanza of this song is the refrain of a well-known vaudeville song of twenty years ago. The second stanza may be a Negro addition. A bit of the refrain has been attracted into the song of the "Traveling Coon" (XI, no. 55, and Odum,1926, p. 59). Cf. also IV, no. 50.

I am indebted to Professor Kittredge for noticing that lines 6 and 7 are from the English traditional song of "The Derby Ram," a Mississippi version of which occurs in Arthur Palmer Hudson's *Ballads and Songs from Mississippi*, J. A. F. L., xxxix (1926), 173. Palmer's bibliography lists a number of English, Scotch, and American versions, the earliest reference being Kinloch's *The Ballad Book*, 1827, pp. 80–81.

He rambled, he rambled,
He rambled all around,
In and out of town,
Well he rambled, he rambled,
He rambled till de butcher cut 'im down.

De rambler had two horns,
Dey reached up to de moon,
He went up in September
And did n't get back till June.
Well, he rambled, etc.

15

REPORTED from Auburn, Ala., 1915–1916, MS. of D. L. Madeira, as heard in Alabama.

This, like some songs in practically every collection of Negro songs, is a mélange, consisting of five unrelated songs, connected by a popular refrain which did not belong originally to any of them. For the refrain as used in other songs in this collection, see VI, no. 34, III, nos. 8 ff.; in other collections, cf. Perrow, 1915, p. 135 (as from Mississippi in 1909) where it connects seven or eight entirely separate songs; Odum, 1925, p. 233, where it connects seven separate songs; Scarborough, 1925, p. 163 (as from Virginia), where it connects three; Ibid., p. 176 (as from Texas), where it connects three; Ibid., p. 194 (as from Texas), where it connects three; and Ibid., p. 197 (as from Alabama), where it connects two separate songs.

The first stanza is a variant of the well-known "Dummy Train" song. Cf. Scarborough, 1925, p. 245 (from North Carolina, with music); also Tiersot, 1911(?), p. 212.

With the second stanza, cf. VI, no. 34, in this collection; also Odum, 1925, p. 234 and Scarborough, 1925, p. 235 (as from Alabama) both with the "You shall be Free" refrain.

With the fifth stanza cf. VI, no. 13 and XIII, no. 17.

Some folks say dat de dummy won' run,
But jest let me tell you what de dummy done done:
Left New Yo'k at de risin' ub de sun
Run into Birmingham at ha'f past one.
Runnin' dummy some,
You shall be free,
G'wan dummy,
You shall be free,
When de good Lawd sets you free.

Nigger and a rooster had a fight,
Rooster kicked de nigger plumb out er sight;
Nigger gits up, says, "Dat's all right,
Meet yo' in de hen-house termorrow night,
With a crocus sack."
You shall be free,
Dead rooster,
You shall be free,
When de good Lawd sets you free.

Hawse and a flea and a couple o' mice,
Sittin' in er corner shootin' dice;
Hawse slipped up an' fell on de flea.
Flea says, "Dat 's a hawse on me."

Chorus

Way down yonder in de ole corn fiel',
Black snake bit me on de heel;
Ah backed right back fo' ter do mah best,
An' backed right back into a hornet's nest.
Runnin' nigger,
You shall be free,
G'wan nigger,
You shall be free,
When de good Lawd sets you free.

Nigger an' er white man playin' seven-up,
Nigger won de money, scared to pick it up,
Nigger drew back and de white man fell,
Nigger grab de money, an' run like hell.
G'wan nigger,
You shall be free,
When de good Lawd sets you free.

For the sake of any reader who might wish to see how Negro dialect looks in French, I quote Tiersot's version, with his translation (Tiersot, 1911[?], pp. 212–213):

Some folks say that a dummy can't run,
But I done tell you what a dummy done done.
It left at-a Memphis at-a half-past ten
Arrived in Natchez at de settin' of de sun!
       Wan't she movin', chil'?
       Well I reckon so!
       Git up de good Lawd home.

Il y a des gens qui disent qu'un "mannequin" ne peut pas courir,
Mais moi, je vous dis ce qu'un "mannequin" a fait, a fait:
Il a quitté Memphis, à dix heures et demie,
Est arrivé à Natchez au coucher du soleil!
       Est-qu'il ne courait pas, enfant?
       Certes, je l'affirmais!
       Amenez le bon Seigneur à la maison.

16

REPORTED from Auburn, Ala., 1915–1916, MS. of W. S. Black.

This song is a combination of the "Dummy Train" song and the various songs beginning "Standin' on the corner not meaning no harm." Cf. in this collection, VII, no. 78, XII, nos. 10, 45, and the notes.

> Got on the dummy, did n't mean no harm,
> Police grabbed me by my arm;
> Asked me for my fare, then led me to the door;
> I ain't been on the dummy no more.

17

A

REPORTED from Auburn, Ala., 1915–1916, MS. of J. W. Persons, as heard in Montgomery, Ala. "Must have at least seventy-five verses."

This song is evidently modern and probably originated on the vaudeville stage. Is the hero a descendant of the "Willum de weaber" described in *Dixie* as a "gay deceiber"?

Cf. Sigmund Spaeth: *Read 'Em and Weep*, 1927, p. 116.

> Willie the weeper was a chimney sweeper,
> He had the dope habit and he had it bad.
> Listen while I tell you about a dream he had:
> The Queen of Sheba was the first he met.
> She called him darling and loving pet.
> She bought him a great big automobile,
> It had a diamond headlight and a silver wheel.
> He went to Monte Carlo and he never made a bet,
> But he won a million dollars playing roulette.
> He had a million dollars in nickels and dimes;
> He knew he had 'em because he counted 'em over a million times.
> The war in Cuba had just begun;
> He had a million cannons and a gatling gun,
> He had a million vessels on de ocean so deep,
> He had a million cattle and he had a million sheep.

B

Reported from Auburn, Ala., 1915–1916, MS. of R. E. Davis, as heard in Georgia.

Consists of lines 10, 11, 14, 15 of *A*, with slight verbal variations.

18

REPORTED from Auburn, Ala., 1915–1916, MS. of A. H. Williamson, as heard in Lowndes County, Ala.
Probably of modern minstrel origin. One of the commonest types of vaudeville jokes about the Negro, probably of white origin, is the joke in which the frightened Negro outruns various fleet animals and comments on or to them as he passes, generally telling them to "get out de way an' let a man run what can *run*." A more recent version of the joke makes the Negro pass a running race horse and register the spot as marked by the statue of a horse.

The refrain, " 'T aint no disgrace to run when you git skeered," occurs independently and in other songs.

A haunted mansion stood
Down in a Southern town.
Sam Johnson was the bravest coon
'T was known for miles around.
A hundred bills to anyone
Who'd in that mansion stay.
Sam says, "Dat's ezy money,
Dat reward dey'll have to pay."
So to that mansion Johnson went
To make himself at home.
When midnight came a spooky said,
"Now Sam, we're all alone."
"Don't make dat WE so strong," says Sam
While reaching for the shelf;
"Jus' let me get my clothes on, dear,
An' you'll be by yo'se'f,
Cause 't ain' no disgrace to run
When you git skeered."
The ghost said, "I've run till I am sore."
"Dat's nothin'," said Sam, "Yo' goin' ter run some more,
Cause 't ain' no disgrace to run
When yo' git skeered."

Sam's lady love he loved so dear
Lived down a country lane.
Sam says, "I'll go ter her dis night
An' to her I'll explain."
But just before he reached the door,
A form he saw in white,
Sam turned around, ran down the lane,
And soon was out of sight.

The noise he made while running fast
Scared up a big wild deer;
That deer and Sam ran nose and nose,
Both running full of fear.
Sam beat that deer ten feet or more
And yelled back full of glee,
"Yo' better take dat rockin' chair off'n yo' head
An' try to keep up wid me.
'Cause t'ain no disgrace to run
When you git skeered."

19

THE VOODOO MAN [1]

REPORTED from Durham, N. C., 1919, MS. of James E. Lyon, Jr., as "heard from uncle in High Point, North Carolina."
I have the same song, with only two or three minor verbal variations, from Auburn, Ala., 1915–1916, MS. of L. T. Smith.
It is apparently of comparatively recent vaudeville origin.

I've been hoodooed,
I've been hoodooed, hoodooed,
Hoodooed by a nigger voodoo;
I've been hoodooed, hoodooed,
Hoodooed by a big black coon.

Oh! coon for me had a great infatuation;
He wanted me to marry but he had no situation.
As soon as I refused,
That coon he got wild.
Says he, "I'm bound for to hoodoo this child."
He went out and got a rabbit's foot
And burned it with a frog
Down in the hollow of an old burnt log,
Right by the road where I had to pass along.
Ever since that time my head's been wrong;
My bones began to ache
And my teeth began to chatter,
Went to the Doctor and he could n't tell the matter.
Says he, "You are a gone coon, gone up the spout."
He looked at my head and my hair fell out,
Nobody knows how funny I feel —
Even the husk fell off my heel.

[1] Local title.

Chorus

I've been hoodooed,
I've been hoodooed, hoodooed,
Hoodooed by a nigger voodoo;
I've been hoodooed, hoodooed,
Hoodooed by a big black coon.

That same black coon had an awful disposition,
He could do more tricks than Hermann the magician.
My Daddy went out for to kill this black moke;
That coon only laughed for he thought it was a joke,
He had all the other coons afraid to look him in the eye,
He had a lot of niggers that he taught to fly.
All the police for this coon had to search;
He robbed a nigger right at church;
He would grab up a chicken and it would n't even holler,
He would throw down his gopher and most everything would follow.
It may seem strange but it ain't no lie,
I hope in my heart that coon will die,
For I can't sleep, walk, talk, nor eat,
Guess I'm dead, my heart don't beat.

Chorus

20

BLUE [1]

REPORTED from Auburn, Ala., 1915–1916, MS. of S. A. Allen, "Sung by Negro construction gang."

    Cf. VI, nos. 15, 16, 17, 18, the last of which seems to be an off-shoot of this song. Perrow, 1913, p. 128, prints a variant as from Mississippi in 1909. The first two lines of stanza 3 are a variant of a couplet common both in contemporary Negro songs and in the minstrel songs of the eighteen-forties. Cf. IV, no. 1 in this collection, and Perrow, 1915, p. 138; Scarborough, 1925, pp. 106, 165, 179, 194, 223, 224, 225; Odum, 1926, pp. 173, 176; also *Ethiopian Glee Book*, 1850, p. 218; *Negro Singers' Own Book*, 1846(?), pp. 112, 359, 408.

    Line 4 of stanza 4 is a variant of a line in the spiritual "Sis Mary wore three links of chain" (II, no. 3 A), and lines 2 and 3 of the same stanza occur in both spirituals and secular songs. Cf. Kennedy, 1925, p. 70 (in a spiritual from Louisiana); Odum, 1926, p. 129 (in a work song) and p. 198 (in a "workaday religious song"). The lines belong originally to the traditional folk-songs of the whites; cf. *J. A. F. L.*, xi, 22, and xxiii, 438.

    This song has too much form and unity to be quite convincing as of Negro popular origin, in its present form.

---

[1] Local title.

My old blue dog
'll make a 'possum walk a log,
Make a 'possum clim' a tree,
Then set down and bark for me.
G'on! Blue, you rascal you,
Ketch another 'possum for me and you.

He'll make a 'possum walk a lim',
Then set down and laugh at him;
I'd get the 'possum and carry him home,
Blue'd get nothing but the bones.
G'on! Blue, you rascal you,
Ketch another 'possum for me and you.

My old blue dog is dead and gone,
Left this nigger here to moan;
I went to the barn one sunny day,
There my good old blue dog lay.
Blue! Blue! Blue! Blue! You rascal you,
I wish it was me instead of you.

I buried him in a beautiful shade,
Dug his grave with a silver spade;
Let him down on a golden chain;
At every link I'd call his name:
Blue! Blue! Blue! Blue! You rascal you,
I wish it was me instead of you.

Going to Heaven some Sunday morn,
Going to tell you what I'll do:
Get St. Peter's golden horn,
Then go out and blow for Blue;
Blue! Blue! Blue! Blue! You rascal you,
Ketch another 'possum for me and you.

21

REPORTED from Auburn, Ala., 1915–1916, MS. of R. R. Beard, as heard in northern Mississippi. "Sung by very old Negro."
    Although I can cite no previous publication of this song, I feel sure that it is to be found in the old minstrel books in pretty much its present form. The opening lines are like those of numerous old minstrel songs, the reference to Old Jim Crow and to playing on the bones and tambourine, and to dancing on the green are all commonplace enough in the old minstrel songs and unknown in Negro

songs of modern composition. The general tenor of ninety per cent of the old minstrel songs is fully as Caucasian as is that of the present song, and many of them set forth the gaiety of Negro life on the plantation very much as this song does.

Oh, 'way down in South Carolina,
Where the cotton and the sugar cane grow,
It is funny 'mong the honey
For to see the niggers laugh and crow.
We'll git up early in de mornin',
For to work we singin' all do go,
Always singin', voices ringin',
I tell you we're not slow.

Chorus

Oh! We do have our fun,
On a holiday we feel so gay,
An' dis is what we do:
An' den we play upon de banjo,
De bones an' de tambourine,
In de mornin' or in de evenin'
While dancin' on de green.

Ebery month we have a party,
Where de niggers an' dear ladies go;
Aunt Jemima from Car'lina
Comes along wid de funny Old Jim Crow;
Dar's old Josephus Orange Blossom
Wid his sweet gal, Ann Liza Jane,
Sister Mary, so contrary,
Had dancin' on de brain.

22

REPORTED from Auburn, Ala., 1915–1916, MS. of L. N. Rivais.
   Apparently descended from the popular song, "The Cat Came Back," current in the eighteen-nineties.

Ole Mr. Johnson had a trouble of his own,
He had a yellow cat that would n't leave home,
He tried and tried and tried his best,
And give er to a man who was travelling west.

De train came aroun' er curve and struck a broken rail,
Nobody left fer to tell de tale,
But de cat came back de very next day,
Fer he was a rounder and could n't stay away.

He gave a little boy a dollar fer to set de cat afloat,
And he carried him up de river in a little ole boat,
He tied a rock aroun' his neck weighed 'bout a hundred pounds,
Such a fishin' roun' 't was, fer the little boy was drowned.
But de cat came back de very, very next day,
For he was a rounder and could n't stay away.

23

REPORTED from Auburn, Ala., 1915–1916, MS. of A. M. Kearly.
This is an incomplete and somewhat corrupted version of a minstrel song that was popular between 1900 and 1910 and was among the first songs of which phonograph records were made.

The preacher went out hunting on one Sunday morning,
And it was against his religion but he carried his gun along;
He killed a couple of quails and one little hare,
And upon his way returning home he meets a grizzly bear.
The preacher raced up a persimmon tree,
And the bear behind him, the limb broke and they come tumbling
    down,
The bear grabbed him and squoze a little too tight,
He cast his eyes on the Lord and said, "Good Lord,
If you won't help me, put a muzzle on the grizzly bear."

24

REPORTED from Auburn, Ala., 1915–1916, MS. of R. M. Beasly.
Whether or not this is a vaudeville song, as I suspect, it employs an opening formula common in the folk-songs of both whites and Negroes. For many other songs in this collection beginning, "I went," "As I went" (or "was going"), "I'm going," see Index. The formulas are equally common in the old minstrel books.

I went to the smoke house to get a little toast,
A dad blamed rat jumped down my throat;
My brother got skeered and run and lef' his hat,
Brought back a piece of cheese and a big Tom cat;
Put the cheese on my lip and the cat on my chest,
When the rat came up I was doing my best.

The cat came to get a little bite,
The dad-blamed rat jumped outer sight,
Cat slipped and the rat made a fall,
Swallowed the rat, cat, cheese and all.

25

REPORTED from Auburn, Ala., 1915–1916, MS. of R. M. Beasly. "Sung at night or before the dinner hour."

I have stanza 1 from Auburn, Ala., 1915–1916, MS. of L. E. Jenkins, as sung "by an old Negro barber" in Birmingham.

Cf. "I got mine," no. 8 A in this chapter, for another song about a crap game.

There's a coon right down in the furniture room
Layin' flat on Lazy Street;
Times had got hard with him,
He could n't get a bite to eat.

He marched right into a big crap game,
Not a penny to his name;
He bet a thousand dollars he will win,
And a swell coon backs the game.

He bet ten thousand dollars more
Just at the crack of day;
He bid farewell to the hard luck coons,
Says, "I'm not po' no more."

26

REPORTED from Auburn, Ala., 1915–1916, MS. of R. M. Beasly. "Sung by Negroes at dinner or night time."

The first two lines are a variant of two lines from the "Creation Song" as found in Cox, 1925 (as from West Virginia, in 1915), p. 502, and in *Negro Singers' Own Book*, 1846(?), p. 73; Gumbo Chaff's *Ethiopian Glee Book*, 1848, p. 126; Christy's *Nigga Songster*, n. d., p. 132; White's *New Book of Plantation Melodies*, n. d., p. 23. These Creation songs, under various titles, generally start with "I'm right from ole Virginny with a head full of knowledge" (cf. III, nos. 24 F and 25, which are from the same song), and include a burlesque account of the Creation, flood, various Biblical characters, and such well-known, non-scriptural heroes as Julecum Caesar and Jack the Giant Killer. Probably the whole of the present stanza is a variant of one of the older stanzas which I have not seen.

Lines 3 and 4 seem to be related to Perrow's variant of the same stanza (1913, p. 159, as from Mississippi in 1909). Cf. also "Dese Bones Gwine Rise Again," II, no. 24, which seems to be related to the old "Creation Song"; also XIII, no. 14, which is another off-shoot of the same song.

In his note on the "Creation Song," Cox (p. 501) lists twenty-three different publications of the song, in eight distinct versions, between 1847 and 1861; and cites also Perrow, 1913, pp. 159–160, and F. C. Brown, *Ballad Literature in North Carolina*, 1914, p. 13. Most of the versions include the "Walk in de parlor" refrain.

To Cox's references, add *Ethiopian Serenaders*, 1847(?), p. 66, and Scarborough, 1925, p. 181.

Ole Eve was the first 'oman, Adams was the man,
Put 'em in the garden of the Promised Lan';
Ole Eve tol' Adam to go up the tree,
"Throw down a apple, one for you, one for me,"
Eve bit the apple, Adam broke the limb,
That broke up the tree of sins.

27

MY GAL [1]

REPORTED from Auburn, Ala., 1915–1916, MS. of J. G. Nall. "Heard at Negro minstrel."

This was originally a white man's song. Professor Kittredge informs me that under the title of "The Fifty Cents" it was a general favorite in the late eighteen-seventies and early eighteen-eighties, and adds the following bibliography: *Wehman Brothers' Good Old-Time Songs, No. 1*, p. 31; *Partridge's National Songster*, p. 31; Wehman broadside, No. 422; *Barlow Wilson's Waltz Me Again Songster*, p. 48; *Singer's Journal*, II, 488 (with music); *Delaney's Song Book, No. 8*, p. 24; *Hi Henry's Superb Operatic Minstrel Songster*, p. 4.

For an old song not directly related to the following, but dealing with the extravagant appetite displayed in a restaurant by the singer's "gal," see "Now Hold your Horses, Will You," p. 8, in *George Christy and Wood's Melodies* (*New Song Book*), n. d.

I took my gal to a fancy ball,
It was a social hop;
We stayed until the lights were out, and then the music, it did stop.
In a restaurant we went, the finest on the street.
She said she was n't hungry,
But this is what she eat:

A dozen raw, a plate of slaw,
A chicken, and a roast,
Apple sass, with asparagrass,
Sof' shell crabs on toast.
Next she tried was oysters fried,
Her appetite was immense.
When she called for pie, I thought I'd die,
For I had but fifty cents.

[1] Local title.

She took it in so crazy, she had an awful tank,
She said she was n't thirsty,
But this is what she drank:
A whiskey shinn, a glass of gin,
A schooner or two of beer,
A ginger pop with rum on top,
That made me quake with fear.
Said she would bring her family around some day
And we would have some fun.
I handed the man the fifty cents and
This here is what he done:

He broke my nose, tore my clothes,
He hit me in the jaw,
He give me a surprise with a pair of black eyes,
With me he scrubbed the floor,
He took me by my clothes unloose,
Threw me over the fence.
Take my advice, don't try it twice,
When you got but fifty cents.

28

REPORTED from Durham, N. C., 1919, MS. of David T. House, Jr.
This song is apparently the same as the jig song, "Little Brown Jug," which
has been printed and is properly a song of the country and mountain whites.
Cf. VI, no. 14.

> Me and my girl and the bob-tail dog,
> Started across the creek on a rotten log;
> The log broke and we fell in
> And there's where I lost my gin.

29

FRANKIE AND ALBERT

"FRANKIE AND ALBERT" is well known, under various titles. In 1917 I heard
a version from Florida, with the refrain "He was my man, but he done me
wrong," but was unable to write it down at the time. Since that time I have
heard several stanzas like those that Mr. Harrison says below (very conserva-
tively) "cannot be written."
Perrow, 1915, p. 178, prints a version of four stanzas as from Mississippi
country whites in 1909. Odum, 1925, p. 228, prints a long version of twenty-one

stanzas, apparently much corrupted, under the title of "Lilly." Cox, 1925, pp. 218–220, prints two versions of seven and nine stanzas, from West Virginia in 1918 and 1916, under the title of "Maggie Was a Lady," and notes twelve other versions in print and MSS, 1911–1923. Scarborough, 1925, pp. 80–84, gives six variants (one with music), all from Texas, and lists one from North Carolina.

According to Sigmund Spaeth (*Read 'Em and Weep*, New York, 1927, p. 34) the song originated in St. Louis between 1850 and 1860.

A

Reported from Durham, N. C., 1919, MS. of Blake B. Harrison. "Other stanzas cannot be written."

For variants of stanza 1, without refrain, see Cox, 1925, p. 219; Odum, 1925, p. 228; Scarborough, 1925, pp. 80, 82, 83. For variants of stanzas 2 and 3, cf. Cox, 1925, pp. 218, 219; Odum, 1925, p. 228; Scarborough, 1925, p. 81. For a possible variant, cf. X, no. 36.

Amy was a good woman, everybody knows.
She spent ten thousand dollars to buy her Albert's clothes.

Refrain

He was her man, but he done her wrong.

Amy went to de bar-room, to git a bottle ob beer.
Amy said to de bartender, "You seen my Albert here?"

Bartender said to Amy, "I ain't gwine tell you no lie,
I seen your Albert down here wid a woman what had blue eyes."

B

Reported from Auburn, Ala., 1915–1916, MS. of H. C. Kilpatrick. Tune: "Nigger Blues." "Negro song heard from various Negroes."

For variants of the first four lines, see Cox, 1925, pp. 218, 219; Scarborough, 1925, p. 81.

Susie went down to de bar room,
Called for a bottle of beer;
Walks up and says to de bar-man:
"Hab my luvin' man been here?
Oh, won't you tell me, please,
Fo' he's de one I love."

C

DELIE [1]

Reported from Durham, N. C., 1924, MS. of M. L. Hamlin, "from memory of a song taught Frank Goodell of Spartanburg, S. C., Amherst, '08, by an old Negro to whom he paid $1.00 to teach him to play the guitar. Learned probably between 1900 and 1904."

The third stanza with slight variations occurs in "Frankie," Perrow, 1915, p. 178; "Maggie Was a Lady," Cox, 1925, p. 220; "Lilly," Odum, 1925, p. 230; "Frankie and Albert," Scarborough, 1925 (as from Texas), pp. 81–82. The first two stanzas are somewhat related to two stanzas in Scarborough, p. 82.

Note that in the "Delie" songs, which are obviously closely connected with "Frankie and Albert," if not originally the same song, the situation is reversed and the woman is shot by the man, instead of *vice versa*.

> Delie, Delie, was a-goin' her last round,
> When ole coon came by
> An' shot her to the groun'.
> All I done had done gone.

> Delie, Delie, why did n't yo' run,
> When yo' seen dat coon a-comin'
> Wid his forty-fo' caliber gun?
> All I done had done gone.

> Rubber-tired cayage, rubber-tired hack
> Done took poor Delie to de bone yard,
> Ain't never brought her back.
> All I done had done gone.

> Men in Atalanta tryin' to pass fo' white,
> Delie's in de bone yard
> Six foot out o' sight.
> All I done had done gone.

> Men in Atalanta drinkin' out a silver cup,
> Delie's in de bone yard,
> Ain't never goin' to get up.
> All I done had done gone.

[1] Local title.

D

Reported from Auburn, Ala., 1915–1916, MS. of E. L. Harper, as heard in Pickens County, Ala. "Sung by Negro to guitar."

This song is hardly complete enough to connect it definitely with "Delie" (that is, "Frankie and Albert"), but the connection seems likely.

> Delia! Delia! raise up your head,
> Try and take your medicine just like the doctor said.
> Poor gal, she gone! Poor gal, she gone!

E

Reported from Durham, N. C., 1919, MS. of J. W. Ellis, "Heard sung by old farm Negroes at one of their dancing and singing meetings."

Some similarity to stanzas 14 and 15 of "Lilly" (Odum, 1925, p. 229) makes it seem likely that this song belongs to the "Frankie and Albert" ballads.

> Benny was arrested upon one Sunday afternoon,
> He was sentenced to be hanged for the crime that he done.
> He climbed upon the scaffold just as brave as brave could be,
> Crying, Lord have mercy on my soul,
> For 't was murder in the first degree.

30

THEOLOGY IN THE QUESTION [1]

REPORTED from Durham, N. C., 1919, MS. of Charlie C. Jordan. "I used to hear this from an old Negro woman who used to be a slave . . . but I do not remember the tune."

Except for the bracketed line that I have inserted from the printed version in stanza 6, this is word for word the same as "Theology in the Quarters," pp. 93–94, in *Uncle Gabe Tucker, or Reflection, Song, and Sentiment in the Quarters*, by J. A. Macon, Philadelphia, 1883. "Theology in the Quarters," however, is in continuous couplets, without stanza divisions, and hence contains just half as many lines as the form here printed.

Odum, 1926, p. 185, prints about a third of the lines, without stanza form and in slightly different sequence.

> Now I'se got a notion in my head
>   Dat when you come to die,
> And stand de 'xamination
>   In de Cote House in de sky,

[1] Local title.

You'll be 'stonished at de questions
  Dat angels gwine to ask us,
When dey gits you on de witness stan'
  And pin you to de facts;

Cause He'll ask you mighty closely
  'Bout your doin's in de night,
And de watermillion questions
  Gwine to bodder you a sight.

Den your eyes'll open wider
  Dan dey eber done before;
When he chats you about a chicken scrape
  Dat happened long ago.

De angels on de picket line
  Erlong de Milky Way,
Keeps a watchin' what you're dribin' at,
  And hearin' what you say.

No matter what you want to do,
  [No matter whar you gwine,] (*printed version*)
Dey's mighty apt to find it out
  And pass it long de line.

And often at de meetin'
  When you make a fuss and laugh,
Why dey send de news a kitin'
  By de golden telegraph.

Den de angels in de orfis
  What's a settin' by de gate,
Jes' reads de message wid a look,
  And claps it on de slate.

Den you better do your duty well
  And keep your conscience clear
And keep a lookin' straight ahead
  And watchin' where you steer.

'Cause arter while de time'll come
  To journey from de land.
And dey'll take you up in de air
  And put you on de stand.

Den you'll hab to listen to de clerk
And answer mighty straight,
If you ebber 'spect to trabble
Froo dem alaplaster gates.

31

MR. FROG WENT A COURTIN' HE DID RIDE [1]

REPORTED from Durham, N. C., 1919, MS. of Thomas Litaker, as heard in Cabarrus County, N. C. "This song is in print; I used to sing it in High School."

The North Carolina Folk-Lore Society has a record of the music from another singer. I recollect the tune myself, from childhood. It is not originally a Negro song at all.

Cf. Talley, 1922, p. 190 (as from Tennessee); Scarborough, 1925, pp. 46–50, three versions from Texas and one from Kentucky, with music. Miss Scarborough locates its probable origin in "A Most Strange Wedding of the Frogge and the Mouse" (1580), and cites Professor Kittredge's comment on its antiquity in *J. A. F. L.*, xxxv, 394.

Mr. Frog went a courtin' he did ride,
      Ahum, Ahum.
Mr. Frog went a courtin' he did ride.
Took a pistol by his side,
      Ahum, ahum.

He rode up to Miss Mice's door,
      Ahum, ahum.
He rode up to Miss Mice's door;
Said, Miss Mice, won't you marry me?
      Ahum, ahum.

Where shall the wedding supper be?
      Ahum, ahum.
Where shall the wedding supper be?
Way down yonder in an old holler tree,
      Ahum, ahum.

What shall the wedding supper be?
      Ahum, ahum.
O what shall the wedding supper be?
Sweet potato and a roasted flea,
      Ahum, ahum.

[1] Local title.

32

POMP'S SOLILOQUY [1]

REPORTED from Durham, N. C., 1919, MS. of John Holton.

This song, evidently the work of some writer of dialect poems or songs, has one curious literary connection. In 1897 Daniel Webster Davis, one of the best of the Negro poets contemporary with Dunbar, published in Cleveland his second volume, *Weh Down Souf*, consisting mainly of dialect poems, one of which was "Pomp's Case Argued." It is a poem of twenty lines, based upon the same situation as "Pomp's Soliloquy." The speaker, one of Pomp's church brothers, states the case and concludes:

> "But I moves for to 'sclude him, cause he never had to ought,
> Ef he stole dem breeches, go an' git hisself caught."

The most obvious connections between "Pomp's Soliloquy" and "Pomp's Case Argued" are seen in the first two lines of stanzas 1 and 4 of the latter:

> Pomp stole dem breeches, an' 'lowed 't won't sin,
> 'Cause he stole de breeches to be baptized in;
> But I doubts dat, brudders! le's argify de case,
> For we can't hab de young lams a-fallin' frum grace.

> True, his moughter bin busted, an' de seat to'ed out —
> Fur 'tiz kinder strainin', dis leadin' ub de shout;
> But, den, he could er patched 'um, an' wid coat tails long
> Hab cut a lubly figger 'doubt doin' enny 'rong.

The whole of "Pomp's Case Argued" may be found in N. I. White and W. C. Jackson, *An Anthology of Verse by American Negroes*, 1924, p. 102.

I suspect that "Pomp's Soliloquy" is one of those dialect "recitation pieces" so popular in the eighteen-nineties, and that Davis, whose other work is saturated with the spirit of these pieces, simply gave an old case a new interpretation.

> I stole dem breeches,
> I 'noledged de corn;
> It were n't no crime,
> Sho' as you're born.

> If de motive am right,
> Den where's de sin,
> If I stole dem breeches
> To be baptized in?

> My only'st par
> Had clean worn out,
> Dey gib de ghost,
> When I gin to shout.

[1] Local title.

But 'ligion is mighty
And must prevail,
If it land dis nigger
In de county jail.

Yes de chain gang's got me
And de coal mines too,
But what's a 'fenseless colored man to do,
When de judge and de jury all 'lowed it was a sin
To steal dem breeches to be baptized in?

Tell de folks all howdy and goodbye, too,
I'll meet dem in heben,
When my work am fru.

When de Lord am judged,
I know he's gwine to say,
Pomp's straight as a shingle,
And far as de day.

He'll shout to de world,
That it t'aint no sin,
To steal dem breeches
To be baptized in.

33

ENGINEER RIGG [1]

REPORTED from Durham, N. C., 1919, MS. of D. T. Miller. "This old song was made up directly after the Negro excursion completely packed with Negroes from Greenville, N. C., and bound for Norfolk, Va., happened with the misfortune as to run into the Western Branch on account of the bridge keeper did not know of the excursion's schedule. There are many more verses but this is the only amount available at this time."

Except for the first two lines, which are found in "Casey Jones" and "Joseph Mica" (see Scarborough, 1925, pp. 249–250), this song seems to be independent of other railroad ballads. Perhaps the following stanza is connected with this episode. I have had it since 1924 from several sources in Durham and Wake County, N. C., without being able to obtain any other stanzas. If for no other reason, this stanza deserves preservation for its rhyme and imagery:

The niggers was all excited, like hot ashes poured on worms,
There was two carloads from Oxford, an' three carloads from Dur'ms.

---

[1] Local title.

Engineer Rigg was a good engineer,
He told his fireman 't was not while to fear,
But to pull off his overalls and put on his pants,
And get ready to dump them niggers in the Western Branch.

The fireman looked him square in the face,
As if he wanted a moment for grace.
The fireman said just as quick as could be,
To stop that train and make me life free.

The drawbridge was open when they rounded the bend,
And to have stopped that train, oh! an awful sin,
So he let her go with still more steam,
Till all but two cars went down in the stream.

They pulled niggers out of there for six long days,
And sent them home to be put in their graves.
Oh! sad it was for the women to see,
That their only nigger was just as dead as could be.

34

REPORTED from Durham, N. C., 1919, MS. of W. B. Jeffrey. "Heard sung by a cripple Negro on the street in Clayton, N. C."

This is a part of a longer song, semi-narrative in nature, the tune of which I have heard. "Shorty," one of the Negro janitors at Trinity College, has recorded the whole song for the North Carolina Folk-Lore Society.

Lines 3 and 4 occur in stanza 7 of "The Rovin' Gambler," a song of the mountain whites, of which a phonograph record exists.

I wonder if my mother's on that train.
I wonder if my mother's on that train.
O she 's coming round de curve
And she's straining every nerve.
O I wonder if my mother's on that train, um um.

35

REPORTED from Durham, N. C., 1919, MS. of Walter J. Miller, "Heard at a minstrel show a few years ago."
Cf. IV, no. 37.

Dis mornin' I gets up and puts on my Sunday clothes,
And down de street I goes.
I meets old brother Mose;
He hits me on my nose,
And down I goes,
And dat's all I knows.

36

REPORTED from Auburn, Ala., 1915–1916, MS. of J. C. Lawton, as heard in Seminole County, Fla.
This is evidently not of Negro popular composition; but whether it is a traditional popular song of the whites, a modern vaudeville song, or a vaudeville song that has somehow survived from thirty or forty years ago, I cannot say. I suspect it is the last.

I've seen in my life some very funny folks,
But the funniest of all I know,
Is a huckleberry nig, just as sure as you're alive,
Just as black as any black crow.
You can talk until you're tired, but you'll never get a word,
From this very, very queer old coon,
Heez er knock-need, double-jointed, hippy hacky make,
And he whistles up the same old tune.

Well he whistles thru de day and he whistles thru de night,
And he whistled when his wife was dead;
He whistled like a locomotive engine in his sleep,
And he whistled like the devil going to bed.
One day a nigger hit him with a brick upon the mouth,
And his lip swell up like a big balloon,
He did n't favor the huckleberry nig,
But he whistled up the same old tune.

37

BROTHER EBEN'S GOT A COON [1]

REPORTED from Durham, N. C., 1919, MS. of Walter J. Miller. "Heard sung by father. Sung in memory of a Negro who had committed murder and had been taken by a mob and hanged. 'Brother Eben' was, I suppose, what you might call a leader of the mob."

Mr. Miller's note is probably the explanation of the song believed in the neighborhood where he heard it, but it is hardly the true explanation. The lines are probably the refrain from one of the old minstrel songs. In Perrow, 1913, p. 158 (as from Mississippi in 1909), I find the following variant, used as a refrain after a stanza that has antecedents in several old minstrel books:

> Uncle Eph'm got de coon and gone on, gone on, gone on,
> Uncle Eph'm got de coon and gone on,
> And left me watching up de tree.

With a variation in the last line, this is the same as the refrain to "Brother Ephram Got de Coon and Gone on," given as an old song from Virginia, and containing stanzas from ante-bellum minstrel songs, Scarborough, 1925, p. 101.

While hunting the coon is almost unknown in the Negro folk-songs of to-day, it was a commonplace in the old minstrel song-books of the eighteen-forties and fifties.

> Brother Eben's got a coon,
> And gone on, gone on,
> Brother Eben's got a coon,
> And gone on, gone on.

[1] Local title.

VI

SONGS ABOUT ANIMALS

IN Africa the Negro had many songs and stories about animals. These were, of course, jungle creatures and were soon forgotten in America. The only African beasts found in American Negro folk-songs are the elephant and the monkey, and these are very plainly not from the jungle, but from the "animal fair," whence also the Australian kangaroo. The Jamaican Negroes, mostly of different racial stock from the American Negro, preserved many of their native *annansi* (spider) stories; but such stories and songs as the American Negroes preserved were transferred to animals native to America. Thus the Uncle Remus stories, dealing with American animals, have many African analogies in which jungle beasts are the characters. It should be noted, too, that the Uncle Remus stories, with their interpolated songs, correspond in form to the song-interpolated animal story of Africa and Jamaica.[1] The significant fact is that the American Negro retained his African interest in animals, in accord with the deep conservatism of his nature; but he showed his equally deep tendency to adapt himself to the white man's world by promptly substituting American animals for those of his ancestors.

The animal songs are among the oldest and most conservative of all the Negro folk-songs. In slavery times they must have been especially suitable to the Negro's need, for they were a familiar channel of expression, and they were nonsense to the white man. They were not nearly so apt to get an ignorant slave into trouble as comment upon people or events. Comment upon people, unless of the flattering sort that Fanny Kemble, Bishop Andrew, and others have quoted was dangerous.[2] Nonsense was the quality of ante-bellum Negro folk-rhymes on which most observers commented; and a very sensible nonsense it was. The necessity for nonsense in the Negro song has long since vanished, but the white auditor still

---

[1] Such interpolations, however, are also common in European folk-tales, probably the best-known example being the tale of "Jack the Giant-Killer."

[2] Frances Anne Kemble, *Journal of a Residence on a Georgia Plantation* (London, 1863), p. 106; and C. F. Deems, ed., *Annals of Southern Methodism for 1856*, chap. 9.

puts a premium on it, and the Negro singer, enjoying nonsense himself, unusually sensitive from long experience to what will please the
white man, and unusually true to the conservative channels of racial
habit, still sings a great deal of nonsense.

At least twenty-eight songs in this group are referable, either in
whole or in part, to the ante-bellum minstrel stage.[3] The same animals are treated in the same convention and often in the identical
words. Since there is no extant body of Negro animal songs preceding the minstrel stage, and since there is abundant evidence that
many songs of certain Caucasian origin infiltrated into the Negro
folk-song from the same source, the most reasonable conclusion is
that the minstrel songs are themselves the ancestors of the Negro
songs, which resemble them, rather than collateral descendants of a
common folk-ancestor. It seems likely, however, that the minstrel
songs of this type, composed by white men as they were, had some
basis in authentic Negro folk-song. One song in this collection,
no. 48, which may be dated [4] 1810–1812 (at least a decade before
Negro minstrelsy arose, and two decades before it became popular),
is of exactly the same nature as the minstrel songs and occurs as a
stanza of IV, no. 8, another stanza of which actually occurs in the
minstrel books.

The song just cited, if its history is correctly given, is the oldest
Negro song in my collection for which an actual date can be given.
Other old songs in the same group, if touches from old Caucasian
folk-song may be considered presumptive evidence of age, are numbers 1 *A* and *B*, 11, 14, and 47.

Originally these songs were probably social songs rather than
work songs. Certainly this is true of the early minstrel songs. Their
principal functions were to accompany dances, or to afford entertainment at social gatherings, whether in a minstrel theatre, in the
slave quarters, or at the "big house" to amuse the white folks.
Most of them are still used primarily as dance songs, "banjo songs,"
or songs of entertainment, but some are used as work songs, particularly by agricultural laborers and workers at miscellaneous occupations.

The songs of this group are very much alike in their general nature. Most of them are short. It seldom happens that an individual
of any particular species is singled out and given a definite character
or history as in the case of the mule Simon Slick (or Simon Slick's
mule, for the matter is not quite clear) or the dog Blue or True. The

---

[3] Nos. 7, 9, 10, 13, 19, 23, 24, 25, 27 *A* and *B*, 28, *A* and *B*, 30, 32 *A* and *B*, 37,
40 *A*, *B*, *C*, and *D*, 41, 42, 43, 47, 48, 49, 50.

[4] See the note to IV, no. 8.

great majority consist of short, pithy remarks about the species in general. The conventional element is very strong; observation runs in conventional channels and contents itself generally with the obvious. Few species take on a definite character in these songs. The rabbit, so highly individualized in the Uncle Remus tales, becomes merely a peg to hang a song on, his rich personality shrunk to "just a little bunch of hair." The mule comes out more strongly; he is both sly and cantankerous. The jay-bird, too, has personality — a humorous and decidedly "sassy" one, which the woodpecker sometimes approximates. The bull-frog is simply ridiculous without any definite character. The dog has more variety of type than of character; he is generally extolled for his prowess as a hunter, whether he be rabbit, coon, or possum dog. The "houn' dawg," not mentioned specifically in this group of songs, may be any one of the three varieties just named, or all of them. The boll-weevil, however, the only creature in the lot who is beyond question not a legacy from the early minstrels, has the fullest character of all — persistent, humorous, pestiferous. His history, character, and songs appear in the chapter on "Recent Events."

Many other animals and "varmints" appear in the Negro's song. Among domestic animals he notices the horse, cow, sheep, goat, hog; he hunts the rabbit, possum, coon, and squirrel, and comments briefly on a number of wilder beasts with which he is quite unfamiliar — the wild-cat, bear, monkey, hippopotamus, kangaroo, and elephant. He notices the snake, toad, frog, terrapin, and cat-fish. Most of the domestic fowls are mentioned — hen, rooster, goose, and duck; other birds present in his song are the jay-bird, crow, hawk, buzzard and (very incidentally) lark and dove. About the only insects noticed are the bedbug, ladybug, and boll-weevil.

Sometimes there is a hint of a story in the short animal song, as in "Well Mr. Peckerwood" and "Snake bake a hoecake"; [5] more often the song is limited to a pithy remark or a bit of humorous observation or burlesque fancy. The conventional device of exaggerated contrast, very common in other types of Negro song, is common also in the animal songs. Typical contrasts of this kind are that of the rabbit, possum, and coon as to their tails and that of the bedbug, ladybug, and firefly as to their wings, with the conventional conclusion (let the psychoanalysts make what they will of it) that the least-favored one "gets there just the same."

The songs in which the Negro sings about animals show not so many outright humorous touches as a basic undertone of humorous

[5] Nos. 45 and 48.

insouciance on the part of the singer. They show some careless bits
of observation of the creatures concerned, but they show only a faint
ability to give individual or even typical character to the creatures
celebrated. In fact, the character of the observation is in most of
them just what it is in the work songs — trivial comment upon the
obvious, with a predilection for the humorously grotesque.

SONGS WITH ANNOTATIONS

The following songs, classified in other groups, might also be included in the
present class: III, 4, 6, 12, 13, 18, 21, 22, 24; IV, 3 *E*, 4, 6, 8, 9, 17, 18, 28 *E*, 29,
31, 40; V, 4, 7, 8 *F*, 10, 13, 15, 20, 22–24, 31, 37; VII, 53, 54, 56, 80; VIII, 1, 3,
5–10, 23; IX, 17, 19, 47; X, 1–8, 10, 19; XII, 3, 31, 33, 34, 40–44; XIII, 2;
XIV, 11, 12, 13 *B*.

I

SIMON SLICK [1]

A

REPORTED from Auburn, Ala., 1915–1916, MS. of Hammond, as heard in southeastern Alabama. "Peculiar gestures are used with this song, imitating the
driving of Simon."

I have another, slightly different, version from Alabama.

Perrow, 1913, p. 125, gives two variants, one from Mississippi country whites
in 1909, and one from East Tennessee mountain whites in 1908, in both of which
the mule's name is Jack, as also in Scarborough, 1925, p. 185. In Talley, 1922,
p. 47, Simon Slick is the name of the mule's owner, as in *B* following and in
Odum, 1925, p. 238. In Odum, 1925, p. 237, the mule's name is Simon Slick.
In none of these variants are any of the lines identical except line 4 of *B* following, which occurs in Talley and both the Odum variants. Variations of the first
two lines of *A* occur in all the variants cited. Perrow cites Chambers's *Popular
Rhymes of Scotland*, 1870, p. 19, for a similar opening. In this connection it will
also be observed that the opening line of *B* is a variant of a familiar Mother
Goose opening.

Cf. VIII, no. 23.

> I had a mule one time,
> His name wuz Simon Slick;
> He met dat Railroad Texas train
> And kicked it off de track,
> Kicked de feathers from dat goose,
> He broke de elephant's back,
> "Woah mule," I say, "Woah."
> Ain't got no time ter fool wid you
> For fooling wid dis mule.

[1] Local title.

B

Reported from Auburn, Ala., 1915–1916, MS. of L. N. Rivais.
   Closely similar to Talley, 1922, p. 47, and Odum, 1925, p. 238. See note to *A*.

> There was a man lived in our town,
> His name was Simon Slick;
> He owned a mule wid a dreamy eye,
> And O how dat mule could kick!
> He'd shut one eye and shake his tail
> And greet you wid a smile,
> He'd gently telegraph his leg and raise you half a mile.

2

REPORTED from Durham, N. C., 1919, MS. of D. B. Newton, as heard in Scotland County, N. C. "Work song."
   For a variant, cf. Odum, 1926, p. 120, with music on p. 250.

> I'se got a mule, I'se got a mule on de mountain
>   And his name is Jerry.
> Take him down, take him down,
>   And ride him when I want to.

3

REPORTED from Auburn, Ala., 1915–1916, MS. of R. M. Beasly.
   Cf. Scarborough, 1925, p. 171 (as from Texas).

> My marster had er little grey mule,
> He bought 'im on er Christmas day;
> The very first word that scoundrel beast said
> Was, "I want my oats and hay,"
> Oh Lord, Oh Lord, you orter heered that scoundrel beast moan,
> Oh Lord, Oh Lord, I wish I'd let him erlone.

4

REPORTED from Auburn, Ala., 1915–1916, MS. of F. W. McMeans, as heard at Wolf Creek, Tenn. "Banjo song."
   Closely similar throughout to "Whoa Mule," Perrow, 1913, p. 126, as from Mississippi in 1909; and "Whoa, Mule," Scarborough, 1925, p. 186, with music, as from Texas; line 2, with slight verbal variations, occurs in Odum, 1925, p. 237. With the first line cf. "Whoa Mule!" Odum, 1925, p. 155.

Whoa! mule; whoa! mule, I holler.
I'll tie a knot in the end of his tail
And hitch him to the collar.

5

REPORTED from Auburn, Ala., 1915–1916, MS. of M. S. Perdue.

I have practically the same song from Auburn, Ala., 1915–1916, as from Georgia.

Practically the same as the first two lines of "Our Old Mule," Talley, 1922, p. 112, and lines 10 and 11 of "Mule Song," Odum, 1925, p. 154, where it is suggested that they come "from a child's rhyme long current among the Negroes."

I had a mule and he would n't gee,
And I hit him in the head with a singletree.

6

REPORTED from Auburn, Ala., 1915–1916, MS. of A. H. Williamson, as heard in Lowndes County, Ala.

There are many songs in which various things "run so fast." I have an unprintable one about a black cat and a sewing machine. Cf. Scarborough, 1925, pp. 199, 239, as from Texas.

In spite of the window glass, I suspect that Old Geneva was a race horse.

Old Geneva
Run so fast
Could n't see nuthin'
But de winder glass.

7

REPORTED from Auburn, Ala., 1915–1916, MS. of R. R. Beard, as heard in Mobile County, Ala. "Very old."

Cf. V, no. 7 and note. For variants of this stanza, see Perrow, 1913, p. 124 (as from Mississippi country whites in 1909); Talley, 1922, p. 6; Scarborough, 1925, p. 185 (as from New Orleans).

I went to de ribber an' I could n't get across,
I gave fo' bits for an old blind hoss,
I rode him in, en he could n't swim,
An' I gave five dollars to get him out ag'in.

8

REPORTED from Durham, N. C., 1919, MS. of K. W. Litaker. "Heard in the cotton fields in Cabarrus County, N. C., within the last two years."

I have known this song since childhood as a song of the whites, and have heard it in the Maine woods, never with any suggestion that it was a Negro song. Perrow, 1913, pp. 123–124, gives one Old Gray Mare song (with music) and two Old Gray Horse songs, all as sung by mountain whites, but they do not seem related to the present song.

> Oh! the old gray mare she ain't what she used to be;
> She ain't what she used to be,
> She ain't what she used to be.
> Oh! The old gray mare she ain't what she used to be
> Ten or twenty years ago.

9

REPORTED from Auburn, Ala., 1915–1916, MS. of H. C. Kilpatrick.

Stanzas beginning "Way down yonder" are common both in ante-bellum minstrel songs and in current secular songs. They occur both independently and as stanzas in songs of the potpourri type. See in the collection, III, no. 20; IV, no. 11; VI, nos. 10, 19, 40, 42; IX, no. 3; X, no. 78; also Perrow, 1913, pp. 134–135 (as from Mississippi in 1909); and cf. "Away down Souf," Gumbo Chaff's *Ethiopian Glee Book*, 1848, pp. 61, 117, and Christy's *Nigga Songster*, n. d., pp. 69, 239.

With the first line, cf. Christy's *Nigga Songster*, p. 239:

> Way down souf on de beaver kreek.

For a Virginia version of the cow's death, see Perrow, 1913, p. 128; and Scarborough, 1925, p. 107 (as from Virginia, with music).

> 'Way down yonder, in de forks o' de creek,
> De ole cow died in de middle o' next week.

10

REPORTED from Auburn, Ala., 1915–1916, MS. of R. R. Beard, as heard in Mobile County, Ala. "Sung by an ex-slave."

> 'Way down yonder in de growin' corn,
> De old cow died wid de holler horn.

11

REPORTED from Auburn, Ala., 1915–1916, MS. of A. M. Kearly. Evidently the
Negro version of

> Little Boy Blue come blow your horn,
> The sheep are in the meadow, the cows in the corn.

Sheep in the meadow, don't you hear them bells
And the cows in the corn just raising hell.

12

REPORTED from Auburn, Ala., 1915–1916, anonymously.
This is a modification of part of a vaudeville song of the whites, popular
about fifteen years ago, in which the goat "Coughed up them shirts and flagged
the train."

A goat one day was feeling fine,
He ate ten shirts from off de line;
Sal took a stick and broke his back
And tied him to de railroad track.

13

REPORTED from Auburn, Ala., 1915–1916, anonymously.
Cf. V, no. 4; also III, no. 22; VI, no. 13; XIII, nos. 13 and 17.

Nigger an' white man
Settin' on a log,
Finger on de trigger,
Eye on de hog.
Gun said bip,
Hog said flipp,
Both of 'em gripped on 'im with all their grip.

14

REPORTED from Auburn, Ala., 1915–1916, MS. of R. R. Beard, as heard in
Mobile County, Ala. "Sung by his grandfather."
Cf. V, no. 28.
This is an echo of "Little Brown Jug," a folk-song popular among the white
people about 1850.

Me an' my wife an' little fice dog
Slept togedder in a hickory log.

15

REPORTED from Auburn, Ala., 1915–1916, MS. of C. M. Hurt. Tune: "All Night Long." "Sung by old Negro piano-player."

"All night long" is a refrain common to many Negro songs.

For other songs illustrating both the worth and the worthlessness of the Negro's dog, see Perrow, 1913, pp. 127, 128, 132; Talley, 1922, p. 150; Scarborough, 1925, p. 171; and V, no. 20, VI, nos. 16, 17, 18, and VII, no. 80.

> My daddy had a rabbit dog,
> That was n't worth a rap;
> He treed a rabbit in Tennessee
> And run him to Birmingham.
> Run him all night long,
> Babe, all night long.

16

REPORTED from Durham, N. C., 1919, MS. of Sam E. Marsh, as heard in North Carolina.

I have the same song from South Carolina.

Cf. "Hyar, Rattler," in Burlin, 1919, iv, 38.

> I carried old Raddler out,
> Thought I'd catch a coon.
> Every time old Raddler barked,
> I found he'd treed the moon.

17

REPORTED from Auburn, Ala., 1915–1916, MS. of W. S. Black, as heard near Athens, Ala.

The same as in Perrow, 1913, p. 128 (as from Mississippi in 1909).

> Somebody stole my old coon dog,
> Wish they'd bring him back.
> Runs the old coons over the fence
> And the little ones through the crack.

18

REPORTED from Auburn, Ala., 1915–1916, MS. of R. R. Beard, as heard in Mobile County, Ala. "Sung by grandfather."

Cf. V, no. 20.

> I had a little dog an' his name was True;
> He showed me a hole in de crack ob de fence
> Where de hog went fru.

19

REPORTED from Auburn, Ala., 1915–1916, MS. of W. S. Black, as heard in northern Alabama. "Sung on plantation."
The same, with slight verbal variations in the last two lines, as in Scarborough, 1925, p. 167, where it is given as an ante-bellum song from Arkansas. Cf. Ibid., p. 166, for an ante-bellum variant from Virginia.

> Rabbit is a cunning thing
> Rambles in the dark,
> Never knows what trouble is
> Till he hears old Rover bark.

20

REPORTED from Auburn, Ala., 1915–1916, MS. of A. H. Williamson, as heard in Lowndes County, Ala.
The first two lines are as in Perrow, 1913, p. 127 (as from South Carolina in 1909). Cf. no. 21 in this chapter, and VIII, no. 5.

> Oh! de rabbit on de log
> An' I ain't got my dog;
> I'm gwine ter shoot 'im wid my pistol way back;
> I'm gwine ter shoot 'im wid my pistol way back.
> Oh! de rabbit on de log,
> An' I ain't got my dog;
> I'm gwine ter shoot 'im wid my pistol way back.

21

REPORTED from Auburn, Ala., 1915–1916, MS. of A. E. Hammond, as heard in southeastern Alabama.
With stanza 1, cf. no. 20 in this chapter, and VIII, no. 5 and notes; with stanza 3, cf. VIII, no. 6, XII, no. 42 and notes. I am certain that I have seen variants of all these stanzas in print, but can cite no variant for stanza 2.

> Rabbit on de lawg,
> Ain't got no good rabbit dawg,
> But I gonna ketch dat rabbit,
> By George,
> By George! By George!
>
> Went down de valley one day,
> Heard er possum sneeze,
> Hollered back to Suzaine,
> "Put on a pot er peas."

Um gonna ketch dat rabbit,
Um gonna ketch dat rabbit,
By George! By George!

De hound's on my track,
De rabbit's on my back,
Um gonna make it to my shack —
Kazed I ketched dat rabbit,
By George! By George!

22

LITTLE BUNNY RABBIT [1]

REPORTED from Durham, N. C., 1919, MS. of L. W. Israel. "Work song."

In the garden
Stealing cabbage.
White man's gun,
Rabbit run.
Rabbit stew,
That'll do.

23

REPORTED from Auburn, Ala., 1915–1916, MS. of F. Cooper, as heard in Tus-caloosa County, Ala. "Sung by farm hand."

I have the same stanza, with slight verbal variations, from Auburn, Ala., 1915–1916, MS. of W. S. Black; from Durham, N. C., 1919; MS. of J. E. Lyon, Jr., as heard in High Point, N. C., in 1911; and from Durham, N. C., 1919, MS. of Eugene C. Crawford, as heard in Orange County, S. C.

The song is practically the same as in Abbot, 1924 (with music); Scarborough, 1925, p. 165 (as an old song from South Carolina, with music), Ibid., p. 169, as from Virginia, Ibid., p. 165 (a variant, from Natchez, Miss.).

That it has an ante-bellum origin is shown by stanzas 1 and 2 of "Do Come Along, Ole Sandy Boy," *Negro Singers' Own Book*, 1846(?), p. 309, the second stanza of which also occurs in other minstrel songs, for example, "Uncle Gabriel":

Mr. Coon he is a mighty man,
He carries a bushy tail,
He steals old massa's corn at night,
And husks it on a rail.

The squirrel has a bushy tail,
Stumpy grows de hair,
De old coon's tail am ringed all round —
De possum's tail am bare.

[1] Local title.

Other stanzas of this song deal with the tails of fox, peacock, and pig; to which "Uncle Gabriel" adds the sow and tadpole and the conclusion that white folks and niggers have no tails.

> Raccoon got a bushy tail
> Opossum's tail is bare;
> Rabbit ain't got no tail at all,
> But jes' a bunch o' hair,
> But jes' a bunch o' hair.

24

REPORTED from Auburn, Ala., 1915–1916, MS. of S. A. Allen, as heard in Shelby County, Ala. "Sung by Negro hunters."

For stanza 1, see note to no. 23, in this chapter. Stanza 2 has a number of variants, with "rabbit" and "possum" for "coon," and "my bull-dog" and "my little dog" for "old sliana," as in Scarborough, 1925, pp. 167 (from Arkansas, as "before the war," with music) and 166 (from Virginia as ante-bellum) respectively.

Both stanzas 2 and 3 have an ante-bellum origin as shown by the last stanza of "Do Come Along, Ole Sandy Boy" (*Negro Singers' Own Book*, 1846[?], p. 309):

> De mink he is a mighty thing,
> He rambles in de dark;
> The only ting disturbs his peace
> Is my old bull dog's bark.

Cf. nos. 19 and 29 in this chapter.

> The coon's tail am a streaked tail,
> The 'possum's tail am bare,
> The rabbit's tail is no tail at all,
> Nothing but a little bitty bunch ob hair.

> The coon am a cunning thing,
> He rambles in the dark,
> He nebber knows what trouble is
> Till he hears old sliana [1] bark.

> The rabbit am a cunning thing,
> His tail is nothing but a bunch of hair,
> He nebber knows what trouble
> Till the broomsage catches fire.

[1] *Sic* in MS. Probably a slip for Dinah.

25

REPORTED from Auburn, Ala., 1915–1916, MS. of J. J. Harriss, as heard in eastern North Carolina.
Cf. nos. 23 and 24, in this chapter.

> De squir'l he totes a bushy tail,
> De 'possum tail am bah;
> Coon, he got de rings all roun',
> An' no tail hab de har.

> Put yo' foot in de water,
> Water mighty col'.
> Hear de terrapin whistle,
> He whistle mighty bol'.

> Coony on a rail,
> Possum by his side,

> (*Two lines not recalled.*)

26

A

REPORTED from Auburn, Ala., 1915–1916, MS. of W. S. Black, as heard near Athens, Ala.
    I have the same song from Auburn, Ala., 1915–1916, MS. of Ard, as heard in Ozark, Ala.
    The same as in Scarborough, 1925, p. 173 (as from Louisiana). For variants with "possum" for "raccoon," see Perrow, 1913, p. 131 (as from Mississippi in 1906); Scarborough, 1925, pp. 170 (as from Texas, with music), 172.

> Raccoon up the 'simmon tree,
> Rabbit on the ground;
> Rabbit says you son-a-gun,
> Shake them 'simmons down.

B

Reported from Auburn, Ala., 1915–1916, MS. of F. Mitchell, as heard in southeastern Alabama. "Negro hunting song."
    I have the same song with slight verbal differences from Clay County, Ala., 1915, and from North Carolina, 1919.
    The same with slight verbal variations, as in Scarborough, 1925, p. 172 (as from Virginia and elsewhere, with music).

Raccoon up the 'simmon tree,
Possum on the ground;
Says the possum to the coon,
You shake dem 'simmons down.

C

Reported from Auburn, Ala., 1915–1916, MS. of T. H. Bonner, as heard in Clay County, Ala.

I have the same from Durham, N. C., 1919, MS. of Walter J. Miller, as heard "several years ago," with part of the last line omitted.

The same, with slight verbal variations, as in Perrow, 1913, p. 131 (as from Mississippi in 1906); Scarborough, 1925, p. 170 (as from Texas, with music).

Possum up a 'simmon tree, raccoon on the ground,
Raccoon say, you rascul you, shake some 'simmons down.

27

A

REPORTED from Auburn, Ala., 1915–1916, MS. of F. Mitchell, as heard in southeastern Alabama. "Negro hunting song."

I have the same song, with "rabbit" for "coon," from Auburn, Ala., 1915–1916, MSS of R. E. Donis and M. E. Bryant.

Cf. Barrow, 1882, p. 875; Perrow, 1913, p. 132 (as from Mississippi in 1909); Talley, 1922, p. 3; and Scarborough, 1925, p. 177, as follows:

Possum up de gum-stump,
Cooney up de hollow,
Little gal at our house
Fat as she can wallow.

Older variants occur in the minstrel books, for example, Christy's *Nigga Songster*, n. d., p. 62, stanza 1 of "Opossum Up a Gum Tree"; also in "Black Shaker's Song," p. 50 of White's *New Illustrated Ethiopian*, n. d., as follows:

Possum up a gum tree,
His tail has body follow;
Raccoon quickly see him
Looking out ob hollow.

For the first line, see also note to IV, no. 36.

Possum up the gum stump,
Coon up the holler;
Git him down, little boy,
I'll give you half a dollar.

B

Reported from Auburn, Ala., 1915–1916, MS. of W. S. Black.
   I am confident that I have encountered "Work snake and Juny bug" in the old minstrel books, but cannot cite the passage.

> Possum in gum stump. Cooney in the hollow.
> Work snake and Juny bug and I'll give you half a dollar.

28

Reported from Auburn, Ala., 1915–1916, MS. of R. R. Beard, as heard in Mobile County, Ala. "Sung by grandfather."
   See note to no. 27 A, in this chapter.

> De raccoon up de gum stump,
> De possum in de holler,
> De squirrel in de pine top
> As fat as he can wallow.

29

A

Reported from Durham, N. C., 1919, MS. of J. D. Johnson, Jr. "Heard sung by an old Negro, who accompanied himself on the banjo, in small town in eastern North Carolina."
   Cf. no. 24, note, in this chapter.

> The raccoon is a cunning thing,
>   He walketh in the dark,
> And never thinks to curl his tail
>   Till he hears old Ranger bark.

B

Reported from Auburn, Ala., 1915–1916, MS. of R. R. Beard, as heard in Mobile County, Ala. "Sung by grandfather."

> De raccoon am a cunnin' t'ing,
> He hopped hisself in de winder;
> Ef it had not been for de fiddle an' de bow
> I'd killed him wid my finger.

30

REPORTED from Auburn, Ala., 1915–1916, MS. of R. R. Beard, as heard in Mobile County, Ala. "Sung by grandfather."

With stanzas 1 and 2, cf. no. 37; and with stanza 3, cf. nos. 26 *A*, *B*, and *C*, all in this chapter.

The general plan of disconnected observations about different creatures and their whereabouts is a common one in work songs, animal songs, songs about women, and songs involving race consciousness. It generally involves some contrast as well as mere enumeration. For an example of the same method from the ante-bellum minstrel songs, cf. the last stanza of "Neber Do to Gib it Up," p. 227 in *Negro Singers' Own Book*, 1846(?), and p. 152 in Christy's *Nigga Songster*, n. d.:

> Master 's on de woodpile barkin' like a dog,
> Toad in de mill pond settin' on a log,
> Possum up a gum tree, saucy, fat, and dirty,
> Come kiss me gals or I 'll run like a turkey.

> Hog in de 'taters,
> Crow in de corn,
> Cow in de cabbage patch
> Widout either horn.

> Niggers in de melon patch,
> Ole boss wid er gun;
> Nigger say, "I ain't guilty,"
> Ole boss say, "You better run."

> Possum in de 'simmon tree,
> Coon in de holler,
> Nigger in de melon patch
> Full as he can waller.

31

REPORTED from Durham, N. C., 1919, MS. of David T. House, Jr.

If I had my rather, I rather be a squirrel,
I would curl my tail on top of my back and run all round this world.

32

A

REPORTED from Auburn, Ala., 1915–1916, MS. of W. D. Kimbrough, as heard in Camden, Ala.

With the first two lines, cf. stanza 6 of "Jenny Get Your Hoe Cake Done," *Negro Singers' Own Book*, 1846(?), p. 360:

The old hen and chickens at the stack,
An old hawk flew down amongst the pack,
An' struck de old hen whack middle ob de back,
I really do believe dat 't is a fact.

A variant of this stanza occurs, *Ibid.*, p. 407, and in Gumbo Chaff's *Ethiopian Glee Book*, 1848, p. 41, both in "Jenny Get Your Hoe Cake Done":

De hen and chickens went to roost,
De hawk flew down and bit de goose,
He bit de old hen in de back;
I really believe dat am a fac.

An old hen sitten' in the fodder stack,
A hawk flew down and pecked her in the back;
If you can't thread a needle, come wind the ball,
If you can't thread a needle, come wind the ball.

ℬ

Reported from Auburn, Ala., 1915–1916, MS. of J. E. Hillhouse.

The old hawk flew up in the roof,
Bit the goose in the middle o' the back,
And made the old duck go quack, quack.

33

REPORTED from Auburn, Ala., 1915–1916, MS. of L. E. Jenkins, as heard in a fraternity house, Auburn, Ala. "Sung by porter."

What did the rooster say to the little red hen?
"I ain't seed you since God knows when."
What did the hen say to the little red rooster?
"You don't come round as often as you uster."

34

REPORTED from Auburn, Ala., 1915–1916, MS. of O. C. Bryan, as heard on an Alabama farm.

I have practically the same song, without the "You Shall be Free" refrain, from Auburn, Ala., 1915–1916, MS. of J. H. Owens. Cf. V, no. 15, also Odum, 1925, p. 234, and Scarborough, 1925, p. 235 (from Alabama), all with the "You Shall be Free" refrain. For the refrain, see note to V, no. 15.

De rooster and de nigger got in a fight,
De rooster slapped de nigger slam out o' sight.

De nigger says, "Dat will be all right;
I'll meet you at de hen-house tomorrow night,
Wid a cracker sack, den you shall be free,[1]
Wid a cracker sack, den you shall be free,
When de good Lawd sets you free.

35

REPORTED from Auburn, Ala., 1915–1916, MS. of J. Chapman.

    I have the same from Auburn, Ala., 1915–1916, anonymously, with "Mammy" for "Sally." Perrow, 1913, p. 127 (as from South Carolina in 1909), preserves "Sally," but gives "turkey" for "chicken." Talley, 1922, inverts the order and gives "Auntie" for "Sally." Scarborough, 1925, p. 194, gives "granny" for "Sally."

Chicken in the bread tray
Scratching out dough;
Sally, will your dog bite?
No, child, no.

36

REPORTED from Auburn, Ala., 1915–1916, MS. of R. R. Beard, as heard in Baldwin County, Ala. "Sung by Negro servant."

Daylight's a-breakin', hear de rooster crowin',
Wake up ebberbody, see de sun rise;
Mornin' lark's a callin', dew drops a fallin'
Like diamonds frum de skies.

37

REPORTED from Auburn, Ala., 1915–1916, MS. of R. R. Beard, as heard in Mobile County, Ala. "Sung by old Negro."
    Cf. no. 30, in this chapter.

Crow in de corn field,
Nigger in de patch;
Chicken in de egg-shell,
'Bout ready ter hatch.

---

[1] Cracker sack is for crocus sack, which occurs in other versions of the song.

38

REPORTED from Auburn, Ala., 1915–1916, MS. of H. W. Chaddick, as heard in
Knoxville, Tenn. "Sung by Negro serenaders."
    This song has all the earmarks of a modern vaudeville song.

> Stand back pork chops,
> Side track ham,
> Let the chicken ooze through.
> I knows I ain't no high-priced coon
> From turkey down to stew,
> But chicken is the only thing I really like,
> 'Cause chicken am de only thing that suits my appetite.
> So stand back pork chops,
> Side track ham,
> And let the chicken ooze on through.

39

REPORTED from Auburn, Ala., 1915–1916, MS. of R. E. Donis, as heard in
Georgia.
    The first line belongs properly to one of the variants of "Ain't No Use Workin'
So Hard" (IX, no. 33), in which it occurs in Scarborough, 1925, p. 235 (as
from Alabama).
    "O babe" is a common refrain.

> Kill that chicken and give me wing,
> I going home on the morning train,
> O babe.

40

A

REPORTED from Auburn, Ala., 1915–1916, MS. of C. B. Crow, as heard in
"Levee Camp on Mississippi River in Louisiana."
    Line 2 is as in Perrow, 1913, p. 133 (from Mississippi country whites in 1909),
and Talley, 1922, p. 36. Cf. also Campbell and Sharp, 1917, p. 312.
    The songs of this type are descended from the ante-bellum minstrels. Cf.
stanza 8 of "Jim Along Josey," p. 286, in *Negro Singers' Own Book*, 1846(?):

> Over de hills an a great way off
> De jaybird died with de hookin' cough,
> An a way down in a big muddy pon'
> Oh dis jaybird died wid his breeches on.

In the "New Jim Along Josey," *Ibid.*, p. 419, it is the bullfrog who dies of the whooping cough; and in "Go Away, Go Away. Don't Come Nigh," (*Ibid.*, p. 104 and Christy's *Nigga Songster*, n. d., p. 107), it is the bulltoad.

Cf. nos. 9 and 42, in this chapter.

> 'Way down yonder, and a long way off,
> Jaybird died wid der whoopin' cough.[1]

B

Reported from Auburn, Ala., 1915–1916, MS. of G. Clark, as heard in Crenshaw County, Ala. "Sung by Negro cook."

I have the same from Auburn, Ala., 1915–1916, MS. of C. H. Adams.

With line 2, cf. the following from "De Bran New Old Dan Tucker," *Negro Singers' Own Book*, 1846(?), p. 214:

> De toads dey jumped an' de tadpoles danced,
> De hogs dey squealed an' de possum pranced.

> Away down yonder in the forks of de branch
> The jaybird whistled and de buzzard danced.

C

Reported from Auburn, Ala., 1915–1916, MS. of M. E. Bryant.

For practically the same, combined with "'Tain't Gwine Rain No Mo'," see Scarborough, 1925, p. 107 (as from Virginia, with music).

Cf. no. 9, in this chapter.

> De ole cow died in de head of de branch,
> De jay birds whistled and de buzzards danced.

D

Reported from Auburn, Ala., 1915–1916, MS. of R. R. Beard, as heard in Mobile County, Ala. "Sung by grandfather."

> 'Way down yonder in de fork ob de branch
> De jaybird say he ain't got much chance.

---

[1] For the equally old "Jaybird sat on a hickory limb," not included in this collection, see Perrow, 1913, p. 133; Campbell and Sharp, 1917, p. 312; Talley, 1922, p. 15; Scarborough, 1925, pp. 111, 191, 218. Perrow cites other jaybird verses in *J. A. F. L.*, ii, 300, and *Dialect Notes*, iii, 324.

41

REPORTED from Auburn, Ala., 1915–1916, anonymously.
From childhood I have known a variant of this as:

> 'Way down yonder in Pasquotank
> Bull frog jumped from bank to bank.

Cf. also Perrow, 1913, p. 135 (as from Tennessee in 1905 and from Mississippi whites in 1909); Scarborough, 1925, p. 198 (as from Texas), and p. 199 (as from Mississippi); Odum, 1925, p. 251.[1]

> Banjo goes, "Ker-blank, ker-blank ";
> Spring frog holler, "Yankete-yank."
> Bull frog jump from bank to bank
> An' skinned his nose on a hick'ry plank.

42

REPORTED from Auburn, Ala., 1915–1916, MS. of W. H. Blake, Jr.
Cf. no. 40 A, in this chapter.

> Way up yonder on the ole green lake
> The bull frog died with the belly ache,
> Just cause he had nothin' else to do,
> Just cause he had nothin' else to do.

43

REPORTED from Auburn, Ala., 1915–1916, MS. of M. E. Bryant, as heard in Alabama. "Sung on a farm."

> I went down to de mill pond
> And heard such a racket;
> It was a bull frog trying on his jacket.

44

REPORTED from Auburn, Ala., 1915–1916, MS. of R. Chambers, as heard in Giles County, Tenn.
Probably connected with gambling. Cf. XII, nos. 18–22.

> Bottom bone, bottom bone,[2]
> Sit on de hill and hear de dove moan.

---

[1] For other bull-frog songs, see Perrow, 1913, pp. 134, 136; Talley, 1922, p. 20, and in this collection, V, no. 31 and note. Bull-frog stanzas and lines are rather frequent in the old minstrel books.

[2] "Bottom bone" means last dollar.

45

REPORTED from Auburn, Ala., 1915–1916, MS. of R. Langdon, "Sung by Negro block-setter in a sawmill."

Variants occur in Talley, 1922, p. 203; Scarborough, 1923, p. 136 (as from Texas), and Scarborough, 1925, p. 193 (as from western North Carolina). The last is practically the same as stanza 1 of XI, no. 13, in this collection, with "peckerwood" for "boll-weevil."

> W-e-ll Mr. Peckerwood,
> What yo'r head doing red?
> Somebody done stole my derby,
> The sun done turned me red.

46

REPORTED from Auburn, Ala., 1915–1916, MS. of R. A. Carroll.

> Get up coon, let's go fishin',
> Catch mud cat and cook him in de kitchen.

47

REPORTED from Auburn, Ala., 1915–1916, MS. of Childree, as heard in southern Alabama.

I have a variant of the first four lines, with "old straw field" for "field" and "blacksnake" for "rattlesnake," from Auburn, Ala., 1915–1916, MS. of J. H. Owens.

The last three lines are not properly a part of the song, but are the chorus of "Raise a Rukus Tonight," (IV, no. 38) which Odum (1926, pp. 172–175) describes as "an old song now popular in various forms," of which his three versions "represent Georgia, Tennessee, and North Carolina."

The first two lines occur in Burlin, 1919, iv, 38, with music, as part of the song, "Hyar Rattler." These lines seem to be connected with stanzas 2 and 3 of "Springfield Mountain" as reported by Cox (1925, p. 292), or the first four lines of a version given me in Alabama (N. I. White, Harvard MS. ii, 596). According to Cox's note, "Springfield Mountain" is based on an incident that occurred at Wilbraham, Mass., in 1761, the song spreading over the country soon after that date.

The first four lines occur in Perrow, 1915, p. 138, as from Virginia in 1909, each of the two couplets being followed by the refrain of the well-known Patteroller song (see IV, no. 23, in this collection). They occur also in Scarborough, 1925, p. 197, as from Alabama, as stanza 2 of "There Was an Old Nigger, His Name Was Dr. Peck" (cf. IV, no. 22, in this collection) with the well-known "You Shall be Free" refrain; and in "Johnny Booker," Ibid., p. 100.

Lines 3 and 4 seem to have been commonly attracted into the Patteroller song, as in Perrow, cited above, and Scarborough, 1925, p. 24.

The four lines as a unit seem to have their original in a stanza of the ante-bellum minstrels:

> I went for to mow down in the field
> A black snake bit me on de heel
> To cut my dirt I thought it best
> And fell caswhash in a hornet's nest.

This stanza occurs in three songs in *Negro Singers' Own Book*, 1846(?), as follows: "I Wonder Whar He Went To," p. 246; "Whar Did You Come From," p. 317; and "Jim Along Josey," p. 410.

The connection with "Springfield Mountain" suggested above becomes clearer by comparing this older form of the stanza with Cox's version of "Springfield Mountain," or with the first four lines of my version, which are:

> One Sunday morn a lad did go
> Into the meadow for to mow,
> When all at once he thought he fell [for felt or feel?]
> A pizen sarpent bite his heel.

> As I wus goin' cross de field,
> Rattlesnake bit me on de heel.
> As I turned for to run me best,
> I rammed my head in a hornet's nest.
> Goin' raise a rukus tonight,
> Get on boat, down river float,
> Goin' raise a rukus tonight.

48

Reported from Auburn, Ala., 1915–1916, MS. of H. C. Kilpatrick, as heard in southern Alabama. "Sung by Negroes on plantation."

Practically the same (with "frog" for "toad," as in all the variants I have seen) as stanza 2 of "Hoecake," Talley, 1922, p. 49, and stanza 4 of "De Original Jim Crow," *Negro Singers' Own Book*, 1846(?), p. 329. Professor W. H. Wannamaker, of Duke University, tells me that in Calhoun County, S. C., he used to hear it sung by both white children and Negroes.

In "The Literary Lantern," a syndicated weekly column published by many Southern newspapers, under date of August 8, 1926, appeared a note by Professor Stanley Williams, of Yale University, quoting a close variant of the stanza from Washington Irving's notebook for 1817, and asking for further information, with the remark that "our colored maid said she used to sing it at school." In a letter to me he adds, "The verses are in an unpublished notebook. . . . Ostensibly it is a journal of a Tour in Scotland, but he evidently used the notebook in later years for miscellaneous entries. At present I believe that he gained knowledge of this verse during a trip through the South in the 'thirties. Within a year, I hope, the diary will be published."

If there is no error in the tradition reported by Miss White for IV, no. 8 (*q. v.*), in which the stanza occurs, its origin may be dated as before 1810–1812.

Snake bake a hoe-cake,
And set de toad to mind it;
Toad went to noddin'
Lizard came a ploddin'
And right dar he find it.

Oh, bring back my cake, you long-tailed Nanny, you!

49

REPORTED from Auburn, Ala., 1915–1916, MS. of M. S. Perdue, as heard in southern Alabama.

Practically the same as in Scarborough, 1925, p. 162 (as quoted from Allen's *Slave Songs*, 1867); Ibid., p. 164 (as an ante-bellum song from Virginia). Ibid., p. 106 (as an old song from Virginia), is a slight variant, with the old "Jim Along Josey" refrain.

This is practically the same as stanza 2 of "Jinny Come Along," p. 250, in Christy's *Nigga Songster*, n. d.:

Dar was a terrapin and a toad
Both come up de new-cut road,
An ebery time de toad did sing
De terrapin cut de pigeon wing.

It is related to stanza 2 of "Jenny Get Your Hoe Cake Done," *Negro Singers' Own Book*, 1846(?), p. 407:

As I was gwain long de road,
Pon a stump dar sat a toad.
De tadpole winked at pollywog's dauter
And kicked de bullfrog plump in de water.

It is one of the songs sung by Uncle Remus to the little boy.

As I went down the new-cut road
I met Miss Possum and I met Miss Toad.
Every time Miss Possum would sing,
Miss Toad would cut that pigeon wing.

50

REPORTED from Auburn, Ala., 1915–1916, MS. of J. A. Peterson, as heard in Coosa County, Ala. "Sung at a Negro concert."

The chorus is that of "Jenny Get Your Hoe Cake Done," a very common song in the old minstrel books; for example, in *Negro Singers' Own Book*, 1846(?), pp. 360, 407; Gumbo Chaff's *Ethiopian Glee Book*, 1848, p. 41; Christy's *Nigga Songster*, n. d., p. 128.

Stanza 1 is practically the same as Scarborough, 1925, p. 190 (as from Mississippi). It occurs, with "my sister Rose" for "Miss Mary," "cry" for "sigh," and "picked" for "kicked," as stanza 3 of "Jim Along Josy," Gumbo Chaff's *Ethiopian Glee Book*, 1848, p. 61. The last line of the stanza occurs in varouis minstrel songs in the following couplet:

> Ginger puddin and punkin pie,
> Black cat kicked out de black cat's eye.

This couplet occurs in "Jinny Git Your Hoe Cake Done," *Negro Singers' Own Book*, 1846(?), p. 408, and (with "gray cat" for "black cat") the same title in Gumbo Chaff's *Ethiopian Glee Book*, 1848, p. 41. With "green peach" for "ginger," it occurs in "White Cat and Black Cat" in *Negro Singers' Own Book*, 1846(?) p. 218, and White's *New Illustrated Ethiopian*, n. d., p. 49, where it is given as "composed and sung by Dan Emmett." With "Indian pudding" for "ginger pudding" and the rôles of the cats reversed, it occurs in "Jenny Git Your Hoe Cake Done," *Negro Singers' Own Book*, 1846(?) p. 360. Cf. also Talley, 1922, p. 2.

Stanza 2 is practically the same as in Scarborough, 1925, p. 106 (as an old song from Virginia). Cf. also no. 49 and note, in this chapter.

Stanza 3 is probably of equal age, though I can cite no previous publication of it.

Miss Mary, she did dream a dream
That she was a floatin' down de stream.
When she woke, she began a sigh,
The old grey cat had kicked out the black cat's eye.

Chorus

Sallie, get your hoe-cake done, my love,
Oh! Sallie get your hoe-cake done.

As I was a goin' up the new-cut road,
I met Mr. Tarpin and Mr. Toad.
The toad gave a jump, and the tarpin
Lodged behind the stump.

I went up the road and met Brother Tucker ridin' a goat,
And leadin' a dog. The dog gave a bark, and the goat gave a jump,
And throwed Brother Tucker right straddle of a stump.

51

REPORTED from Auburn, Ala., 1915–1916, MS. of A. L. Holloway, as heard in Monroe County, southern Alabama. "Sung at a race in work."
Cf. Odum, 1926, p. 4:

> Ever see a wild cat
> Hug a lion, Lawd, Lawd?

Woo look er, look er yonder,
Woo look er, look er yonder,
Woo look er, look er yonder,
At de wild cat huggin' dat bear.

52

Reported from Auburn, Ala., 1915–1916, MS. of A. M. Kearly. "Heard at commencement speeches."
    Cf. X, no. 44, and note.

I give fifteen cents to see the elephant jump the fence;
He jumped so high he touched the sky
And never got back till next July.

VII

WORK SONGS — GANG LABORERS

THE Negro sang work songs long before he came to America, and in America he sang work songs long before there was any widespread interest in what he sang. Travellers in Africa frequently commented upon the songs sung by the natives at work.[1] Travellers in the ante-bellum South noticed these songs earlier and more frequently than they noticed the religious songs.[2] Both the travellers in Africa and those in the Slave states made constant reference to boat songs. These songs, necessarily timed to the work in hand, were frequently of a religious nature. They were plentiful as long as boats remained an important means of communication, but they died out completely when railways and good roads supplanted the old plantation long-boat. Their chief reminders to-day are the boats themselves, several splendid specimens of which are to be seen in the Charleston City Museum.

The work song, however, has persisted, and will persist as long as the Negro retains his dominant racial traits. It is by far the most numerous group of Negro folk-songs. When songs in the present collection had already reached an unwieldly number and I was devoting several consecutive summers, in Durham, N. C., to their classification and analysis, I heard almost every day various Negro work songs that I had never heard before, mixed with songs that I had heard years before, hundreds of miles away.

The earlier work song seems very often to have been a work song in the strict meaning of the word; that is, a song actually timed to the work in hand and setting a rhythm for it, like many sailor chanties. The boat songs were of this type. Charles Peabody told of slaves protesting that their song-leader sang songs that made them work too hard.[3] Songs of this type are still used by the Negroes, for example, numbers 27 and 87 in this chapter.

[1] See chapter I, pp. 20–21. Mrs. Natalie Curtis Burlin, in *Songs and Tales of the Dark Continent*, New York and Boston, G. Schirmer, 1920, records several African work songs from the singing of two African students at Hampton Institute.

[2] E. g., Charles Peabody, as quoted in the article, "American Music," in the *American History and Encyclopedia of Music;* C. F. Deems in *Annals of Southern Methodism for 1856* (Nashville, Tenn., 1857) chap. 9; William H. Russell in *My Diary North and South* (Boston, 1863), p. 207, etc.

[3] "American Music."

By far the greater number of work songs, however, are not timed particularly to the work in hand; they are merely sung in a way that keeps them from interfering with the work. Their primary function is mental rather than physical; they are to keep the worker's mind contented with at least the illusion of thought while his body is allowed to work mechanically. No doubt this great function of the work song was one reason why the white man so early discovered the advantage of encouraging the Negro to sing, and why the song-leader is sometimes still given extra pay for his vocal services. Probably it is also one of the reasons why most Negro songs are of such simple metrical structure and such short, episodic nature, and why the longer songs of minstrel and "ballet" origin tend so constantly to break up into shorter songs. For while the Negro is working, any song may become a work song of this type. Having become so, it must accommodate itself somewhat to the work. In this and various other printed collections, both spirituals and social songs are often found doing duty as work songs. This is particularly true of the large number of songs that developed out of the early minstrel songs, none of which were originally work songs.

The adaptation of almost any Negro song to the purposes of work also partly explains the trivial nature of so many Negro songs. Some of the triviality and nonsense is partly a heritage from the time when the broken English of the slave often made nonsense in spite of his best intentions, and, being laughed at, was persisted in. More of it is undoubtedly a survival of a later time, when the slave's safest rôle was that of buffoon, since nonsense was amusing to the master, while serious thought might tread upon his sensibility. But much of it is due to the fact that in a work song it is the tune and rhythm that count, rather than the words, and that any song may be seized upon and made to do service as a work song. Thus it is no more incongruous to find spirituals used as work songs than to find "Uncle Ned" serving as a religious song, nor is it at all unusual to find songs that began in the kitchen or on the farm being sung by construction-gang laborers, or *vice versa*. By the very nature of these songs their words are those which naturally rise most easily to the surface of consciousness. The songs that survive long enough to be repeated by the Negro or observed by the collector probably constitute a minority of Negro work songs, the majority being too trivial even for the singer to remember.

In the present group I have included only the songs of the gang laborer, because, despite the general interchangeability of work songs, they contain some qualities which make them, in the mass, a little different from other work songs. Certainly they are more free-spoken, probably because of the singer's greater boldness when surrounded by others of his race, and, in the case of the sex songs, the absence of auditors who might be offended by obscenity. The songs about women which the gang laborer so revels in are treated in a separate section and need not here be discussed. His random thoughts, too, are very similar to those discussed elsewhere, except that they contain a somewhat larger flavor of drinking, gambling, and rowdyism than do the songs of most other labor groups.

Since the gang laborer may sing practically any song as a work song, he sometimes sings songs that are older than they seem and are heritages rather than improvisations. Examples of songs which contain touches of the ante-bellum song are numbers 44, 45, 57, 59, 82 *A*, and 85. None of these songs, or number 71, which was in print in 1900, belongs to the type of song most characteristic of the gang laborer — the song which reflects his immediate environment. In the present collection there is no song of this latter type for which I have been able to establish an existence earlier than 1905. The probability is that few of them are older than the last decades of the nineteenth century.

It is in just these songs growing out of his work that the gang laborer is most interesting. They express a great variety of transient moods about his captain, his partner, his pick or hammer, his work, and his pay. Next to his woman, the most important person in the gang laborer's song is his "Cap'n," or boss. The "Cap'n" is the man who hires and fires him, who keeps him working, sometimes "cusses" and abuses him, and sometimes helps him out of difficulties. The captain's methods are not delicate; while not often a "nigger-hater," he is always a man who believes that "a nigger should keep his place." It is of some value, therefore, in the question of racial antagonisms, to know what the laborer thinks of him. He knows, of course, that the captain may hear and understand his songs, while assuming not to notice them. Many of his remarks are intended for the captain to hear, or rather to half-hear, in the manner familiar to most Southerners, wherein the Negro wishes to signify a state of disgruntlement but is unwilling to make a clear-cut issue of the matter. In all the gang songs dealing with the captain, it must be understood that the captain himself is a possible half-auditor and that the singer may know that he "got a forty-fo'" within reach.

To the captain's demand for harder work he protests, "Captain, I'm drivin', but de steel won't stand it," or "You work me so hard,

Captain, I'm bound to rat [that is, loaf], sometime." In bolder mood, with the captain out of earshot, he sings, "Captain says hurry; I says take my time." Again he wishes his captain would go blind so that he could arrive late at work. A slightly humorous grievance is the captain's obtuseness to all signs of quitting time. The worker delights in singing that the whistle is blowing, or it is raining and the captain won't knock off. The captain "must be cross." More desperately, "Gwine to be twelve o'clock in Hell, boys, when de Captain knock off." He compliments the captain on his mules — whether in good faith or sly sarcasm, who can say? Putting on a bolder face, but probably singing *sotto voce*, he asks the captain to hand down a chew of Battle Axe tobacco. Probably for the ear of his partner rather than the captain, he sings significantly: "Woke up this morning with a knife in my hand — Good morning, young man." "Work don't hurt me" he tells his captain; and, no doubt with John Henry's famous exploit in mind,[4] he proclaims that though he is nothing but a man he will die hammer in hand, "before I'd let dat steam-drill beat me down." Yet in another mood (no. 14) he sings that the captain won't have mercy and that this very hammer killed his partner, doubtless through overwork. When he gets tired of the job, "Captain gwine to call me an' I'll be gone." If he demands his time because he is "tired of working in damned old mine," he is unusually outspoken; a much more characteristic resignation is when he *sends* his hammer to the captain, with the message that he is gone, but adds, to preserve his self-respect, "If he ask you was I running, tell him no, tell him no."

Next to his captain, the gang laborer sings of his partner, bragging of their joint prowess, grieving at his death, threatening him for his laziness in getting up late, and telling how he and his partner "raised hell roun' de pay-car do'." He sings constantly of his hammer or his pick, being very critical of both the weight and ring of his hammer and often addressing both hammer and pick directly. He does not seem to be greatly interested in his pay, but he sometimes hints that he is being humbugged, that pay-time has come and the captain "won't pay off," and that he can't see how his money gets away from him. "All for the white man, nothing for the nigger" is a sentiment common to work songs of all types. "If you don't work your time out, you don't get your pay." One singer "hopes I get my full week's pay," with which he is "going to get my babe some shoes"; another, on pay day, "is going to drink my fill."

---

[4] See nos. 23 etc., in this chapter.

As to the work itself the singer "don't mind working in hot sunshine." He taunts his partner: "You gwine to kill yo' fool self a-workin'; tryin' to work like me." On the other hand, "I can't hold 'em," and "De road is rocky, Lord." The comments on his work which he addresses directly to his captain are generally indirect replies either to actual or to anticipated efforts to speed up the work.

In general, he is suspicious of the captain, because he has often been exploited and he knows he is easy game. He does n't want to be humbugged, or to work overtime. He likes to quit a job, but he hates to be asked his reasons. He does n't want to be thought afraid of the captain, yet the truth shines out clearly that he *is* afraid. His blessed privilege is to mouth and grumble, and to hint threats *sotto voce:* it is a valuable salve to his self-respect. He is "bound to rat" some time, but nevertheless he likes to brag of his prowess as a workman. Sometimes his songs convey a hint that he is a "bad nigger"; and he sings more openly of the doings of other desperadoes. He sings "blues" both when in an occasional blue mood and when feeling anything but blue. Behind most of it there is a stoical acceptance of things as they are, and behind much of it there is more than a suggestion of humor. Surely this is the genuine Negro laborer revealed in his songs as he has revealed himself to numerous employers through other channels.

SONGS, WITH ANNOTATIONS

The following songs classified with other groups might also be included in the present class: II, 5, 7 *C*, 10 *B*; III, 5, 15, 16, 33; IV, 3 *F*; V, 1, 3, 8 *E*, 20, 40 *A*; IX, 1–6, 8, 10–47, 51, 52, 54, 57; X, 1–30, 39, 40–59, 61, 62, 64, 68–78; XI, 2, 3, 6–8, 14; XII, 1–4, 8–13, 16, 18, 21, 23–25, 29; XIII, 8, 12, 18; XIV, 10, 17, 18.

I

REPORTED from Durham, N. C., 1919, MS. of N. I. White.

Heard "sung by a gang of street laborers at work digging a ditch."

Evidently made over from a steel-driving song. The words of the fifth and tenth lines are inaccurately quoted, though metrically correct. I heard the song several times but could never catch the exact words. The "*huh*" here and hereafter represents a grunt as hammer or pick is driven home. It is commonly employed in many of the work songs when the nature of the work allows.

Odum, 1926, pp. 94–106, gives ten songs addressed to the captain, with a discussion. Most of the songs quoted are much longer than mine and seem to be combinations. There are very few lines in common between Odum's songs of this type and mine, though the form and general sentiments are similar.

Captain, I'm drivin' — *huh*
But de steel won't stand it — *huh*.
Captain, I'm drivin' — *huh*
But de steel won't stand it — *huh*.
Let dem picks go down.

My ol' captain — *huh*
Got a fo'ty-fo'-forty [1] — *huh*.
My ol' captain — *huh*
Got a fo'ty-fo'-forty — *huh*.
Let dem picks go down.

2

REPORTED from Auburn, Ala., 1915–1916, MS. of B. A. Wooten, as heard in Marengo County, Ala.
Cf. Odum, 1926, p. 100. Odum, 1925, pp. 176–177, gives an eight-stanza song with the refrain, "Take yo' time, take yo' time."

Cap'n says, hurry, I say take my time.

3

REPORTED from Auburn, Ala., 1915–1916, MS. of C. C. Certain, as heard in Jackson, Miss. in 1906. "Sung by construction gang."

Ain't gwine let you humbug me.

4

REPORTED from Auburn, Ala., 1915–1916, MS. of E. D. Bartlett, as heard near Lineville, Ala. "Sung by railroad and mining negroes."

Captain! Captain! yo' mules look fine
With the big red bridle and the loaded line.

5

REPORTED from Auburn, Ala., 1915–1916, MS. of C. C. Certain, as heard at Jackson, Miss., in 1906. "Sung by construction gang."
Cf. Odum, 1925, p. 275.

Lawd, Lawd, you hear dat, Captain?
De whistle done blow'd, de whistle done blow'd.
It gwine be twelve in Hell when de captain knock off —
When de captain knock off.

[1] A "forty-four"; that is, a pistol of large caliber.

6

REPORTED from Auburn, Ala., 1915–1916, MS. of J. P. Creel, as heard in Jefferson County, Ala. "Sung by negroes on railroad work."
The first two lines are substantially identical with IX, no. 41.
Cf. also Odum, 1926, p. 102.

Captain, Captain, you must be cross,
It's done four o'clock and you won't knock off.
Captain, Captain, you must be cross,
For the money's done come and you won't pay us off.

7

REPORTED from Auburn, Ala., 1915–1916, MS. of R. Langdon. "Sung by two negroes in lumber yard during rain."

Well, it keeps on raining
But the cap-tain won't-knock-off.

8

REPORTED from Auburn, Ala., 1915–1916, MS. of C. C. Certain, as heard at Jackson, Miss., in 1906. "Sung by construction gang."

Captain, Captain, don't you know,
Work don't hurt me nowhere I go.
Ain't sick to-day, but I don't feel so well.

9

REPORTED from Auburn, Ala., 1915–1916, MS. of C. C. Certain, as heard in Jackson, Miss., in 1906. "Sung by construction gang."

Lord, you work me so hard, Captain,
I'm bound to rat some time.

10

REPORTED from Auburn, Ala., 1915–1916, MS. of C. C. Certain, as heard at Jackson, Miss., in 1906. "Sung by construction gang."

Hello, Captain,
How do you do?
If you got any Battle Axe,[1]
Send me down a chew.

[1] A special brand of chewing tobacco.

11

REPORTED from Auburn, Ala., 1915–1916, MS. of H. M. Kilpatrick, as heard in Pickens County, Ala. "Sung when old Negro works hard and then loses his money. Tune loud."

> Captain, Captain, I can't see
> How my little money gets away from me.

12

REPORTED from Auburn, Ala., 1915–1916, MS. of C. J. Perryman, as heard in northern Alabama. "Very little tune. Rock quarry song."
Cf. "John Henry," V, nos. 1 ff., and nos. 23 ff. in this chapter.

> Captain, Captain, nothing but a man,
> But 'fo' I let dat steam-drill beat me down,
> I'd die wif er hammer in my hand.

13

REPORTED from Auburn, Ala., 1915–1916, MS. of C. C. Certain, as heard in Jackson, Miss., in 1906. "Sung by construction gang."

> I woke up this morning with a knife in my hand —
> Good morning, young man,
> Good morning, old Captain.

14

L & N SPECIAL [1]

REPORTED from Auburn, Ala., 1915–1916, MS. of Hammond, as heard near Montgomery, Ala. "Sung by a railroad hand. 'Wham' is used with a sling of the hammer."
Odum, 1925, p. 223, gives an entirely different version "as sung to the Frisco Rag-Time described in Chapter V." Cf. also, Odum, 1925, p. 111. The last four lines with slight variations constitute a work song reported to Miss Scarborough as heard in Florida "years ago," Scarborough, 1925, p. 220 (with the music).

> I ask de captain — *wham!*
> Won't he hab mercy — *wham!*
> Naw boy! — *wham!* — Naw boy! — *wham!*
> Dat dere hammer — rung like mine.

[1] Local title.

Dis dat hammer, killed my partner,
Killed 'em dead — *wham!*
Killed 'em dead — *wham!*

15

December 5, 1919, MS. of Thomas Litaker, as heard in Cabarrus County, N. C.
Cf. Odum, 1925, p. 252.

I wish my captain would go blind.
Would n't go to work till half-past nine.

16

A

Reported from Auburn, Ala., 1915–1916, MS. of R. E. Donis, as heard in Georgia.
Practically the same as in Lomax, 1917, p. 143, and Odum, 1926, p. 139.
Cf. also Odum, 1926, pp. 41, 202.

Some o' these mornings, and 't won't be long,
Capt'n gwine ter call me and I be gone.

B

Reported from Durham, N. C., 1919, MS. of Howell J. Hatcher. "Heard sung by old negro working on father's farm."
Same as *A*, with "days" for "morning" and "You're" for "Capt'n."

17

Reported from Auburn, Ala., 1915–1916, MS. of J. G. Hall, as heard in a mining camp.

Captain, Captain, give me my time
Tired of workin' in damned old mine.
Miner, miner, you got no home here to-day,
To-morrow you will be gone.
Captain, Captain, can't you see
This pick and shovel is killing me?

18

REPORTED from Auburn, Ala., 1915–1916, MS. of J. H. Reynolds.
I have the same song, with slight verbal variations and without the last
two lines, from Auburn, Ala., 1915–1916, anonymously.
Cf. nos. 23 D and 24, in this chapter.

> Take my hammer,
> Carry it to my captain,
> Tell him I'm gone,
> Tell him I'm gone.
> If he ask you was I running,
> Tell him no,
> Tell him no.
> Tell him I was going across the Blue Ridge Mountains
> Walking slow, yes, walking slow.

19

REPORTED from Auburn, Ala., 1915–1916, MS. of C. C. Certain, as heard at
Jackson, Miss., in 1906. "Sung by construction gang."
Cf. Odum, 1925, pp. 257, 276.

> Me an' my pardner
> Picked through de mountain
> In twenty-one days,
> In twenty-one days.

20

REPORTED from Auburn, Ala., 1915–1916, MS. of C. C. Certain, as heard at
Jackson, Miss., in 1906. "Sung by construction gang."
Practically the same as Odum, 1911, and 1925, p. 258, and closely related
to Perrow, 1913, p. 172 (as from Mississippi, 1909, with music). Odum thinks
the singer killed his partner; my version and Perrow's suggest that work killed
him.

> I remember last summer,
> 'T was de month of June,
> My partner fell sprawling
> An' dey laid 'im in de tomb.
> Ain't dat 'nough, boys,
> To grieve my mind?

21

REPORTED from Auburn, Ala., 1915–1916, MS. of A. L. Holloway, as heard in
Monroe County, southern Alabama. "Sung at work time."

> I done called you
> And Captain done warned you,
> If you don't git up
> I'm goner jump in on you.

22

REPORTED from Auburn, Ala., 1915–1916, MS. of C. C. Certain, as heard at
Jackson, Miss., in 1906. "Sung by construction gang."
    Practically the same as Odum, 1925, p. 257. Cf. also Odum, 1925, p. 276.

> Me and my pardner done made a plot
> To take all de money de white folks got.
> Me and my pardner and two or three mo'
> We raised hell, boys, roun' de pay car do'.

23

A

JOHN HENRY [1]

REPORTED from Durham, N. C., December 16, 1919, MS. of W. L. Hampton.
"Heard from convicts working on a road near Bahama School, N. C., 1911."
    John Henry is the subject of both ballads and work songs. For three incomplete variants of the ballad, and note on John Henry, see V, nos. 1 ff.
    Cf. Odum, 1926, pp. 226, 230.

> Poor John Henry — *hic*
> Was a steel-driving man — *hic*,
> Old John Henry — *hic*
> Was a steel-driving man — *hic*.
> Drove that steel — *hic*,
> Steel would n't stand — *hic*.

---

[1] No local title given.

B

THIS OLD HAMMER [1]

Reported from Durham, N. C., 1919, MS. of Harvey Harward, as from Huntington, W. Va., 1910.

"This song had its origin in the Big Ben tunnel in West Virginia. John Henry was a laborer in this tunnel and became famous on account of the great amount of work he could do in one day. It is claimed he could do the work of six ordinary men in one day. He died while on duty, this giving rise to the thought that work killed him. The one stanza which was written is repeated over and over by laborers who sing it."

Cf. Perrow, 1913, p. 164 (as from Tennessee whites in 1905, Mississippi in 1909, Kentucky in 1912); H. C. Davis, *J. A. F. L.* (1914), XXVII, 249, lists it as a work song; Berlin, 1919 (Hampton Series, iv, 24), with music; Scarborough, 1925, p. 220 (as from Virginia), p. 219 (as from Virginia and Mississippi, the former to the tune of "Come Thou Fount of Every Blessing"); Odum, 1926, p. 236. In W. C. Handy's *Blues*, 1926, it is the only expression taken literally either from the ballads or songs about John Henry.

> This old hammer killed John Henry,
> But this old hammer won't kill me.

C

Reported from Auburn, Ala., 1915–1916, MS. of A. L. Holloway, as heard in Monroe County, southern Alabama. "Sung while driving posts."

> This ole hammer, mos' too heavy — *huh,*
> Killed John Henry, killed 'im dead — *huh.*

D

Reported from Auburn, Ala., 1915–1916, MS. of H. M. Kilpatrick, as heard in Pickens County, Ala. "Railroad work song." "Incomplete."

I have heard the same song, with minor variations, from another source in Alabama, 1915–1916.

Cf. nos. 18 and 24, in this chapter.

The tune is given in Appendix I, p. 409.

> This old hammer killed John Henry,
> But it can't kill me.
> Take this old hammer, take it to the Captain,
> Tell him I'm gone, babe, tell him I'm gone.
>
> If he asks you what wuz the matter,
> Tell him you don't know, babe,
> Tell him you don't know.
>
> If he asks you wuz I running,
> Tell him no, tell him no.

[1] Local title.

24

REPORTED from Durham, N. C., 1919, MS. of J. D. Johnson, Jr. "Heard sung by an old negro, who accompanied himself on the banjo, in a small town in eastern North Carolina."

I have substantially the same song from Marion, western North Carolina, 1919.

Burlin (Hampton Series, 1919, iv, 24) gives practically the same song, with the music, and a final stanza similar to no. 23 *B*.

Cf. Nos. 18 and 23 *B*.

The tune is given the same as no. 23 *D*, in Appendix I, p. 409.

> Ain't no hammer in this mountain,
> Ring like mine, babe, ring like mine.
> Take this hammer, give it to the walker,
> Tell him I'm gone, babe, tell him I'm gone.
> If he ax you, where's I'm gone to,
> Just tell him I'm gone, babe, tell him I'm gone.

25

REPORTED from Durham, N. C., 1919, MS. of Walter J. Miller.
Cf. Anna K. Odum, *J. A. F. L.* (1914), XXVII, 265.

> Dis here hammer won't ring;
> Throw it in the river, throw it in the river.
> Dis here old hammer is too heavy;
> Throw it in the river, throw it in the river.

26

REPORTED from Auburn, Ala., 1915–1916, MS. of C. C. Certain, as heard at Jackson, Miss., in 1906. "Sung by construction gang."

The tune is the same as that of no. 87, given in Appendix I, p. 410.

> Pick, I'll drive you,
> Pick, I'll drive you
> So low down.
> Pick, I'll drive you
> So low down.

27

REPORTED from Durham, N. C., 1915, MS. of N. I. White, as heard in Greensboro, N. C. "Sung by laborers laying a car track."

Cf. Odum, 1926, p. 107.

The tune is given in Appendix I, p. 410.

Put de dawgs on him. (*Solo by leader. Gang grapples a rail.*)
Put 'em on me. (*All, swinging the rail half-way into position.*)
Put 'em on me. (*All, with a drop in tone, swinging rail into final
    position.*)

(*Repeated with each rail handled.*)

28

REPORTED from Auburn, Ala., 1915–1916, MS. of W. S. Black, as heard at
Athens, Ala.

> Don't min' workin',
> Don't min' tryin',
> Don't min' workin' in hot sunshine.

29

REPORTED from Auburn, Ala., 1915–1916, MS. of C. C. Certain, as heard at
Jackson, Miss., in 1906. "Sung by construction gang."

Lor', de hotter de sun shine de better I feel.

30

REPORTED from Auburn, Ala., 1915–1916, MS. of C. C. Certain, as heard at
Jackson, Miss., in 1906. "Sung by construction gang."

> You gwine to kill yo' fool self a workin',
> Tryin' to work like me,
> Tryin' to work like me.
> You gwine to kill yo' fool self pickin',
> Tryin' to pick like me,
> Tryin' to pick like me.

31

REPORTED from Auburn, Ala., 1915–1916, MS. of J. P. Creel, as heard in Jefferson County, Ala.

"Sung by Negroes while they were sliding track on the railroad. Sometimes
there were as many as fifty men at work in one group. Each man had to lift at
the same time in order to move the track, and this song was used as a means of
keeping the men together. They would give two short taps with their bars and
then lift. The lifting and tapping was just like keeping time in marching or
singing."

Cf. Odum, 1925, p. 262, for the first two lines.

Jack the rabbit! Jack the bear!
Can't you line him just a hair,
Just a hair, just a hair?
Annie Weaver and her daughter
Ran a boarding house on the water.
She's got chicken, she's got ham,
She's got everything I'll be damned.
Old Joe Logan he's gone north
To get the money for to pay us off.

32

REPORTED from Auburn, Ala., 1915–1916, MS. of C. C. Certain, as heard at Jackson, Miss., in 1906. "Sung by construction gang."

June, July, and August,
June, July, and August,
De three hottest months I know.
I can't hold 'em,
I can't hold 'em.
Captain, how in hell can you?
How in hell can you?

33

REPORTED from Durham, N. C., 1919, MS. of E. C. Lovell. "Heard sung by road gang, Memphis, Tenn., 1915."
Cf. II, no. 61.

De road is rocky, Lord,
But it won't be rocky long.

34

REPORTED from Auburn, Ala., 1915–1916, MS. of C. C. Certain, as heard in Jackson, Miss., in 1906. "Sung by construction gang."

Water-boy, water-boy,
Bring de water roun';
If yo' don't like yo' job,
Set de bucket down.

35

REPORTED from Auburn, Ala., anonymously.

Water Jack! you oughter been here and half-way back.

36

REPORTED from Auburn, Ala., 1915–1916, MS. of T. M. Brannon, as heard in Barbour County, Ala. "Sung by Negroes digging ditches."

> I been hammering — *huh*
> All over Georgia — *huh*
> Alabama too — *huh*
> Alabama too — *huh*.
>
> (*Repeat*)

37

REPORTED from Auburn, Ala., 1915–1916, MS. of F. Mitchell, as heard in southeastern Alabama. "Sung by Negro wood cutters and is wood cutters' song."

> Hey, Bull and Ben tally — *wham!*
> How long, how long — *wham!*
> Fo' the sun goes down — *wham!*
> Poor boy cryin', all day long — *wham!*
> Can't heah no train — *wham!*
>
> Can't heah no whistle blow — *wham!*
> All I can heh — *wham!*
> The Boss man say — *wham!*
> "Let the chips fly " — *wham!*

38

REPORTED from South Carolina, 1919, MS. of J. R. Davis. "Heard by J. R. D. from a Negro who was serving a term on the Public Works."

> Oh let the sun go down — *hunk,*
> And we'll get rest — *hunk.*
> Oh let the sun go down — *hunk*
> And we'll be blest.

39

REPORTED from Auburn, Ala., 1915–1916, MS. of C. C. Certain, as heard from Jackson, Miss., in 1906. "Sung by construction gang."

When you git lazy and want ter lay off,
You have a little talk with the walking boss.

40

REPORTED from Durham, N. C., 1919, MS. of J. G. Neal. "From Marion, a small town in the western part of North Carolina."

Working on the railroad
Ten cents a day,
   Working to get my babe some shoes.
Hopes I get my full
Week's pay,
   And don't spend it for liquor or booze.

41

REPORTED from Durham, 1919, MS. of Walter J. Miller.

Working on the railroad at forty cents a day,
If you don't work your time out, you don't get your pay.
Working on the railroad at forty cents a day,
You can make more money a-working in the hay.

42

REPORTED from Durham, N. C., 1919, MS. of Percy F. Dilling. "Heard sung by Negroes at work in King's Mountain brick yard (Cleveland County, N. C.)"

Takes two thousan' brick to top this kiln,
Pay day is Sat'day, then I drink my fill.

43

REPORTED from Durham, N. C., 1919, MS. of Percy F. Dilling. "Sung by road gang at King's Mountain, Cleveland County, N. C."

So long, nigger, so long I say.
You don' get none of my money till nex' pay day.

44

<small>REPORTED</small> from Auburn, Ala., 1915–1916, MS. of Childree, as heard in Russelville, Ala. "last year."

The last stanza of "Get Up in the Morning," as given in *Ethiopian Serenaders*, 1857(?), p. 207, runs:

> Sal one day she gave a sigh,
> Her mouth would hold a pumpkin pie,
> A bushel of potatoes, two quarts of gin;
> She gaped one day and her head fell in.

Cf. also, *Ibid.*, p. 147, the last stanza of "The Gal from the South."

> As I was goin' down de street,
> Met my black Sally Sweet.
> She backed her ears fur to make me grin,
> Her mouth flew open and her head fell in.

45

<small>REPORTED</small> from Auburn, Ala., 1915–1916, MS. of C. C. Certain as heard at Jackson, Miss., 1906. "Sung by construction gang."

This song is an outgrowth of the old Skewbald ballad, originally Irish. For its history and an 1822 English broadside version, see Scarborough, 1925, pp. 61–64. Miss Scarborough quotes John Mason Brown's Negro version (*Lippincott's Mag.*, Dec., 1868) and cites Perrow (1915, p. 134) as from Mississippi in 1909.

Cf. also Odum, 1926, p. 133.

> I don't mind race riding,
> If 't wa'n't for my wife,
> Old Skubald might stumble
> And away goes my life.

46

<small>REPORTED</small> from Auburn, Ala., 1915–1916, MS. of C. C. Certain, as heard at Jackson, Miss., 1906. "Sung by construction gang."

> Dat ole black gal,
> Dat ole black gal
> Keeps on a-grumbling,
> Keeps on a-grumbling
> 'Bout a new pair o' shoes,
> 'Bout a new pair o' shoes.
> Foots on de ground!
> Foots on de ground!

47

REPORTED from Auburn, Ala., 1915–1916, MS. of E. D. Bartlett, as heard near Lineville, Ala. "Sung by railroad and mining gangs."
The first line shows the influence of "Casey Jones," and the whole will sing to the "Casey Jones" tune.

> Come all you rounders if you want to flirt;
> Yonder comes a yellow gal in a hobble skirt.
> You can hug her, you can kiss her, and do all you please
> But you can't get the hobble above her knees.

48

REPORTED from Auburn, Ala., 1915–1916, MS. of E. D. Bartlett, as heard near Lineville, Ala. "Sung by railroad and mining gangs."

> I've got a woman and a sweetheart too,
> My woman don't love me but my sweetheart do.

49

REPORTED from Auburn, Ala., 1915–1916, MS. of J. W. Persons. "Sung by railroad crews."
Cf. no. 61, in this chapter and X, no. 9.

> It takes gravel and rock to make a solid road,
> But it takes a chocolate baby to satisfy my soul.
>
> I'm going to build me a railroad from Birmingham to Rome,[1]
> Ain't nobody going to ride but a chocolate baby to the bone.

50

REPORTED from Auburn, Ala., 1915–1916, MS. of J. P. Creel, as heard in Jefferson County, Ala. "Sung by Negroes who were shoveling dirt into cars on L. & N. construction cuts."
Cf. Odum, 1926, p. 37.

> I woke up early dis mornin',
> I could n't keep from cryin',
> Oh! Lawd.
>
> I'se a gwine down de road 'fore long
> To see dat brown-skinned Tommie o' mine.

[1] Probably Rome, Ga.

51

REPORTED from Auburn, Ala., 1915–1916, MS. of J. L. Pitts, as heard in central Alabama. "Sung about depot."

> I waked up this morning
> With the same thing on my mind,
> Thinking about my high brown
> Down on the Seaboard line.[1]

52

REPORTED from Auburn, Ala., 1915–1916, MS. of C. C. Certain, as heard at Jackson, Miss., in 1906. "Sung by construction gang."

> I'll a'knowledge, Honey, I done wrong,
> I'll a'knowledge, Honey, I done wrong.
> Come, 'oman let's live right.
> Come, 'oman let's live right.

53

REPORTED from Auburn, Ala., 1915–1916, MS. of L. A. Nall, as heard in New Orleans. "Sung by street car track-layers (Negro)."

De rooster crowed in Paris and de hen she laughed in France,
De old gals ob dis town won't gib me a chance.

54

REPORTED from Auburn, Ala., 1915–1916, MS. of E. D. Bartlett, as heard in Tallapoosa County, Ala. "Sung by gang on public road."

> Rooster crows for midnight,
> Rooster crows for day,
> Wish to God there'd come a wind
> And blow that chicken away.
> Rooster crows for midnight,
> Rooster crows for day,
> Niggers with another man's wife,
> You had better get away.

[1] That is, the Seaboard Air Line Railroad.

55

REPORTED from Auburn, Ala., 1915–1916, MS. of L. A. Nall, as heard in New Orleans. "By track layers."

> If you in love and yo' girl don't treat you right,
> Pick up a big stick and hit her all yo' might.

56

REPORTED from Auburn, Ala., 1915–1916, MS. of E. D. Bartlett, as heard in Birmingham, Ala. "Sung by mining Negroes."

> Going to the race track
> To see my pony run;
> If I win any money
> Gonna give Caldonia some.

57

REPORTED from Auburn, Ala., 1915–1916, MS. of J. E. Hillhouse, as heard in Georgia close to boundary of Alabama and Tennessee. "Sung by Negro convicts in mines."

This song smacks strongly of the ante-bellum minstrel books, but I have not seen it in print.

> Corn-shuck fiddle and a shoestring bow,
> Gal stuck a needle in her toe, by Joe.
> No matter where I go, I'll take Sal to the party-o-o,
> Take Sal to the company store, dress Sal up in calico.
> Oh! no matter where I go, I'll take Sal to the party-o-o.

58

REPORTED from Durham, N. C., 1919, MS. of J. R. Davis, as heard in South Carolina.

"Between each part of this song, this Negro would stop singing at the end of each sentence until the sound of his pick could be heard. This sound became a part of his song. It sounded like this:

> "I'se gwina leave here (*hunk*), etc."

> I'se gwina leave here, and I ain't coming back,
> I'se gwina carry my yellow gal on my back.

59

REPORTED from Auburn, Ala., 1915–1916, MS. of J. E. Hillhouse, as heard in northern Alabama. "Sung by driver in mine. Tune slow and drawn out."
"I'se gwine to a nation" is probably a diluted survival from the many references to "the wild-goose nation" in the old minstrels. Originally the reference was apparently to the newly developed slave territory of the southwest. Singers were often either "going to" or "just back from" the wild-goose nation.

I'se gwine to a nation, I'm goin' to ride the cannon ball,[1]
To free my woman from the prison wall.

60

REPORTED from Auburn, Ala., 1915–1916, MS. of E. D. Bartlett, as heard near Lineville, Ala. "Sung by railroad and mining gangs."
Cf. Handy, 1926, p. 27, where it is given as traditional in Florence, Ala.

Sal's got a meat skin laid away,
To grease that wooden leg, so they say,
To grease that wooden leg, so they say.

61

REPORTED from Auburn, Ala., 1915–1916, MS. of H. Carder, as heard "at T. C. I. Dolomite quarry at Ketona, Ala."
Cf. no. 49, in this chapter, and X, no. 9.

Takes rock and gravel
To make a solid road.
I love you woman but
Your husband is a man
I do despise.

62

REPORTED from Auburn, Ala., 1915–1916, MS. of E. D. Bartlett, as heard in Tallapoosa County, Ala. "Sung by gang on public road."
Cf. Scarborough, 1925, p. 35:

Ships in de ocean,
Rocks in de sea
Bone-headed woman, etc.

[1] A fast train.

I have the same, contributed anonymously from Auburn, Ala., 1915–1916. For a variant stanza, see X, no. 83.

> Rocks on the mountains,
> Fish in the sea.
> Good-looking woman
> Make a fool out of me.

63

REPORTED from Auburn, Ala., 1915–1916, MS. of C. C. Certain, as heard at Jackson, Miss., in 1906. "Sung by construction gang."

> I wrote a letter,
> "Honey, send me my clothes."
> And she wrote me
> She'd throw'd 'em en de road.

64

REPORTED from Auburn, Ala., 1915–1916, MS. of E. D. Bartlett, as heard at Birmingham, Ala. "Sung by mining Negroes."

> Gona get me a pistol with a shiny barrel,
> Gona kill the first fellow
> Fooling with my long-haired girl.

65

REPORTED from Auburn, Ala., 1915–1916, MS. of S. R. Huey, as heard in "mining camp near Birmingham."

> Honey, when I'se had youse,
> You wore tans;
> Now, the man dats got youse,
> You wears brogans.

66

REPORTED from Auburn, Ala., 1915–1916, MS. of E. D. Bartlett, as heard near Lineville, Ala. "Sung by railroad and mining gangs."

> If you don't believe I'll treat you right
> Let down your windows and blow out the light.

67

Reported from Auburn, Ala., 1915–1916, MS. of B. Y. Pennington, as heard at Andalusia, Ala. "Sung by Negro digging sewer ditch."

> I had er good woman
> But she took morphine and died.
> Oh! if your good woman leave you,
> Honey, don't you wear no black
> For you do bad
> Her ain't er comin' floatin' back.

68

Reported from Auburn, Ala., 1915–1916, MS. of E. D. Bartlett, as heard near Lineville, Ala. "Sung by railroad and mining gangs."

> The only thing I ever done wrong,
> I went to see my honey and stayed too long;
> The only thing I ever done right,
> I went to see my honey and stayed all night.

69

Reported from Auburn, Ala., 1915–1916, MS. of R. E. Donis, as heard in Georgia.

I have the first two lines, substantially the same, from Athens, Ala., 1915–1916.

Cf. Odum, 1925, pp. 221, 275.

> Thought I heard that K. C. whistle blow,
> She blowed like she never blowed before.
> Thought I heard that K. C. whistle blow,
> She blowed like my honey she's on board.

70

Reported from Auburn, Ala., 1915–1916, MS. of C. B. Crow, as heard at levee camp, Mississippi River, La.

> Dis ain't no lie, jes' a natchel fact,
> I lost my breeches on de railroad track.

71

REPORTED from Auburn, Ala., 1915–1916, MS. of E. Oliveira, as heard in New Orleans. "Sung by workmen (Negro) on railroad."

These are the opening lines of a song known all over the country. I have heard it sung by college and high school quartettes as early as 1908. Miss Scarborough (1925, p. 248) prints the full text of sixteen lines, with a note that an arrangement of the song was published in 1900 by Hinds, Noble, and Eldridge.

Cf. the following song.

I've been working on the railroad all the livelong day,
I've been working on the railroad just to pass the time away.

72

REPORTED from Auburn, Ala., 1915–1916, MS. of E. Oliveira, as heard in New Orleans.

Originally a part of the preceding, but given to me as complete. It is a variant of the last four lines of the version quoted by Miss Scarborough, 1925, p. 248.

Baltimore for its oysters,
Boston for its beans,
New York for its pretty girls,
But for niggers — New Orleans.

73

REPORTED from Durham, N. C., 1919, MS. of W. W. McDougle. "Sung by a gang of Negroes working on a railroad in Buncombe County (N. C.). They were not local Negroes. I think the railroad company brought them there from South Carolina and Georgia. They sang this song while they worked, repeating the same lines over and over again. The tune is very weird and sudden minors are characteristic."

The longest train I ever saw
Was on the Seaboard Air Line,
The engine pas' at a' ha' pas' one,
And the caboose went pas' at nine.

74

REPORTED from Auburn, Ala., 1915–1916, MS. of C. H. Adams.

The last line is common in the songs beginning "Don't you leave me here," and in "Alabama Bound" songs.

Cf. Odum, 1926, p. 147; Scarborough, 1925 (as from Mississippi), p. 239.

> If the train go leave me
> I got a mule to ride,
> I got a mule to ride.

75

REPORTED from Auburn, Ala., 1915–1916, MS. of J. W. Persons, as heard at Montgomery, Ala.

If the train breaks down, baby, I've got a mule to ride.

76

REPORTED from Auburn, Ala., 1915–1916, MS. of C. J. Perryman, as heard in northern Alabama. "Sung by section gang."
   I have the same songs from Birmingham, Ala.
   Printed by Niles, *New Republic*, 1926, p. 292; Handy, *Blues*, 1926, pp. 7, 34. Cf. XII, nos. 33, 34, 35.

> If der river wus whiskey an' I wus a duck,
> I'd dive to der bottom an' I'd neber come up.

77

REPORTED from Auburn, Ala., 1915–1916, MS. of J. G. Nall. "Sung by work-house crew."
   The first two lines are practically the same as in Odum, 1926, pp. 22, 24; Perrow, 1915, p. 190. Odum, 1926, p. 24, cites "Thirty days in jail and my back turned to the wall" as a line in a recent popular blues.

Laid in jail with my face turned to the wall;
Dirty black gal she caused it all.
Judge he fined me, the clerk he wrote it down;
Took me to the work house on the other side of town.
I'm worried now but I won't be worried long.

Bear down on that pick, nigger, and bring something up on that
   handle for your captain.

78

REPORTED from Auburn, Ala., 1915–1916, MS. of L. E. Jenkins, as heard at Edgewater, near Birmingham. "Sung by coal miners."
   I have the same song in four lines, without the last line below, from Auburn, Ala., 1915–1916, MS. of R. M. Beasly.
   With the first two lines, cf. Lomax, *Nation*, 1917, p. 144, and Scarborough, 1925, p. 164.

Standing on a corner smoking a cheap cigar,
Waiting for a freight to catch some car,
If the brakeman sees me
He'd throw me overboard.
"Where you going, young fellow?"
"I'm going down the road."
"O! you hobo."

79

REPORTED from Durham, N. C., 1919, MS. of Percy F. Dilling. "Heard sung
by Negroes working in brick yard at King's Mountain, Cleveland County,
N. C."

The nigger is happy,
His load off his back.
But when the policeman comes snoopin',
He's gotta ball the jack.[1]

80

REPORTED from Auburn, Ala., 1915–1916, MS. of C. J. Perryman, as heard in
northern Alabama. "Sung by section crew."

I got a bull-dog in my back yard,
When he barks he row [2] like thunder.

81

REPORTED from Auburn, Ala., 1915–1916, MS. of C. C. Certain, as heard at
Jackson, Miss., in 1906. "Sung by construction gang."

My buggy it needs greasing,
Git in de buggy, let's take a ride,
Git in de buggy, let's take a ride.

82

A

REPORTED from Auburn, Ala., 1915–1916, MS. of R. B. Ashe, as heard in
Alabama.

Cf. Perrow, 1915, p. 130 (one variant from East Tennessee whites in 1907
and two from Mississippi in 1909); Handy, 1926, p. 36. In these versions, however, the singer's demand is not for molasses, but "Just pickle my bones in

---

[1] That is, leave in a hurry. Literally, "ball the jack" is a particular dance.
[2] That is, roar.

alcohol." Talley, 1922, p. 26, agrees with my version. Cf. in this collection
XII, nos. 32, *A* and *B*.

The "when I die" motif is probably taken over from the spirituals. See note
to XII, no. 32 *A*.

> When I die, don't bury me deep,
> Put a jug of 'lasses at my feet,
> And a piece of corn bread in my hand,
> Gwine to sop my way to the promised land.

B

Reported from Durham, N. C., 1919, MS. of H. H. Hanchey, as heard "in
southeastern part of N. C."

The same as *A*, with very slight verbal differences.

C

Reported from Auburn, Ala., 1915–1916, MS. of W. D. Kimbrough, as heard in
Camden, Ala.

> When I die, bury me deep,
> Place a jug of 'lasses at my feet,
> Give me a few biscuits in my hand,
> And I'll sop my way to the promised land.

D

Reported from Durham, N. C., 1919, MS. of James E. Lyon, Jr., as heard at
High Point, N. C., 1916.

> When I die,
> Plant a water melun
> On my grave,
> An' let the juice come seepin' through.

E

Reported from Auburn, Ala., 1915–1916, MS. of L. A. Nall, as heard in New
Orleans. "Sung by track layers. Tune same as 'Jogo Blues.'"

> Cf. Handy, 1926, p. 36.

> If I die in de state of Arkunsaw,
> Ship my bones back to my mudder-in-law,
>
> but
>
> If I die in de state of Kentuckee,
> Just trow me in de ribber, let de fish make a meal of me.

83

REPORTED from Auburn, Ala., 1915–1916, MS. of E. D. Bartlett, as heard near Lineville, Ala. "Sung by railroad and mining gangs."

> I'll just swear and swear to damn,
> Everybody is doing it in Birmingham.

84

REPORTED from Durham, N. C., 1919, MS. of A. W. McDougle.

"I heard this song sung by a gang of Negroes working on a railroad in Buncombe County (N. C.). They were not local Negroes. I think the railroad company had brought them there from South Carolina and Georgia. They sang this song over and over again. The tune is very weird and sudden minors are characteristic."

> I'm goin' far away
> Where the tall trees grow,
> An' shiver when the cold wind blows,
> An' shiver when the cold wind blows.

85

REPORTED from Auburn, Ala., 1915–1916, MS. of B. Y. Pennington, as heard in Andalusia, Ala. "Sung by Negro ditch diggers."

> Well the funniest thing I ever seen,
> My daddy got drunk and walked to New Orleans.

86

REPORTED from Auburn, Ala., 1915–1916, MS. of B. Y. Pennington, as heard in Andalusia, Ala. "Sung by Negro ditch diggers."

> Well they took him up on the smoky road,
> But dey brought him back on de coolin' board.

87

REPORTED from Durham, N. C., MS. of N. I. White, as heard in Statesville, N. C., about 1908. "Heard sung by ditch diggers."

Scarborough, 1925, p. 151, gives the following, with music, as the opening lines of a Lynchburg, Va., version of "Shortnin' Bread":

> Run here, mammy, run here quick,
> Shortnin' bread done made me sick.

The tune is given in Appendix I, p. 410.

> Run here, Doctor — *huh,*
> Run here quick — *huh*;
> Little Mary — *huh*
> Swallowed a stick — *huh*.

88

REPORTED from Greensboro, N. C., in 1920, MS. of N. I. White, as sung by Mr. M. B. Tutt.

"Work song, sung by Negro laborers in Augusta, Ga. Judge Pequette, of the Recorder's Court, had a reputation among the Negroes for severity of sentences. His usual sentence was 'forty-five dollars fine or 90 days on the roads.'"

The tune is given in Appendix I, p. 410.

> Thought I heard — *huh!*
> Judge Pequette say — *huh!*
> Forty-five dol-lars — *huh!*
> Take him away — *huh!*

89

A

REPORTED from Auburn, Ala., 1915–1916, MS. of E. D. Bartlett, as heard near Lineville, Ala. "Sung by railroad and mining gangs."

The same as in Odum, 1926, p. 216. I have the same from W. M. Mobley (Alabama, 1915–1916); and from K. W. Litaker (North Carolina, 1919) as heard "sung by an old Negro when he was going to preaching."

> If you don't believe I'm sinking down,
> Look what a hole I'm in.

B

Reported from Auburn, Ala., 1915–1916, MS. of C. J. Perryman, as heard in northern Alabama. "Sung when sun is very hot, in saw-mill."

> If you don't believe I'm sinkin',
> Just look what a hole I'se in.
> I don't see no fiah
> But I sho' is burning down.

90

REPORTED from Auburn, Ala., 1915–1916, MS. of E. D. Bartlett, as heard near Lineville, Ala. "Sung by railroad and mining gangs." Cf. in this collection, X, no. 84; also IX, no. 49, and Scarborough, 1925, p. 236:

> Boat 's up de ribber an' she won't come down
> B'lieve to my soul she's water-boun';
>   Oh, my ragtime Liza Jane.

Handy, 1926, p. 3, quotes a blues stanza beginning: "O de Kate's up de river, Stack is in de ben'" with a note identifying the Kate and the Stack as two Mississippi River boats of twenty years ago, the Kate Adams and the Stackolee.

The boat is up the river and she won't come down,
She must be heavy loaded and water bound.

91

A SOUTHERN JACK [1]

REPORTED from Durham, N. C., 1919, MS. of W. T. Huckabee, Jr., as heard in Albermarle, N. C.

> I got a southern jack,[2]
> I got a southern jack;
> First thing I do, shovel in the coal,
> Next thing I do, watch the drivers roll.
> I got a southern jack,
> I got a southern jack;
> All aboard on the southern jack.

[1] Local title.
[2] An engine on the Southern Railway.

VIII

RURAL LABOR

THE songs of Negro workers in the field reveal the same qualities of boastfulness, the same reliance upon "a gal in de white folks' yard," the same desire to move on to another job, — to "wash my face an' eat my breakfast on another white man's place," — the same inconsequential utterances, that are characteristic of all the work songs; but the vicious qualities, particularly the preoccupation with "big-legged women," and "brown-skins," "long-haired women," and women who "got bad hair" are conspicuously absent in the songs which comprise this division in my collection.

The song that is timed to the work in hand is not so much needed as in gang labor, though the reaping song (no. 16) is apparently timed to the swing of the cradle. Domestic animals, particularly the mule, play a larger part, and so, naturally, does the weather. There is also an indication that some of the songs are older; four of them [1] have distinct ante-bellum touches. The songs smack more strongly of the country and stick more closely to the immediate milieu of the worker; for while the gang worker may have been once a country Negro, it does not happen so often that the rural worker may have been a construction-gang worker.

On the whole, the songs of the rural worker seem to be more decent and more conservative than those of the gang laborer.

SONGS, WITH ANNOTATIONS

The following songs classified with other groups might also be included in the present class: III, 13, 14; IV, 3 F; VI, 8, 23, 34, 43, 48; VII, 74; X, 46, 48, 57, 58, 67; XI, 4, 6–13; XII, 6, 19, 20, 26, 39; XIII, 2, 11–13; XIV, 5 C.

I

REPORTED from Durham, N. C., 1919, MS. of N. H. Hanchey, as heard about 1915. "Song sung by slaves when they went back to work after a rainy day. It was said to be a sign of dry weather to see a rabbit sitting in the fence corner."

An old song that has recently had its popularity revived by the radio and

---

[1] Nos. 1, 3, 17, 22.

phonograph. It was at the height of its popularity at the Democratic National Convention in New York in 1924.

Scarborough, 1923, pp. 286, 288, gives two variants, and, 1925, p. 107, a long composite version, with music, from Texas, as "another famous old dance-song, well known especially in Texas."

It ain't er gwine ter rain, it ain't er gwine ter rain,
It ain't er gwine ter rain no mo'; it rained last night an' de night befo'.
Rabbit settin' in de jamb ob de fence, it ain't er gwine ter rain no mo'.
He's settin' thar for de like ob sense, it ain't er gwine ter rain no mo'.

2

REPORTED from Durham, N. C., 1919, MS. of K. W. Litaker. "Heard in the cotton fields in Cabarrus County, N. C., within the last two years."

This song is apparently an off-shoot of various Judgement Day spirituals. Cf. Uncle Remus's song, "What you gwine do when de great day comes?" I remember hearing Negroes sing something like the following:

> What you gwine do when de world's on fire?
> Pra-a-ay for me!

I give it here rather than among the songs derived from spirituals because it illustrates the singing habits of rural workers.

The first line occurs in Odum, 1926, p. 195, as part of a spiritual used as a work song.

What you gwina do when the world's on fire?
I'm gona jump in a hole o' water.

What you gwina do when the water gets to boilin'?
I'm gona kick and squeal and hollo'.

3

REPORTED from Durham, N. C., 1919, MS. of K. W. Litaker. "Heard sung by Negro while shucking corn for my grandfather, in Cabarrus County, N. C., within the last two years. The Shankletown mentioned in this song is a Negro settlement about two miles from my home. It is a hangout for all the Negroes on Saturday night."

The chorus suggests somewhat vaguely a favorite old minstrel chorus found in "Lynchburg Town" (*Ethiopian Serenaders*, 1857[?], p. 80, and *Negro Singers' Own Book*, 1846[?], p. 157) and in "A Going Along Down" (*Negro Singers' Own Book*, 1846[?], p. 56). See note on IV, no. 33. Stanza 2 is given by Perrow, 1913, p. 128, as from Mississippi in 1909.

Sally went to preachin', she shouted and she squalled,
She got so full religion she tore her stocking heel.

Chorus

An a git a long home, nega, nega,
An a git a long home, nega, nega,
An a git a long home, nega, nega,
I'm bound for Shankletown.

Somebody done stole ma ol' coon dawg,
Wish I had 'im back.
Chased the big ones over the fence,
And the little ones through the cracks.

Chorus

I'm gona git some bricks, and build my chimny high,
To keep my neighbors' tomcats from wettin' out the fire.

Chorus

4

REPORTED from Auburn, Ala., 1915–1916, MS. of V. P. Carter, with no note as to where heard. "Sung as a field song."

If a horse had wool and a sheep had hair,
Automobile coming a-flying through the air,
Watermelons growing on huckleberry vine,
We would have snow in summer [time?].

5

REPORTED from Auburn, Ala., 1915–1916, MS. of T. B. Chambers, as heard in Giles County, Tenn. "Sung by farm hands."
As in Perrow, 1913, p. 170, quoted in no. 6, in this chapter.
Perrow, 1913, p. 127, quotes a variant (as from South Carolina in 1909). See in this collection VI, nos. 20 and 21, and notes. I have the same song from R. Chambers (1915–1916), also from Giles County, Tenn., as "sung by blacksmith and farm hands."

Rabbit on the log,
Got no rabbit dog,
Gonna shoot him with my pistol forty-four.

6

REPORTED from Auburn, Ala., 1915–1916, MS. of T. B. Chambers, as heard in Giles County, Tenn. "Sung by farm hands."

Possibly suggested by the preceding song. Cf. Perrow, 1913, p. 170, as from Mississippi:

> Chickens on my back and bloodhounds on my track,
> I've got to make it to my shanty, if I can.

> Rabbit on the log, got no rabbit dog,
> Shoot him with my pistol forty-four.

Chicken in de tree,
Nobody here but me,
Spozen I gets hungry to-day.

7

REPORTED from Auburn, Ala., 1915–1916, MS. of J. A. Peterson, as heard in Coosa County, Ala. "Sung by Negroes picking cotton."

Cf. Scarborough, 1925, p. 236:

> Me 'n' my baby an' my baby's frien'
> Can pick mo' cotton dan a cotton gin.

Me and my partner, partner Jack,
Can pick more cotton than a press can pack.

8

REPORTED from Auburn, Ala, 1915–1916, MS. of H. Caldwell, as heard in Jackson County, Ala. "Sung by Negro farm hand."

Oh dat ole mule,
He was a fool,
You could n't get a saddle,
Oh, you could n't get a saddle
On dat ole mule.

9

REPORTED from Auburn, Ala., 1915–1916, MS. of M. E. Bryant, as heard in Alabama. "Sung on farm."

These two lines combine elements from two stanzas quoted by Scarborough, 1925, pp. 171 (as from Texas), 185.

Jack's ole mule, Jack's ole mule,
I can't get der bridle on Jack's ole mule.

10

REPORTED from Durham, N. C., 1919, MS. of W. B. Jeffreys. "Heard . . .
around sawmills."
  I have the same song from W. L. Hampton, Durham, N. C., 1919, as sung
by a Negro farm hand; and from D. B. Newton, Durham, N. C., 1919, as heard
in Marlboro County, S. C. In the latter the third line is:

> Oh bud, bud, bud, oh, bud, oh bud.

For the last line, see note to IX, no. 4

> I won't go to preaching, ain't got no shoes.
> I can't get the bridle on the darned old mule,
> Oh, bud.

11

REPORTED from Auburn, Ala., 1915–1916, MS. of M. E. Bryant, as heard in
Alabama. "Sung on farm."
  Cf. "Run, Nigger, Run," IV, nos. 23 (*A–D*).

> Over der fence and through de pasture
> White man run, but de nigger run faster.

12

REPORTED from Auburn, Ala., 1915–1916, anonymously, as heard in Houston
County, Ala. "Sung by Negroes picking cotton."

> Nigger in de cotton patch picken' out cotton,
> Cotton in de boll an' de boll half rotten.

13

REPORTED from Durham, N. C., 1919, MS. of Howell J. Hatcher. "Heard sung
by an old Negro on father's farm."

> I've bin to the 'Bama and I just got back,
> I did n't bring no money but I brought the sack.

14

REPORTED from Durham, N. C., 1919, MS. of W. L. Hampton. "Heard from
a Negro farm hand in Durham County, N. C."

> Shut your mouth and hold your breath
> Until you faint and fall to death.

15

REPORTED from Auburn, Ala., 1915–1916, MS. of A. M. Kearly, with no note as to where heard.

Practically the same as in Perrow, 1915, p. 140 (as from Mississippi in 1909). Cf. in this collection, XI, no. 9.

> The times are hard and money is sca'ce;
> Soon as I sell my cotton and corn
> I am bound to leave this place.

16

REPORTED from Auburn, Ala., 1915–1916, MS. of J. P. Creel, as heard in Georgia. "Sung by Negroes while they were cutting wheat; swing of cradle furnished time for song. Repeated for hours at a time."

The "O! Alle! O!" may be either a yodel or a simple "call," both of which I have heard from Negro field-workers.

> Watch me whet my cradle, O! Alle! O!
> I'll make it beat de beater, O! Alle! O!
> Watch me throw my cradle, O! Alle! O!
> I'se been all over Georgia, O! Alle! O!
> I nebber saw but one man, O! Alle! O!
> Who could cut it better'n I can, O! Alle! O!
> Watch'er lie before me, O! Alle! O!
> Come on my binder, O! Alle! O!
> Watch de bundles behind her, O! Alle! O!
>
> De stormy clouds arising, O! Alle! O!
> De dinner'll soon be here, O! Alle! O!
> De rain it am a coming, O! Alle! O!
> Better save de grain, sah! O! Alle! O!

17

REPORTED from Auburn, Ala., 1915–1916, MS. of J. P. Creel, as heard in Georgia. "Sung by Negroes in fields."

This is a variant of "Dandy Jim of Caroline," a favorite with the antebellum minstrels. In the *Negro Singers' Own Book*, 1846(?), p. 210, it occurs as follows:

> Dar's dandy niggas in each place,
> Wid beefsteak lips dat work wid grace,
> But none among de gals can shine
> Like Dandy Jim ob Caroline.

Refrain

All de colored virgins tell me, Oh!
I'se de best-lookin' nigger in de country, Oh!
I looked in de glass and found it so
Just as de virgins tell me, Oh!

I'se de handsomest nigger in de county, O,
For my master's told me so.
Among dem niggers I'se bound to shine
Case I'se Dandy Jim from de Caroline.

Dem Georgia niggers cannot shine
Case dey heels stick out away behind,
Ha! Ha! Ha! I'se bound to shine
Case I'se Dandy Jim from Caroline.

18

REPORTED from Auburn, Ala., 1915–1916, MS. of S. J. Nadler, as heard in southern Alabama. "Sung by farm hands."

Som' ob dese mo'nin's I'm gwaine a git up an' wash my face,
An' eat my breakfast on another white man's place.

19

REPORTED from Auburn, Ala., 1915–1916, MS. of S. J. Nadler, as heard in northern Alabama. "Sung on a farm by wood-cutters."

I wen' up a persimmon
And come down a pine,
And I split my breeches
Right square behind.

20

REPORTED from Auburn, Ala., 1915–1916, MS. of J. E. Hillhouse, as heard in southern Alabama. "Sung in the fields."
The latter part of this song seems to have some faint connections with the spirituals and their degenerate off-shoots.

If you don't let my brown-skin babe alone,
I'se gwine to start me a grave-yard of my own.
Sticks and stones gwine to break yo' bones,
You can talk about me when I'se gone,
But I'se goin' to live in the harvest anyhow till I die.

21

REPORTED from Auburn, Ala., 1915–1916, MS. of J. E. Hillhouse, as heard in southern Alabama. "Heard in fields."

Professor Kittredge informs me that this was a popular song among white children in Boston about 1865, with "Walking on the railroad track" for line 3.

> Mary Mack is dressed in black,
> Silver buttons all down her back,
> O-o-oh! babe.

22

REPORTED from Auburn, Ala., 1915–1916, MS. of J. E. Hillhouse, as heard "in Georgia fields."

I feel almost certain that I have seen old massa's story house, sixteen stories high, in the old minstrel books, but cannot cite the passage. It does occur in "Karo Song" (Scarborough, 1925, p. 171, as from Texas), which contains several old stanzas; and in the *Literary Digest*, 1916, p. 1558, as stanza 2 of the ante-bellum "Massa bought a Yaller Gal," from northern South Carolina, 1876–1886. The phrase suggests to me why it is that "The train she rode" is always "sixteen coaches long." Drinking the river dry is only one of the bizarre achievements of Jim Crow in the ante-bellum minstrel books, long before Paul Bunyan was exploited.

Cf. Scarborough, 1925, p. 126, for a version of Jim Crow, containing this and other boasts.

> Old master had a story house, sixteen stories high,
> A'n dat house was filled with chicken pie.
> He sent me down to the river, I ain't goin' to tell you no lie,
> I took dat steamboat on my back and drunk dat river dry.

23

REPORTED from Auburn, Ala., 1915–1916, MS. of D. Q. McCord, as heard in southern Georgia. "Sung in the fields."

Cf. Scarborough, 1925, p. 171.

> Ole master had a little grey mule,
> An' he bought him on Christmas Day,
> An' de very fust word dat scound'l beast said,
> Was "I wants a little oats and hay."
> Oh Lord, you oughter hear him moan,
> Lord, I wish I had a let him alone.

24

REPORTED from Auburn, Ala., 1915–1916, MS. of J. W. McKinstry, as heard in eastern Mississippi. "Sung by Negroes in the field."

On a Monday bright and fair the hearse came rolling by,
Six white horses side by side to bear me to my tomb.
And a certain little house on Twenty-Fourth Street,
I am going in and take my seat.
So throw me down my dirty clothes and valise
For I am going away and I am going to stay, never to return.

25

REPORTED from Auburn, Ala., 1915–1916, MS. of C. H. Adams.
In 1918 I heard this song sung by white boys from Richmond, Va., who said it was current there among both Negroes and white people.

I'd rather be in the cottonfield
Working hard,
Than be a buck-private in the
National Guard.

IX

GENERAL AND MISCELLANEOUS LABOR

NEGRO work songs are in general very much alike, whether sung by gang laborers, or by individual laborers on the docks, in saw-mills, in the garage, or on the farm. So far as the structure of the song is concerned, no useful purpose is to be served by dividing the work song into groups according to the nature of the labor that accompanies them. A work song originating from one type of labor quickly becomes assimilated to another type. However, the number of work songs in this collection is so large that their mere bulk seemed to make sub-division advisable; moreover, although the songs are interchangeable between various types of labor, there are some differences in the labor groups which are reflected in the sentiments which their songs express. For these reasons the songs used in general, miscellaneous occupations and those used in rural labor are placed in separate classes in this collection.

The function of the work songs used in both these groups is seldom the primary work song function of establishing a rhythm for the work in hand; yet it will be noticed that most of them are short and are so constructed as not to interfere with the rhythm of work. They are all capable of indefinite extension, either by repetition, or by the tacking-on of improvised stanzas or of well-known unrelated stanzas from other songs. Their function is primarily to keep the singer's thoughts from interfering with his work, to pacify his mind with the semblance of thought without yielding to any of the distractions which more serious thoughts would involve. Knitters, chewers of the cud, and some talkers are well acquainted with the physical and psychological value of similar processes.

Naturally, the thoughts expressed are of no particular individual weight. The first trivial thought that comes to mind finds an easy, unreflecting expression. But the psychoanalysts have taught us that the most spontaneous, unreflected thought is, after all, the most deeply significant when properly understood, that it is the key to the real self which we occupy our more conscious thoughts with dissembling. Susceptible as this principle is of grotesque distortion, it has an undoubted value in the understanding of Negro folk-song. The mass of Negro work songs shows the same large proportion of insignificant, momentary impression that exists but fails to find expression in less naïve people while they are in full control of their thoughts; but the majority of these songs are solidly based on what are subconsciously the real interests of the singer. These are, mainly, his work, his food, his woman, and his occasional restlessness. There is nothing peculiarly racial about any of these interests in the abstract, yet the Negro's thoughts on each of these fundamental interests of life are, after all, genuinely and naïvely Negro and thus highly significant of racial character.

The Negro of miscellaneous occupation does not sing about his work as often as the gang laborer does, nor does he sing, like Goethe, to one clear strain in divers tones. In one mood "a working man ain't nothing but a dog," and "Done and worked till my hands got sore — ain't goin' to work no more"; but the more cheerful mood is the dominant. "All the nigger's lookin' for is fat meat and sundown," both of which are confidently expected. "I don't bother work, work don't bother me"; "De Lord is good, your sins will be forgotten"; "De Lord will bless your good corn bread"; and, anyhow, "I'll get to heaven when I die." The gang laborer speaks more specifically about his work, but despite occasional dark moods, his reaction, also, as shown in the previous chapter, is predominantly cheerful.

This is not to say that the singer is not often restless. He does not need to feel that the present task is oppressive in order to desire a change. For the irresponsible laborer a change of employment is the principal means of obtaining the variety of life and experience which people less limited in opportunity secure in more regular ways. He has some reason to be, as he proclaims himself, "a winding ball." The travel he is so fond of talking about comes mainly when he decides to "eat breakfast in a bran'-new place." Sometimes, too, when "something gone wrong," the easiest solution is to "leave here jumping." He loves to be "goin' down the road." Very commonly he is "Alabama bound" on a mule, but that is merely a conventional particular expression of a general state of mind — he does not commonly travel on a mule nor does he show a special preference for Alabama except as a popular refrain. He travels on a train if he can. The train seized hold upon the Negro imagination in the mid-nineteenth century, when it was a "bullgine" on the minstrel stage, and it is still the folk Negro's symbol of romance. The "lonesome road" is more a figure of speech expressing something to be dreaded than something often encountered, for the folk Negro is too sociable ever to be lonesome long.

Food runs constantly in his mind. Generally it is his customary diet that he relishes in anticipation rather than the food that can be enjoyed in imagination only. "I got peas in de pot ten days old," "Make me a biscuit every hour," "Bile them cabbage down," "hoecake a bakin'," and collard greens from which "the grease runs down, babe," are all instinct with appetite, and are more representative than the determination to "eat beef-steak jus' as long as it las'," though that sentiment, too, expresses an authentic mood.

With the laborer at miscellaneous occupations, the thought of woman is connected with food (at least in utterance) more often than with the sex desire which predominates in the woman song of laborers whose utterance is less restricted by circumstance. His woman in the shanty, "bakes good collard greens," or is warned to turn her damper down and so avoid culinary and perhaps conjugal disaster. His trump-card, however, is the woman in the white folks' yard, who may or may not have been hired with the time-honored privilege of "totin'," but who always provides him with meat, lard, or a chicken wing, and sometimes maintains him out-right for periods when "white folks think I'm workin', I ain't doin' nothin'."

By their very nature, most of the songs in this group are of recent origin. Though many of them have surprisingly persisted for twenty or thirty years, there are few of older date. And yet the older songs have left some impress even here. Number 37 was sung to the tune of an old spiritual, and nos. 19, 29, and 55 are based mainly upon well-known spiritual lines. The "way down yonder" opening of no. 3 is at least as old as the earliest minstrels, and nos. 17, 26, and 36 are direct descendants of ante-bellum songs, the first two having easily recognizable ancestors in more than one of the old minstrel books.

SONGS, WITH ANNOTATIONS

The following songs classified with other groups might also be included in the present class: III, 14, 24 *D*; V, 1, 5, 8 *D*; VI, 2, 5, 6, 9, 22, 33, 36, 39, 40 *B*, 45, 51; VII, 7, 16 *B*, 23 *C*, 37, 42, 44, 51, 69, 79, 85, 86, 89 *B*, 90; X, 1–30, 40, 41, 46, 59, 61, 62, 64, 68–78; XI, 2, 3, 6–8; XII, 2, 3, 4, 8–13, 16, 21, 23, 25, 29, 30; XIII, 14; XIV, 10, 12, 13 *B*, 17, 18.

I

REPORTED from Auburn, Ala., 1915–1916, MS. of A. H. Williamson, as heard in Lowndes County, Ala.

> Well er workin' man
> Ain't nothin' but a dawg;
> Well er workin' man
> Ain't nothin' but a dawg.

Well I'm worried now,
Well I won't be worried long.
Well I'm worried now,
Well I won't be worried long.

2

REPORTED from Auburn, Ala., 1915–1916, MS. of W. S. Black, as heard at
Athens, Ala.

All the nigger is looking for is fat meat and sundown.

3

REPORTED from Durham, N. C., 1919, MS. of David T. House, Jr.
The "Way down yonder" opening is about as common as the "Some folks
say" and "As I was going" openings, from the ante-bellum minstrels to the
present time.

Way down yonder where the wind blows cold,
You can't make a dollar to save yo' soul.

4

REPORTED from Durham, N. C., 1919, MS. of David T. House, Jr.

I worked to-day, I worked mighty well,
I would n't work to-morrow if you'd ring your bell.

5

REPORTED from Durham, N. C., 1919, MS. of Jesse M. Livingston. "Heard
sung by Negroes working in saw-mill in Scotland County, N. C., 1918."
I have the same from Durham, N. C., 1919, MS. of D. B. Newton, as heard
in Scotland County, N. C.

Born in No'th Carlina,
Raised in Tennessee,
Worked like Hell in Georgia,
Died in Germinee.

6

REPORTED from Auburn, Ala., 1915–1916, MS. of W. S. Black, as heard in northern Alabama.

"I'm going back" and "I'm going away" are common expressions in work songs. Cf. Odum, 1925, pp. 178, 217; also Odum, 1926, pp. 38, 40, 43, 75, 85, 96, 112, 124.

> I am going back to Georgia
> Before long, Baby.

7

REPORTED from Durham, N. C., 1919, MS. of J. D. Johnson, Jr. "Heard from old Negro, who accompanied himself on the banjo, in a small town in eastern North Carolina."

This looks like an offshoot of "It Ain't Gwine Rain no Mo'," VIII, no. 1.

> I ain't a gonna work a no mo'!
> I ain't a gonna work a no mo'!
> Done an' work-ed 'til my hands got sore.
> I ain't a gonna work a no mo'!

8

REPORTED from Durham, N. C., 1919, MS. of W. T. Huckabee, Jr. "Heard . . . in the eastern part of North Carolina, while watching a gang of Negro boys who were in swimming."

Hugh Wiley used practically this same song in one of his "Wildcat" stories published originally in the *Saturday Evening Post*. This MS. antedates the story, I believe, by a month or two.

> I don't bother work and work don't bother me,
> I'm just as happy as a b-b-bumble bee.
> Eat when I can git it, sleep most all de time,
> I don't give a doggone if de sun don't never shine.

9

REPORTED from Durham, N. C., 1919, MS. of J. G. Neal. "From Marion, N. C."

> Wash those clothes, my honey child.
> Your old man's at the
> Wood pile.
> Work, my honey, work,
> Work, my honey child.

10

REPORTED from Durham, N. C., 1919, MS. of E. C. Lovell. "Heard sung by a gang unloading cotton from a river steamboat, Vicksburg, Miss., 1915."

> Roll dat bale, roll dat cotton,
> De Lord is good, your sins will be forgotten.

11

REPORTED from Durham, N. C., 1919, MS. of E. C. Lovell. "Heard sung by a gang unloading a river steamboat. New Orleans, La., 1915."

> Carry dat load on your head,
> De Lord will bless your good corn bread.

12

REPORTED from Auburn, Ala., 1915–1916, MS. of R. Langdon. "Sung by Negro block setter in sawmill."

The same as in Odum, 1926, p. 126, stanza 1 of "Turn Your Damper Down," with "Raise" for "H'ist" and "Turn" for "Tuck." In Handy, 1926, p. 3, it occurs in the typical "blues" form:

> When you see me comin' h'ist yo' window high,
> When you see me comin' h'ist yo' window high,
> When you see me goin' hang yo' head an' cry.

> When you see me coming
> H'ist [1] your window high,
> When you see me leaving
> Tuck your head and cry.

13

REPORTED from Auburn, Ala., 1915–1916, MS. of R. M. Beasley. "Sung by Negroes at dinner hour."

I can't explain Shakespeare's function as a trouble-maker or his appearance in town. Perhaps the line is suggested by the once-popular "Doctor Cook's in town." In the ante-bellum minstrel books the arrival "in town" of various people, from Jim Crow to Dickens, was frequently the starting-point of various stanzas of topical allusion.

---

[1] That is, hoist.

Good-bye, darling, I am leaving,
Won't you come and go with me?
Everybody got to take out after me.
Lord, I have so much trouble
When Shakespeare comes to town.

14

REPORTED from Durham, N. C., 1919, MS. of D. B. Newton. "Work song heard in Marlboro County, South Carolina."

The "gal" in Baltimore, Kalamazoo, and other places was the starting-point of many vaudeville stage verses in the early nineteen-hundreds. As a boy I heard Negroes singing many of these verses, the one about the "gal" in Kalamazoo being unprintable. The early minstrels sang of numerous "gals" with fanciful un-Negro names, but I think the present version probably arose not earlier than the eighteen-eighties, or nineties. A modified form of the stanza occurs in "Miss Mary Jane" (with music), Scarborough, 1925, p. 117, as from South Carolina. The song "I Got a Gal an' I can't Git Her (Odum, 1926, p. 147) may have started from these songs.

The refrain, "Oh bud," is found in several other songs in this collection (namely nos. 27 and 28, in this chapter and VIII, no. 10), but I do not think I have seen it elsewhere. I have been told by North Carolina Negroes that "bud" is really "Bud" the obscene hero of a number of work songs current thirty years ago, some of which were repeated to me.

I'se got a gal in Baltimo',
De street car runs right by her door.
Oh bud, bud, bud, oh, bud, oh bud.

15

REPORTED from Durham, N. C., 1919, MS. of D. B. Newton. "Work song heard in Scotland County, North Carolina."

I'se gwina save all of my nickles and dimes
To buy me a Mary Jane,
To buy me a Mary Jane.
I'se gwina save all of my nickels and dimes
To buy me a Mary Jane.

16

REPORTED from Durham, N. C., 1919, MS. of D. B. Newton. "Work song heard in Marlboro County, South Carolina."

I have the same song from John Bridgers as heard in Raleigh, N. C., in 1923. With the usual variations and without the "how long" refrain, it has become a common "blues" stanza.

Cf. Handy, 1926, p. 2.

I layed me head on de railroad track.
Me thought about me yaller gal, and me took it back.
Oh honey, how long?

17

REPORTED from Auburn, Ala., 1915–1916, MS. of D. G. Barnes, as heard in Dale
County, Ala. "Sung by laborers."
Slightly different variants of the first four lines occur in *Negro Singers' Own
Book*, 1846(?), p. 329; Perrow, 1913, p. 127; Scarborough, 1925, p. 110. In the
first it occurs as a stanza in "De Original Jim Crow, sung by the celebrated
Tom Rice," with the regular "Jim Crow" refrain. In Perrow it occurs as stanza
6 of "Hook and Line," as sung by Kentucky mountain whites in 1905, without
refrain; and in Scarborough it is given as stanza 2 of an old version of "Ole
Virginny Never Tire, attributed to Tom Rice," with the "Clare de Kitchen," or
"Ole Virginny Neber Tire" refrain.

> I went to de river,
> And I couldn't get across,
> I paid five dollars
> For an old blind hoss.
> I pushed him in
> And he could n't swim,
> And I give him Hell
> With a hickory limb.

18

REPORTED from Durham, N. C., 1919, MS. of R. S. Jones. "Heard sung by
Negroes in a laundry in Durham, N. C., about 1918."

> That's all right,
> I'll get to heaven when I die,
> That's all right.

19

REPORTED from Auburn, Ala., 1915–1916, MS. of E. Oliveira, as heard in New
Orleans. "Sung by Negro deck hand on a boat."
With the first two lines compare the spiritual, "What kind of shoes you goin'
to wear? Golden slippers," II, no. 53.

What kind of clothes do the angels wear, Ugh! Ugh!
What kind of clothes do the angels wear, Ugh! Ugh!
Oh, my —
With a heepy dog prune he runs like loon,

And looks a like a 'possum boiling in de pot.
Roolety, toot, toot, down by the chutes,
De hen lays an egg with her belly on the hay.
Listen to my same old tune.

20

REPORTED from Auburn, Ala., 1915–1916, MS. of R. Langdon. "Sung by Negro block setter in sawmill."

When I leave here jumping
There's something gone wrong.

21

REPORTED from Auburn, Ala., 1915–1916, MS. of R. Langdon. "Sung by Negro block setter in sawmill."

Well my home ain't here,
But it's further down the road.

22

REPORTED from Auburn, Ala., 1915–1916, MS. of R. Langdon. "Sung by two Negroes in lumber yard during rain."

Oh, well, it's raining here,
It's shore God gloomy on the sea.

23

REPORTED from Auburn, Ala., 1915–1916, MS. of A. L. Holloway, as heard in Monroe County, southern Alabama.

Starch my jumper and patch my overalls,
So if I miss de local I ken ketch de cannon ball.[1]

24

REPORTED from Durham, N. C., 1919, MS. of Thomas Litaker. "Heard sung by Negro on father's place. Cabarrus County, N. C."

Hikin' down the main line,
Gasoline burner don't stop here,
Don't stop here.

[1] A fast train.

25

REPORTED from Durham, N. C., 1919, MS. of D. B. Newton, as heard in Scotland County, N. C.

"Don't you leave me here," with its sequent "If you leave me here," along with "I've got a mule to ride" and "Alabama bound," are all extremely common.

Cf. nos. 46–48, in this chapter, XI, no. 14, XII, no. 31; also Lomax (*Nation*), 1917, p. 142; Scarborough, 1925, p. 239; Odum, 1926, p. 155.

> If you goes and leaves me here,
> I'se got a mule to ride,
> I'se got a mule to ride;
> And if you goes and leaves me here,
> I'se got a mule to ride.

26

REPORTED from Durham, N. C., 1919, MS. of Thomas Litaker, as heard in Cabarrus County, N. C.

Stanza 8 of "Hop Lite Loo," *Negro Singers' Own Book*, 1846(?), p. 14, concludes:

> Whenever de white folks go to bed,
> De devil is working in de nigger's head.
> Oh, hop lite Loo, etc.

Cf. also stanza 6 of "What's de Matter, Susey," in White's *New Illustrated Ethiopian* (n. d., probably early eighteen-fifties), p. 38:

> Ole folks and young folks you'd better go to bed,
> You only put de debble in de little nigger's head.

> Old folks better up and git to bed
> Before the young folks git the debil in der head.

27

REPORTED from Durham, N. C., 1919, MS. of D. B. Newton, as heard in Marlboro County, S. C.

For the last line, see note to no. 14, in this chapter.

> Git up in de mawning and kill dat calf.
> I'se gonna eat beefsteak jus' as long as it las'.
> Oh bud, bud, bud, oh bud, oh bud.

28

REPORTED from Durham, N. C., 1919, MS. of D. B. Newton, as heard in Marlboro County, S. C.

The first line is familiar and is, I think, old, but I can cite no previous publication. It appears to be a variant of the first line of "Keemo Kimo" (IV, no. 30).
This supposition is supported by the version given by Scarborough, 1925, p. 201,
as from Richmond, Va., beginning:

> Milk and de veal
> Six weeks old
> Mice and skippers
> Gettin' mighty bold!

For the last line, see note to no. 14.

> I got peas in de pot ten days ol',
> I could n't touch de bottom wid a ten-foot pole.
> Oh bud, bud, bud, oh bud, oh bud.

29

REPORTED from Durham, N. C., 1919, MS. of R. S. Jones. "Sung by Negroes
at work on city streets."

An offshoot of the various chariot spirituals. Odum, 1926, pp. 188–205, has
a chapter on "Workaday Religious Songs."

> We'll ride the chariot wheel,
> We'll ride the chariot wheel.
> We'll ride the chariot wheel,
> We'll ride the chariot wheel.

30

REPORTED from Durham, N. C., 1919, MS. of L. W. Israel. "Heard in western
North Carolina, sung by Negroes at work. The song goes on indefinitely. The
leader supplies the first word and all the rest is repetition."

Cf. Odum, 1926, chapter on "Songs of the Lonesome Road," pp. 35–46. The
nearest direct parallels in Odum are the lines "Look down dat lonesome road
an' cry" (p. 37), and "Going down dat lonesome road" (p. 46).

> Doan' go down that lonesome road,
> Weeping down that lonesome road,
> Weeping down that lonesome road.
>
> Doan' go down that lonesome road,
> Gambling down that lonesome road,
> Gambling down that lonesome road.

Doan' go down that lonesome road,
Crying down that lonesome road,
Crying down that lonesome road.

Doan' go down that lonesome road.

31

REPORTED from Durham, N. C., 1919, MS. of W. L. Hampton. "Heard from a Negro farm-hand in Durham County, N. C."

Riding of the sheep, and leading of the goat,[1]
I won't be back until the middle of the week.

32

REPORTED from Auburn, Ala., 1915–1916, anonymously.

A very common "blues" stanza that has been taken over into various other songs. See X, no. 83.

Cf. Scarborough, 1925, p. 276 (as from Texas), p. 277; and Handy, 1926, p. 34. In the "Hesitating Blues" (Handy, 1926, p. 95) a slight variation of these lines constitutes the only folk stanza.

Tell me how long will I have to wait,
Or will I have to do a little hesitate.

33

A

REPORTED from Auburn, Ala., 1915–1916, MS. of H. M. Kilpatrick, as heard in Pickens County, Ala. "Sung in corn field when under shade."

I have the first two lines, reported from Auburn, Ala., 1915–1916, MS. of T. H. Bonner, as heard in Clay County, Ala.

Practically the same as in Perrow, 1915, p. 135, as from Mississippi in 1909. A combination of elements from this song and the following is found in Scarborough, 1925, p. 235, as from Alabama:

Ain't no use o' my workin' so hard, darlin',
Ain't no use o' my workin' so hard, darlin';
I got a gal in de white folk's yard.
She kill a chicken
She bring me de wing;
Ain't I livin' on an easy thing,
Honey Babe?

Cf. also Odum, 1926, p. 145.

---

[1] This line is probably given here in reverse order.

Ain't no use in working so hard,
I got a woman in the white folk's yard,
She totes me meat, she totes me lard,
Ain't no use in working so hard.

B

Reported from Auburn, Ala., 1915–1916, MS. of O. C. Bryan, as heard on an Alabama farm.

I got a 'oman in de white folk's yard,
She give-er me meat and she give-er me lard.
Whenever dey kill a chicken, she give-er me de stuffin',
Ev'body thinks dat I is working, but I ain' doin' nothin'.

34

REPORTED from Auburn, Ala., 1915–1916, MS. of B. A. Wooten, as heard in Marengo County, Ala.
    The second stanza belongs to the John Henry songs. See V, nos. 1 ff., and VII, nos. 23 ff.

Buy me a ba'l of flour,
Make me a biscuit every hour,
En I'll keep my skillet greasy
If I kin.

Big old hammer kill John Henry,
    Kill John Henry.
Goin' to kill me, goin' to kill me,
    Goin' to kill me.

Mama tole me, papa showed me,
Hard labor — makes a man.

35

A

REPORTED from Auburn, Ala., 1915–1916, MS. of W. H. Blake, Jr., as heard in Sheffield, Ala. "Sung by Negro chopping cotton."
    "Turn yo' damper down" is a popular refrain and seems to have acquired a symbolic meaning of "go easy," "be careful." Cf. Odum, 1926, p. 126:

An' if you two-time me, daddy,
Turn yo' damper down.

If yo' bread is burning,
Turn yo' damper down;
If yo' bread is burning,
Turn yo' damper down.

B

Reported from Auburn, Ala., 1915–1916, anonymously, as heard in Atlanta, Ga. "Sung by a crowd of street pavement workers."

Oh Babe! I smell your bread a-burnin',
Turn your d-a-m-p-e-r d-o-w-n.

C

Reported from Auburn, Ala., 1915–1916, MS. of R. Langdon. "Sung by Negro block setter in sawmill."

When you smell yo' cabbage burnin',
Turn yo' damper down.

D

Reported from Auburn, Ala., 1915–1916, MS. of J. L. Pitts, as heard in central Alabama.

Come out of that kitchen,
Quit your hanging around.
I smell your cabbage scorching,
O, turn your damper down.

36

REPORTED from Auburn, Ala., 1915–1916, MS. of F. W. McMeans, as heard in Wolf Creek, Tenn.

This song and the next are fairly common and are of the same age, I feel sure. However, I can cite only Scarborough, 1925, pp. 124, 168. In the former it occurs, lacking the second line below, as the chorus of an ante-bellum dance song from Virginia. In the latter, an old song from South Carolina, the second line is present:

Boil dem cabbage down
An' tu'n 'em roun' an' roun'.
Stop dat foolin', little nigger gal,
An' boil dem cabbage down.

Stanza 1 of "Cooking Dinner" (Talley, 1922, p. 156) combines elements from this song and the following one, thus:

Bile dem cabbage down,
Turn dat hoecake 'round,
Cook it done an' brown.

Bile them cabbage down,
Stir them 'round and 'round.

37

REPORTED from Auburn, Ala., 1915–1916, MS. of J. B. Christian, as heard in Tallahassee, Fla. "Sung to the tune of 'I'll lay down my life for my Lord.'"

Bake dem biscuits, bake 'em brown,
Bake dem biscuits 'round and 'round.

38

REPORTED from Auburn, Ala., 1915–1916, MS. of R. Langdon. "Sung by Negro block-setter in sawmill."

If you think I'm goin' to
Put my head on that red hot stove,
You've done gone and lost yo' mind.

39

REPORTED from Durham, N. C., 1919, MS. of Walter J. Miller. "Heard several years ago."

Peas in the pot, hoecake a bakin',
Sally in de kitchen with her shift-tail a shakin'.

40

REPORTED from Auburn, Ala., 1915–1916, MS. of H. I. Killingsworth, as heard in southwest Georgia. "Sung by farm Negroes."

She cooks good cabbage,
But O dem collard greens!
The grease runs down, babe,
Just like de col' ice c-r-ream.

41

REPORTED from Auburn, Ala., 1915–1916, MS. of S. J. Nadler, as heard in southern Alabama. "Sung on a farm. Sung just before dinner."

This is properly a song of gang labor, practically the same as VII, no. 6, but is given here as showing the various uses to which a work song may be put.

> Cap'n, cap'n, yo' must be cross.
> Time fo' the w'is'le an' yo' won't knock off.

42

REPORTED from Auburn, Ala., 1915–1916, MS. of G. Clark, as heard in Crenshaw County, Ala. "Sung by Negro cook."

The first three lines were probably suggested by the gospel trains and gospel ships of the spirituals, whose passengers were customarily listed individually, a stanza at a time.

> Same train car'ed my papa,
> Brought my mamma, car'ed my sister
> Brought my brother.
> I looked out de winder and seed the train a coming.
> I stepped on board and de train kept a running.

43

LULU GAL [1]

REPORTED from Greensboro, N. C., 1915–1916, MS. of Mrs. J. J. W. Harriss, as heard in Guilford County, N. C. "Sung by washerwoman."

This seems to be related to the chorus of the old minstrel song, "Jawbone walk and Jawbone talk" as in Scarborough, 1925, p. 104:

> Lulu gal, Lulu gal, Lulu gal!
> Tie ma shoe, boy, tie ma shoe,
> Tie ma shoe, boy, tie ma shoe.

> Lulu gal, Lulu gal.
> Mama make Lulu 'have herself.

44

REPORTED from Durham, N. C., 1919, MS. of Jesse M. Livingston. "Heard sung by a Negro girl . . . while she was picking cotton."

> Pore ol' me, pore ol' me,
> Ev'ybody talkin' 'bout pore ol' me.

[1] Local title.

45

REPORTED from Auburn, Ala., 1915–1916, MS. of B. Y. Pennington, as heard in Andalusia, Ala. "Sung by Negroes working on courthouse."
An example of the song from the feminine point of view sung by men, rather uncommon before the advent of the blues.

> I'm goin' to der co'thouse,
> I'm goin' to der co'thouse,
> Wid er thousand skillets in my hand.
> I'm gonna walk right up to der Judge
> And tell 'em gimme back my do-right man.

46

REPORTED from Auburn, Ala., 1915–1916, MS. of H. I. Killingsworth, as heard in southwestern Georgia.
Cf. nos. 47 to 53, in this chapter, and XI, no. 14.

> If de train goes and leaves me here,
> I got a mule to ride, I'm Alabama bound.

47

REPORTED from Auburn, Ala., 1915–1916, MS. of W. M. Mobley, as heard in Birmingham, Ala.
The first line is extremely common as a refrain, also the first stanza. See XI, no. 14 and note. The second stanza, with variations of the last line, is also common. See note on VII, no. 90, also X, no. 89, and no. 49, in this chapter.

> I'm Alabama bound,
> I'm Alabama bound.
> Ef de train don't run,
> I got a mule to ride,
> Fur I'm Alabama bound.
>
> De boat's up de ribber
> An' she won't come down.
> I b'lieve to ma soul
> She's Alabama bound.

48

REPORTED from Auburn, Ala., 1915–1916, MS. of P. W. Pitts. "Sung in cotton fields around a railroad."

For the first two lines, see XI, no. 14, XII, no. 31 and note. With lines 3 and 4, cf. Odum, 1926, pp. 42 and 98.

I'm Alabama bound,
If de train don't run, I am got a mule to ride;
My home ain't yere,
It's further down de road.
If you catch me getting sober,
Make me drunk again;
I'm a winding ball, and
Don't deny my name.

49

REPORTED from Auburn, Ala., 1915–1916, MS. of J. W. Persons. "Sung on Tennessee River by deck hands."

Stanza 1 is practically the same as in VII, no. 90, X, no. 84, and no. 47, in this chapter.

The boat's up the river
And she won't come down;
I believe to my soul
She must be water bound.

The boat's up the river
And she won't come down;
One-long-lonesome-blow
And she's Alabama bound.

50

REPORTED from Auburn, Ala., 1915–1916, MS. of W. V. Wellons.
Cf. X, no. 4 and XI, no. 14.

She is a long tall yellow gal,
She wears a Mary Jane,
She wears a Mary Jane.
If that train don't leave dat rail
I am Alabama bound.

51

REPORTED from Auburn, Ala., 1915–1916, MS. of P. W. Pelts.

Preacher in a pulpit,
Jumping up and down,
Negroes in the cornfield,
Shouting, "I'm Alabama bound."

52

REPORTED from Auburn, Ala., 1915–1916, MS. of E. Oliveira, as heard in New
Orleans. "Sung by deck hand."
The first line comes from the common type of songs about women, in which
a good-looking woman, a blondy woman, a brunette woman, etc., "make a
preacher lay his Bible down." Cf. X, nos. 1–11.

De preacher in de pulpit put his bible down,
And all the niggers in the cotton field shouted,
"I'm Alabama bound."

53

REPORTED from Auburn, Ala., 1915–1916, MS. of R. R. Beard, as heard in
Baldwin County, Ala. "Sung by Negro cook."
Many of the Negroes who migrated to the North in the years following the
outbreak of the World War returned to the South after a brief stay. This seems
to be the Odyssey of a returned wanderer from Hackensack, N. J.

Las' year I was from Rack-in-sack,
An' dis year I'se er rack-en-back.

54

REPORTED from Auburn, Ala., 1915–1916, MS. of R. E. Donis, as heard in
Georgia.

I got up this morning and I wash my face,
Goin' to eat breakfast in a bran' new place.

55

REPORTED from Auburn, Ala., 1915–1916, MS. of W. C. Sills, as heard in Wilcox
County, Ala.
Cf. Kennedy, 1925, p. 40, as from Louisiana:

Down in the valley,
In the valley on my knees.

Cf. also XIII, no. 40.

Down in the hollow 'pon my knees,
Prayin' to the Lord to send me cheese.

56

REPORTED from Auburn, Ala., 1915–1916, MS. of W. V. Wellons.
Cf. X, nos. 54, 82.

I went up on de mountain to see de *sun* go down.

57

REPORTED from Auburn, Ala., 1915–1916, MS. of B. A. Wooten, as heard in
Marengo County, Ala.
For a variant of the first two lines, cf. Odum, 1926, p. 93.

If I live and don't get killed,
Make my home in Thomasville,
And I'm now one thousand miles from my home.

58

REPORTED from Auburn, Ala., 1915–1916, MS. of C. A. Ashcraft, as heard in
Florence, Ala. "Sung at a fertilizer plant."

If yo' house ketch on fire
And they ain't no water 'roun',
Pitch yo' trunk out the window,
Let the whole damn row burn down.

59

REPORTED from Auburn, Ala., 1915–1916, MS. of A. H. Williamson, as heard in
Lowndes County, Ala.

If I had it you could get it
For fifty dollars every minute,
But I'm all in, down an' out.
If I ever get my han' on er dollar ergin
I'm gwine ter hol' to it, I gwine ter hol' to it,
Just because I'm all in, down an' out.

60

REPORTED from Durham, N. C., 1919, MS. of Howell J. Hatcher. "Heard sung by old Negro on father's farm."

You've been talking 'bout you coming, you going, you *gwine*.
Why don't you go on and hush your lying.

X

SONGS ABOUT WOMEN

THE songs in which the Negro sings about women come from all sources — from the mine, the construction gang, the jail, the dance, the minstrel show, the farm, the levee, even sometimes from the popular songs of the white man. Wherever the Negro is at work on a task which allows his mind to wander, — and most of his tasks are of this description, — it wanders sooner or later to his woman. Most commonly these songs are sung by gang laborers with whom most of the coarser songs originate. To-day they enter into quite a considerable part of the "blues," which Mr. Handy says originated in low dives, but which certainly served the ends of labor before they came upon the vaudeville stage, and thence again to the laborer through the phonograph. They had little place, however, on the mid-nineteenth century minstrel stage, where the songs about women were of so decidedly different a character that one is forced to conclude either that the Negro has changed his psychological nature since 1850, or (what we know from other evidence to be the case) that the early minstrel songs were almost purely Caucasian.

Although the great mass of Negro songs about women are of recent origin, a few are degenerate descendants of the old minstrel stage. The "yaller gal" of grotesque appearance (no. 33), who was brought from the south by "ol' Massa," was a contemporary, and probably a near relative of "Darling Nelly Gray." Unfortunately endowed by nature to begin with, both her character and her appearance have suffered in the tradition of the song. Some of her physical defects have been inherited direct from the black-face minstrels by the "yaller gal" or "black gal" whom the modern singer "would n't marry" (no. 317). It was on a minstrel stage of the eighteen-forties or fifties that the singer first "went down to Sally's house" (no. 65). The "sho-fly lady" (no. 59) probably belongs to the same period. One song in this group, no. 61, is composed of stanzas from two different songs of the old minstrels. And a very common motive in number of modern songs — the comparison of three women — probably originated [1] in the similar comparison of three animals by the old minstrels.

[1] See no. 16, in this chapter.

Probably there are other bits of traditional influence, but undoubtedly most of the songs are of recent origin. Many of them, obviously, are of quite trivial inception; and yet an apparently trivial song, born to-day to die to-morrow, often shows a surprising vitality and geographical range, as the notes to some of them will show, while some, like number 61, are not at all the modern extemporisings they appear to be. Nevertheless, what we know of the trivial songs sung by the slaves makes it quite apparent that their thoughts of women, at least as expressed in their songs, are not those expressed by most of the songs sung to-day.

It is in his songs about women that the modern folk Negro reveals the most unpleasing side of his nature. What slight traces of deference and affection are shown by a few songs, such as number 85, are obscured by the dominant tone of brutal selfishness. The romantic love of the poets is not for him. Love is always an appetite, almost never an abstraction. His attitude toward woman is cynical and utilitarian. She is useful in bringing him food; he expects little constancy in her and apparently finds little. Certainly he himself makes no bones about deserting or beating a woman. Sometimes the songs show pride in the possession of a woman, or admiration for her physical qualities or her ability as a "provider." Very rarely indeed do they show a real or genuine affection. On the contrary, between a third and a fourth of the songs in my collection that would normally fall into this group are unprintable, as crude and filthy as brutal tastes could make them.

It is to be realized, of course, that the low-class laborer, of whatever race or nationality, is not habitually delicate either in his sentiment or in his language. Stating the plain truth about these songs is not an effort to ticket the Negro laborer as a peculiar moral leper. The same men who sing these songs also sing the spirituals, sometimes even as they work. I have never heard of a Negro laborer bringing white women into such songs, as I have read poems by one or two well-known Negro poets on illicit relations with white women. Sailors, cowboys, and lumbermen of the white race are equally obscene in some of the songs they sing. It is not to be assumed that a lack of finesse in talking of animal passions is more indicative of moral decadence than a highly sophisticated deftness in discussing the same feelings. And yet, after all legitimate palliation is admitted, it is hardly to be denied that the Negro's song about his woman constitutes a most unflattering exhibit.

SONGS, WITH ANNOTATIONS

The following songs classified with other groups might also be included in the present class: IV, 20, 28; V, 10, 27; VII, 45–69; VIII, 20, 21; IX, 12–16, 32–40, 50; XI, 14; XII, 23, 30, 45; XIV, 1, 3, 5 *A*, 9–11, 14, 21.

I

REPORTED from Auburn, Ala., 1915–1916, MS. of R. Langdon. "Sung by Negro block-setter in sawmill."

In songs of this type the same amazing powers are attributed to the good-lockin' woman, the yaller gal, the black gal, the blondy woman, the brunette woman, the black-headed woman, the red-headed woman, the dark-skin baby, the long, lean lanky gal, and the long tall, yaller gal. In other collections I find only two of the strong effects described in this song and those following; namely, the bull-dog breaking his chain (Perrow, 1915, p. 190, as from Mississippi in 1909; Scarborough, 1925, p. 278, as from Texas), and the preacher laying his bible down (Scarborough, 1925, p. 278, as from Texas).

Stanzas of this type were commonly sung in the earlier blues; among the later blues several of these stanzas are to be found in "Saint Louis Blues," Handy, 1926, p. 74.

> A good-looking woman make a rabbit
> Move his family to town.

2

REPORTED from Auburn, Ala., 1915–1916, MS. of W. C. S lls, as heard in Wilcox County, Ala.

> A good-looking woman
> Will make a bull dog join the church.

3

REPORTED from Auburn, Ala., 1915–1916, MS. of R. Langdon. "Sung by Negro block-setter in a sawmill."

I have the same song from Ozark, Ala., about a good-looking woman of still greater potency, who makes the bull dog *chew* his chain.

Cf. Perrow, 1915, p. 190 (as from Mississippi in 1909) and Scarborough, 1925, p. 278 (as from Texas) in both of which it is the brown-skin woman who makes the bulldog break his chain. The preference for the brown-skin shown in the songs of Perrow and Miss Scarborough is also shown in Odum, 1926, where the chapter on "Man's Song of Woman" (pp. 135–152) shows a decided majority for the brown.

> A good-looking woman
> Make a bull-dog break his chain.

4

REPORTED from Auburn, Ala., 1915–1916, MS. of B. Y. Pennington, as heard in
Andalusia, Ala. "Sung by Negro ditch diggers."

This song and the following constitute a link between the comparison of
three women (see nos. 15 ff., in this chapter) and the preceding bizarre tributes
to one.

Oh! er yaller gal'll make er houn' dog quit his trail,
But er black gal'll make er tadpole hug a whale.

5

REPORTED from Auburn, Ala., 1915–1916, anonymously.

A blondy woman, a blondy woman
Make a po' man go to jail,
But a brunette woman will make
A tadpole fight a whale.

6

REPORTED from Auburn, Ala., 1915–1916, MS. of J. L. Pitts, as heard in central
Alabama. "Sung by working Negroes. Tune: 'Nigger Blues.'"

O, a brunette woman
Will drive a good man insane,
O, a brunette woman
Will drive a good man insane;
But a blond woman
Will make a bulldog break his chain.

7

REPORTED from Auburn, Ala., 1915–1916, MS. of H. C. Kilpatrick.

Oh, a black-headed woman
Make a tadpole hug a whale,
But a red-headed woman
Send a po' man straight to jail.

8

REPORTED from Auburn, Ala., 1915–1916, MS. of J. W. Persons, as heard in Montgomery, Ala.

> It takes a dark-skinned baby
> To make a preacher throw his Bible down.
>
> It takes a long, lean, lanky gal
> To make a rabbit fight a hound.

9

REPORTED from Auburn, Ala., 1915–1916, MS. of C. A. Ashcraft, as heard in Florence, Ala. "Sung at fertilizer plant."
   Cf. VII, nos. 49 and 61.

> It takes the rock and gravel
> To make a solid road,
> It takes a good-lookin' woman
> To satisfy my soul.

10

REPORTED from Durham, N. C., 1919, MS. of Blake B. Harrison.
   The tune is given in Appendix I, p. 411.

It takes a long, tall yaller gal to make a preacher lay his Bible down.
It takes a long, tall yaller gal to make a bulldog break his chain.

11

REPORTED from Durham, N. C., 1919, MS. of W. L. Hampton. "Heard from Negro farm hand in Durham County, N. C."

> Old black gal is my living, old yellow gal is my home.

12

REPORTED from Auburn, Ala., 1915–1916, MS. of W. M. Mobley, as heard in Birmingham, Ala.
   I have the same song with slight differences from southwest Georgia (1915), Ozark, Ala. (1915), and Cabarrus County, N. C. (1917–1919).

> I had a good-lookin' 'oman,
> But de fool laid down an' died.

13

REPORTED from Auburn, Ala., 1915–1916, MS. of R. Langdon. "Sung by Negro block-setter in a sawmill."

> I had a good-looking woman,
> But she took morphine and died.
> I had to drag her home.

14

REPORTED from Auburn, Ala., 1915–1916, MS. of J. O. Lizenby, as heard in Houston County, Ala.

> I had a tall, long, kinky-headed woman,
> But the fool laid down and died;
> She cooked good cabbages
> Also collud greens.

15

REPORTED from Auburn, Ala., 1915–1916, MS. of M. E. Bryant.

> Some says yellow
> While others say brown,
> But for me I'll take the blackest in town.

16

REPORTED from Auburn, Ala., 1915–1916, anonymously, as heard in Alabama.
I have stanzas 1, 5, and 6, with "white shirt" for "hobble skirt," reported from Alabama as heard "sung by Negro actors in a small show"; also stanza 6 from another contributor in Alabama, both as heard about 1915.
The chorus suggests the influence of the spiritual.[1]

---

[1] The comparison motif is one of the commonest conventional devices in the Negro secular song. Sometimes the comparison is of two subjects, e. g., the white man and the Negro, but generally it is threefold, as in the following songs. For similar threefold comparison songs dealing with animals, insects, etc., see Chapter VI. The stanzas comparing three women seem to be later imitations of the threefold insect comparison, the last line of which, "but it gets ther just the same," is slightly modified in the woman-stanzas to fit the particular stanza. Both the uniform fourth line and its modification seem to be later additions to songs of this type. The original, found frequently in the old minstrel books, seems to have been the comparison of three animals, usually the raccoon, 'possum, and rabbit, without a uniform fourth line.
From an old song called "Do Come Along, Ole Sandy Boy," in *Negro Singers' Own Book*, 1846(?), p. 309, may be seen the comparisons — of three subjects (animals)

Well a white lady wears a hobble skirt,
A yaller gal tries to do de same,
But a poor black gal wears a Mary Jane,
But she's hobbling just de same.

Well a white lady wears her teddy bear coat,
A yaller gal tries to do de same,
But a poor black gal ain't got no teddy at all,
But she's teddying just de same.

Well a white lady sleeps in a feather bed
A yaller gal tries to do de same,
But a poor black gal makes a pallet on de floor,
But she's sleeping just de same.

Well a white lady wears her diamond ring,
A yaller gal tries to do de same,
But a poor black gal wears an old brass ring,
But she's ringing just de same.

Well a white lady rides in an automobile,
A yaller gal tries to do de same,
But a poor black gal rides in an old ox-cart
But she's riding just de same.

and of two subjects (white folks and Negroes) — that are common in modern Negro songs:

Mr. Coon he is a mighty man,
He carries a bushy tail,
He steals old Massa's corn at night,
And husks it on a rail.

Do come along, ole Sandy boy,
Do come along, Oh, do!
Oh, what did uncle Gabriel say?
Oh, Kitty, can't you come along too.

De squirrel has a bushy tail,
Stumpy grows de hair,
De old coon's tail am ring'd all round —
De possum's tail am bare.

Do come along, etc.

Practically every line of the stanzas quoted is echoed in modern songs in this and other recent collections.

For the triple comparison of animals in modern songs, see VI, no. 23 and note. For the comparison of women, see Lomax (*Nation*), 1917, p. 144; Scarborough, 1923 (as from Texas), pp. 271, 275; and for related songs, with the comparison and refrain omitted, cf. Odum, 1926, pp. 153–154.

Well a white lady smells like toilet soap,
A yaller gal tries to do de same,
But a poor black gal smells like a ram billy goat,
But she's smelling just de same.

Chorus

I'm going away to see aunt Dina,
I'm going away to see my Lord.

17

REPORTED from Durham, N. C., 1919, MS. of David T. House, Jr.

White gal rides on an automobile,
Yellow gal rides on a train,
Black gal rides on a bull and cart,
But she rides just the same.

18

REPORTED from Durham, N. C., 1919, MS. of H. O. Waltz.

White gal rides in automobile,
Yellow gal does the same,
Black gal rides in an old ox-cart,
But she gets there just the same.

The white gal uses good cold-cream,
The yellow gal does the same,
But the black gal uses pure hog-lard,
But she gets there just the same.

The white gal uses perfume soap,
The yellow gal does the same,
But the black gal uses no soap at all,
But she smells just the same.

19

REPORTED from Auburn, Ala., 1915–1916, MS. of J. C. Nall.

The *Montgomery Advertiser* of April 4, 1916, quoted a variant of stanza 2, which had appeared in a current popular magazine as "a delightful little essay in verse," by Mark Twain, because scribbled on the fly-leaf of one of Mark Twain's books. The *Advertiser* pointed out that it was a current Negro song, probably remembered from Mark Twain's pilot days on the Mississippi.

For three stanzas similar to stanza 2, see Talley, 1922, p. 96.

White gal rides in an automobile,
Yallow gal does the same,
Black gal don't ride none at all,
But she gets there jest the same.

The blue jay has the wings so blue,
The butterfly has the same,
The bed bug ain't got no wings at all,
But he gets there jest the same.

20

REPORTED from Cambridge, Mass., 1917–1918, by Mr. and Mrs. Gideon, as recently heard at Camp Zachary Taylor, Louisville, Ky.

De white girl smell like Castile soap,
De yaller gal try to do de same,
De po' black gal smell like little billy goat,
But she get dere just de same.

De white gal rides in the Pullman car,
Yaller gal try to do de same,
De po' black girl rides in the old Jim Crow car,
But she get dere just de same.

21

REPORTED from Durham, N. C., 1919, MS. of E. C. Lovell. "Heard sung by street minstrel, King's Mountain, Cleveland County, N. C., 1911."

I have another song, contributed in Durham, N. C., 1919, MS. of Edwin Gibson, which is practically the same as stanza 4 below.

The chorus suggests the spirituals.

Brown gal she is a pretty queen,
Yellow gal she is de same,
Old black gal's a pictur' of home-made sin,
But that's a lookin' jus' de same.

Chorus

Goin' o'er de mountain, John an' Betsy,
Goin' o'er de mountain, Cora-Lee;
If you get dar befo' I do,
Do Lord, 'member me.

Brown gal she dress like Paris,
Yellow gal she do de same;
Old black gal wears a burlap sack,
But that's dressin' jus' de same.

Brown gal she sing like Galli-cu,
Yellow gal she do de same;
Old black gal brays like a corn-fed mule,
But that's singin' jus' de same.

Brown gal she smell like sweet soap,
Yellow gal she do de same;
Old black gal smells like a billy-goat,
But that's smellin' jus' de same.

22

REPORTED from Durham, N. C., 1919, MS. of Harvey Harward.

A white gal sleeps in a folding bed,
A brownskin does the same.
A black gal makes a pallet,
But she's sleeping just the same.

A white gal rides in an automobile,
A brownskin rides on the train,
A black gal rides in an ox-cart,
But she's riding just the same.

A white girl wears a hobble skirt,
A brownskin wears a plain,
A black gal wears a guano sack,
But she's hobbling just the same.

23

REPORTED from Auburn, Ala., 1915–1916, MS. of C. M. Hurt.

The high brown rides a Pullman car,
The yellow gal rides the same,
The old black gal rides a hand-car,
But she gets there just the same.

24

REPORTED from Durham, N. C., 1919, MS. of R. B. Edwards. "This Negro song about women was heard in a minstrel [show]."

> The rich girl wears the ten-dollar shoes,
> The brown skin gal does the same,
> The poor black gal ain't got no shoes at all,
> But she gets there just the same.

25

REPORTED from Auburn, Ala., 1915–1916, MS. of F. W. McMeans, as heard in Wolf Creek, Tenn.

> Rich gal drinks the snipped wine,
> Poor gal drinks the plain,
> My gal drinks Hiller Brothers' best,
> But she gets drunk just the same.

26

REPORTED from Auburn, Ala., 1915–1916, MS. of B. Y. Pennington, as heard at Andalusia, Ala. "Sung by Negro ditch diggers."

> Oh! yaller gal she drinks wine and champagne,
> But er a black gal she drinks gin,
> But gets there just the same.

> Oh! er yaller gal she smells like toilet soap,
> Oh! er yaller gal she smells like toilet soap,
> But er black babe she smells like a billy goat.

27

A

Reported from Auburn, Ala., 1915–1916, MS. of P. J. Bowab, as heard in Escambia County, Ala.

I have the same from another contributor in Alabama.

I have heard this sung with the favorite "Honey, how long" refrain. It is connected with the earlier "blues."

Practically the same as Odum, 1926, p. 171. Cf. also *Current Opinion*, 1919, p. 165, and Handy, 1926, pp. 4, 74.

From ashes to ashes
And from dust to dust,
I ain't seen a woman
That a man could trust.

B

Reported from Auburn, Ala., 1915–1916, MS. of J. R. Rutland, as heard in
Auburn, Ala. "Sung by Negro minstrels."

Ashes to ashes, dust to dust,
I got a woman I can't trust.

C

Reported from Auburn, Ala., 1915–1916, MS. of B. A. Wooten, as heard in
Auburn, Ala. "Sung by Negro boy on street."

Ashes to ashes, dust to dust,
'Taint but one woman it'll do to trust.

D

Reported from Auburn, Ala., 1915–1916, MS. of C. B. Crow, as heard "in
Levee Camp on Mississippi River in Louisiana."
   The common variant of this stanza substitutes "cocaine" for "woman," as
in Handy, 1926, p. 4.

Ashes to ashes and dust to dust,
Ef whiskey don' kill you
Den the woman must.

28

Reported from Durham, N. C., 1919, MS. of Jay L. Jackson, as "heard in the
vicinity of Farmville, N. C."
   This is a variant of IX, no. 33, *q.v.*

I'se gotta gal in de white folks' yard,
She kill'er chicken and she bring me de wing;
She's thinkin' I'm workin'
But I ain't doin' er thing.
Goodbye, honey, I'm gwain home.

29

REPORTED from Durham, N. C., 1919, MS. of Blake B. Harrison.

> I got a long, tall yaller gal
> On de road somewhere.

30

REPORTED from Auburn, Ala., 1915–1916, MS. of J. H. McIntosh. "Sung in mines."

> I gotta woman, she lives down by the sea,
> Ever time my boat lands, she comes a runnin' to kiss me.

31

REPORTED from Auburn, Ala., 1915–1916, MS. of A. H. Williamson, as heard in Lowndes County, Ala.

Some of the details of personal description in the "I would n't marry" songs are borrowed from the "Massa had a yaller gal" song of the old minstrels. Cf. "The Gal from the South," in *Ethiopian Serenaders*, 1857(?), p. 147; and for modern descendants of the same, cf. Odum, 1925, p. 236; Odum, 1926, p. 197; Scarborough, 1925, pp. 66–68 and 112.

From Mr. Perrow's collection, which contains many "I would n't marry" stanzas, it appears that the song is better known among white people than among Negroes. His Negroes would n't marry "a yaller gal," "a black gal," or "a widow" (Perrow, 1915, pp. 136, 137, 176, all as from Mississippi in 1909). His mountain whites and country whites would n't marry "a city girl," "a country girl," "a schoolteacher," "a widow," "a preacher," "a pore gal" (Perrow, 1915, p. 176, as from North Carolina in 1905, East Tennessee in 1908, Mississippi in 1909, Kentucky in 1913). For other Negro variants, cf. Lomax (*Nation*), 1917, p. 143; Scarborough, 1923, pp. 12–13; Odum, 1925, p. 191.

Cf. the North Carolina mountain-white song:

> I won't go home with ole Joe Clark
> I'll tell you the reason why, etc.

A parallel to these songs occurs among Jamaican Negroes. Cf. Walter Jekyll's *Jamaican Song and Story*, London, 1907, p. 244:

> Breezy say him no want Brown lady.

> I would n't marry a yaller gal,
> I'll tell yo' de reason why:
> Her hair's so dad-blamed nappy
> She'd break all de combs I buy.

I would n't marry a yaller gal,
I 'll tell yo' de reason why;
Her neck so long and stringy
I 'm 'fraid she 'd never die.

32

REPORTED from Auburn, Ala., 1915–1916, MS. of A. M. Kearly.

I don't like a black gal, I tell you the reason why;
Her hair is so long and kinky she will break every comb I buy.
I don't like a yellow gal, I tell you the reason why:
Her neck is so long and stringy I am afraid she will never die.

33

REPORTED from Durham, N. C., 1919, MS. of J. D. Johnson, Jr. "Heard sung by an old Negro, who accompanied himself on the banjo, in a small town in eastern North Carolina."
A corrupted descendant of the "Massa bought a yaller Gal" song, IV, nos. 3 ff.
In the *Ethiopian Serenaders*, 1857(?), p. 147, "The Gal from the South" begins:

"Ole Massa owned a colored girl,
    He bought her from the South.
Her hair it curled so very tight
    She could not shut her mouth;

and the third stanza is:

One morning, Massa, going away,
    He went to get his coat,
But neither hat nor coat was there,
    For she had swallowed both;
He took her to a tailor shop
    To have her mouth made small,
The lady took in one long breath,
    And swallowed tailor and all.

She's my yaller gal,
    I brought her from the South.
Took her down to the blacksmith shop,
    To have her mouth made smaller,
But bless your soul she swallowed shop and all.

34

REPORTED from Auburn, Ala., 1915–1916, MS. of R. Allen, as heard in Jackson
County, Ala.

Professor Kittredge informs me that this is a popular stage song and cites
William C. Cameron's *Volk's Theatre Songster*, p. 11.

> Oh get away from the window,
> My lover and my dove,
> Oh get away from the window,
> Don't you hear?
> Oh my love yes,
> Come some other night,
> For there's going to be a fight;
> There'll be razors a flying in the air.

35

REPORTED from Auburn, Ala., 1915–1916, anonymously.

The first two stanzas, with slight verbal variations, constitute all except the
chorus of "The Hesitating Blues, words and music by W. C. Handy," Handy,
1926, p. 94. But Handy's version lacks the last two stanzas here given and has
a chorus that is not related to these stanzas. The third stanza, with slight verbal
differences, occurs in "Blind Man Blues," Handy, 1926, p. 114. Cf. XIV,
nos. 1, 3, 19.

This and the three following songs are somewhat unusual in that they are
from the feminine point of view.

> Hello Central!
>
> What's the matter with the line?
> I want to talk to that brown of mine.
> Tell me how long I will have to wait;
> Can I get you now or will I have to hesitate?
>
> What's that you say, I can't talk to my brown;
> A storm last night blew all the wires down.
> Tell me how long I will have to wait;
> Can't I get him now or will I have to hesitate?
>
> My man's mouth looks like a lighthouse on the sea,
> And every time he smiles he shines the lights on me.
> How long will I have to hesitate,
> Can I get him now or will I have to wait?

Ain't crazy 'bout no high yellows, worried about no brown,
Come to picking my choice, gimme
The blackest man in town.
How long will I have to wait?
Can I get him now or will I have to hesitate?

36

REPORTED from Auburn, Ala., 1915–1916, MS. of W. H. Williamson, as heard in
Lowndes County, Ala.
   Cf. "Frankie and Albert," V, no. 29.

> I went down to de "slop" joint
> Wid a razor in my han'.
> "Open up dis gang way,
> I'm a lookin' fo' my man,
> I'm a lookin' fo' my baby,
> Why don' you come home?"

37

REPORTED from Greensboro, N. C., 1919, as sung to N. I. White by Miss Guelda
Elliott, who learned it some years before from a Negro washerwoman in Lexing-
ton, N. C.
   I have the same song, with slight variations, reported in Durham, N. C.,
1919, MS. of James E. Lyon, Jr., who heard it in Greensboro, N. C., in 1918.
   The tune is given in Appendix I, p. 411.

> Po' gal take a warnin',
> The men they will fool you,
> They'll tell you more lies
> Than the crossties on the railroad
> Or the stars in the skies.

38

REPORTED from Durham, N. C., 1919, MS. of L. W. Israel, as heard in North
Carolina.
   An interesting variant of this song (Odum, 1926, p. 157) is composed of two
stanzas, the first a modification of line 1, used three times and followed by a
modification of line 4. Another variant occurs as stanza 2 of "Careless Love"
blues, Handy, 1926, p. 55.

> When my aporn tied in a bow
> You was always hanging roun' my door.

Now my aporn barely will pin,
You pass by and won't stop in.

When my money you could blow,
You was always hanging aroun' my door.

Now my money 's all blowed in,
You pass by and won't look in.

39

REPORTED from Auburn, Ala., 1915–1916, MS. of W. M. Mobley, as heard in
Birmingham, Ala.

'Oman, 'oman, who can yo' reg'lar be?

40

REPORTED from Auburn, Ala., 1915–1916, MS. of W. M. Mobley, as heard in
Birmingham, Ala.

I lub dat 'oman,
I tell de world I do.

41

REPORTED from Auburn, Ala., 1915–1916, MS. of A. M. Kearly.

The woman I love is struck on a married man.

42

REPORTED from Durham, N. C., 1919, MS. of Percy F. Dilling. "Heard at
King's Mountain, Cleveland County, N. C. Sung by Negro passing through on
freight train."

I don't want no jet black woman for my regular.

43

REPORTED from Auburn, Ala., 1915–1916, MS. of W. D. Kimbrough, as heard
in Camden, Ala.

Talk about yo' gal, but you ought to see mine,
She don't drink whisky, but she sho' kills the wine.

44

REPORTED from Auburn, Ala., 1915–1916, MS. of A. M. Kearly, as heard de-claimed at a Negro school commencement.
This occurs as stanza 2 of "A Few Negroes by States," Talley, 1922, p. 117, with "South Ca'lina nigger" for "Alabama gals."

Fifteen cents in the panel of the fence,
The Alabama gals ain't got no sense.

45

REPORTED from Auburn, Ala., 1915–1916, MS. of J. A. Peterson, as heard in Coosa County, Ala. "Tune: Chopping Wood."

Sure as the vine grows up the wall,
Me and you goiner marry this comin' fall.

46

REPORTED from Durham, N. C., 1919, MS. of Howell J. Hatcher. "Heard sung by old Negro working on father's farm."

You made me love you and now your man have come;
I'll see you later when I've got my gun.

47

REPORTED from Auburn, Ala., 1915–1916, MS. of J. R. Rutland, as heard in Auburn, Ala. "Sung by Negro street singers."

Now look here woman, I can't stand
You runnin' aroun' wid another man.

48

REPORTED from Durham, N. C., 1919, MS. of Howell J. Hatcher. "Heard sung by old Negro working on father's farm."
I have the same from Andalusia, Ala., 1915–1916.
The same as in Odum, 1926, p. 216. Cf. VII, nos. 66, 89.

If you don't believe I'm sinking, just look what a hole I'm in.
If you don't believe I love you, just look what a fool I've bin.

49

REPORTED from Durham, N. C., 1919, MS. of David T. House, Jr.

I can shimmy, she wabble, I can ball-the-jack.[1]
I know what it takes to get my good gal back.

50

REPORTED from Auburn, Ala., 1915–1916, MS. of W. W. Culver, as heard in Houston County, Ala. "Sung by cotton chopper."

You swing Sally and I'll swing Sue;
Who swing the gal with the run-down shoe?

51

REPORTED from Auburn, Ala., 1915–1916, MS. of E. Oliveira, as heard in New Orleans, La.
Other love philtres recommended by the blues are "If you want to keep yo' baby, better get yourself a lock and key," and "Leave her alone till her lovin' heart gets good and sore." (Handy, 1926, pp. 4, 149.) **Also,**

Ef yore gal gits mad an' tries to bully you-u-u,
Jes' take yore automatic an' shoot her through an' through.

(Scarborough, 1925, p. 275, as from Texas.)

If you're in love and your gal don't treat you nice,
Just pick up a big old stick and beat her all your might.

52

REPORTED from Durham, N. C., 1919, MS. of Blake B. Harrison.

If my wife don't treat me right,
I'll knock her teeth down her throat
And walk the streets all night.

53

REPORTED from Durham, N. C., 1919, MS. of Blake B. Harrison.

If my wife comes home wid whiskey on her breath,
I'll pick up a stick and beat dat heifer to death.

[1] All three are comparatively recent dance steps.

54

REPORTED from Auburn, Ala., 1915–1916, MS. of C. A. Ashcraft, as heard in Florence, Ala. "Sung at fertilizer plant."
    Cf. stanza 1 of no. 82, in this chapter.

> Went upon the mountain,
> Look down on the risin' sun.
> Did n't see nobody do me like my woman done.

55

REPORTED from Durham, N. C., 1919, MS. of Blake B. Harrison.

> Took my gal to de milk-shake stand,
> Fool fell in love wid de milk-shake man.

Refrain

> She called him honey, she called him baby.

56

REPORTED from Auburn, Ala., 1915–1916, MS. of B. A. Wooten, as heard in Marengo County, Ala.

> Lord, I put you in the shade,
> I give you all I made;
> Woman, woman, you sho' have done me wrong.

57

REPORTED from Auburn, Ala., 1915–1916, MS. of W. S. Black, as heard in northern Alabama. "Sung on plantation."

> Woman, woman, look what you done,
> You took my money and stole my gun.
> Come on, Baby, Papa ain't mad with you.

58

REPORTED from Auburn, Ala., 1915–1916, MS. of R. R. Beard, as heard in northern Mississippi. "Sung by farm hand."

> 'Tain't no use to greab about it,
> Kase yer gotter do widout it;
> By, by, my honey, I'm gone.

59

REPORTED from Auburn, Ala., 1915–1916, MS. of F. W. McMeans, as heard in Wolf Creek, Tenn. "Banjo song."

Professor Kittredge writes me that this is "a variant of a song popular among white folks when I was a youngster. It simply illustrates the vogue of the original 'Shoo Fly' — which led that phrase to be generally applied in humorous fashion." The phrase occurs in the title *Dan Bryant's Shoo Fly Songster* (1869) and in a song from Mississippi quoted in Scarborough, 1925, p. 200.

The uncompleted chorus is probably the one often found with "Eliza Jane" (see IV, no. 28):

> Whoa, mule, whoa, I say,
> Keep yo' seat Miss Liza Jane, hold on to de sleigh.

Cf. Perrow, 1915, p. 180, as from Mississippi in 1909.

> I had a sho-fly lady
> And she had a sho-fly hat,
> And she had a sho-fly baby,
> But I did n't give a damn for that.

Chorus

> Whoa! mule, etc.

60

REPORTED from Durham, N. C., 1919, MS. of Blake B. Harrison.

I have also heard it as "Mary wore a hobble skirt." Possibly this started as one of the parodies of "Mary had a little lamb" that were popular on the vaudeville stage in the nineteen-tens.

> Mary wore an X-ray dress,
> Mary wore an X-ray dress,
> Mary wore an X-ray dress,
> And she left off all the rest.

61

REPORTED from Auburn, Ala., 1915–1916, MS. of B. A. Wooten, as heard in Marengo County, Ala.

With stanza 1, cf. stanza 5 of "What's de Matter, Susey" ("Composed and sung with unbounded applause, at White's Melodeon, by the original Old Dan Emmett"), White's *New Illustrated Ethiopian*, n. d., p. 38:

> Massa on de cellar door, a mendin' ob his shoes,
> De nigger on de telumgraph, a readin' ob de news.

With stanza 2, cf. stanza 1 of "Ol' Virginny Never Tire," Scarborough, 1925, p. 109 (as an ante-bellum dance song from Virginia) and p. 110 (as from West Virginia):

> There is a gal in our town,
> She wears a yellow striped gown,
> And when she walks the streets aroun'
> The hollow of her foot makes a hole in the groun'.

The stanza is related, somewhat less closely, to stanza 4 of "Nigger Pompey," p. 74, in White's *New Illustrated Ethiopian*, n. d.

> Angel rubber overcoat, patent leather shoes,
> Nigger in the telegram readin' of the news.

> I got a yaller gal in dis town,
> The holler in heel cut a hole in de groun'.

62

REPORTED from Auburn, Ala., 1915–1916, MS. of R. Allen.

The echo from Burns may have come from hearing the song sung by white people. Another Burns echo occurs in the "Ever After On" blues, arranged by W. C. Handy (Handy, 1926, p. 59):

> But I'll love my baby till the seas run dry,
> Till the rocks all dissolve by the sun.

> My love is like a red red rose,
> Her eyes mahogany brown;
> She the color of a sorrel horse,
> Meet her when the sun goes down.

63

REPORTED from Auburn, Ala., 1915–1916, MS. of H. I. Killingsworth, as heard in Clay County, Ga.

The unusual internal rhyme looks suspicious, but I have found no printed version.

> Dey say dat spring is the loving time,
> When birds am singing sweet;
> But, after all, I laks de fall,
> Hit's pow'ful hard to beat.

64

REPORTED from Auburn, Ala., 1915–1916, MS. of C. A. Ashcraft, as heard in Florence, Ala. "Sung at fertilizer plant."

> Good lookin' woman,
> Le' me be your teddy bear;
> Put a rope aroun' my neck
> An' lead me anywhere.

65

REPORTED from Auburn, Ala., 1915–1916, MS. of C. M. Hurt. "Sung by old Negro pianist."

This song and the two following are related to the old minstrel songs. Cf. stanza 3 of "Sally is de Gal for Me" ("sung by old Jim Carter with monstrous applause"), *Negro Singers' Own Book*, 1846(?), p. 34:

> I'se gwine down to Sally's house,
> If Sally ain't at home,
> I'll set myself in de big armchair
> And play on de old jawbone.

"All night long" is a familiar refrain in blues and work songs.

> I went down to Sally's house,
> And Sally was n't home;
> I sit right down in Sally's chair,
> And I rocked tell Sally come home,
> Rocked all night long, Babe, all night long.

66

REPORTED from Auburn, Ala., 1915–1916, MS. of W. S. Black, as heard in Athens, Ala.

Cf. IV, no. 28 *F*.

> Went to see my Susan Jane,
> She met me at the do',
> Shoes and stockings in her hand
> Foot all over the floor.

67

REPORTED from Durham, N. C., 1919, MS. of Howell J. Hatcher. "Heard sung by an old Negro on father's farm."

> I went down to my *gul's* house las' night,
> She met me at the *doh*,
> She knocked me in the head with a rollin' pin
> And I ain't been back no moh.

68

REPORTED from Auburn, Ala., 1915–1916, anonymously.

> I went down to my gal's house,
> But could n't get in at all;
> I went round to de winder,
> There was another mule in my stall,
> All night long, baby, all night long.

69

REPORTED from Auburn, Ala., 1915–1916, MS. of B. A. Wooten, as heard in Marengo County, Ala. "Slave song."
Cf. Odum, 1925, p. 235 (stanza 3 of "Pan o' Biscuits"):

> Had a sweet pertater
>   Roastin' in de san';
> Saw my mother comin' —
>   How I burnt my hand!

> I had ole Irish potato,
> I roast it in de sand,
> I put it in my pocket,
> To give to Lizabeth Ann.

70

REPORTED from Auburn, Ala., 1915–1916, MS. of W. M. Mobley, as heard in Birmingham, Ala.

> Thru de winder,
> Thru de blind,
> See dat 'oman?
> She's mine.

71

REPORTED from Auburn, Ala., 1915–1916, MS. of M. S. Perdue, as heard in southern Alabama. I have the same from another contributor in Alabama.

> I wonda where my brown gone,
> She been gone away for a year and a day.
> I hope she hain't gone to stay.
> I wonder where my brownskin gone.

72

REPORTED from Auburn, Ala., 1915–1916, anonymously.
   Cf. Lomax (*Nation*) 1917, p. 144; Scarborough, 1925, p. 164, also V, no. 16, in this volume.

> Standing on de corner,
> Waiting for my brown.
> First thing I knowed
> I was jail-house bound.

73

REPORTED from Auburn, Ala., 1915–1916, anonymously. "Sung by Sam Davis during the construction of gymnasium." (The gymnasium of the Alabama Polytechnic Institute was built two or three years before this song was contributed.   N. I. W.)

> Been working in the cotton and corn all day,
> Hands and feet so sore.
> Well if I thought those gals was coming this way
> Dogged if I'd work any more.

74

REPORTED from Durham, N. C., MS. of F. S. Bennett. "Heard in eastern Tennessee, about fifteen years ago."
   The tune is given in Appendix I, p. 411.

> Yonder come a yaller gal,
> All dressed up in red —
> Well, I wish my wife was dead,
> Well, I wish my wife was dead.

75

REPORTED from Durham, N. C., 1919, MS. of Eugene C. Crawford, as heard recently on the streets of Durham.

I have heard or seen this song with "white folks" for "old folks." I think it is an old dance song of the whites, later adopted by the Negroes. The rhyme, based on the obsolescent "gwine," is significant of some age.

Cf. a variant from Mississippi, in Scarborough, 1925, p. 165, as part of "an old song":

> Monday mornin' break o' day,
>> White folks got me gwine.
> Saturday night when de sun go down,
>> Dat yaller gal am mine.

> Saturday night and Sunday too,
> Pretty little gal is on my mind;
> Monday morning at break of day,
> The old folks have me going.

76

REPORTED from Auburn, Ala., 1915–1916, MS. of L. A. Nall, as heard in New Orleans, La.

It ain't no use a pleadin' now, lady, yo' done played your las' trump card,
Just go an' git another man, yo' said hit wer'n't hard.

77

REPORTED from Durham, N. C. (anonymously) by a student. "Probably heard in N. C."

Jones is a "creeper." Odum, 1926, contains a number of songs dealing with similar situations, on pp. 147, 151.

> Jones, he's got my gal an' gone;
> When I get him I'm goin' to cut him, bite him,
> I'm goin' to cut him through an' through —
> Jones, he's got my gal an' gone.

78

REPORTED from Durham, N. C., 1919, MS. of Edwin P. Gibson. "Heard in childhood."

"Rock, rock," evidently refers to the "Rock candy" dance. Old Joe Clark is a figure in the folk-song of the mountain whites. I recall two stanzas from mountain whites heard fifteen years ago:

(1) I won't go home with old Joe Clark,
        I'll tell you the reason why —
     Blowed his nose in a cornbread crust
        An' called it punkin pie.

(2) Old Joe Clark is dead,
     The last thing he said
     Was, never let a woman have her way.

Cf. Perrow, 1912, p. 152, and 1915, p. 176, where Joe Clark has no Negro connections.

Way up on the mountain top I gave my horn a blow,
I thought I heard my yaller gal say,
    "Yonder comes my beau."

Refrain

        Rock, rock, old Joe Clark,
        Rock, rock, I say.
        Rock, rock, old Joe Clark,
        For I'm going away.

If you see that gal of mine, I'll tell you what to tell her,
Tell her not to fool her time with me, but look out for another feller.

79

REPORTED from Auburn, Ala., 1915–1916, MS. of R. M. Beasly.

        She goes out fishin' ev'ry night,
        I'm goin' fishin' too.
        I'm gwinter tell my lovin' wife,
        Gointer get mo' fish than you.

        Here's a proposition that we all must make
        Honey ef them fish will bite;
        (Eny fish will bite if you get good bait),
        And my wife's goin' fishin' tonight.

80

REPORTED from Auburn, Ala., 1915–1916, MS. of F. Mitchell, as heard in south-eastern Alabama. "Sung by Negroes when leaving town for long time or to start on chain gang."
    For several variants of the last four lines, cf. Perrow, 1915, p. 130 (one from East Tennessee whites, 1907, two from Mississippi, 1909), Handy, 1926, p. 36. There seem to be two common types of mortuary directions:

(1) "If I die" in a certain place, commonly Arkansaw.
(2) "When I die," no place specified.

See VII, no. 82 and XII, no. 32.

> Oh, goodby, gal, honey, fare you well,
> Believe I'll go down to the ribber,
> Jump overboard and drown.
> Oh, if I die in the state of Arkansaw
> Ship my body to my ma-in-law;
> Oh, if I die please throw my body in the sea
> So nobody will worry after me.

81

REPORTED from Auburn, Ala., 1915–1916, MS. of C. B. Barker.
Lines 6 and 7 occur in "The Rovin' Gambler," a song of the mountain whites, of which there is a phonograph record. Cf. also Odum, 1925, p. 258.

> I went on to Macon,
> I had a dollar to spend.
> I fell in love wid a pretty yellow girl,
> She's in love wid me.
> She taken me in her parlor,
> She cooled me wid her fan,
> She sez I has the purtiest hair!

82

REPORTED from Auburn, Ala., 1915–1916, anonymously.
Cf. no. 54, in this chapter.

> I went up on the mountain
> To see the rising sun;
> Ain't found nobody
> To treat me like my woman done.
>
> Oh, tell me good woman
> Who might your regular be;
> If you ain't got no regular,
> Won't you please take me?
>
> Oh, tell me good woman
> Who might your regular be;
> I want some good woman
> To ball-the-jack [1] with me.

[1] A Negro dance.

83

REPORTED from Auburn, Ala., 1915–1916, anonymously.
    For a variant of stanza 1, see VII, no. 62.
    The "Honey how long" refrain is very common in this and other collections.
See IX, no. 32.

De rocks in de mountains,
    Or fish in de sea,
Can't make dem no nigger
    What won't love me.

Honey, how long,
Have I got to wait?
Why can't I have you now —
Why do you hesitate?

84

REPORTED from Auburn, Ala., 1915–1916, MS. of W. H. Williamson, as heard
in Lowndes County, Ala.
    For stanza 1, cf. Odum, 1926, p. 156, Handy, 1926, p. 7. Stanzas 1 and 2
often occur both independently and in combination with other stanzas. For
stanza 2, cf. VII, no. 90.

The Alabama river
It is so deep and wide,
And my woman
Is on de other side.

Oh! de boat's up de river
And she won't come down;
I believe to my soul, babe,
Dat she's water bound.

Oh! de boat's a-reelin'
She rockin' to and fro,
But if she sinks, baby chile,
I'm gwine to swim to sho'.

85

REPORTED from Durham, N. C., 1919, MS. of James E. Lyon, Jr. "Heard in High Point, N. C., 1916."

I rather be dead
An' laid in de dirt
Than to see ma gal
With her feelin's hurt.

I rather be dead
An' laid in de sand
Than to see my gal
With another man.

I rather be dead
An' laid in de ground
Than to see my gal
In anoder weddin' gown.

XI

RECENT EVENTS

THE songs in which the folk Negro takes note of the larger world by which he is surrounded are sung in the fields, in the kitchen, in the section gang, on the streets, and in minstrel shows. Few of them in their present state are of any great age, since they could hardly anticipate the events by which they were inspired. They are related, of course, to some of the songs classified under Narrative Songs, when the songs in that group have to do with actual occurrences. This group deals only with those events of national or general significance, but there are numerous songs all over the South which deal with events of only local significance. The well-known ballad on the wreck of the Southern train No. 97 is an example of these. Some years ago Dr. Frank C. Brown found such a ballad growing up among the Negro workers in the "Bull Durham" tobacco factory in Durham, shortly after the wreck of a Negro excursion train.

Trivial comment upon the events of the day has always characterized Negro song. It is true of many of the songs quoted by travellers in Africa, of the songs heard by travellers and novelists who occasionally recorded ante-bellum songs, and of the ante-bellum minstrel songs, which, while generally not really Negro songs, pretended to be, and did influence later songs of the Negro. These songs seldom have enough weight to outlast the interest in the event by which they were provoked. If there were ever many genuinely Negro songs inspired by even so weighty an event as emancipation, I have failed to find a single one in oral tradition to-day.

Within the last twenty years the events which have most impressed the Negro folk-singer's imagination have been the sinking of the Titanic, the advent of the boll weevil, the spurious discovery of the North Pole (strangely, the authentic discovery moved him not), and the World War. The great Northern migration of Negroes in 1917–1918 about which Southern editors grew so excited seems to have left little record in Negro song, the only echo in this collection being IX, no. 53, in which the singer seems to proclaim his disillusion with Hackensack, New Jersey — even though the Yankees did not cut off his moustache, as they did for his migrating ancestor, according to IV, no. 24.

The sinking of the Titanic was a shock great enough to penetrate even the comparative insulation in which the folk Negro lives; moreover, it was a wreck, and Negroes will always thrill to wrecks. The "ballet" singer was sobered by it and tuned it to tragedy after the manner of his kind, but the folk Negro soon turned it to jest. He was not there, but on the back of a mule; his alibi is convincing, so why worry. The panic of 1906 affected him more nearly, but he took that misfortune good-humoredly, if not in jest. Dr. Cook is a joke to the Negro, out and out; the joke is on the explorer for not realizing the discomfort of a polar climate. As for the boll weevil, the joke is on the Negro, but the Negro's reaction is typically racial. Many small Negro farmers were ruined by the boll weevil. Their credit was destroyed and they were forced into other kinds of work, often into other parts of the country. This side of the story is plainly evident in what the merchant told the farmer, — "Boll weevils in your field," — and the farmer's reply — "Down the road I'm gone." Yet the Negro cherishes no malice toward the boll weevil; he plainly admires his persistence, endows him with a rich personality, and makes of him a home-seeker, a hardy traveller, and a bold, ready fellow at conversational give-and-take. All at the Negro's expense, be it observed, but not at all to his dismay. Like the "seeker" in the old spirituals (and in the very same words) the boll weevil is a fellow-traveller, "jes' a-huntin' for a home."

The World War made a slight impression on Negro song, but nothing like the impression that its aftermath made on the educated and semi-educated portion of the Negro race. Despite the undoubted patriotism of that race, the World War must have impressed the illiterate Negro (strange as it may seem) as entirely a white man's affair. There is no evidence that it touched the really sympathetic depths out of which enduring folk-song is born. The War Department made an effort to capitalize Negro singing in the training camps; spirituals were encouraged, together with patriotic songs to the old spiritual tunes; but when the Negro soldier sang in France, he sang the old spirituals, the old secular songs, and modifications and parodies of familiar songs. Nothing that he sang shows that the war really touched his folk consciousness. It was the white man's show, to which the Negro was admitted in consideration of carrying water for the elephants.

In a Georgia training camp Professor U. B. Phillips heard one singing, unconscious of its irony in the situation, that strangely unmar-

tial old spiritual, "Ain't gonna study war no more." [1] A Negro welfare worker heard it again behind the battlefields. [2] The French
heard it also. Of other songs Mrs. Burlin quotes a French general as
saying, "It was not alone the colored troops that were helped by the
songs of the Negro, but the white people as well. Far and near, the
black soldiers cheered with their singing all who came within sound
of their voices; officer and private, villager and peasant alike — none
will ever forget the stirring effect of those old Negro songs." [3]

The effect on the Negro himself, or on his songs, was not particularly lasting. The Hindenburg line impressed him not half so deeply
as the boll weevil. In a poem called "Gee-Up Dar, Mules," Mr.
Edwin Ford Piper shows how it might have touched his song when
he represents a returned soldier encouraging his mules with the
following: [4]

"General Foch is a fine old French,
He puts us niggers in a front line trench;
The barb wire down, and the barrage begun, —
Boche see a nigger and the Boche he run.

"O po' mourner,
You shall be free
When the good Lord sets you free!

"O, I hitched up the mules, and the mules worked fine;
I hitched 'em up to that Hinnenburg line,
I drawed her back till I snagged her on the Rhine,
An' the boss come along, and he give me my time.

"O po' mourner
You shall be free
When the good Lord sets you free!

"Gwan-n mules! Gee-up dar, mules."

If these lines were never actually sung by returned Negro soldiers,
they only prove once more how superior is the truth of poetry to
that of history.

Though the songs in this group are comparatively recent, they
have ancestors, and some of them had midwives. As in the case of

---

[1] Preface to *American Negro Slavery*, New York and London, D. Appleton & Co.,
1918.

[2] Charles Halston Williams, *Side Lights on Negro Soldiers*, Boston, B. J. Brimmer
Co., 1923.

[3] Natalie Curtis Burlin, *Hampton Series, Negro Folk-Songs* (New York and Boston,
G. Schirmer, 1918–1919), iv, 7.

[4] In *Contemporary Verse* for April, 1919, p. 51. Quoted by permission of the editors.

the travelling coon, the midwives may have been the vaudeville stage of the white man. In others, quite definitely, they were professional street singers and "ballet" writers. Only a few days before writing these lines I was trying to get a more complete version of "John Jasper" (II, no. 85) from "Shorty" Love, the Negro handy-man at the Duke University Library. "I wish I knowed that ballet," said Shorty. "'Bout two years ago at a Fourth of July picnic a man was selling them. It's a purty ballet and it did n't cost but ten cents; and I knowed then I oughter bought one." One of my students in Alabama gave me a song which I thought a little doubtful, and when I questioned him, he said that he had once sung in vaudeville, and that he wrote the song in question and had written a number of others for Negro street singers. Songs in the present group that point either slightly or strongly to the street musician and the professional folk-song composer are numbers 1, 5, and 20.

The presence of immediate ancestors is very closely indicated by the considerable tendency to parody. Almost all groups of Negro songs show this tendency, but the present group shows it very plainly indeed. The World War apparently produced few entirely original Negro songs, but it produced numerous parodies. The songs quoted in Mr. Niles's *Singing Soldiers* [5] contain a very high percentage of parodies both of old Negro songs and of the songs of the whites. In the present collection number 18 is quite plainly a parody of "Tipperary," while in number 16 the German who lays his rifle down is merely substituted for the preacher who laid down his bible, in the earlier songs, under the bizarre spell of "a long, tall, brownskin girl." Number 17 is also a parody of a pre-war Negro song. There is a similar relationship between number 7, hinting at the potency of the panic in Birmingham, and

> If you don't believe I'm sinking,
> Just look what a hole I'm in.

The presence of these almost contemporary ancestors suggests older ones of the same nature. The ancients who never knew they were ancients may have had wine that we know not of, which these supposedly recent songs merely decant into new bottles. The panic of 1906 was preceded by "hard times" which made their impress upon the minstrel great-grandfathers of contemporary Negro song, the most conspicuous example being Stephen Foster's "Hard Times, Come Again No More." When we come to the inquiry in number 7 about the boll weevil's red head (*is* it red?) we touch upon an older

[5] John J. Niles, *Singing Soldiers*, New York, Charles Scribner's Sons, 1927.

song (VI, no. 45), very much like it in expression and sentiment, in which the red-headed woodpecker answers the same question by saying

> "Somebody done stole my derby,
> De sun done turn me red."

Even in "just lookin' for a home" the weevil is repeating an old spiritual line.

When we read (no. 15) that "Doctor Cook's in town" with his discouraging opinions on polar temperature, we suspect a connection with those old black-face singers of eighty years ago, who were always "in town" or "just come to town," with strange comments and accomplishments. On this branch of the family tree, but rather far out, roosts even the cavalier Mr. Charles Dickens:

> Old Boz came to America
> And got fat pickers by de way.
> Den he turned and picked de Yankee press,
> But dey'll make him pick bull bones, I guess.
> O get out de way,
> O get out de way, old Johnny Tucker
> You're too late to come for your supper.[6]

One of the most interesting examples, however, is the group of songs about the sinking of the Titanic, which illustrates most of the typical processes of Negro secular song development.

In 1909, before the sinking of the Titanic, Mr. Perrow printed the following in the *Journal of American Folk-lore* as a Negro song from Mississippi:

> O where were you when the steamer went down, Captain?
> O where were you when the steamer went down, Captain?
> O where were you when the steamer went down, Captain?
> I was with my honey in the heart of town.[7]

Where the captain should have been is plain; by all traditions of his class he should have been holding her head ag'in the bank till the last galoot got ashore. But where was the Titanic at this time? Not yet in existence. So much for the first stage, the probable existence of an ur-Titanic on the Mississippi River, possibly the very boat that went down trying to break the record of the Robert E. Lee or the

---

[6] Stanza 4 of "Get Out de Way, Old Johnny Tucker," p. 318 in the *Negro Minstrels' Own Book* (c. 1850). This same song, it will be noticed, is the ancestor of Old Dan Tucker as sung by Negroes to-day.

[7] Note that the verse form is the same as one of the two typical blues forms, several years later.

boat in which Mark Twain's brother was mortally injured. These lines, and not anything written about the Titanic, are unquestionably the origin of all three versions of number 2 in this group.

It will be noted, however, that all three versions also contain the ubiquitous "Alabama Bound" refrain, which started independently. Not only has an old song picked up the Titanic and become apparently a new one; it has also picked up part of an entirely different song.

These songs, however, are really folk-songs and probably came into existence after "The Great Titanic" (no. 1), which is obviously the individual effort of a "ballet" writer. "The Great Titanic," too, is a folk-song, sung in different localities of the South with slight variations due to imperfect memory. Four lines of it were reported from Mississippi in 1926 as an example of "improvised singing" by Negroes. Yet it is obviously quite distinct from the shorter Titanic songs which represent a union of the Mississippi steamboat and "Alabama Bound." This parallel existence of two distinct types of folk-song about the same subject is repeated in the case of the John Henry narrative songs and the John Henry work songs discussed in chapter V.

Thus the sinking of the Titanic is represented in Negro folk-song by most of the elements of composition that occur from time to time in other songs; namely, individual "ballet" compositions taken over by the folk, older folk-songs revamped to fit a contemporary subject, and intrusions from unrelated songs. Finally, in number 5, the Titanic becomes mixed with another song, that of "The Travelling Coon," itself a song of "ballet" origin which has borrowed something from "O Did n't He Ramble," copyrighted by Bob Cole in 1921 but sung for at least ten years before that date. And here the question first asked of the Mississippi captain when his boat went down is answered (but not asked), as to the whereabouts of the travelling coon — he was on deck when the vessel struck, but when she sank he was "shootin' craps in Liverpool."

SONGS, WITH ANNOTATIONS

The following songs classified in other groups might also be included in the present class: VIII, 25; IX, 5, 53.

I

THE GREAT TITANIC [1]

REPORTED from Auburn, Ala., 1915–1916, MS. of A. A. Lauderdale, as heard in Marion County, Ala. "Sung by Negro on streets of Hackleburg in Northwest Ala."

I have the same song from Auburn, Ala., 1915–1916, MS. of W. H. Avery, as heard sung in Tuscumbia, Ala. (about fifty miles from Marion County), "by a blind Negro." The only differences are two slight verbal variations in the Tuscumbia version and the insertion of the clause "that sits in Heaven," between "God" and "told," in stanza 5. Also from Auburn, Ala., 1915–1916, MS. of B. Coplan, as sung by a blind white man in Fayetteville, Tenn., a song composed of lines 5, 19–20, 5, 7, 5 of the present version, in order. The North Carolina Folk-Lore Society has the same song as sung by a Durham Negro about 1920.

It apparently belongs to the class of songs, like most of the longer narrative songs in this collection, composed by and for a professional singer rather than by and for a group. There are many songs of this class, some originating on the vaudeville stage and some with street musicians. Often they are taken up and modified by a folk group. One or two unusually accurate details in the various versions may be due to an illustrated book on the Titanic which enjoyed extensive sales among the Negroes soon after the disaster.

Puckett, 1926, p. 64, gives the chorus as an example of "improvised singing" by a Mississippi Negro.

The tune is given in Appendix I, p. 412.

It was on one Monday morning just about one o'clock
When that great Titanic began to reel and rock;
People began to scream and cry,
Saying, "Lord, am I going to die?"

Chorus

It was sad when that great ship went down,
It was sad when that great ship went down,
Husbands and wives and little children lost their lives,
It was sad when that great ship went down.

When that ship left England it was making for the shore,
The rich had declared that they would not ride with the poor,
So they put the poor below,
They were the first to go.

While they were building they said what they would do,
We will build a ship that water can't go through;
But God with power in hand
Showed the world that it could not stand.

[1] Local title.

Those people on that ship were a long ways from home,
With friends all around they did n't know that the time had come;
Death came riding by,
Sixteen hundred had to die.

While Paul was sailing his men around,
God told him that not a man should drown;
If you trust me and obey,
I will save you all to-day.

You know it must have been awful with those people on the sea,
They say that they were singing, "Nearer My God to Thee."
While some were homeward bound,
Sixteen hundred had to drown.

2

A

REPORTED from Auburn, Ala., 1915–1916, MS. of B. Y. Pennington, as heard in Andalusia, Ala.

I have the same with slight verbal differences from Durham, N. C., 1919, MS. of H. J. Hatcher, as heard near Mt. Airy, N. C., in 1919.

There are quite a number of Titanic songs beginning like this one. Compare with a song reported to E. C. Perrow from Mississippi in 1909 (Perrow, 1913, p. 123), before the sinking and indicating that the Negro merely took the Titanic story and attached it to a river sinking:

> O where were you when the steamer went down, Captain?
> O where were you when the steamer went down, Captain?
> O where were you when the steamer went down, Captain?
> I was with my honey in the heart of town.

For "Alabama Bound," see no. 14, in this chapter and XII, no. 31 and note.

> Oh! where was you when de old Titanic went down?
> I wus on de back of er mule singing "Alabama Bound."

B

Reported from Auburn, Ala., 1915–1916, MS. of W. H. Blake, Jr.

Without the repetition this is practically the same as Scarborough, 1925, p. 213 (as from Texas), with "boat" for "Titanic."

> Where wus you when the big Titanic
> Went down?
> Where wus you when the big Titanic
> Went down?
> Standing on the deck singing
> "Alabama Boun'."

C

Reported from Auburn, Ala., 1915–1916, MS. of J. L. Pitts, as heard in central Alabama. "Sung by working Negroes."

> O, what were you singing
> When the Titanic went down?
> O, what were you singing
> When the Titanic went down?
> Sitting on a mule's back,
> Singing, "Alabama Bound."

3

REPORTED from Auburn, Ala., 1915–1916, MS. of H. T. Killingsworth, as heard in southwestern Georgia. "Sung by boat hands."

> Out on dat ocean,
> Dat deep, wide ocean,
> Out on dat ocean de Titanic is sinking down.

4

REPORTED from Auburn, Ala., 1915–1916, MS. of H. Caldwell, as heard in Jackson County, Ala. "Sung by Negro farm hand."

> Oh, the captain must 'er been drunk
> When the big ship sunk,
> You could hear her whistle blowing
> Forty miles or more.

5

THE TRAVELLING COON [1]

REPORTED from Durham, N. C., 1919, MS. of Percy F. Dilling. "Song sung by travelling minstrel at King's Mountain, Cleveland County, N. C."

An interesting variant occurs in Odum, 1926, pp. 59–61, as from South Carolina. Only two lines of the present version are the same as in Odum, but every stanza, except the fifth, of the present version is very similar to a stanza in Odum. Stanza 5 does not occur in Odum, and several stanzas in Odum do not occur in the present version. The chorus of the present version occurs in a four-line arrangement as stanza 3 of Odum's version, which has another chorus.

---

[1] No local title given.

These lines seem to be based on the chorus of the modern minstrel song, current from about 1905 to 1915:

> He rambled, he rambled, he rambled all around town.
> He rambled, he rambled, he rambled till the butcher cut him down.

Cf. IV, no. 50.

The song is obviously of vaudeville or street-singer origin. Several years ago the song circulated in Durham, N. C., as a printed "ballet."

> Once there was a travelling coon
> Who was born in Tennessee,
> Made his living stealing chickens,
> And everything he could see.

> *Chorus*

> Well he travelled and was known for miles around,
> And he did n't get enough, and he did n't get enough,
> Till the police shot him down.

> Well the police got in an automobile;
> They got right after that coon;
> No matter how fast that freight train past,
> That coon was sho' to get on board.

> That coon got on the Titanic steamship,
> And sailed across the ocean blue.
> When he saw that iceberg a-comin',
> Right overboard he flew.

> The people standin' aroun',
> Said that nigger was sure a fool,
> But when the Titanic ship went down,
> He was shootin' craps in Liverpool.

> They sent for his mother down in Georgia,
> She was all carried 'way with tears.
> When she opened up the coffin for to see her boy,
> He had done a' disappeared.

6

REPORTED from Auburn, Ala., 1915-1916, MS. of A. M. Kearly.

With this and the following, cf. Perrow, 1915, p. 140 (as from Mississippi in 1909). The panic in question is that of 1908-1909.

The old minstrel books contain a number of songs about "hard times," but there seems to be no direct connection with the modern songs.

> A nickel worth of meal and a dime of lard
> Will do while the panic's on.

7

REPORTED from Auburn, Ala., 1915–1916, MS. of R. Langdon. "Sung by Negro block-setter in sawmill."

> If you don't know the panic's on,
> Just go to Birmingham.

8

A

REPORTED from Auburn, Ala., 1915–1916, MS. of A. H. Williamson, as heard in Lowndes County, Ala.

> Save up yo' money,
> Don' you buy no corn
> Cause de panic's on.
> I wear shoes made of all kinds of leather,
> I wear clothes made for all kinds of weather
> Cause de panic's on.

B

Reported from Auburn, Ala., 1915–1916, MS. of W. M. Mobley, as heard in Birmingham, Ala. "Sung by a cook."

> Save yo' money,
> Don't buy no gun,
> 'Cause de panic's on.

9

REPORTED from Auburn, Ala., 1915–1916, MS. of R. Langdon. "Sung by Negro farmer."

The boll-weevil songs may be dated from about 1900, when the boll weevil first appeared in Texas and rapidly spread northward, bringing disaster to cotton growers. The songs appear to have originated in Texas and spread to other states with the weevil. They seem to be largely confined to the more southern cotton-producing states, since no songs of this cycle appear in Perrow, Talley, or Odum, whose songs are mostly from the more northerly states which were not so heavily dependent upon cotton. Miss Scarborough argues for communal composition of these songs, but quotes a correspondent (p. 79) who believes that they were started "by a man in Merivale [Miss.]." On pages 76–79 she gives five of these songs from Texas, all different from those in this volume, and generally related by the common line, "Jes' a-lookin' for a home," which I suspect has a spiritual origin. Cf. also Scarborough, 1923, p. 136, and Handy, 1926, p. 3.

I have the same song as the following, with slight verbal variations, from Auburn, Ala., 1915–1916, MS. of M. J. Hollingsworth, as heard in Pickens County, western Alabama; also stanza 1, with slight verbal variations, from Auburn, Ala., 1915–1916, MSS both of A. H. Williamson, as heard in Lowndes County, Ala., and of A. M. Kearly.

> Well, the farmer told the merchant,
> "I want some meat and meal";
> Well, the merchant told the farmer,
> "Boll weevil's in yo'r field."
>
> "I done chopped out my cotton
> And my new ground corn.
> If you don't let me have it
> Down the road I'm gone."

10

REPORTED from Auburn, Ala., 1915–1916, MS. of A. L. Holloway, as heard in Monroe County, southern Alabama.

> "Boll weevil, boll weevil,
> Where did you come from?"
> "Texas, Mississippi, Louisiana,
> On a bum."
>
> De fus' time I saw de boll weevil,
> 'T was in Arkansaw;
> De next time I saw de boll weevil,
> He was arguin' wid my father-in-law.
>
> The farmer went to the merchant
> To get some meat and meal;
> De merchant said, "Go way from here, you dirty farmer,
> You got boll weevils in your field."

11

REPORTED from Auburn, Ala., 1915–1916, MS. of A. M. Kearly.

> The boll weevil told the farmer,
> "You can bury me in the sand,
> But I'll see you in next Spring
> When you break your land."

12

Reported from Auburn, Ala., 1915–1916, MS. of A. M. Kearly.

> The boll weevil told the farmer,
> "You had better let me alone;
> I will eat all your cotton
> And jump down on your corn."

13

Reported from Auburn, Ala., 1915–1916, anonymously.
Cf. VI, no. 45 and note.
With the last line of each stanza, cf. the spiritual line, "I'm a-huntin' for a home, home," Fenner, 1901, p. 8.

> Farmer said to boll weevil,
> "What makes your head so red?"
> "Working in the hot sun — wonder I ain't half dead;
> Trying to make a home, trying to make a home."
>
> Farmer took the little boll weevil
> And put him in a block of ice.
> Boll weevil said to farmer, "Ain't it cool and nice?
> Trying to make a home, trying to make a home."

14

Reported from Auburn, Ala., 1915–1916, MS. of D. L. Madeira, as heard in Florida.
This song is a combination of "Alabama Bound" (in the chorus), the boll-weevil songs, and a common type of songs about women. For the first element, cf. various other songs in this collection (for example, VII, nos. 74, 75; IX, nos. 46–52; XII, no. 30; and nos. 2 and 15, in this chapter); Lomax (*Nation*) 1917, p. 144; Scarborough, 1925, p. 213 (from Texas) and p. 239 (from Mississippi); Odum, 1926, pp. 146–147. For the second element, cf. preceding boll-weevil songs and notes. For the third element, cf. in this collection X, nos. 1–11 and notes. Stanza 3 is practically the same as in Odum, 1926, p. 147.

Chorus

> Don' yo' leave me here,
> Don' yo' leave me here,
> But if yo' has ter leave me, sweet baby,
> Leave a dime for beer.

'Cause Ah'm Alabama bound
Ah'm Alabama bound.
If de train break down,
I'se got a mule to ride.

A farmer wants some meat and meal;
Merchant says, "Dere nothin' doin', boss,
Boll weevil's in yo' fiel'."
For I'se Alabama bound.

Boll weevil bug de farmers do despise;
Backs way down in de cotton boll,
Yo' jest can see his eyes.

She's down on de road somewhere,
On de road somewhere,
Long, tall, slim chocolate drop,
She's on de road somewhere.

She's long and tall an' she's thin an' slim,
Got a hump in her back like a camel, boss;
She make a panther squall;
Don' yo' leave me here.

Fo' she make a rabbit spit in a bull dawg's face,
Make a bull dawg break his chain,
Make a preacher lay his bible down,
Deacon in de amen corner howl out,
Don' yo' leave me here.

15

Reported from Auburn, Ala., 1915–1916, MS. of C. J. Perryman, as heard in
northern Alabama. "Sung by section gang."

For the "Alabama Bound" refrain, see the preceding song, also XII,
nos. 30, 31.

Doctor Cook's in town; Doctor Cook's in town,
He says, "The North Pole's too dog-goned cold,
I'm Alabama bound, I'm Alabama bound."

16

REPORTED from Durham, N. C., 1919, MS. of Eugene Crawford. "One would often hear the Negro soldiers as they hiked along the road, singing this song. Heard in France."

This is a parody of the popular song, "It takes a long, tall, yaller gal to make a preacher lay his bible down." See X, no. 10.

It takes a long, tall, slim, black man to make a German lay his rifle
    down.

17

REPORTED from Durham, N. C., 1919, MS. of Eugene C. Crawford. "Heard from Negro soldiers in France."

This is a parody of an older song. Cf. XIII, no. 8 *A* in this collection, and Perrow, 1915, p. 401, two variants (as from Mississippi in 1909 and Virginia).

> Mamie in the kitchen,
> Cooking pink beans;
> Dadie on the ocean,
> Dodging submarines.

18

REPORTED from Auburn, Ala., 1915–1916, MS. of E. L. Harper, as heard in Pickens County, Ala. "Sung by Negro who made living singing and playing songs. Tune: Tipperary."

This parody on "Tipperary" is probably not originally Negro.

> It's a long way to old Kentucky,
> It's a long way to go,
> It's a long way to old Kentucky,
> Since Alabama went dry.
> Farewell to Tom and Jerry,
> Farewell to Rock and Rye,
> It's a long way to old Kentucky
> For Alabama gone dry.

THE SEAMIER SIDE

THE songs that reflect the folk Negro's sins and peccadillos are almost all of comparatively recent origin. Those dealing with typical "bad men," like "Railroad Bill" and "Cotton-Eyed Joe," are probably a little older than the rest, except those dealing with petty theft. The latter, however, have a very long ancestry. In slavery days travellers and pro-slavery writers frequently spoke of the thieving propensities of the slaves.

There have been few civilizations in which the petty thefts of servants or a servant class have not been a stock joke. Even to-day the expressions "you lying scamp" or "you thieving rascal" are applied by old-fashioned Southerners (at least in fiction) when no actual lie or theft is being charged. The Negro himself to-day views the situation humorously more often than not, as the songs in this group show.

> Pomp stole them britches but 't wan't no sin
> Case he stole them britches to be baptised in,

wrote one Negro poet, taking quite naturally the white man's point of view.

The well-known "Some folks say dat a nigger won't steal" is directly descended from the ante-bellum minstrels. Nor is it at all surprising, considering what various travellers have written of theft among some of the African tribes, to find the folk Negro, even without the white man's influence, regarding petty theft as humorous. Consider the moral status of Br'er Rabbit. "A daimen icker in a thrave 'S a sma' request" is a proposition in which both races in the South have pretty generally concurred.

With these possible exceptions, however, the songs in this group all originated after the Civil War. Some of the sins they celebrate are of comparatively recent adoption. No slave, obviously, could carry a gun, much less dare to sing about a "forty-four." Nor did he have access to whiskey. He lived under a more effective Prohibition régime than his grandchildren. Cocaine was not even in existence. Chickens and watermelons no doubt enjoyed little more security in slave days than at present, but their disappearance was not a proper subject for song. Most of the songs of this type that the Negro sings to-day probably originated with the black-face comedians of the white race and were taken up by the Negro because they appealed to his sense of humor. The ante-bellum Negro may have had his vices, but it was not his idea of tact to sing about them.

Many of these songs are connected with the blues, which were mainly of an underworld origin. Others, particularly those reflecting a humorous point of view on the matter of theft, probably owe a good deal to the conventionalized vaudeville idea of Negro humor. The readiness with which the folk-Negro accepts the white man's idea of Negro humor has always been an exasperation to the leaders who wish to improve the Negro's self-respect.

The most typically Negro songs in this group are those which have the fatalistic good humor in the face of misfortune for which the Negro is distinguished. The reverses of the crap game disturb him very little. Jail is a destiny that might as well be accepted cheerfully. The attitude of the Negro toward the law under which he lives but in which he has small part is so interesting that I could wish it better represented by the songs in this collection. The situation is undoubtedly humorous to the Negro himself at times, but it also trembles on the verge of pathos. This side is well illustrated by the following bit of dialogue quoted from a recent volume of Negro sketches: [1]

Voice — Way you been, Scip?
Scip — I been to de trial.
Voice — Who trial?
Scip — Un Fed boy, Jonas.
Voice — When dey guh finish?
Scip — Dey done finish.
Voice — Wha' dey do wid him?
Scip — You talk like a fool. Ax me what dey guh do wid him. Ain't I tell you dey try him? Ain't I tell you dey done finish try him? You ax me wha' dey do wid him. Ai'nt you know who set on de jury?
Voice — White folks.
Scip — Yes, white folks, and dat ain't all — poor white folks — poor buckra, cracker — ain't dat nuff? Dat who set on de jury.
Voice — But Jonas ain't do nuttin'.
Scip — Dat ain't make no difference. I done tell you who set on de jury.

---

[1] *Congaree Sketches*, by E. C. Adams (University of North Carolina Press, Chapel Hill, N. C., 1927), pp. 4-5. Quoted by permission of the author and publishers.

Voice — Is he pa fret much?

Scip — No he ain't fret. He know dey ain't no nuse to fret. He raise he chillun right and he ain't fret. He got sense. He know wha' guh be, guh be, en he ain't fret.

The "eastman," of course, and the bad man who brags of his prowess are both at home in songs of this class, but it would be restricting human nature too much to assert that they are peculiarly Negro types; they are simply racial variations of a universal type.

Nor will anyone who really knows the Negro take these songs, or the related songs about women treated elsewhere, too seriously as representing the whole of the Negro race. They are sung mainly by gang laborers, men engaged in hard and brutalizing work. They represent truly the thoughts of the singers in a particular mood at a particular time, but not necessarily the thoughts of the same men at home or in church. Even so, it is not a matter of color, as anyone familiar with the songs of white sailors and lumberjacks will readily testify. That a depraved singer is by no means to be argued from a depraved song, is a fact which must have been quite clear even to Hobo John, when he uttered those distinctly pious lines:

> And all niggers what rides de rods
> Got to put their trust in de hands of God,
> Hands of God, hands of God,
> Got to to put their trust in the hands of God.

SONGS, WITH ANNOTATIONS

The following songs classified in other groups might also be included in the present class: III, 1, 4 *A*, 6; IV, 23; V, 3, 8–11, 16, 25, 29, 32; VI, 44; VII, 76–79; IX, 48; X, 13, 27 *D*, 36, 43, 46, 53, 68, 72, 77.

I

REPORTED from Auburn, Ala., 1915–1916, MS. of C. C. Certain, as sung by construction gang in Mississippi in 1906.

Perrow, 1912, p. 155, prints four variants and fragments of "Railroad Bill," one as from Alabama in 1909 and three as from Mississippi in 1909. Odum, 1925, pp. 198–203, prints five variants of from ten to thirty lines in length. Scarborough, 1925, p. 252, quotes from Odum and Perrow and adds a variant from Mississippi. According to Perrow, Ibid., "Railroad Bill was a 'bad nigguh who terrified Alabama some years ago.' According to the song cited above, McMillan was an officer whom Railroad Bill killed."

> Railroad Bill did not know
> Dat Jim McMillan had a forty-fo'.

2

REPORTED from Auburn, Ala., 1915–1916, MS. of A. M. Kearly.

Roborus appears to be the same as Railroad Bill. The first line seems to be a variant of a common line, "Railroad Bill mighty bad man" (Perrow, 1912, p. 155, and Odum, 1925, pp. 200, 201, 202). The second line is a variant of two Railroad Bill lines (Perrow, 1912, p. 155): "Killed McMillan like a lightnin'-flash," and "He killed Bill Johnson with a lightning-flash."

> Roborus was a mighty mean man,
> He killed my son by the lighten flash.

3

REPORTED from Auburn, Ala., 1915–1916, MS. of A. H. Williamson, as heard in Lowndes County.

With the first line, cf. Odum, 1925, p. 134, "Shanghai Rooster."

> Shang-hi rooster ain't got no comb,
> Some of dese women ain't got no home,
> An' did n't it rain, rain, rain, rain, rain.
>
> Railroad Bill did not know
> That Jim McMillan had a forty-fo',
> And did n't it rain, rain, rain, rain, rain.

4

COTTON-EYED JOE [1]

REPORTED from Auburn, Ala., 1915–1916, MS. of B. A. Wooten, as heard in Marengo County, Ala.

Miss Scarborough, 1925, p. 69, gives a thirty-line version of "Cotton-Eyed Joe," — with music, — as "an authentic slavery time song," from Texas and Louisiana. Lines 5 and 6 are as in the present song, with "forty" for "twenty-five." Talley, 1922, p. 32, gives a ten-line version containing a variant of the present fragment.

> I'd been married twenty-five years ago,
> If it had n't been for Cotton-Eyed Joe.

[1] Local title.

5

REPORTED from Auburn, Ala., 1915–1916, anonymously.

Jones, I got my butcher knife and gattling gun and 't ain't no use for
    you to run,
I 'm gonna kill you an' bury you and dig you up for fun;
I 'll let the buzzards pick the meat off your bones, bum, bum;
An' your people will sadly moan, bum, bum,
Where is Jonese-e-u-m?

6

REPORTED from Durham, N. C., 1919, MS. of Howell J. Hatcher. "Heard sung
by old Negro working on father's farm."

    You've got your big gun, and I've got mine,
    Just rap on the cartridge if you don't mind dying.

7

REPORTED from Durham, N. C., 1919, MS. of Howell J. Hatcher. "Heard sung
by old Negro working on father's farm."

    A thirty-two special on a forty-four frame;
    How can I miss you when I've got dead aim?

8

REPORTED from Durham, N. C., 1919, MS. of Blake B. Harrison.
    The lines, "Who dar knockin' at the door," and "Who's dat knockin' at de
door," are common both as titles and choruses in the old minstrel songs. Cf.
Gumbo Chaff's *Ethiopian Glee Book*, 1848, p. 76; Christy's *Nigga Songster*, n. d.,
p. 117; White's *New Illustrated Melodeon*, n. d., p. 10; *Ibid.*, p. 73, "as composed,
arranged and sung by Charles White, the unrivalled Ethiopian performer."

    Who dat knockin' at de do' belo'?
    Ole uncle Eben wid a forty-fo'.

9

REPORTED from Durham, N. C., 1919, MS. of Sam E. Marsh. "Frequently
heard when you see a bunch of Negroes."
    I have the same song from Durham, N. C., 1919, MS. of J. R. Davis, as from
South Carolina.
    "Mr. Brown" is probably "my brown," as in Lomax (*Nation*) 1917, p. 144.
Variants of this song, and especially of the first line, are common. Cf. in this

collection, V, no. 16, VII, no. 78, X, no. 72, XII, nos. 10, 45; also Odum, 1926, pp. 26, 78, and Scarborough, 1925, p. 164.

> I was standing on the corner
> Talkin' to Mr. Brown,
> Along came the sheriff,
> Says, "Jail-house bound."

10

REPORTED from Durham, N. C., 1919, MS. of H. H. Hanchey. "Heard in summer of 1919, in New Hanover County, N. C. I think it originated from Negroes going to the city drunk."

> Standin' on de conah did n't mean no hawm.
> Long come a 'liceman an' grabbed me by de awm,
> Took me to de station to hab my trial,
> De judge gimme thirty days on de ole rock pile.

11

REPORTED from Durham, N. C., 1919, MS. of Percy F. Dilling, as heard at Bessemer City, Gaston County, N. C. "Sung by Negroes working on the railroad. He meant to get one hundred dollars saved up. He would bother no man but the policeman."

> I want to century just one more time.
> I don't bother no man but the man with the headache stick.

12

REPORTED from Auburn, Ala., 1915–1916, anonymously, as heard at Fort Payne, Ala., "during town boom of 1890 because of Negroes' fright from Police Dept."

Between 1900 and 1905 I heard small boys in North Carolina taunt recently arrested prisoners with

> Police, police, turn me loose
> Got no money but a good excuse,

adding other lines better calculated to infuriate the policeman. These two lines occur in "The Negro and the Policeman," Talley, 1922, p. 66.

The song is probably an off-shoot of May Irwin's "Mr. Johnson Turn Me Loose," one of the coon songs of the 1880–1910 period.

> O police, police, turn me loose,
> I'se got a home in de buzzard roost.
> Police, police, can't you see
> Dat I'se cripple in de knee?

13

REPORTED from Auburn, Ala., 1915–1916, MS. of A. H. Williamson, as heard in Lowndes County, Ala. "Sung by Negroes about going to jail. Bob Brenson was Chief Deputy of Lowndes County and Eaton Haynes was High Sheriff of Lowndes County."

> Yonder come Bob Brenson,
> Eaton Haynes behind.
> Get yo' tickets ready
> For on to jail yo' gwine.

14

REPORTED from Auburn, Ala., 1915–1916, MS. of E. Oliveira, as heard in New Orleans.

Evidently based on the following lines of the well-known song, "I've Been Working on the Railroad," which is quoted in Scarborough, 1925, p. 248, with the note that it was printed in 1900:

> Sing me a song of the city,
> Roll them cotton bales,
> Darky ain't half so happy
> As when he's out of jail.

> Clean that corn a coming,
> Hoe that cotton bale,
> Niggers always talking when they out of jail.

15

REPORTED from Auburn, Ala., 1915–1916, MS. of S. A. Allen, as heard in Shelby County. "A favorite among Negroes in Shelby County jail."

"Coming out of the wilderness" is really a religious expression somewhat similar to "coming through."

> Oh, how did you feel when you come out of the wilderness?

16

REPORTED from Auburn, Ala., 1915–1916, MS. of W. S. Black.

> I am so glad de cops dey don't know where I'm is.

17

REPORTED from Durham, N. C., 1919, MS. of James E. Lyon, Jr., as heard in High Point, N. C., 1916, "from Paul and Silas."

Mr. Lyon's comment that this is from "Paul and Silas," a well-known spiritual, illuminates somewhat the strange uses to which Negro songs may be put. The only similarities between the authentic spiritual and the present song are that Paul and Silas were "bound in jail" and that "one sang and the other one prayed." See II, no. 31.

The first two lines of the present song seem related to the song popular with college glee-clubs some years ago:

> First she gave me coffee,
> Then she gave me cake,
> Then she gave me ginger-bread
> And kissed me at the gate.

They give me coffee,
They give me tea,
They give me everything I wanted
But the jail-house key.

18

A

REPORTED from Auburn, Ala., 1915–1916, MS. of D. Q. McCord. "Sung by Negroes in road crews."

I have the same song, with slight verbal variations, from Auburn, Ala., 1915–1916, MS. of G. E. Lumpkin, as heard in "different parts of Ala."; also the last four lines in somewhat corrupted form, from Auburn, Ala., 1915–1916, MS. of R. W. Davis.

This is a well-known glee-club song, probably not of Negro origin. The interline refrain, "Way down," etc., belongs properly to "Some Folks Say Dat a Nigger Won't Steal" (cf. no. 39 *A–E*, in this chapter) and takes the place of the authentic lines, "Come you seven, come e-leven."

My baby needs a new pair shoes,
Way down, way down, way down, yonder in de corn fiel'.
How'm I gointa buy 'em if I lose?
Way down, way down, way down yonder in de corn fiel'.
Roll dem bones, roll dem bones, roll 'em on de square,
Roll 'em on de sidewalk, de streets or any whar.
Roll 'em in de evenin', roll 'em in de night,
Roll dem bones, when de cops are out of sight.

B

Reported from Auburn, Ala., 1915–1916, MS. of B. Y. Pennington, as heard at Andalusia, Ala. "Sung by Negro ditch diggers."

The first three lines illustrate the characteristic Negro practice of condensing a well-known song that cannot be accurately remembered at the time of singing. The last four lines are well known and occur both independently and with the "Alabama Bound" refrain. Cf. IX, nos. 47, 48, XI, no. 14, and no. 31, in this chapter.

> I'm gonna roll dem dice
> And I ain't gonna lose,
> 'Cause my baby need a new pair of shoes.
> Don't you leave me here,
> Don't you leave me here,
> But if you leave me here,
> Please leave me a dime for beer.

C

Reported from Durham, N. C., 1919, MS. of Thomas T. Neal.

In this song only the first and last lines of the refrain belong to the "Roll Them Bones," song.

> My chilluns on de ground,
> My wife is out of work,
> Ain't got no shoes for de chillun,
> Can't find my wife no work.

Refrain

> So come you seben,
>   Oh! bones will you 'leben?
> Can't find my wife no work
>   And baby needs a new pair ob shoes.

19

REPORTED from Durham, N. C., 1919, MS. of Howell J. Hatcher. "Heard sung by old Negro working on father's farm."

> Shoot your dice and have your fun,
> I'll have mine when the police come.
> Police come, I did n't wanta go
> I knocked him in the head wid a forty-fo'.

20

REPORTED from Durham, N. C., 1919, MS. of Howell J. Hatcher. "Heard sung by old Negro on father's farm."
   This couplet occurs most commonly in the spirituals, as in the Fisk University quartet's phonograph record of "Little David."

> I told you once and I told you twice
> That you can't get to Heaven by rolling dice.

21

REPORTED from Auburn, Ala., 1915–1916, MS. of A. M. Kearly.

> I don't play the dozen
> And don't you ease me in.

22

A

REPORTED from Auburn, Ala., 1915–1916, MS. of H. T. Killingsworth, as heard in southwestern Georgia. "Sung by Negro crap shooters."

> Lickety splup, lickety splup,
> De more you put down de less you pick up.

B

Reported from Auburn, Ala., 1915–1916, MS. of W. W. Allen.

> Chuck a luck,
> The more you lay down
> The less you pick up.

23

REPORTED from Auburn, Ala., 1915–1916, MS. of W. M. Mobley, as heard in Birmingham, Ala.
   For other songs dealing with racing, see IV, no. 40, VI, no. 6, VII, no. 45, XIV, no. 23.

> I'se gwine to de race track
> To see my pony run,
> An' ef I win some money
> I'se gwine to gib ma honey some.

24

REPORTED from Durham, N. C., 1919, MS. of R. S. Jones. "Heard sung by Negroes at work on city streets."

> Give me whiskey when I die.

25

REPORTED from Auburn, Ala., 1915–1916, MS. of R. E. Donis, as heard in Georgia.

> Kentucky water drinks like sherry wine.

26

REPORTED from Durham, N. C., 1919, MS. of W. L. Hampton, as heard in Durham County, N. C. "Heard from a Negro farm hand in Durham County, N. C."
Evidently part of the old song of the white people:

> Well I ain't been sober since last October,
> And I don't know the reason why.

> Have n't been sober since the last October.

27

REPORTED from Auburn, Ala., 1915–1916, MS. of R. R. Beard, as heard in Mobile County, Ala. "Sung by an ex-slave."

> When I got good ole egg-nog an' 'simmon beer,
> An' I git tight, yer need not keer,
> 'Case Christmas comes but once a year.

28

REPORTED from Auburn, Ala., 1915–1916, MS. of F. W. McMeans, as heard at Wolf Creek, Tenn. "Banjo Song."
A variant of the old song, "Massa had a storey house," VIII, no. 22.

> The rich man has a big fine house
> Fifteen stories high,
> And every story in that house
> Is full of rock and rye.

29

REPORTED from Auburn, Ala., 1915–1916, anonymously.

> I'm gwine back to Birmingham,
> Dat's de place where whiskey am.

30

REPORTED from Auburn, Ala., 1915–1916, MS. of C. Clark, as heard in Crenshaw County, Ala. "Sung by Negro cook."
  With the last line, cf. various other "Don't you leave me here" songs, as the
following one, and XI, no. 14.

> De preacher in de pulpit
> Drinking champagne and beer,
> Women in de amen corner
> Singing don't you leave me here.

31

REPORTED from Auburn, Ala., 1915–1916, MS. of De Witt Holder, as heard in
Jackson, Miss. "Sung by Negroes."
  The first four lines belong to the "Don't you leave me here" songs. With the
rest of the song, cf. various songs on different complexions of women: VII, no. 90,
IX, nos. 47–49, XI, no. 14.

> Doan you leave me here,
> Oh doan you leave me here;
> If you leave me here, boys,
> Leave a dime for beer.
>
> My mammy and my daddy am brown skin,
> De lices in my head am brown skin,
> De horses in my stable am brown skin,
> De possum on my table am brown skin,
>
> De chicken in my coop am brown skin,
> De turtle in my soup am brown skin.

32

A

REPORTED from Durham, N. C., 1919, MS. of French W. Graham, "as heard in Newburgh, N. Y., 1919."

The "when I die" motif, and the comment on a burial place are both found in the Negro spirituals and in the revival songs of the white people of the early nineteenth century; for example, the common couplet:

> When I die I wanta die right,
> Wanta go to heaven all dressed in white (Kennedy, 1925, p. 132),

and the spiritual, "You may bury me in the East, you may bury me in the West."

Cf. VII, no. 82.

> When I die don't bury me a-tall,
> Just kiver my body with alcohol.

B

Reported from Auburn, Ala., 1915–1916, MS. of E. A. Caldwell, as heard in Jackson County, Ala.

> When I die bury me good and deep,
> Bottle of booze at my feet,
> Pair of dice in my hand;
> Throw seven and eleven
> In the Promised Land.

33

REPORTED from Auburn, Ala., 1915–1916, MS. of De Witt Holder, as heard in Jackson, Miss. "Sung by Negroes."

I have the first stanza from Auburn, Ala., 1915–1916, as heard in Alabama, with "sea" for "ribber" and "beer" for "booze"; also from Auburn, Ala., 1915–1916, as heard in northern Alabama, with "whiskey" for "booze" and "duck" for "mallard duck." Cf. also VII, no. 76 and note, and nos. 34 and 35, in this chapter.

> If de ribber was booze,
> An' I'se a mallard duck;
> I'd dive to de bottom, boys,
> An' I'd neber come up.
>
> Oh, when I die,
> Doan you bury me 'tall;
> Jes' soak my bones
> In alcohol.

Oh, when I die,
Doan you bury me deep;
Put a jug of molasses
By my head and feet.

Put two big biscuits
Right in my hands,
And I am on my way
To de Promised Land.

34

REPORTED from Auburn, Ala., 1915–1916, anonymously.
　With the first stanza, cf. no. 33, in this chapter and note; with the second, cf.
XIV, no. 12.

If de river was whiskey,
En if I was er duck,
I'd go down and never come up.

If de blues was whiskey,
I'd stay drunk all de time.

35

REPORTED from Auburn, Ala., 1915–1916, MS. of J. R. Rutland, as heard in
Auburn, Ala. "Sung by Negro minstrel."
　Cf. no. 33, in this chapter and note.

If the ocean were whiskey and the seas were rye,
I'd swim 'cross the ocean and drink the seas dry.

36

REPORTED from Auburn, Ala., 1915–1916, MS. of P. J. Bowab, as heard in
Escambia County, Ala.,
　Cf. X, no. 27 *B*, *C*, *D*, XIV, no. 4.

From ashes to ashes
And from dust to dust;
If de whiskey don't kill me
De morphine must.

37

REPORTED from Auburn, Ala., 1915–1916, MS. of R. R. Beard, as heard in Mobile County, Ala. "Sung by an ex-slave."

> Dey mixed dem roun' an' stirred dem up
> Like rum an' 'lasses in er cup.

38

REPORTED from Auburn, Ala., MS. of A. H. Williamson, as heard in Lowndes County, Ala.

> Oh! I'm goin' er way
> Er thousand miles fum home,
> I'll drink my good "bottled in bond"
> But I'll let the cocaine 'lone.

39

SOME FOLKS SAY [1]

NUMEROUS stanzas of this sort have been in circulation for years. I have heard:

> Some folks say dat a girl won't climb,
> But I caught one up a long-leaf pine.

I have always heard it sung by white people, with the interline refrain:

> Way down, way down, way down yonder in de cornfield.

Perrow, 1915, p. 135, gives one stanza of *A* below, with the "You shall be free" refrain. Peabody, 1903, and Odum, 1926, p. 174, give it "preacher" as in *E* below. In Odum the lines are combined with "Raise a Rukus Tonight."

The song was known to ante-bellum minstrels. Cf. "'Whar You Cum From,' by J. B. Harper, the Celebrated Delineator of Comic and Aethiopian characters. Copyright secured," in *Negro Singers' Own Book*, 1846(?), p. 411:

> Some folks say dat niggers won't steal,
> I kotch one in my cornfield.
> I ax him 'bout de corn, he call me a liar,
> I up wid a chunk and knock him in de fiar.

If this is the original version, the song probably came from the tidewater region of Virginia or North Carolina, where "chunk" means to throw.

It is probably this song that is largely responsible for the many songs, including numerous blues, beginning "Some folks say."

A variation of the refrain to "Way down-in de cott'n field" occurs in "Cott'n Dance Song," given in Burlin, 1918–1919, iii, 21, as "from Slavery Times, Florida."

---

[1] No local title given.

A

Reported from Durham, N. C., 1919, MS. of Jesse M. Livingston. "Heard sung by Scotland County cornfield Negroes (about 1912)."
I have the first stanza from Durham, N. C., 1919, MS. of David T. House.

Some folks say a Negro won't steal,
I caught two in my cornfield.
One had a shovel, the other had a hoe,
If that ain't stealing I don't know.

Some folks say a Negro won't steal,
But I caught three in my cornfield.
I ran dem through a pine thicket,
Stove my head in a yellow jacket nest.

B

Reported from Auburn, Ala., 1915–1916, MS. of R. E. Davis, as heard in Georgia.

Some folks say a Negro won't steal,
I caught two in my tater fiel'.
One had a shovel and the other had a hoe,
If that ain't stealin' I don't know.

C

Reported from Auburn, Ala., 1915–1916, MS. of S. J. Nadler, as heard in Etowah County, northern Alabama. "Sung by Negro laborers on farm."

Some folks say dat niggers don't steal,
But I caught three in my cornfield.
One had a bushel, one had a peck,
One had a water-million straddle his neck.

D

Reported from Auburn, Ala., 1915–1916, MS. of M. J. Hollingsworth, as heard in Pickens County, western Alabama.

Some folks say that a Negro won't steal,
I caught ninety-nine in my corn field.
One had a bushel and one had a peck;
One had an ear tied around his neck.

E

Reported from Auburn, Ala., 1915–1916, MS. of H. T. Killingsworth, as heard in southwestern Georgia. "Sung by cornfield Negroes."

> Some folks say dat er preacher won't steal,
> But I caught one in my cornfield.
> He had er bushel, his wife had er peck,
> De baby had a roastin' ear hung er round his neck.

40

REPORTED from Durham, N. C., 1919, MS. of Blake B. Harrison.

With "chicken" for "rooster," the lines occur in Talley, 1922, p. 95; Odum, 1925, p. 237; Scarborough, 1925, p. 194, as from Texas, with the "You shall be free" refrain. In all these modern versions it is the opening couplet of a short narrative called by Talley and Odum "Frightened Away from a Chicken Roost." In the ante-bellum minstrel books, however, the identical lines exist as an independent jingle:

> Behind de hen house on my knee
> Tinks I hear a chicken sneeze.
> Turkey playin' cards on de pumkin vine,
> Goose chaw backer and duck drink wine.

This stanza, with very slight verbal variations, occurs in "Git Along John" (*Negro Singers' Own Book*, 1846[?], p. 312, and Christy's *Nigga Songster*, n. d., p. 238), and "Cum Along John the Piper's Son" (Christy's *Nigga Songster*, n. d., p. 68). A variant occurs in "Singing Darkies of Ohio" (White's *Serenaders' Song Book* [copyright, 1851], p. 54).

For what is probably a parody, see IX, no. 55.

> Down in de hen-house on my knees,
> Thought I heard dat rooster sneeze.

41

REPORTED from Auburn, Ala., 1915–1916, MS. of M. E. Bryant.
Cf. the next three songs, also VIII, no. 6.

> Chicken in dis tree and dere's nobody here but me,
> Gwine to get me a chicken 'fore day.

42

A

REPORTED from Auburn, Ala., 1915–1916, MS. of M. E. Bryant.
Perrow, 1913, p. 170, gives three variants, one from East Tennessee mountain whites in 1909, with music; two from Mississippi Negroes in 1909. Odum, 1926, p. 128, gives one variant. Cf. VI, no. 21, XI, no. 6.

Chicken in dis sack and de hounds is on my track,
Am going to make it to my shanty 'fore day.

B

Reported from Auburn, Ala., 1915–1916, MS. of J. W. McKinstry, as heard in southwestern Alabama.

Hounds on my track,
Chickens on my back;
Oh, Lord, if they don't hurry up and catch me,
I will make it to my shack.

43

REPORTED from Auburn, Ala., 1915–1916, MS. of A. H. Williamson, as heard in Lowndes County, Ala.
Probably from a minstrel song of the present century.

Well I wonder whut de po' nigger gwinder do,
Well I wonder whut de po' nigger gwinder do.
Tell me oh! tell me! Whut de niggers gwinder do
When de chickens roos' so high,
Well de chickens dey roos' so high,
Well de chickens dey roos' so high.
Tell me, *please* tell me, whut de nigger gwinder do,
When de chickens roos' so high.

44

REPORTED from Auburn, Ala., 1915–1916, MS. of A. M. Kearly.
Cf. Odum, 1925, p. 133. Both songs probably sprang from the popular minstrel song of the early nineteen hundreds, "Chicken, chicken, you can roost behind the moon," of which Perrow quotes a part (1913), p. 130, as from Mississippi in 1909.
Cf. in this collection V, nos. 8–11, VI, nos. 34–39.

Chicken, come down out of that sycamore tree,
You cannot roost too high for me.
The white folks get up late and the Negro early and soon,
And the man with the chicken has gone over behind the moon.

45

REPORTED from Auburn, Ala., 1915–1916, MS. of R. M. Beasly.
Cf. V, no. 16, VII, no. 78, and nos. 9 and 10, in this chapter.

Standin' in some corner, hongry as can be,
I ask some kind young lady to soke some bread in me.
She throwed her arms around me, she loved me like a fren',
"If I give you this samwidge you'll be here bummin' ergin."

46

REPORTED from Auburn, Ala., 1915–1916, MS. of R. A. Chambers.

Tuesday mornin' after a shower of rain,
Round de bend I saw a passenger train.
On de pilot lay a hobo Jawn,
He been a good old rounder but he's dead and gone,
Dead and gone, dead and gone,
He been a good old rounder, but he's dead and gone.

Pore old Jawn said befo' he died,
He'd fix it so no nigger could ride,
And all niggers what rides de rods
Got to put their trust in de hands of God,
Hands of God, hands of God,
Got to put their trust in the hands of God.

47

REPORTED from Auburn, Ala., 1915–1916, MS. of R. M. Beasly.

Looker yonder comin'! comin' down the track,
Must be hoboes with a bulget on his back,
One must be my brother, the other my brother-in-law,
Tramped all the way from Missouri or state of Arkansaw.

48

REPORTED from Auburn, Ala., 1915–1916, MS. of A. H. Williamson, as heard in Lowndes County, Ala.
    For a variant, cf. Odum, 1925, p. 211. An eastman is a Negro man who is supported by the women.
    A variant of the last three lines occurs as the chorus of "I'm a Nachel-bawn Reacher," Scarborough, 1925, p. 233, as from eastern Tennessee.

> Ol' Aunt Dina dreampt a dream,
> She dreampt she bought a sewin' machine,
> She sewed de stitches
> An' de needle was broke,
> I'm a natchel-born eastman
> An' it ain't no joke,
> Eastman an' it ain't no joke,
> I'm a natchel-born eastman
> An' it ain't no joke.

XIII

RACE–CONSCIOUSNESS

THE songs in which the Negro singer is race-conscious are generally work songs, though some of them, especially the older ones, may be social songs. Race-consciousness may be present even in his religious songs. It was present in the songs sung on the early minstrel stage and preserved by the Negro.[1] It would be almost impossible, in fact, for any American Negro not to be race-conscious at times.

But race-consciousness is one thing and race-sensitiveness and racial self-pity are others. Many Negro writers and leaders are highly race-sensitive. A large number of poems have been written by Negro poets to protest against the white man's injustice.[2] The commonest explanation to-day of the Negro spiritual is that it is a racial sorrow-song — an idea good for at least one purple patch of prose sympathy in almost any treatise. This idea, which I hope I have already demonstrated to be misleading, finds an occasional complement in the consideration of the secular songs also as an expression of self-pity. Both ideas have had the support of Negro writers— for one reason, because they gained sympathy for the Negro; for another, because the writers themselves sincerely believed them. This fact only suggests, what anyone who knows the folk-songs and the writings of Negro leaders could easily believe, that the more radical-minded Negro leaders and the extremely conservative folk Negro do not understand each other as fully as they might be supposed to do.

Beyond question there are some secular folk-songs in which the Negro does indulge in self-pity, also some in which he expresses resentment of the treatment accorded him by the white race. "All for the white man and nothing for the nigger" is the sentiment of several songs in which the white man and Negro are compared as to their opportunities, their pleasures, and their status before the law. Of course, there is some bitterness in the comparison. But to stop

---

[1] Cf. nos. 2, 3, 5, 6, 11, 14.

[2] See "Racial Feeling in Negro Poetry," by the present author, in the *South Atlantic Quarterly*, January, 1922.

here, as has been the common practice, is to leave the story but half-told. The very small number of such songs in my whole collection of nearly a thousand (and the proportion holds true of all the other collections I have seen) is a matter of really primary significance. To base a general conclusion upon them would be like concluding that all Americans in the nineteenth century were polygamists because the Mormons were. Moreover, such a conclusion would ignore the very obvious truth that many of these songs show a humorous acceptance of facts that to a white man would be anything but humorous. Some of this humor is even borrowed from the "coon-songs" of the white man, as in the first song given below. For the folk Negro "it's no disgrace to run when you git skeered" (another sentiment probably borrowed from the whites); more commonly than not he laughs at himself for running from the white man. This may be a state of mind carried over from slavery times, when it was certainly no disgrace to run from the "pateroller"; or it may be another adoption of the white man's idea of humor as expressed in the old minstrel songs; but it is certainly present in the songs the Negro has sung since slavery times. He laughs at himself running because it is another man that he sees; he seldom sees his own disasters except at the very moment of their incidence. If we ignore the twinkle in a man's eye when he tells a story at his own expense, it is easy to misinterpret or over-interpret the story.

It is very easy, in fact, to over-interpret all Negro folk-songs through forgetting that to the folk Negro the music, and not the words, is the important matter. Words to the folk Negro are more apt to be mere incidents, or ornaments, than instruments of precise meaning. They express a general feeling in his songs, but not the accurate idea with which we associate them in sophisticated songs. Nonsense and triviality have supplied many of the words and ostensible sentiments of the Negro song from the time they were first reported by early nineteenth-century travellers down to the present day. If the Negro singer comments upon his own inferiority to the white man in much the same manner and mood in which he comments upon women, work, obvious animal traits, and trivial personal experiences, and in less proportion, then it is hard to see that he takes one subject more seriously than the others. If he borrows and preserves the white man's so-called humor on this supposedly sensitive topic, I am even less impressed with his self-pity. And if he is consistent in contrasting raccoon, 'possum, and rabbit, the yaller gal and the black gal, the ladybug and the bedbug, sometimes in the very same song in which he contrasts Negro and white man and always in the same manner, I am led to suppose that the real importance of the circumstance is not self-pity, but a fondness for the rhetorical device of antithesis, let the sentiments be what they may. Of course the Negro laborer is sometimes surly; of course, he sometimes growls and is dissatisfied with his lot. But the real significance of his songs expressing race-consciousness is the fact that they show so little of this mood. Fundamentally they are striking evidence of the deep conservatism, humor, patience, and sense of present realities with which the Negro has contributed probably more than his full share to the concord of the two races in the South.

SONGS, WITH ANNOTATIONS

The following songs classified in other groups might also be included in the present group: III, 23; IV, 37; V, 15; VI, 13, VIII, 11; X, 16–20.

I

REPORTED from Durham, N. C., 1919, MS. of J. D. Johnson, Jr. "Heard sung by an old Negro, who accompanied himself on the banjo, in a small town in eastern North Carolina."

This is evidently a descendant of a modern minstrel song which was popular about 1905:

> Coon, coon, coon, and I wish my color would fade;
> Coon, coon, coon, I like a brighter shade;
> Coon, coon, coon, in morning, night or noon,
> I'd rather be a white man than a coon, coon, coon.

Ho! ho! and I wish my color would fade.

(To be repeated over and over again.)

2

REPORTED from Durham, N. C., 1919, MS. of Jesse M. Livingston. "Heard sung by cornfield Negroes in Scotland County, about 1912."

Miss Scarborough prints several songs about the monkey and the baboon, (1925, p. 180), but without the comparison. Stanza 23 of "De Original Jim Crow," *Negro Singers' Own Book*, 1846(?), p. 329, begins:

> A ring-tailed monkey and a ribb'd-nosed baboon.

I think the comparison of the Negro and the monkey goes back to the old minstrels. In 1843, William Cullen Bryant described a "monkey song" as sung on a South Carolina plantation. *Prose Writings of William Cullen Bryant*, edited by Parke Godwin, 1901, ii, 32.

The original for this stanza, as well as for the "God made a nigger" song
(see no. 14,in this chapter) is to be found in stanza 5 of the "Creation Song"
as printed by Cox, 1925, p. 502:

> Then he made a nigger, made after night,
> Made him in a hurry, and forgot to make him white.
> Then he made a monkey and set him on a rail,
> You could n't tell the difference, but the monkey had a tail.

Cox's version is as sung in West Virginia about 1915, but the "Creation Song"
is found in most of the minstrel books from 1846 to 1861. See Cox's note, p. 501;
also notes to III, no. 25, and V, no. 26, in this volume.

> I saw a negro and a monkey
> A riding of a rail.
> The only difference I could tell
> The nigger did n't have no tail.

3

A

REPORTED from Auburn, Ala., 1915–1916, MS. of W. D. Kimbrough, as heard
in Camden, Ala.
  Cf. two lines from "Hop Lite Loo," *Negro Singers' Own Book*, 1846(?), p. 14;
also *Ibid.*, p. 412, in "Whar You Cum From":

> Now brandy is brandy anyway you mix it
> Niger is niger any way you fix him.

> A nigger be a nigger, don't care what he do,
> Tie a yellow ribbon in the bottom of his shoe.

B

Reported from Auburn, Ala., 1915–1916, anonymously.
  An interesting variant occurs in Odum, 1925, p. 233, where "Button up his
galluses" becomes "Snatch his britches up," and the shirt and coat are omitted
to make room for the "You shall be free" refrain.

> Er a nigger 'll be a nigger
> Don't keer what you do.
> Tie a bow of ribbon in the toe of his shoe,
> Button up his gallowses around his throat,
> Don't wear no shirt, don't need no coat.

4

REPORTED from Auburn, Ala., 1915–1916, MS. of R. M. Beasley. This is an off-shoot of the spiritual:

> If 'ligion wuz a thing that money could buy
>   Reign, Marse Jesus, oh, reign.
> The rich would live an' the poor would die
>   Reign, Marse Jesus, oh, reign.

If-a 'ligion wuz er thing that money could buy,
The rich would live and the po' would die.
I'm so glad things jes' like dis,
Dere's 'nother good chance for the po' coon yet.

5

REPORTED from Auburn, Ala., 1915–1916, MS. of W. W. Allen, as heard in Florida.

The comparison of the white man and the Negro, on which the following songs are mainly based, is present in the old minstrel books. In addition to passages cited with the songs upon which they bear, two stanzas may be quoted from "What's Going On," *Negro Singers' Own Book*, 1846(?), p. 245.

> White folks hab good brain,
> Negro hab sense like punkin;
> I kotch de debil todder night
> Eating apple dumpling.

> White folks say de debil's dead,
>   An buried in a tan vat;
> De nigger says he's raised again,
>   And turned into a ramcat.

White man kill Muskogee duck,
Give the nigger the bones to suck.

6

REPORTED from Auburn, Ala., 1915–1916, MS. of R. R. Beard, as heard in Mobile County, Ala. "Sung by grandfather."

Ginger Blue was apparently a dangerous character whose history belongs to pre-minstrel obscurity. Cf. stanza 2 of "Tom Walker," *Negro Singers' Own Book*, 1846(?), p. 12:

> De first was on de walk,
> A nigga singing walk chalk,
> Ginger Blue in de street,
> He made nigger's gizzard beat.
> Walk Tom Walker, etc.

also, *Ibid.*, p. 348, "Ginger Blue," stanza 1 of which ends:

> Walk, chalk, Ginger Blue, get over double trouble,
> And Old Varginny neber tire.

Cf. VIII, no. 11.

> Walk, talk, ginger blue,
> De white man jumped an' de nigger flew.

7

REPORTED from Auburn, Ala., 1915–1916, MS. of A. M. Kearly.

This song is probably a corrupted form of a stanza printed by Perrow, 1915, p. 140, two variants as from Mississippi in 1909; and Lomax (*Nation*) 1917, p. 144:

> White folks go to college, niggers to de fiel'.
> White folks learn to read and write, nigger learn to steal.

> A white child goes to school and learns to read and write,
> And a negro goes to the field and learns how to steal.

8

A

REPORTED from Auburn, Ala., 1915–1916, MS. of J. W. McKinstry, as heard in southwestern Alabama. "Heard at Negro concert."

That this song and its variants are descended from songs sung by slaves as early as 1838 is strongly indicated by Fanny Kemble. See Appendix V, p. 457.

For two variants, from Mississippi in 1909 and Virginia, cf. Perrow, 1915, p. 401.

> White man in the dining-room eating cake and cream,
> Negro in the kitchen eating those good old greasy greens.

B

Reported from Auburn, Ala., 1915–1916, MS. of E. D. Bartlett, as heard near Lineville, Ala. "Sung by railroad and mining gangs."

> White folks in the parlor eating ice cream,
> Negroes in the kitchen scraping over
> Good old greasy greens.

C

Reported from Auburn, Ala., 1915–1916, MS. of J. W. McKinstry. "Sung by Negro boys at a concert at close of school." "This is only a part of the 'Good Old Turnip Greens' song."

> White man in the parlor reading latest news,
> Negro in the kitchen blacking Roosevelt's shoes.

9

REPORTED from Auburn, Ala., 1915–1916, MS. of A. M. Kearly.

> If a white man kills a negro, they hardly carry it to court,
> If a negro kills a white man, they hang him like a goat.

10

REPORTED from Auburn, Ala., 1915–1916, MS. of J. E. Hillhouse, as heard in southern Alabama.

This song goes back to the early minstrels. In "Who Dare," *Negro Singers' Own Book*, 1846(?), p. 339, the singer advises his friends (stanza 1) "Neber live with white folks, dey neber use you well," and in stanza 3 specifies:

> Den a little cold pancake and a little hog fat, Ah!
> And dey grumble like de debil, if you eat too much ob dat, Ah.

For later variants see Perrow, 1915, p. 140 (as from Tennessee in 1909); Scarborough, 1925, p. 207 (as from an old cornshucking song).

> A cold cup o' coffee and the meat's mighty fat,
> The white folks growl if I eat much o' dat.

11

REPORTED from Durham, N. C., 1919, MS. of Jesse M. Livingston. "Heard in 1914, on plantation in Scotland County, N. C."

I have the same, with trifling verbal differences, from Auburn, Ala., 1915–1916, MS. of P. Pickard.

Practically the same as in Scarborough, 1925, p. 165. Cf. Ibid., p. 228, where it is given as sung "before the war," with the first two lines slightly different. With only slight differences, it was sung by slaves during the early eighteen-fifties. See Appendix V, p. 455.

> The old bee makes de honey-comb,
> The young bee makes de honey;
> Colored folks plant de cotton and corn,
> And de white folks gits de money.

12

REPORTED from Auburn, Ala., 1915–1916, MS. of A. M. Kearly.
I have the same from Auburn, Ala., 1915–1916, MS. of W. W. Allen, with
"naught" for "ought"; from Auburn, Ala., 1915–1916, MS. of H. Carder, as
heard in a dolomite quarry at Ketona, Ala., with "the company" for "white
folks"; and from Durham, N. C., MS. of David T. House, Jr.
It is a very common stanza, both as an independent song and in combination. Cf. Perrow, 1915, p. 140 (as from Virginia in 1909); Ibid., pp. 144–145;
Lomax (*Nation*), 1917, p. 144; Talley, 1922, p. 207. For a variant, see Scarborough, 1925, p. 228, from Mississippi:

> Here sits de woodpecker,
> Learnin' how to figger,
> All for de white man
> And nothing for de nigger!

Ought's a' ought and a figure's a figur',
All for the white folks and none for the nigger.

13

REPORTED from Auburn, Ala., 1915–1916, MS. of O. C. Bryan, as heard in
Coffie County, Ala. "Sung by old Negro on farm."
Cf. VI, no. 13, and nos. 12 and 17, in this chapter.

The white man and the nigger
Had a hunt on cold Christmas night.
They caught de 'possum five,
Nothing would do but to have a fight.
Oh what a growl over the poor sum,
Why do I care to have a settlement by figures?
Aught's a' aught, figure is a figure,
All for de white man and none for the nigger.

14

A

REPORTED from Auburn, Ala., 1915–1916, MS. of P. W. Pelts.
Practically the same as in Lomax (*Nation*) 1917, p. 144, and Cox, 1925,
p. 502 (from West Virginia in 1915), as the first two lines of stanza 5 in the
"Creation Song," which is found in many of the minstrel books from 1846 to
1861. See Cox's note, p. 501; and notes to III, no. 25; V, no. 26; and XIII, no.
2, in this volume.

God made a nigger,
He made him in the night,
He made him in a hurry,
And forgot to make him white.

ℬ

Reported from Auburn, Ala., 1915–1916, MS. of L. G. Duggar. "Sung by Negro hitching up horse."

God made white man,
God made nigger,
God made nigger,
And forgot to make him white.

God mixed de paint,
God painted white man,
God painted white man,
And de paint give out.

15

REPORTED from Auburn, Ala., 1915–1916, MS. of W. H. Williamson, as heard in Lowndes County, Ala.
This song combines a modification of the "God made a nigga" song with the lullaby. For other lullabies, see the next song, and XIV, nos. 15 and 16.

Chorus

Bye-bye, little black baby,
Bye-bye, go to sleep;
The angels am watchin' you baby,
So why don't you go to sleep?

God made yo', yo' little black baby,
Yes! God made yo' in the night,
An' when de mornin' come, baby,
He forgot to make you white.

But God loves yo', yo' little black baby,
Jes' de same as if yo' wuz white,
God made yo', yo' little black baby,
So I jes' says yo 's all right.

16

REPORTED from Auburn, Ala., 1915–1916, MS. of R. Allen, as heard in Jackson County, Ala.

Line 4 is taken from the well-known hymn, "In the Sweet Bye and Bye."

Oh little nigger baby,
Black face and shiny eyes,
Better than the po' white trash
In the sweet bye and bye;
Black face born that way, brains all in his feet.
That's the song of the little nigger baby
Down on Market Street.[1]

17

A

REPORTED from Auburn, Ala., 1915–1916, MS. of R. B. Ashe, as heard in Alabama.

I have the same song from Auburn, Ala., 1915–1916, contributed anonymously; from Auburn, Ala., 1915, MS. of J. H. Owens; and as a stanza of the "Dummy Train" song, VI, no. 16. Practically the same song is printed by Odum (*J. A. F. L.*, xxiv, 255, no. 7), whence it is quoted by Odum, 1925, p. 255, and Scarborough, 1925, p. 227. The first two lines occur independently in Odum, 1925, p. 7. Scarborough, p. 180, prints a variant from Louisiana, with "Monkey and baboon" for "Nigger and white man."

The song seems to be slightly related to the "Nigger and rooster had a fight" song, VI, no. 34.

Nigger and a white man playing seven up,
Nigger won the money, scared to pick it up;
Nigger made the motion, the white man fell;
Nigger grabbed the money and run like hell.

B

Reported from Auburn, Ala., 1915–1916, MS. of J. W. McKinstry, as heard in southwestern Alabama. "Sung at big Negro meeting, to the tune of 'All My Sins,' etc."

This song is an interesting example of the way in which even a very short Negro song may combine the most diverse elements. The last line and the tune are from a spiritual (see II, no. 3). The first couplet is from the "Seven up" song; and the second couplet is the same as IX, no. 55, a modification of XII, no. 40, which occurs in Scarborough, 1925, p. 194, as from Texas; Odum, 1925,

---

[1] Probably in Chattanooga, Tenn.

p. 237; and as the first two lines of "Git Along John," *Negro Singers' Own Book*, 1846(?), p. 312.

Negro and white man playing seven up,
Negro wins the money but he is afraid to pick it up.
Down in the hollow upon my knees,
Praying to the Lord to send me some cheese,
All my sins done taken away, all my sins been taken away.

18

REPORTED from Durham, N. C., 1919, MS. of J. P. Jones. "Heard while walking on the railroad . . . in Durham County" [N. C.]. "Sung by gang of Negroes." "Also heard sung by Negroes working on the roads of Durham County." Cf. Puckett, 1926, p. 8.

The coal car is more commonly the Jim Crow car, which the "po' black gal" rides in in the songs comparing girls of different color. Many songs on this same model compare three girls, three animals, or three insects. See VI, nos. 23–26, and X, nos. 17–26.

Rich man rides on a Pullman car,
Poor man takes de plain,
But de ole black nigger rides on de coal car,
But he gets there just de same.

XIV

BLUES AND MISCELLANEOUS SONGS

THE miscellaneous songs concluding this group are so placed because, like the boll weevil, they were "jes' a-lookin' for a home." This section seemed as good a home for them as any. Most of them except the lullabies are in reality work songs which express random thoughts not especially applicable to any particular form of work. They are a part of a large number of work songs in this collection expressing random thoughts; but all such songs except those in this section were referable to some particular branch of work through the conditions under which they were observed as being sung.

The blues in this section are by no means all that the collection contains. A number will be found classified under other groups. Some, again, are not so easily recognizable; for in spite of the typical tunes and the two or three easily recognizable formulas, there are a number of so-called blues that do not conform to the general type. Probably many such in the present collection were not blues when collected and have since been absorbed into that category. For when most of them were collected, the recent craze for blues was just beginning to gather momentum. Any collection made since 1915 would show a much greater influence of blues upon almost all types of Negro songs, as is true of Odum and Johnson's *Negro Workaday Songs*.

The blues are, more definitely than any other Negro songs, the songs of a single singer. They express an individual reaction, usually one of depression, but often, as Mr. Niles has pointed out, one of humorous acceptance of the inevitable. Their early significance is shown by several of the songs in this group; they were "the poor man's heart disease," "a woman on a good man's mind," "a good man feelin' bad" — in other words, personal restlessness or depression. They stressed melancholy, love, misfortune, complaint, homesickness, and often brought in other themes from other songs by the mere impulse of lengthening the present outburst. They varied considerably in length and form, partly because of the inclusion of extraneous elements; but typically they consisted either of one line sung three times or a line sung twice (either with or without a modification the second time), and an entirely different third line. Unlike most Negro songs, they are known definitely by name — the names of states, towns, and countries being employed almost as extravagantly and irrelevantly as various feminine names were employed in the ante-bellum minstrel songs.

Their enormous popularity has caused the blues to receive more attention from recent writers than any other form of Negro folk-song except the spiritual. Miss Scarborough, Abbe Niles, Odum and Johnson, and several writers of popular magazine articles have, considered together, pretty well exhausted the subject.[1] Much of what appears in this chapter repeats what has already been said by them, especially by Mr. Niles in his thorough-going introduction to Mr. Handy's *Blues*.

Blues were in existence some time before they were called blues or before they struck the fancy, first of the cabarets, then of the American and European public, and then of the folk Negro again, with re-doubled force. They had their origin, according to Mr. Handy, in a mayoralty campaign in Memphis, Tennessee, in 1909. At first they were just a nameless tune to which the Negro bystanders promptly provided indelicate words. The words they provided are given by Mr. Niles, but they failed to survive in popular tradition. In 1912, Mr. Handy published his music, which was shortly thereafter fur-nished with other words, and exploited by a white man. But before this, about 1910, the word "blues" had come into use all over the South to describe the song. Hence it would appear quite likely that blues were generally known before Mr. Handy published his music. The words furnished to Mr. Handy's music and later to other blues tunes were undoubtedly furnished in the regular folk manner of the Negro — that is, partly from other songs already current. Miss Scarborough reports pre-Handy blues from Texas, and Odum and Johnson cite several blues verses collected in Mississippi and Georgia as early as 1905 to 1908. Obviously Mr. Handy's primary rôle was that of giving more definite form and character to something that already existed, just as his later rôle in shaping the more modern blues has been to effect a combination of folk verses with verses of his own, with the folk verses drawn from all sources, even spirituals, and used somewhat sparingly in the combination.

Mr. Niles has made it seem very probable that the music to "Joe Turner," which developed between 1892 and 1896, is the source of almost all the typical blues tunes.

[1] See my bibliography, under these names and also under Handy, Lomax, Milhand, Van Vechten, "Enigmatic Folksongs," and "A Negro Explains Jazz."

The original habitat of the blues was the Negro underworld. But they soon spread to the streets and levees, then, branching out from the city, to the construction gangs and rural workers. By the time my songs were collected, they might be found anywhere.

Retaining to the present day much of their underworld "aroma," they became popular in metropolitan cafés shortly after 1912, and spread rapidly over the country. At this stage they were seized upon by the re-vampers and music publishers. They became part and parcel of the developing jazz craze. Hundreds of blues appeared in sheet-music form and phonograph records. According to figures compiled by Odum and Johnson, of the 1320 "race records" issued by three large phonograph companies, nearly 1000 are blues. The blues passed to France in 1917, then to England. In America such vaudeville and cabaret blues singers as Alice Carter, Gilda Gray, Clara Smith ("the World's Greatest Moaner"), and Ma Rainey were enjoying an immense vogue. The powerful effect of some of these singers on their audiences has been very graphically described by Mr. Carl Van Vechten in *Vanity Fair* for August, 1925, and March, 1926. Perhaps the influence of these singers accounts for the predominance of the feminine point of view in the later blues; for before their great popularity the blues were mainly masculine, as shown by those in this collection. Several American composers turned their attention to the form, and in 1925 Albert Chiafferelli produced a symphony, "Jazz America," founded on two blues tunes. A young Negro poet, Langston Hughes, wrote a poem called "Weary Blues," which secured him the enthusiastic patronage of several Negrophile white authors and publishers, who boosted his rather mediocre volume into temporary prominence. Finally, in 1926, one of the leading tobacco companies in the country began advertising a certain pipe tobacco in the *Saturday Evening Post*, under the caption, "No more haunting, taunting, hot-pipe Blues." Popularity could go no further.

The value of the blues as an expression of the folk-Negro's mind is somewhat impaired by the fact that the folk blues and the factory product are to-day almost inextricably mixed. More than anything else, however, they illustrate the singer's desire to comment upon himself, sometimes trivially, sometimes weightily. They do not speak for the groups, but only for the singer. They sometimes show self-pity, but it is most distinctly personal and without racial tinge. The white man, and the Negro *as* Negro, have no place in them.

Once blues became the fashion, their nature was considerably changed. Like most Negro songs, they had no fixed length.

Each singer added, altered, and imported, in the immemorable fashion of the "personal" interpreter of folk-songs. The love element was intensified, probably because the singers were mostly women. They retained some phrases of the old folk blues, but the tendency was to take two or three folk phrases and build a whole new song about them. In this form the blues came back to the folk from whom they had originated. Most blues sung by Negroes to-day have only a secondary folk origin; their primary source is the phonograph record. The process of imperfect memory, with free addition and alteration, begins over again, and a new crop of folk-songs is in gestation for a new generation of song collectors. In examining one of these songs Odum and Johnson (page 27) find that of four stanzas the first is the same as the phonograph record of a stanza from one blues, the second and third are the same as different stanzas from another record, except that the second is slightly changed and the third is a combination and variation of two stanzas, and the fourth is a slight variation from a stanza in still another record.

The significance of this example is plain in its bearing on the future of the blues; its even more significant bearing on the present state of Negro songs should also be comprehended. For the Negro song has already gone through two great periods of influence from without, first between 1830 and 1860, when "Jim Crow" Rice and his contemporaries were making the minstrel song more popular than even the present blues; and again in the eighteen-nineties, when the "coon songs" and ragtime songs of Ernest Hogan, Harry Von Tilzer, May Irwin, and Cole and Johnson enjoyed a more moderate vogue. In each case the folk Negro, who had contributed only slightly to the songs sung about him, immediately adopted the product, and by the familiar process of adding, telescoping, half-forgetting, and altering, transmitted the changed song to a new generation as his own. Examples of this process may be seen in IV, nos. 28, 43, 50; V, nos. 14, 23; XII, no. 12; XIII, no. 1; and no. 32, in this chapter, with reference to the later influence. With reference to the early minstrel songs they are too numerous to require particular citation.

The vogue of the blues is already on the wane, but their influence on Negro folk-song is only in its first stage.

SONGS, WITH ANNOTATIONS

The following songs classified in other groups might also be classified with blues: VII, 67, 76, 77, 82, 90; IX, 16, 32; X, 1, 2, 4–27, 35, 38, 51, 52, 57, 68; XII, 34, 36.

I

REPORTED from Durham, N. C., 1919, MS. of Blake B. Harrison.
The various "hesitating blues" are based upon the "how long must I hesitate" refrain, which has been carried over into many other Negro songs, for
example, X, nos. 35, 83, and nos. 3 and 19, in this chapter. For a modern hesitation blues, see Handy, 1926, p. 94 ("Words and music by W. C. Handy"), where
the refrain is about the only genuine and original element of the folk blues.
The name comes apparently from the Hesitation Waltz, popular about 1914.
For discussions and examples of blues, see Scarborough, 1925, pp. 264–280,
Odum, 1926, pp. 17–35; and W. C. Handy, *Blues*, 1926.

I got de hesitation stockings and de hesitation shoes.
I believe to my soul I got de hesitation blues.

Refrain

Honey, how long will I have to wait?
Kin I git you now or must I hesitate?

2

REPORTED from Auburn, Ala., 1915–1916, MS. of J. B. Christian. "Tune:
Hesitation Blues."
I am told that "balling the jack" is a Negro dance-step, but the use of the
expression in this collection suggests that its meaning may have coalesced somewhat with the slang phrase of the whites, "high-balling" — to run rapidly.

Corn in de field,
Hay in de stack,
Baby in de chicken coop
Ballin' de jack.

3

REPORTED from St. Louis, Mo., 1918, MS. of N. I. White, as sung by Miss
Dorothy Barnett, who learned it in Chicago.
For a variant of the first two lines, see Handy, 1926, p. 7.

Well the grave-yard must be an awful place,
Lay a man on his back an' throw dirt in his face.
Honey, how long have I got to wait,
Honey, how long must I hesitate?

4

REPORTED from Auburn, Ala., 1915–1916, MS. of Alsobrook.
Cf. X, no. 27.

> Ashes to ashes and dust to dust,
> I got an old negro that I could not trust.

5

$\mathcal{A}$

REPORTED from Auburn, Ala., 1915–1916, anonymously.

> De four day blues ain't nuffin',
> But a woman wants a man.

$\mathcal{B}$

Reported from Auburn, Ala., 1915–1916, MS. of A. M. Kearly.

> Some folks say them four day blues ain't bad;
> It must not have been them four day blues I had.

C

Reported from Auburn, Ala., 1915–1916, MS. of S. J. Nadler, as heard in southern Alabama. "Sung by cattle drivers and farm hands."

> Some folks say-a de fo' day blues ain't bad,
> But de fo' day blues am de wust I eber had.

6

REPORTED from Durham, N. C., 1919, MS. of D. B. Newton, as heard in Scotland County, N. C. "Work song."
The "St. Louis Blues" is one of the most widely known of the printed blues. Cf. Handy, 1926, pp. 71, 74.

> Some folks says dat dem St. Louis blues ain't bad,
> So it must er been dem wully, wully blues I had.

7

REPORTED from Auburn, Ala., 1915–1916, MS. of R. E. Donis, as heard in Georgia.
The "Memphis Blues" is one of the first printed and recorded blues, and one of the most widely known.

> Some folks says Memphis Blues ain't bad,
> It must not a been the Memphis Blues I had.

8

A

REPORTED from Auburn, Ala., 1915–1916, MS. of B. A. Wooten, as heard in Marengo County, Ala.

> I got the railroad blues, but I'm too damn mean to cry.

B

Reported from Auburn, Ala., 1915–1916, MS. of W. M. Mobley, as heard in Birmingham, Ala.
This is one of the most commonly known of all blues stanzas. It occurs in Scarborough, 1925, p. 274, as from Louisiana; Odum, 1925, pp. 164, 173; Odum, 1926; p. 18; Handy, 1926, p. 5; cf. Handy, 1926, p. 19.

> I got de blues,
> But I'm too damn mean to cry.

9

CEMETERY BLUES [1]

REPORTED from Durham, N. C., 1919, MS. of Harvey Harward. "Song of mourning."
For a variant of the last four lines, cf. Odum, 1926, p. 40. Cf. also X, nos. 39, 42, 82.

> I went down to the cemetery
> To look my fair brown in the face.
> Said "Fair Brown, I love you,
> But I can't take your place.
> Fair Brown, Fair Brown, who
> Can your regular be?
> The reason I ask you is
> You look good to me."

[1] Local title.

10

REPORTED from Auburn, Ala., 1915–1916, MS. of B. Y. Pennington, as heard in Andalusia, Ala. "Sung by Negro ditch diggers."

I have practically the same song, with lines 1 and 3 lengthened by "and don't know what to do," from Auburn, Ala, 1915–1916, MS. of S. R. Huey, as heard in a mining camp near Birmingham; also from Auburn, Ala., 1915–1916, anonymously; also, with the order of woman and man reversed, from Durham, N. C., 1919, MS. of K. W. Litaker, as heard "in the cotton fields of Cabarrus County, N. C., within the last two years."

> When a woman takes the blues,
> She tucks her head and cries;
> But when a man catches the blues,
> He catches er freight and rides.

11

REPORTED from Auburn, Ala., 1915–1916, MS. of N. C. Johnson. "Any blues tune."

Every stanza of this song, in a slightly varied form, is well known. With stanza 1, cf. X, nos. 12 and 13; with stanza 2, cf. no. 13, in this chapter; with stanza 3, cf. X, nos. 1–11; with stanza 4, cf. nos. 5–7, in this chapter; with stanza 5, cf. X, no. 15.

I had a good woman, I had a good woman,
But the fool laid down and died;
I had a good woman, but the fool laid down and died.
If you got a good woman, you better pin her to your side.

When a man gets the blues, when a man gets the blues,
He jes' catches a train and rides;
When a man gets the blues, he catches a train and rides.
But when a woman gets the blues, she lays her little head and cries.

A blond woman, a blond woman,
Make a tadpole hug a whale,
A blond woman make a tadpole hug a whale;
But a dark-haired woman make you go right straight to jail.

Some folks say, oh, some folks say
That the nigger blues ain't bad.
Oh, some folks say that the nigger blues ain't bad.
Well, it must not have been the nigger blues I had.

Oh, some niggers like, oh, some niggers like
A yaller or a brown.
Oh, some niggers like a yaller or brown.
But for my choice, I'll take the blackest woman in town.

12

A

REPORTED from Auburn, Ala., 1915–1916, MS. of B. Y. Pennington, as heard in
Andalusia, Ala. "Sung by Negroes digging sewer."
    Cf. VII, no. 76, and Handy, 1926, pp. 7, 34.

> Oh! if the blues was whiskey,
> I'd stay drunk all the time;
> 'Er if the river was booze,
> And I was a mallow duck,
> I'd dive to the bottom and
> I'd never come up.

B

Reported from Auburn, Ala., 1915–1916, MS. of A. L. Holloway, as heard in
Monroe County, southern Alabama. "Tune: De Blues." "Sung when feeling
blue."
    I have the same from Auburn, Ala., 1915–1916, MS. of R. E. Davis, as heard
in Georgia.
    Cf. "If de river was whiskey," VII, no. 76.

> If de blues was whiskey,
> I'd stay drunk all de time.

13

A

REPORTED from Auburn, Ala., 1915–1916, MS. of A. L. Holloway, as heard in
Monroe County, southern Alabama. "Tune: Same as 'De Blues.' Sung when
feeling down and out."

> De blues ain't nothing
> But a poor man's heart disease.

B

Reported from Auburn, Ala., 1915–1916, MS. of B. Y. Pennington, as heard in Andalusia, Ala. "Sung by Negro ditch diggers."

> Oh! der blues ain't nothen'
> But the heart dersease,
> But it's er mean old dog
> What won't scratch his mommer's fleas.

C

Reported from Auburn, Ala., 1915–1916, MS. of W. S. Black, as heard near Athens, Ala.

> Blues ain't nothin' but a good man feeling bad.

14

REPORTED from Auburn, Ala., 1915–1916, MS. of J. R. Jackson. With the second stanza, cf. Odum, 1926, p. 41.

> Oh, it's rainin' here,
> But it's stormin' on the sea.
>
> Oh, I'm wear-ry now,
> But I won't be weary long.
>
> My wife done tuk an' quit me,
> Now it's all over town.
>
> The blues ain't nothin',
> But a woman on a pore man's mind.

15

REPORTED from Auburn, Ala., 1915–1916, MS. of H. A. Brown. "Sung by Negro nurse."

For another Negro lullaby, see XIII, no. 15. The lullabies sung by Negroes are generally the old traditional lullabies of the whites. I have had "By o' Baby Bunting" given me as a Negro song (Auburn, Ala., 1915–1916, anonymously). Mrs. Burlin (*Hampton Series*, iv, 31, [1919]) quotes as a Negro lullaby the old English song, still current among Southern whites:

> Go to sleep, etc.
> When you wake
> You will have
> All the pretty little horses, etc.

Talley, 1922, quotes a number of Negro nursery rhymes that are indisputably old songs of the whites; for example, "Stick-a-ma-stew" (p. 155), "Deedle Dumpling" (p. 171), "Frog Went a Courting" (p. 190), "Periwinkle" (p. 201), "Randsome, Tantsome" (p. 202). Cf. Miss Scarborough's chapter, "The Negro's Part in Transmitting the Traditional Songs and Ballads," 1925, pp. 33–64.

Babe is a good little boy sometimes,
Babe is a bad little boy sometimes,
Babe tries to stand on his feet and rule him's mammy,
And rule his mammy.

16

REPORTED from Auburn, Ala., 1915–1916, MS. of A. H. Williamson, as heard in Lowndes County, Ala.

This song has long been sung among white people in the South, and is obviously one of the many songs about the Negro composed by popular-song writers of the white race.

I'm my mammy's little Alabama coon,
I ain't been born very long,
I 'member seeing de big roun' moon,
I 'member learnin' one sweet song.
She took me to de cotton patch,
An' I roll an' I tumble in de sun,
An' my daddy picked de cotton
An' my mammy watched me grow,
And dis am de song she sung.

Chorus

Go to sleep, you little pickaninny,
Brudder Fox'll catch you if you don't,
Slumber on de bosom of yo' ole mammy Jenny,
Mammy gwine ter swotch yer if you don't;
Lu-la-lu-la-lu-la-lu-la-lu,
Under the silver settin' moon,
Hush-a-bye, rock-a-bye, Mammy little baby,
Mammy's little Alabama coon.

I'm my mammy's little Alabama coon,
I'm gwine ter be a big man some day;
I gwine ter be christened very soon,
An' my name's gwine ter be a Henry Clay;

An' I'm gwinter marry a yaller gal,
An' have pickaninnies of my own,
And de yaller gal'll take er pickaninny on 'er knee,
An' dis am de song she'll croon:

Chorus

Go to sleep, yo' little pick-a-ninny, etc.

17

REPORTED from Auburn, Ala., 1915–1916, anonymously.
   For a variant, cf. Scarborough, 1925, p. 277, as from Texas.

I ain't no doctor,
No doctor's son,
But I can doctor you till de doctor comes.

18

REPORTED from Auburn, Ala., 1915–1916, MS. of P. J. Bowab, as heard in
Escambia County, Ala.

I ain't no preacher
Nor a preacher's son,
But I'll hold de congregation
Till de preacher comes.

19

REPORTED from Auburn, Ala., 1915–1916, anonymously.
   The last two lines are the well-known "how long" refrain, found in the blues
and many other songs. Cf. no. 1, in this chapter, and note.

I ain't no miller,
No miller's son,
But do your grinding
Till the miller comes;
Tell me how long will I have to wait,
Or will I have to do a little hesitate.

20

REPORTED from Auburn, Ala., 1915–1916, anonymously.
    Cf. V, no. 23.

> I went out hunting on Sunday morn
> And forgot to carry my gun along.

21

REPORTED from Auburn, Ala., 1915–1916, MS. of S. J. Nadler, as heard in
southern Alabama.

> I'm gwain to town,
> Wat yo' want to bring you back?
> A cake o' chocolate dat my honey sho' do lak.

22

REPORTED from Auburn, Ala., 1915–1916, MS. of J. H. Owens.

> I went down to the old rock mill,
> I fell off the platform half got killed.

23

REPORTED from Auburn, Ala., 1915–1916, anonymously.
    For other songs dealing with racing, see IV, no. 40; VI, no. 6; VII, no. 45; XII,
no. 23.

> My daddy was a miller,
> And he taught me how to grind;
> My daddy was a jockey,
> And he taught me how to ride.

24

REPORTED from Durham, N. C., 1919, MS. of Blake B. Harrison.

> My daddy drives a street car and my brother drives a hack,
> My mammy takes in washin' while I ball de jack.

25

REPORTED from Auburn, Ala., 1915–1916, MS. of A. M. Kearly. "Sung by Negro actors in small show."

> Come after breakfast,
> Bring along your lunch,
> And leave before supper time.

26

REPORTED from Durham, N. C., 1919, MS. of James E. Lyon, Jr., as heard in High Point, N. C., 1919.
The song probably refers to sellers of furniture on the installment plan.

> If there ever was a devil
> Born in the land,
> Why it must hab' been
> The furniture man.

27

REPORTED from Durham, N. C., 1919, MS. of H. H. Hanchey. "Heard in summer of 1916, Duplin County, N. C."

> Did you eber go a fishin' on a hot summer day,
> Set on de bank an' fish yo' time away,
> Wid yo' hands in yo' pockets and yo' pockets in yo' pants,
> An' de skeeters just natchelly got de bitin' dance.

28

REPORTED from Durham, N. C., 1919, MS. of W. Q. Grigg.
Cf. the various stanzas of "Shortnin' Bread" dealing with "two little niggers," III, no. 21; V, nos. 5 A, B, C, and 6.

> Look up yonder in the deep blue sky,
> Two little negroes a eatin' huckleberry pie.

29

REPORTED from Durham, N. C., 1919, MS. of David T. House, Jr.

> Gwine up town and I'se coming right back;
> Baby in the cradle just balling the jack.

30

REPORTED from Auburn, Ala., 1915–1916, MS. of T. H. Bonner, as heard in Clay County, Ala.

Nigger you better come out dose gymsampson weeds,
Fo' you git red wast nest stung.

31

REPORTED from Auburn, Ala., 1915–1916, MS. of H. Carder, as heard in Jefferson County, Ala.

Save up yo' money
And haul out your rocks;
You will always have tobacco
In your own tobacco box.

32

REPORTED from Auburn, Ala., 1915–1916, MS. of H. Carder, as heard in Jefferson County, Ala.

The last two lines probably come from a popular song-hit which I remember as current between 1905 and 1915, with the title and refrain, "Won't you Please Go 'way and Let me Sleep," copyrighted in 1902 by Harry Von Tilzer.

Listen, white folks,
While I tells to you
Coons mit outa habit
Am mighty few.

Some have the habit
Of dressing neat,
While my bad habit
Is sleep and eat.

Sleep and eat,
Sleep and eat,
Please go 'way
And let me sleep.

33

REPORTED from Durham, N. C., 1919, MS. of Blake B. Harrison.

With the first line, cf. Scarborough, 1925, p. 239. For other songs dealing with trains, see II, nos. 4, 5; VII, nos. 73–75.

Train, train, train, train, run so fast,
Could n't see nothing but de trees go past.

Refrain

Don't tell mamma where I'm gone,
Cause I'm on my way back home.

Mister, mister, I don't want to fight,
I got de heart disease, don't feel just right.

Mister, mister, I don't want to fight,
I'm gwine to de functum and stay all night.

APPENDICES

I

SPECIMENS OF TUNES

THE specimen tunes here submitted were chosen with the design of illustrating the Negro folk-song in each of its three large divisions — religious song, social song, and work song. Each one of the larger divisions contains several types which differ both in musical character and in the function of the song. Some of these distinctions I have sought to illustrate by my selections, but it was impossible to illustrate them all. Most of the illustrations chosen have never been printed before, so far as I am aware. Although the social songs and work songs have been sadly neglected by musicians, any student who desires to explore further into the nature of any one of the three main types may come at them easily through the use of the bibliography in this volume.

All of the songs were sung either by myself or Ed Lloyd. Ed, who was called in to supply certain types not in my own memory, proved to be able to sing a considerable number of the songs I had gathered from other sections of the country. A reading of the first line or two was generally sufficient to enable him to take up the rest of the song in tune, often with interesting variations in the stanzas. Whether the music also varied from that of the original singer I have no means of knowing, though it did vary somewhat within itself, in the different repetitions necessary for recording.

For the recording I am indebted to the patience and insight of my wife. Each song was sung repeatedly, both as a whole and phrase by phrase, and was then sung back from the musical notation and tested, phrase by phrase. Each song has also been played or sung from the notes by someone not familiar with the tune, and again subjected to criticism. I believe the result is as accurate versions as any I have heard played or sung from notes. And yet it must be admitted that, like all Negro folk-songs, they require a singer who has heard them sung by Negroes if they are not to lose some of their most characteristic qualities.

I

PHARAOH'S ARMY

II, no. 1, p. 58. The refrain, as I sing the song and have always known it, differs slightly from the text of no. 1. An example of the spiritual that has long enjoyed popularity as a picnic song of white people.

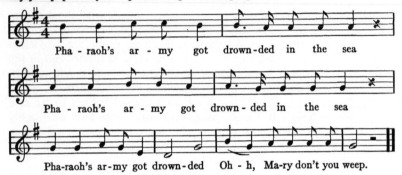

Pha - raoh's ar - my got drown-ded in the sea

Pha - raoh's ar - my got drown - ded in the sea

Pha-raoh's ar-my got drown-ded Oh - h, Ma-ry don't you weep.

2

SHOW ME THE WAY

II, no. 10 A, p. 71. As sung by Ed Lloyd.

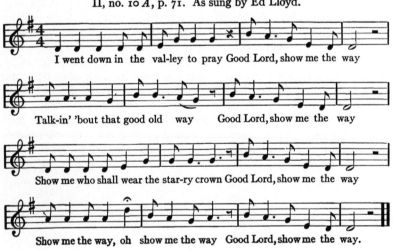

I went down in the val-ley to pray Good Lord, show me the way

Talk-in' 'bout that good old way Good Lord, show me the way

Show me who shall wear the star-ry crown Good Lord, show me the way

Show me the way, oh show me the way Good Lord, show me the way.

3

CITY OF REFUGE

II, no. 31, p. 90. As sung by Ed Lloyd.

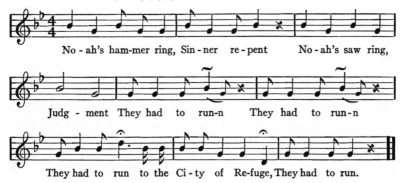

No - ah's ham-mer ring, Sin - ner re - pent No - ah's saw ring,

Judg - ment They had to run-n They had to run-n

They had to run to the Ci - ty of Re-fuge, They had to run.

4

O WE'LL PUT JOHN ON THE ISLAND

II, no. 35, p. 96. A spiritual used by both white people and Negroes.

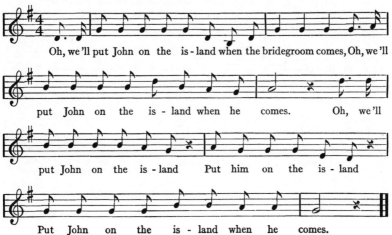

Oh, we'll put John on the is - land when the bridegroom comes, Oh, we'll

put John on the is - land when he comes. Oh, we'll

put John on the is - land Put him on the is - land

Put John on the is - land when he comes.

5

WE'LL ROLL THE CHARIOT ALONG

II, no. 36, p. 97. Typical of the "Negro" spiritual sometimes used by white people.

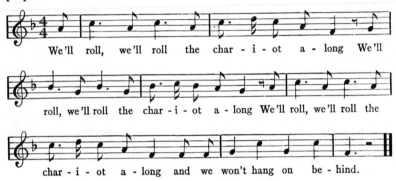

We'll roll, we'll roll the char - i - ot a - long We'll roll, we'll roll the char - i - ot a - long We'll roll, we'll roll the char - i - ot a - long and we won't hang on be - hind.

6

MY OLE MISTIS

IV, no. 2, p. 152. As sung by Ed Lloyd. This is one of the older social songs. Ed says it was a banjo song of the white people and that he learned it from a "white feller who sho' could make a banjo talk."

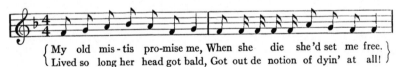

My old mis - tis pro-mise me, When she die she'd set me free.
Lived so long her head got bald, Got out de notion of dyin' at all!

Rail - road, my true love, I'm goin' home in the mor - nin'.

7

RAISE A RUCUS TONIGHT

IV, no. 38, p. 180. As sung by Ed Lloyd. Typical of the social song that serves no particular social function beyond the desire for harmony. Ed says this is really a quartet song, with bass and tenor repetitions of the phrase, "Raise a rucus tonight."

Come a - long, Oh, chil - lun come a - long

Whiles the moon is shin - in' bright. Git on board!

Down the ri - ver flow, We 're goin' raise a ru - cus to - night!

8

THIS OLE HAMMER

VII, no. 23D, p. 261. As sung by Ed Lloyd. Another gang-labor song.

This old ham - mer Kill'd John Hen - ry

Can't kill me, boys Can't kill me.

9

PUT DE DAWGS ON HIM

VII, no. 27, p. 262. Typical of the gang work song in which the leader has a special function, also of the song highly adapted to the work in hand. See description on p. 263.

Put de dawgs on him.   Put 'em on me‑e,   Put 'em on me‑e.

10

RUN HERE DOCTOR

VII, no. 87, p. 279. A regular gang-labor song, with a "huh" at the end of each line to represent the picks striking the earth.

Run   here,   Doc‑tor (Huh!) Run   here   quick! (Huh!)

Lit‑tle   Ma‑ry (Huh!) Swallow'd   a   stick.

11

THOUGHT I HEARD

VII, no. 88, p. 279. Typical of the gang work song adapted from the individual social song. Twenty-five years ago I heard this same tune and almost the same words, with ribald variations, as a Negro street song in Statesville, N. C.

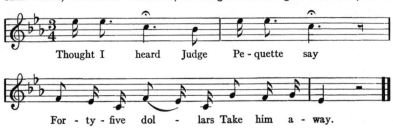

Thought I   heard   Judge   Pe‑quette   say

For‑ty‑five   dol ‑ lars Take   him   a‑way.

12

MAKE A PREACHER LAY HIS BIBLE DOWN

X, no. 10, p. 315. Typical of the songs about women most commonly used as work songs, but generally sung individually, and often sung to fill a momentary pause in the work.

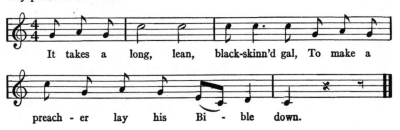

It takes a long, lean, black-skinn'd gal, To make a

preach - er lay his Bi - ble down.

13

PO' GAL

X, no. 37, p. 326. Typical of many social songs not generally sung communally and often sung while at work on some individual occupation.

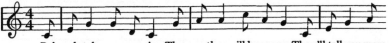

Po' gal, take a war-ning The men they will leave you They'll tell you more

lies than the cross-ties on the rail-road Or the stars in the sky.

14

YONDER COME A YALLER GAL

X, no. 74, p. 335. Typical of the individual song sung on the streets or at individual occupations.

Yon - der come a yel-low gal   All dress'd up in red   Well, I

wish my wife was dead   Well, I wish my wife was dead.

15

THE TITANIC

XI, no. 1, p. 347. As sung by Ed Lloyd. The text varies slightly from the version given in XI, no. 1, as did some of the stanzas sung by Ed, but the tune is the same, so far as my memory can be trusted, as that to which I have heard the song sung. Typical of the narrative social song of ballet origin.

Oh, wasn't it sad about the Ti-tan-ic How it got lost Oh, wasn't it sad a-bout the Ti-tan-ic How it got lost They left the port of Lon-don Bound for the New York shore When a ice-berg struck the ves-sel Caus'd a leak-in' hole And they said to the Cap-tain We'll nev-er reach the shore Oh wasn't it sad a-bout the Ti-tan-ic How it got lost.

II

SPECIMENS OF NEGRO BALLETS AND RELATED SONGS

I

JUDGE THE TREES NOW

GOD SAID SO, NOT MAN

Given to me by Mr. Lockwood, of the Barker-Suggs Printery, Durham, N. C., 1928. Mr. Lockwood was also able to furnish me with the author's original manuscript, on small, coarse tablet paper, ruled. The following verbatim copy of the manuscript, when compared with the original "ballet," illustrates an interesting stage in the history of many songs of this type. I have another printed ballet "composed by Sister Nancy Stukes," which shows the same erratic line arrangement as this manuscript.

Sometimes when you are traveling, you will meet with ups and downs,
But don't get discouraged, work on for your crown.

You can judge the trees by the fruit they bear,
Go and judge the trees by the fruit they bear,
Go and judge the trees by the fruit they bear;
You can tell them anywhere.

When I started out to praying, I did not know much about the way.
Old Satan had so much power he tried me day by day.
But I kept on praying until Jesus came on down;
He blessed my soul from heaven, and the grace turned me 'round.

I know you are a motherless child, and have been driven from door to
    door;
I know you can't feel welcome, and I don't care where you go.
Then I know I have got a religion and trying to work in the gospel,
Still I see so much merrymaking until it's about to run me wild.

I saw the sun come creeping and it was coming from yonder shore;
It was making its way across the blue ether, and it won't shine here any-
    more.
When the rocks and the mountains will be falling and the seas will be
    boiling,
So then sinners will come a running and have no place to go.

God spoke to Adam in the garden, he was standing behind sister Eve,
It is written plainly in the Bible, God wants you to judge the trees.
You say you have religion, but how can the world say so?

You are trying to cheat God's people and will scandalize the poor.
Stop here and judge the trees.

(Composed and sung by one of the Twelve Tribes of Israel.)

BROTHER C. P. STANFIELD,
116 Rowan Alley
Durham, N. C.

PRICE 10c

JUDGE THE TREES KNOW

GOD SAID SO. NOT MAN [1]

Some times when you or traviling. you will meets with ups and down.
But don't you get discorad work own for your Crown.   v. 1.

you Can Judge the trees, By the fruit they Bare.
Go and Judge the trees By the fruit the Bare.
Go and Judge the trees By the fruit the Bare.
you can tell then any where.

when i Started out to praying i did not know mutch about the way.
old Satin had So mutch powder he tried me day By day.
But i keep own praying untill Jesus Come own down.
he Bless my Sold from heaven and the grace turn me around.   V. 2.

i know you is a motherless child. and have Ben drove from door too door.
i know you Can't field welcom and i dont Care where you go.
then i now i have got a religion and trying to work in the Gospel Stile
i Sea So mutch merrysom untill about to run me wile.   V. 3.

I Saw the Sun come Creaping and She was Coming from yarnder Shore
She was making her way Across the Blue eather and She wont Shine here
any more.
when the Rocks. and the montain will Be falling and the Seas will Be
Boilding
So then Sinners will come a running and ant got no place to go.   4.

God Spoke to Adams in the garden he was Staning Behind Sister eave.
it is wrote planly in the Bible God wont you to Judge the trees.   v. 5.

[1] In the manuscript the stanzas are separated by lines left blank, but are written
solid, like prose, without regard to the rhyme.

you Say you have got a religion But how can the world Say So.
you or trying to cheat God's peoples. and will Scandlelies the poore.
Stop here and Judge the trees.

price 10c only.

Composed and Song By one off the twelve tribes off isrul

> Bro. C. P. Stanfield
> 116 Rowan Allie
> Durham N. C.

2

I'LL LIVE ON

Found among the old printing samples of the Morris Printing Co., Durham,
N. C., 1928.

1 'T is a sweet and glorious tho't comes to me,
I'll live on, I'll live on, yes, I'll live on,
Jesus saved my soul from death and now I'm free,
I'll live on, I'll live on, yes, I'll live on.

Chorus

I'll live on, and on, yes, I'll live on, and on,
Thro' eternity I'll live on, and on, yes, I'll live on, and on,
I'll live on, and on,
Thro' eternity I'll live on, yes, I'll live on.

2 When my body's slumbering in the cold, cold clay,
I'll live on, I'll live on, yes, I'll live on,
There to sleep in Jesus till the Judgment day,
I'll live on, I'll live on, yes, I'll live on.

3 When the world's on fire and darkness veils the sun,
I'll live on, I'll live on, yes, I'll live on,
Men will cry and to the rocks and mountains run,
I'll live on, I'll live on, yes, I'll live on.

4 In the glory land with Jesus on the throne,
I'll live on, I'll live on, yes, I'll live on,
Thro' eternal ages singing, home, sweet home,
I'll live on, I'll live on, yes, I'll live on.

3

IF I COULD HEAR MY MOTHER PRAY

Found among the old printing samples of the Morris Printing Co., Durham, N. C., 1928.

1 How sweet and happy seem those days of which I dream,
When memory recalls them now and then,
And with what rapture sweet my weary heart would beat,
If I could hear my mother pray again.

Chorus

If I could hear my mother pray again,
If I could her tender voice as then,
So glad I'd be 'twould mean so much to me,
If I could hear my mother pray again.

2 She use to pray that I on Jesus would rely,
And always walk the Gospel shining way,
So trusting still His love I seek that home above,
Where I shall meet my mother some glad day.

3 Within the old home place her patient smiling face,
Was always spreading comfort, hope and cheer,
And when she use to sing to her eternal King,
It was the songs the angels loved to hear.

4 Her work on earth is done the life crown has been won,
And she is now at rest with Him above,
And some glad morning, she I know will welcome me,
To that eternal home of peace and love.

4

"SIN'S A MESS"

Rescued from the waste samples box of the Morris Printing Co., Durham, N. C. Printed probably in 1928.

When you "air" at home at rest,
Snug and tight in ye cozy nest,
Realize folks that ye "air" blest,
"Kaiz" sin is nothing but a mess.

All de things that ye possess,
To ye Lord ye must confess,
De's things true and all the rest,
For sin is nothing but a mess.

Pa go look in de chest,
Find de Bible and confess,
To de Lord who will bless,
That sin is nothing but a mess.

Gwine down toward the bay,
Pa begins to walk and pray,
I'll be good from dis day,
For sin's a mess.

Our folks go to church to look and dress,
To gaze at sister May's new dress,
I, to you, must distress,
That sin is nothing but a mess.

Flies and bugs "air" an uncounted pest,
Different all times from de rest,
Worry you home at your best,
Sin is nothing but a mess.

Go up town and hang around,
And at home won't sit down,
Making news to tell the rest,
It is sin, that's a mess.

Jest as well do right and do ye best,
In short de Lord will prove de test,
Your old body in de grave must rest,
Sin is nothing but a mess.

Written by

C. Herman Hassell   **F. D. Purcell**
Williamston, N. C.   *Raeford, N. C.*

PRICE 10 CENTS

5

JOB ON HIS WAY
(*Composed by Jessie Jenkins*)

One of several ballets given me by Mr. W. W. Weaver, from the jackets of the Durham Publishing Co., Durham, N. C.

Old Job was the richest man,
He had his affliction all over the land,
Job was afflicted from his head to his feet,
Friends came around, asked Job how do you feel?
Job began to shout:

"I'm on my way to Canaan land;
  I am on my way to Canaan land.
If Jesus will my leader be,
  I'm on my way, praise God;
Oh, there's nothing you can say,

Old Job, what do you suppose
  Satan came around for — to try your soul?
Job asked the Lord to take a day
  Out of his time,
I'm going to the country,
  Where seekers never find.

Is there anybody here that wants to go with me?
Is there anybody here that wants to go with me?
  If there's nobody here, I'll journey on;
I'm on my way, praise God;
  I'm on my way.

Old Job, your cattle are all dead;
  News came in to Job, lying on his bed;
The Lord gave the great,
  The Lord gave the small;
Blessed be the name of the Lord —
  Giveth all.

Oh, there's nothing you can say,
    Can change my mind;
I'm on my way."
    Can change my mind;
Neither can it change this heart of mine.
    I'm on my way, praise God;
I'm on my way.

Old Job what do you suppose,
  If you got your right mind?
Let your faith go,
  Job looked around at his wife with a smile;
You speak as the foolish —
  And not the wise.

Oh, there's nothing you can say
  Can change my mind.
Oh, there's nothing you can say
  Can change my mind.
And neither can it change
  This heart of mine.
I'm on my way, praise God;
  I'm on my way.

6

THE GAMBLER'S DEATH
Composed by L. V. Medlin

One of several ballets given me by Mr. W. W. Weaver, from the jackets of the
Durham Publishing Co., Durham, N. C.

I.

Oh, ain't it an awful pity, very bad and sad,
The mother of a gambler lost the only son she had;
The poor man gambles all night long, until the break of day,
Then he rose up from the table, and threw his cards away.

Chorus.

Where is the gambling man?
Where is the poor man going?
Where is the gambling man?
I wonder where the poor man's going.

2.

The gambler calls to his friends to come and take him home.
He said: "I'm sick and feeling bad and I don't want to go alone."

Chorus.

3.

As soon as the gambler reached his home they laid him on the bed,
He called for a drink of cool water and said: "Put a towel around my
head."

Chorus.

4.

The gambler's mother ran out of doors,
She hollered, screamed and cried:
"My son's been gambling all night long;
I believe he is going to die.

Chorus.

5.

That gambler told his mother to call his friend;
He told her to call them all.
"It won't be many more hours now,
'Till I'll look up the gambling wall."

Chorus.

6.

As soon as his friends reached the place
His face was full of frowns.
He said: "Here comes Death and the sheriff,
With a rope to tie me down."

Chorus.

7.

The gambler's mother began to pray;
She got down on her knees;
She began to call upon the Lord to
Forgive him if He please.

Chorus.

8.

The gambler told his mother:
"Mother, your prayers are all in vain;
I have overstayed the day of grace,
And have made my bed in Hell."

Chorus.

7

ELSIE LEE

From the samples of the Barker-Suggs Printery, Durham, N. C. Given me by
Mr. Lockwood, 1928.

Where the little old Appomatox
Wash along its sandy shore;
Where the nightingales are singing sweet to me.
Through those scenes I seem to wander
As in days of long ago
When I courted my own darling Elsie Lee.

Sweetheart, your tears are falling
I must go where duty's calling.
So dry your eyes and listen, dear, to me.
Let not your heart be yearning
For some day I will be returning
Farewell my own, my darling, Elsie Lee.

Out in the golden west tonight I am dreaming
The wind is whispering memories sweet to me;
I am going south where the harvest moon is shining,
Back home once more to darling Elsie Lee.

DAN M. WHEELER.

8

THE PREACHER

This ballet, which I secured from a colored preacher in Durham, differs from the others in being printed on pale blue paper.

Some preachers are out preaching
Just for a preacher's name
Their doctrine and preaching
Are a scandal and a shame.

Chorus

Do you call that true religion?
Oh, no, 't is a scandal and a shame.

Some deacons in the churches
Are sitting in the deacon's chair.
They drink their beer and whiskey,
And say they don't care.

Chorus

Some deacons in the churches
Are living with two wives.
You tell them of true glory
And you'll see their temper rise.

Chorus

Some members in the churches
They love to talk and grin;
But when you open the services
They won't open their mouths and sing.

Chorus

Some members in the churches
Love to dress and put on airs,
If you can't dress up with them and wear the finest clothes,
They won't associate with you nor ask you in their doors.

Chorus

Some preachers are up preaching
Their voices sound so sweet.
The reason they don't like holiness
They want to court every sister they meet.

Chorus

Some preachers come to your house,
  You ask him to rest his hat.
He sits right down and begins to grin.
  Saying, "Sister, where's your husband at?"

Composed by the blind lady   IDA STEWART

Price, 10 Cents

9

THE BEULAH RAILWAY

Probably of white authorship and intended for white people, since it bears in
small type following the final stanza the following: "Fifty cents a year makes
you a member of this work. Free Tract Society (Inc.) 746 Crocker St., Los
Angeles, Cal., U. S. A. Phone Broadway 3618."
  Printed on both sides, 3¼ by 4⅝ inches.
  Picked up on the streets of Durham, N. C., 1926, by Mr. W. Freeman
Twaddell.

God a great railway to heaven has planned,
He staked out the line with His dear, loving hand;
Away back in Eden the grant was first given,
On Calvary's cross the last spike was driven.
The road was surveyed with a special design,
To make it a practical Holiness line;
The grade was thrown up with the greatest of care,
Directly through Canaan, a country most fair.

Of fasting and praying the ballast was made,
The ties are as solid as when they were laid;
The crossings are guarded, not a curve on the track,
Trains never take siding, nor ever turn back.
The streams are all spanned by bridges of Faith,
The last one we cross is the river of Death.

Vestibule coaches, God's chariots they are;
"Holiness to the Lord" is inscribed on each car;
Trains stop at all stations where signal is given,
And run to the Grand Central Depot in Heaven.
Conviction's the station where sinners get in,
Soon reaching Repentance, confessing their sin;
And Faith is the office where tickets are sold
And baggage checked through to the City of Gold.

Regeneration comes next into view.
The heart is now changed and all things become new;

God's Spirit bears witness with that of our own,
That we are His children, joint heirs to His throne.
The gauge is quite narrow, with rails from above;
Salvation's the engine, 't is driven by love.
Following the Spirit along in the light,
The old Carnal Nature now comes into sight.
"Inbred Sin" the porter calls out through the train,
"Put off the old man, he cannot remain."

But trusting in Jesus and reading His Word,
The all-cleansing fountain is seen in the Blood;
By faith we step in and its waves o'er us flow,
We rise from the pool and are whiter than snow.
What transports of rapture now sweep o'er the plain.
The music of Paradise filling that train.
Oh ecstasy, ravishing! fountain of bliss!
Scenery celestial! Is Heaven like this?

Jesus, the heavenly Bridegroom, is near,
Making perfect in love and casting out fear;
Our hearts are made younger as onward we glide,
Our strength is renewed, our needs are supplied.
All glory to Jesus! Hallelujah! Praise God!
Travel is luxury on the old Beulah Road,
God's railway celestial encircling the globe;
The good of all ages have travelled this road.
Elijah and Enoch by official request,
Ran in on a special, not stopping at Death.

No accident has this railway yet known,
The Dispatcher is He who sits on the throne.
Trains only move at Jehovah's command,
He holds the throttle with Omnipotent hand.
The Holy Spirit is the headlight so clear,
Revealing the track to the wise engineer.
The angels are brakeman, so kind and urbane,
Adding much to the comfort of all on the train.

Dying Love is a town in the Valley of Fear,
The backslider's repair shops are located here,
Are your vows broken, have you been untrue?
Step into these shops and be burnished anew.
Dear sinners, take passage for Heaven today,
Make haste, there is danger and death in delay.
The Spirit is calling, and so is the Bride;
Our train is now coming, and you must decide.

The road you are traveling will land you — well,
In anguish and torment with demons to dwell,
The fare is expensive, just think of the cost,
When Heaven and Jesus and all may be lost!
So many are taking the Try route to Heaven,
When God's great Bee-line is the only route given.
His word is the guide and its teachings are plain,
You'll surely be lost if you take the wrong train.

Then, be not deceived in making your choice,
But follow the Word and the Spirit's small voice,
Take the train they advise, and then stay on board,
And you will ride home to eternal reward.
I've a ticket for home, Hallelujah! Praise God!
My baggage is checked, I am now on the road;
I've said to the world and its honors goodbye;
My soul's on the wing, I'm en route to the sky.

10

THAT INFLUENZA TRAIN

Neither this song nor the one following came to me as a separately printed ballet, though both may very well have been originally printed as ballets. The owner of the volume from which they are taken lent me at the same time the ballet of "The Preacher" and insisted that both the volume and the ballet be returned before Sunday as he used the volume in his Sunday services.

The volume from which this and the following song are taken is a manila-bound pamphlet of thirty-two pages, entitled "The Golden Trumpet Jubilee Hymns. Compiled by Rev. W. M. Jones, Richmond, Va. Price twenty-five cents." It has no date or printer's imprint, but from internal evidence cannot have been printed before 1918. Many Negro preachers, particularly those of the itinerant type, have compiled or composed similar little song-books. Most of those that I have seen, however, are a little less primitive than "The Golden Trumpet." The twenty-eight songs included in this volume, without being the same as the old spirituals, seem to be a blend of the spiritual and the religious ballet, although there are some that contain fragments from various hymns woven together in precisely the same way as some of the old spirituals. In fact, they exemplify every important characteristic of the old spiritual discussed in Chapter II. Though apparently recent in composition, they are being used in a small Negro congregation in Durham to-day just as the old spirituals were formerly used.

> One day while sitting in my home
> I felt very bad,
> My head began to ache me,
> I did n't know what I had.

Chorus

That Influenza, that Influenza
  Come to lay your body down,
  That Influenza.

The first thing the influenza done,
  In the North, I am told
It went in almost every home
  And left somebody cold.

It came rumbling down the line,
  The people were amazed,
They had the doctor come at once,
  But still they filled their graves.

It moved like a cyclone,
  Without fear or dread,
It ran across some doctor's den
  And left their bodies dead.

The Board of Health met one day,
  The churches all were closed,
The saints of God wandering about
  Had to praise God out of doors.

This sent forth doctors all around,
  They did n't know what to do.
A message came from across the sea
  And said it was the flu.

This terrible disease must come from God
  For the Doctors could n't say.
Remember in just two month's time
  Ten thousand filled their graves.

It took away your appetite,
  It made you feel so mean,
Just in three or seven days,
  It left you very lean.

Some time I think it beat the war
  But did n't last as long.
In a short time all over the land,
  Millions were going home.

Some boys were overseas,
  Returning home you know,
But those who left on the influenza train
  Have never come back any more.

II

DAVID, PLAY ON YOUR HARP

Apparently a combination of spiritual and religious ballet. The chorus is that of the spiritual, verbatim. The structure of the stanzas is that of the religious ballet, though their material is that of the spirituals. See introduction to the preceding song.

Old Man Jesse had eight sons,
Little David was the youngest one;
In the presence of Saul, David did stand,
And played on the harp with his hand.

Chorus

Little David play on your harp,
　　Hallelujah! Hallelujah!
Little David play on your harp,
　　Hallelujah!

When I get in the King
I'll march all around,
And have on a long, white robe,
Come streaming down;
Then I am going to move at God's command
With the golden harp placed in my hand.

When we're done toiling here below,
We will step off this earthly shore,
Up to Heaven with the Saints will go,
Take down our harp and begin to blow.

I do acknowledge, I do say so,
I talk with the prophets gone on before —
Jeremiah, Malechia, Stephen and Thomas,
Old brother Noah, ten thousand and more.

III

SPECIMENS OF SPIRITUAL SONGS AND CAMP-MEETING SONGS OF THE WHITE PEOPLE

I

No. 75, pp. 273–274, in *The Christian's Companion;* no imprint, but a "Note to the Reader," signed John P. Lemay, is dated from Granville County, N. C., May 27, 1836.

Hark, listen to the trumpeters,
　　They sound for volunteers,
On Zion's bright and flow'ry mount,
　　Behold the officers —
Their horses white, and garments bright,
　　With sword and bow they stand;
Enlisting soldiers for their King,
　　To march for Canaan's land.

It sets my heart all in a flame,
　　A soldier I will be;
I will enlist, gird on my arms,
　　And fight for liberty.
They want no tories in their band,
　　That will their colors fly;
But call for valiant hearted men,
　　That do not fear to die.

The armies now are in parade,
　　How martial they appear;
All dress'd and arm'd in uniform,
　　They look like men of war.
They follow their brave general,
　　The great eternal Lamb;
His garments stain'd in his own blood,
　　King Jesus is his name.

The trumpet sounds, the armies shout,
　　And drive the hosts of hell,
How dreadful is our God in arms,
　　Th' great Emmanuel.
Sinners enlist with Jesus Christ,
　　The only Son of God,
And march with us to Canaan's land
　　Beyond the swelling flood.

There is a green and flow'ry fleld,
　　Where fruits immortal grow,
There cloth'd in white with angels bright,
　　We'll our Redeemer know.
We'll shout and sing forever more,
　　In that eternal world,
But Satan and his armies too,
　　Shall down to hell be hurled.

Hold up your heads, ye soldiers bold,
　　Redemption's drawing nigh,
We soon shall hear the trumpet sound,
　　That shakes both earth and sky,
In fiery chariots then we'll fly,
　　And leave the world on fire,
And meet around the starry throne,
　　To tune th' immortal lyre.

2

No. 82, p. 288 in *The Christian's Companion.*

I've listed in the holy war; sing glory, glory, glory,
Content with suff'ring soldiers fare; sing glory, etc.
The banner o'er my hand is love; sing glory, etc.
I draw my rations from above; sing glory, etc.

I've fought through many battle sore, sing glory, etc.
And I must fight through many more;
I take my breastplate, sword and shield,
And boldly march into the field.

The world and flesh and Satan too,
Unite and strive what they can do;
On thee, O Lord, I humbly call,
Uphold me, or my soul must fall.

I've listed and I mean to fight,
'Till all my foes are put to flight,
And when the vict'ry I have won,
I'll give the praise to God alone.

Come loving christians join with me,
Come face the foe, and he shall flee,
The heavenly battle's now begun;
Come take the field and win the crown.

With 'listing orders I am come,
Come rich, come poor, come old and young,
Here's gracious bounty Christ has given
And glorious crowns for you in heaven.

Our General he is gone before,
And bids you draw on grace's store;
But if you do not 'list and fight,
You'll sink into eternal night.

3

THE HEBREW CHILDREN

Page 276 in *The Southern Harmony and Musical Companion.* By William Walker. New Edition, improved and enlarged. Philadelphia. Published by E. W. Miller. 1847. The preface to a former edition is dated Spartanburg, S. C., 1835.

Where are the Hebrew children?
Where are the Hebrew children?
Where are the Hebrew children?
Safe in the promised land:
Tho' the furnace flamed around them,
God while in their trouble found them;
He with love and mercy bound them,
Safe in the promised land.

Where are the twelve apostles?
Where are the twelve apostles?
Where are the twelve apostles?
Safe in the promised land:
They went thro' the flaming fire,
Trusting in the great Messiah,
Holy grace did raise them higher,
Safe in the promised land.

Where are the holy martyrs?
Where are the holy martyrs?
Where are the holy martyrs?
Safe in the promised land:
Those who wash'd their robes, and made them
White and spotless pure, and laid them
Where no earthly stain could fade them,
Safe in the promised land.

Where are the holy Christians?
Where are the holy Christians?
Where are the holy Christians?
Safe in the promised land:
There our souls will join the chorus,
Saints and angels sing before us,
While all heaven is beaming o'er us,
Safe in the promised land.

By and by we'll go and meet them,
By and by we'll go and meet them,
By and by we'll go and meet them,
Safe in the promised land:
There we'll sing and shout together,
There we'll sing and shout hosanna,
There we'll sing and shout forever,
Safe in the promised land.

Glory to God Almighty
Glory to God Almighty
Glory to God Almighty
Who called us unto him,
Who are blind by sinful nature,
Who have sinned against our Maker,
Who did send his son to save us,
Safe in the promised land.

Where is our blessed Saviour?
Where is our blessed Saviour?
Where is our blessed Saviour?
Safe in the promised land;
He was scourged and crucified,
He by Romans was derided,
Thus the Lord of glory died,
To raise our souls above.

4

Page 119 in Leavitt's *The Christian Lyre*, Philadelphia, 1830.

I'll try to prove faithful,
I'll try to prove faithful,
I'll try to prove faithful, faithful, faithful,
Till we shall all meet above.

O, let us prove faithful,
O, let us prove faithful,
O, let us prove faithful, faithful, faithful,
Till we all shall meet above.

There'll be no more sinning,
There'll be no more sinning,
There'll be no more sinning, sinning, sinning,
When we all shall meet above.

There'll be no more sorrow,
There'll be no more sorrow,
There'll be no more sorrow, sorrow, sorrow,
When we all shall meet above.

There we shall see Jesus,
There we shall see Jesus,
There we shall see Jesus, Jesus, Jesus,
When we all shall meet above.

There we shall sing praises,
There we shall sing praises,
There we shall sing praises, praises, praises,
When we all shall meet above.

5

JUDGMENT HYMN

Page 91 in *The Christian Lyre.*

O there will be mourning, mourning, mourning, mourning,
O there will be mourning, at the judgment seat of Christ.
  Parents and children there will part,
  Parents and children there will part,
  Parents and children there will part,
  Will part to meet no more.

O there will be mourning, etc.
  Wives and husbands there will part,   (*Repeat twice.*)
  Will part to meet, etc.

O there will be mourning, etc.
  Brothers and sisters there will part,   (*Repeat twice.*)
  Will part to meet, etc.

O there will be mourning, etc.
  Friends and neighbors there will part,   (*Repeat twice.*)
  Will part to meet, etc.

O there will be mourning, etc.
    Pastors and people there will part,   (*Repeat twice.*)
    Will part to meet, etc.

O there will be mourning, etc.
    Devils and sinners there will meet,   (*Repeat twice.*)
    Will meet to part, etc.

O there will be shouting, etc.
    Saints and angels there will meet,   (*Repeat twice.*)
    Will meet to part, etc.

6

A HOME UP YONDER

No. 20, p. 15 in *The Revivalist*, Philadelphia, 1868.

I have some friends before me gone,
For a few days, for a few days,
And I'm resolved to follow on,
For I have a home up yonder.

For I'm going home
For I'm going home,
For I have a home up yonder, Glory, glory.

I think I hear them singing,
Just up there, just up there;
I think I hear them singing,
Up there in Paradise.

If you get there, before I do,
Look out for me, I'm coming too.

My suffering time will soon be o'er,
Thus I shall sigh and weep no more.

Fight on ye conq'ring souls, fight on,
Until the conquest you have won.

Farewell vain world, I'm going home
My Saviour smiles and bids me come.

7

LET US TAKE WINGS

No. 70, p. 41 in *The Revivalist*.

The judgment day is coming, coming, coming,
The judgment day is coming, O! that great day.

Let us take the wings of the morning,
And fly away to Jesus,
Let us take the wings of the morning,
And shout the Jubilee!

I see the Judge descending,
Descending, etc.

I see the dead arising,
Arising, etc.

I see the world assembled,
Assembled, etc.

I hear the sentence uttered,
Uttered, etc.

I hear the wicked wailing,
Wailing, etc.

Chorus

For they took not the wings of the morning, etc.

I hear the righteous shouting,
Shouting, etc.

Chorus

For they took the wings, etc.

8

OH! HE'S TAKEN MY FEET

No. 114, p. 65 in *The Revivalist*.

Chorus

Oh, he's taken my feet from the mire and the clay,
And he's placed them on the Rock of Ages.

I'll praise him while he gives me breath,
I hope to praise him after death.

I hope to praise him when I die,
And shout salvation as I fly.

And I will tell to sinners round
What a dear Saviour I have found.

9

O! THERE WILL BE MOURNING

No. 156, p. 86 in *The Revivalist.*

Parents and children there will part,   (*Repeat twice.*)
Will part to meet no more.

First chorus

O! there will be mourning, mourning, mourning, mourning,
O! there will be mourning at the judgment seat of Christ.

Wives and husbands there will part, etc.

Brothers and sisters there will part, etc.

Friends and neighbors there will part, etc.

Pastors and people there will part, etc.

Saints and angels there will meet, etc.

Second chorus

O! there will be glory,
Glory, glory, glory,
O! there will be glory,
At the judgment seat of Christ.

10

SAY, BROTHERS

No. 173, p. 95 in *The Revivalist.*

Say, brothers, will you meet us?   (*Repeat twice.*)
On Canaan's happy shore?

Say, sisters, will you meet us, etc.

By the grace of God we'll meet you
    Where parting is no more;
That will be a happy meeting
    On Canaan's happy shore.

Jesus lives and reigns forever
On Canaan's happy shore.
Glory, glory, hallelujah!
Forever, evermore!

I I

AWAY OVER JORDAN

No. 255, p. 129 in *The Revivalist.*

My brother's going to wear that crown,   (*Repeat twice.*)
  To wear that starry crown
Away over Jordan with my blessed Jesus,
  Away over Jordan, to wear that starry crown.

You must live right to wear, etc.

John Wesley's going to wear, etc.

My father's going to wear, etc.

My mother's going to wear, etc.

I 2

HOSANNA

From *The Revivalist.*

I have some friends before me gone,
  Who love to sing hosanna,
And I'm resolved to travel on,
  For I love to sing hosanna.

Chorus

For we have one more river to cross,
  And then we'll sing hosanna,
For we have one more river to cross,
  And then we'll sing hosanna.

Ten thousand in their endless home,
  All love to sing hosanna,
And we are to the margin come,
  And love to sing hosanna.

One family we dwell in him,
  We love to sing hosanna;
Though now divided by the stream,
  We love to sing hosanna,

One army of the living God
We love to sing hosanna,
Part of the host have cross'd the flood,
Who love to sing hosanna.

Amen, amen, my soul replies,
I love to sing hosanna,
I'm bound to meet you in the skies,
Where we will sing hosanna.

13

OLD SHIP ZION

No. 375, p. 185 in *The Revivalist*.

What ship is that that is passing by?
O glory, hallelujah!   (*Repeat both lines.*)
Why, it's old ship Zion, Hallelujah!   (*Repeat.*)

O, who is your captain and what is his name?
'T is the meek and lowly Jesus.

Is your ship well built, and her timbers all sound?
Why, she's built of gospel timber.

What colors does she wear in time of war?
Why, it's the bloody robe of Jesus.

Who are those that are going on board?
Why, they're volunteers for Jesus.

Do you think she will safely land her crew?
Why, she's landed thousands over.

O, what shall we do when we all get there?
We will sing and shout forever.

14

MY BIBLE

No. 385, p. 191 in *The Revivalist*.

My Bible leads to glory,   (*Repeat.*)
Ye foll'wers of the Lamb.
Sing on, pray on, foll'wers of Immanuel,
Sing on, pray on, Soldiers of the Cross.

Religion makes me happy.

King Jesus is my Captain.

I long to see my Saviour.

Then farewell sin and sorrow.

We'll have a shout in glory.

We'll wave our palms forever.

15

MY HOME IS OVER JORDAN

No. 390, p. 193 in the *Revivalist*.

My home is over Jordan,   (*Repeat twice.*)
Where pleasures never die.

Where the wicked cease from troubling,
And the weary are at rest.

Farewell to sin and sorrow,
I bid you all adieu.

And you, my friends, prove faithful,
And on your way pursue.

16

ZION'S PILGRIMS

No. 409, p. 200 in *The Revivalist*.

Pilgrims we are, to Canaan bound,
    Our journey lies along this road;
This wilderness we travel round
    To reach the city of our God.

Our robes are washed in Jesus' blood,
And we are travelling home to God.

And if our robes are pure and white,
May we all reach that blest abode?
O yes, they all shall dwell in light
Whose robes are washed in Jesus' blood.

17

CANAAN

No. 424, p. 207 in *The Revivalist.*

How happy is the pilgrim's lot,
   I am bound for the land of Canaan,
How free from ev'ry anxious tho't,
   I am bound for the land of Canaan.

I am bound for the land of Canaan   (*Repeat.*)
Oh, Canaan, bright Canaan, I am bound for the land of Canaan,
Oh, Canaan is my happy home.

Nothing on earth I call my own,
A stranger in the world unknown.

I trample on their whole delight,
And seek a city out of sight.

There is my house and portion fair,
My treasure and my heart are there.

If you get there before I do,
Look out for me, I'm coming too.

I have some friends before me gone,
And I'm resolved to travel on.

Our songs of praise shall fill the skies,
While higher still our joys they rise.

18

OH, BROTHER, BE FAITHFUL

No. 433, p. 213 in *The Revivalist.*

Oh, brother, be faithful,   (*Repeat twice.*)
Faithful, faithful,
Till we arrive at home.

O sister, be faithful,

There we shall see Jesus.

There we shout glory.

There'll be no more parting.

19

ROLL CALL

No. 356, p. 176 in *The Revivalist*.

If you get there before I do,
    When the general roll is call'd we'll be there;
Look out for me, I'm coming too,
    When the gen'ral roll is called we'll be there.

We'll be there, we'll be there, we'll be there,
When the gen'ral roll is called we'll be there.

We're pressing on to Canaan's land,
We'll join the blood-washed pilgrim band.

Then we'll go up the shining way,
We'll praise the Lord thro' endless day.

20

WE 'LL MARCH AROUND JERUSALEM

No. 358, p. 176 in *The Revivalist*.

O brethern, will you meet me
    On that delightful shore?
O brethern, will you meet me
    Where parting is no more?

And we'll march around Jerusalem,
We'll march around Jerusalem,   (*Repeat twice.*)
When we arrive at home.

O sister, will you meet me?

O leader, will you meet me?

O preacher, will you meet me?

Young convert, will you meet me?

Yes, bless the Lord, I'll meet you.

Backslider, will you meet me?

21

I WANT TO BE A SOLDIER

No. 2, p. 17 in *A Collection of Revival Hymns and Plantation Melodies.* By Marshall W. Taylor, Cincinnati, copyright, 1882. In this volume the revival hymns of the white people and the plantation songs of the Negroes are indistinguishable.

We are the sons of Wesley,
We are the sons of God;
We'll stand by our Discipline,
And by God's holy Word.

Chorus

I want to be a soldier,
The Lord hath set me free.
I want to be a soldier,
Fighting for liberty.

God bless our Church and bishop,
And the local brethren, too.
God bless our Church and people,
With all the travelling crew.

We Methodists get happy —
The Lord hath set us free.
We'll shout and give him glory,
To all eternity.

We'll unfold the Gospel banner,
Wherever we do go,
And spread our free communion
While journeying below.

I saw a might army,
Which went along before;
So great no man could number
Through blood and tears no more.

Go preach, ye sons of thunder,
Ye daughters of the Lamb,
For Jesus will be with you
Until the world shall end.

God bless us in the East,
As well as in the West,
Protect us in the North,
Stand by us in the South.

We've fought the mighty battle,
  With the rebellious crew;
Don't you see how many dangers
  The Lord has brought us through?

22

THE GOSPEL TRAIN

No. 91, p. 159 in *A Collection of Revival Hymns and Plantation Melodies.*

The gospel train is moving,
  I hear it just at hand;
I hear the carwheel moving,
  And rumbling through the land.

Chorus

Get on board, children, (*Repeat twice.*)
  For there's room for many more.

I hear the bell and whistle,
  They're coming round the curve;
She's playing all her steam and power,
  And straining every nerve.

O see the gospel engine,
  She's heaving now in sight;
Her steam-valves they are groaning,
  The pressure is so great.

No signal for another train,
  To follow in the line;
O sinner, you're forever lost,
  If once you're left behind.

O see the engine banner,
  She's flut'ring in the breeze;
She's spangled with the Savior's blood,
  But she still floats at ease.

This is the Christian banner,
  The motto's new and old,
Repentance and Salvation
  Are burnished there in gold.

She's nearing on the station;
  O sinners don't be vain,
But come and get your ticket,
  And be ready for the train.

The fare is cheap and all can go,
 The rich and poor are there;
No second class are on board this train,
 No difference in the fare.

We soon shall reach the station,
 O how we then shall sing
With all the heavenly army
 On that celestial shore.

IV

SPECIMENS OF SONGS FROM THE OLD MINSTREL BOOKS

I

COME DAY, GO DAY, OR MASSA IS A STINGY MAN

"Sung with everlasting shouts of applause by the renowned Dan Emmet."
Page 91 in *Marsh's Selection, or, Singing for the Million, Containing the Choicest and Best Collection of Admired Patriotic, Comic, Irish, Negro, Temperance, and Sentimental Songs Ever Embodied in One Work.* Three volumes in one. New York, Richard Marsh, 374 Pearl Street, 1854.

Oh, massa is a stingy man,
   And all his neighbors knows it,
He keeps good whiskey in his house,
   And neber says, here goes it.
     Sing come day, go day,
     God send Sunday,
     We'll drink whiskey all de week,
     And buttermilk o' Sunday.

A stray dog came to town,
   Pon a bag of peaches,
De horse run off, an he fell down,
   And mashed 'em all to pieces.
     Fala du, fala du da du da du da la,
     Fala, du fala du lala du la du la.
     Come day, etc.

Joe cotton, dig corn,
   Den we feed de niggies,
An oh, lord Moses,
   What a liscious time for niggas.
     Come day, go day, etc.

Black Jen's got a holler tooth
   An says it's always aching,
But when she pits de hoecake in,
   Den it stops a plaguing.
     Come day, go day, etc.

Oh, missis says we eat too much,
   And wear out too much trowses,
She'll make us feed on atmosphere,
   And dress in nature's blowses.
     Come day, go day.

She sent consumption Joe one night,
 Tobacco leaf to kiver,
It made him sneeze out de moonlight,
 An cough away his liver.
  Come day, go day.

Oh, massa loves to hug de gals,
 And missus does n't knows it,
But as I like de angels too,
 I believe I won't exclose it.
  Come day, go day.

Oh, missus says we should n't eat,
 Kase we don't work a Sunday,
But natur keeps disgestion's mill,
 Agoin as well as Monday.
  Come day, go day, etc.

Massa sich a stingy man,
 I no more ketch his possum,
I roast and eat him in de wood,
 And den I swear I loss him.
  Come day, go day, etc.

Old Jake went out to shoot,
 And when de gun it go off,
It kicked his right ear out o' joint,
 Den fall and smash his toe off.
  Come day, go day, etc.

2

GOIN OBER DE MOUNTAIN, OR, THE DIFFICULTIES
BETWEEN OLD JAKE AND HIS SWEETHEART

"Sung with great applause by the popular Virginia Minstrels."
Page 93 in *Marsh's Selection*.

A nigga come from Arkansas,
 [*Bone and Banjo Symphony*]
De biggest fool I ever saw,
 Reel o'er de mountain, love,
 I'm gwine for to leab you,
 Reel o'er de mountain, love,
  Don't let me parting grieve you!

3

DANDY JIM FROM DE CAROLINES

"Now published for the first time from the original manuscript in the possession of T. G. Booth."
Page 104 in *Marsh's Selection*.

I'd often heard it said ob late
Dat South Carolina was de State,
Where handsome nigs are bound to shine,
Like dandy Jim from Caroline.

Chorus

For my ole massa tole me, oh,
I'se de best lookin' nig in de county, oh;
I look in de glass an' find it so.
Just what Massa tole me, oh.

Now beauty, dat is but skin deep,
But through my skin it's hard to peep;
Dar's none can soothe de black gal's mine,
Like dandy Jim from Caroline.

Chorus

I dress's myself from top to toe;
To see Miss Dinah I did go,
Wid pantaloons strapp'd down so fine,
Went dandy Jim from Caroline.

Chorus

De bull-dog kept out de yard;
I tink I'd better lebe my card —
I tied it fas' wid a piece of twine,
Signed dandy Jim from Caroline.

Chorus

She got my note, she wrote me a letter;
De more she wrote, she felt de better.
An' ebery word and ebery line
Was dandy Jim from Caroline.

Chorus

De sport ob de story is soon told,
De heart for lub is nebber cold;
She changed her name from lubly Dine
To Miss Dandy Jim from Caroline.

Chorus

Now ebery little nig she's had,
Is de bery image ob dar dad;
Dar heels stick out three feet behine,
Like dandy Jim from Caroline.

Chorus

I took dem all to church one day
To christen dem widout delay;
De preacher christen eight or nine,
Young dandy Jims from Caroline,

Chorus

But when he cum to take his tex,
He seem'd to be so much perplex,
For nothing cum across his mine,
But dandy Jim from Caroline.

Chorus

4

OLD DAN TUCKER

"Composed by Dan D. Emmet, and sung by him with unbounded applause in Howe's Amphitheatre of the Republic, New York."
Page 622 in *Marsh's Selection*.

I come to town de udder night,
I hear de noise den saw de sight,
De watchmen dey were runnin' roun,
Cryin Old Dan Tucker's come to town,
Git out ob de way! [*Banjo*]
Git out ob de way! [*Banjo*]
Git out ob de way old Dan Tucker,
Your too late to come to your supper.

Tucker is a nice old man,
He used to ride our darby ram,
He sent him whizzin down de hil,
If he hadn't got up — he'd laid dar still.
Git out ob de way, etc.

Sheep an de hog walkin in de pastur
Sheep sez "hog can't y'e go a little faster?
Hush! hush honey! hear de wolf howlin!
Ah, ah, de lawd — ole bull dog growlin,
Git out ob de way, etc.

Jaybird in de martins' nest,
To sabe he soul he got no rest,
Ole Tucker run in de fox's den
Out come de young ones — nine or ten.
    Git out ob de way, etc.

Tucker on de wood pile — can't count 'lebben
Put in a fedder bed — him gwine to hebben,
His nose so flat, his face so full,
De top ob his head like a bag ob wool,
    Git out ob de way, etc.

Tucker went round hicory steeple,
Dar he met some colored people,
Some was black, an some was blacker,
Some was de color ob brown tobacur.
    Git out ob de way, etc.

High-hold on de holler tree,
He poke his bill in for to see,
De lizzard cotch 'im by de snout,
He call old Tucker to pull 'im out.
    Git out ob de way, etc.

Tucker he had cash a plenty,
Dressed to death — his old trunck empty,
To kiss de gals he thot was useless,
'Cept he kissed wid a sway-back-looseness,
    Git out ob de way, etc.

Here's my razor in good order,
Magnum bonum — jis hab bought 'er,
Sheep shell de oats, old Tucker shell de corn
I'll shabe you all when de water gets warm.
    Git out ob de way, etc.

I went to meetin de udder day,
To hear Old Tucker preach an pray,
Dey all got drunk, but me alone,
I make ole Tucker — walk jaw-bone,
    Git out ob de way,   [*Banjo*]
    Git out ob de way,   [*Banjo*]
Git out ob de way you harden'd sinner,
Your too late to come to your dinner.

5

GINGER BLUE

Page 157 in *Marsh's Selection*, part 2.

Oh, my name's Ginger Blue, what I tell you is mighty true;
    I come from the Tennessee Mountains;
My paragraph is short, and my life is sweet,
    As the water that flows from the fountain:
The first ting I said when I raised this nigga head
    To the darkies on the plantation,

Chorus

Walk, chalk, Ginger Blue, git over double trouble,
    And ole Varginny never tire.

One night Pete Williams was goin to give a dance
    To the niggas what lived in that quarter;
Says he, Ginger Blue, I want you to come,
    And then you shall have my daughter.
He'd no sooner said the word than I was up like a bird,
    And my feelings 'gan to jangleate.

(*Spoken.*)   Says I, look here Pete, I does n't like to be cutting round that daughter of yours when Clum Grum is throwing his affections at her, besides he's such a mighty consequential nigga, you can smell him half a mile off, because he carries musk, cologne water, and all the perfumications, round him. Well, says Pete, Ginger, I don't care nothing for that; but if de nigga comes cutting round my daughter I be dam if I don't make him.

Walk, chalk, Ginger Blue, etc.

When I got to the dance, the first thing struck my eye,
    Was Clum Grum the consequential nigga;
Oh, he had the damdest heels you ever did see,
    And I see caus I was a better figure.
He was much surprised when he opened his eye
    And see this nigga stand right before him.

(*Spoken.*)   I golly he had to

Walk, chalk, Ginger Blue, etc.

When the dance was done, we gin to lumber home;
  Between you and me we made a splutter,
We looked for all the world jis like a flock of ducks,
  Apaddling and scrambling in the gutter.
I was gwan cross massa's farm id Rosana on my arm,
  When something struck my observation.

(*Spoken.*) I golly, dere was the president and secretary of the darkey temptation society. They couldn't tell their heads from a bag of wool. Thinks I old coons, if any of them temperance members see you they'll make you

  Walk, chalk, Ginger Blue, etc.

6

WHAR DID YOU CUM FROM?

Page 187 in *Marsh's Selection*, part 2.

  1. Some folks say a nigger won't steal,
      But I cotch one in my corn field,
      So I ask him bout dat corn an he call me a liar,
      So I up wid my foot an I kick him in de fire.
        Oh, whar did you cum from, knock a nigger down?
        Oh, whar did you cum from, etc.

  2. I went for to mow down in de field,
      A black snake bit me 'pon my heel;
      To cut my dirt I tought it best,
      So I ran slap up 'gainst a hornet's nest.
        Oh, whar, etc.

7

LUCY LONG

Page 192 in *Marsh's Selection*, part 2.

Oh, I jist come out afore you,
  To sing a little song,
I plays it on de banjo,
  And dey calls it Lucy Long,

    Oh, take your time, Miss Lucy,
    Take your time, Miss Lucy Long.

Miss Lucy she is handsome,
  And Miss Lucy she is tall,
And de way she spreads her ancles
  Is death to de niggers all.

    Oh, take your, etc.

Oh, Miss Lucy's teeth is grinning,
   Just like an ear ob corn,
And her eyes de look so winning,
   I wish I ne'er was born.

     Oh, take your, etc.

Oh, Miss Lucy when she trabbles,
   She always lebes a mark,
Ob her footsteps on de grabble,
   You can see dem in de dark.

     Oh, take your, etc.

My mother's sick a-bed ah!
   My daddy's got de gout,
Good morning, Mr. Jenkins,
   "Does your mother know you're out?"

     Oh, take your, etc.

My daddy is a baker,
   My mother kneeds the dough,
My brother plays de fiddle,
   And I de banjo.

     Oh, take your, etc.

If I had a scolding wife,
   I'd lick her sure as I'm born;
I'd take her down to New Orleans,
   And trade her off for corn.

     Oh, take your time, etc.

8

THE GAL FROM THE SOUTH

Page 147 in *The Ethiopian Serenaders' Own Book*. Philadelphia & New York, Fisher and Brother, 1857.

Ole Massa owned a colored girl —
   He bought her at the South;
Her hair it curled so very tight,
   She could not shut her mouth.
Her eyes they were so very small,
   They both ran into one,
And when a fly lit in her eye,
   'T was like a June-bug in the sun,

Chorus

Ha, ha, ha, ha, ha, ha,
The gal from the South
Her hair it curl'd so very tight
She could not shut her mouth!

Her nose it was so very long,
    It turned up like a squash,
And when she got her dander up,
    She made me laugh, by gosh,
Ole Massa had no hooks nor nails,
    Or nothing else like that,
So on this darkie's nose he used
    To hang his coat and hat.

Chorus

One morning, Massa, going away,
    He went to get his coat,
But neither hat nor coat was there,
    For she had swallowed both;
He took her to a tailor shop,
    To have her mouth made small;
The lady took in one long breath,
    And swallowed tailor and all!

Chorus

9

DO COME ALONG, OLE SANDY BOY

Page 309 in *Negro Singers' Own Book*. Philadelphia, New York, Turner and
Fisher, 1846(?).

Mr. Coon he is a mighty man,
He carries a bushy tail,
He steals old massa's corn at night,
And husks it on a rail.

Do come along, ole Sandy boy,
Do come along, O, do!
Oh, what did uncle Gabriel say,
Oh, Kitty, can't you come along too.

A squirrel has a bushy tail,
Stumpy grows de hair,
De old coon's tail am ring'd all round
De possum's tail am bare.

Do come along, etc.

Other stanzas deal successively with the fox's tail, peacock's tail, pig's tail, but without the triple comparison. The last two stanzas are as follows:

Niggers hair am berry short,
White folks hair am longer,
White folks dey smell very strong,
Niggers dey smell stronger.

Do come along, etc.

De mink he is a mighty thing,
He rambles in de dark,
The only ting disturbs his peace
Is my old bull dog's bark.

Do come along, etc.

10

DE ORIGINAL JIM CROW

"Sung by the celebrated Tom Rice."

Page 329 in *Negro Singer's Own Book*.

Oh, Jim Crow's cum again, as you must all know,
For he wheel about, he jump about, he do just so,
And ebery time he jump about, he jump Jim Crow.
So I wheel about, I turn about,
I do just so,
And ebery time I wheel about,
I jump Jim Crow.

I kneel to de buzzard and I bow to de crow,
An ebery time I wheel about, I jump Jim Crow,
So I wheel about, etc.

Stanzas 4 and 5:

Snake bak'd a hoe cake, and set de frog to watch it,
De frog he fell asleep, an de lizard come and cotch'd it.
So I wheel about, etc.

I cum to a riber, and could n't get across,
So I gib half a dolla for an old blind horse.
   So I wheel about, etc.

Stanza 23:

A ring-tail'd monkey and a ribb'd nosed baboon
Went out de oder day to spend de arternoon
   So I wheel about, etc.

V

SPECIMENS OF SONGS FROM ANTE-BELLUM NOVELS, TRAVEL BOOKS, SLAVE AUTOBIOGRAPHIES, ETC.

1 — 3

THREE DANCE SONGS

Given as examples of the "unmeaning songs" composed for their adaptation to certain measures and to "patting." Pages 219–220 in *Twelve Years a Slave — The Narrative of Solomon Northup*, edited by David Wilson. New York, 1855, copyright, 1853.

Harper's creek and roarin' ribber
Thar, my dear, we'll live forebber;
Den we'll go to de Injin nation,
All I want in dis creation,
Is pretty little wife and big plantation.

Chorus

Up dat oak and down dat ribber,
Two overseers and one little nigger.

———

Who's been here since I've been gone?
Pretty little gal wid a josey on.

Chorus

Hog Eye!
Old Hog Eye,
And Hosey, too!

Never see de like since I was born,
Here come a gal wid a josey on.

Chorus

———

Ebo Dick and Jurdan's Jo,
Them two niggers stole my yo'.

Chorus

Hop Jim Along
Walk Jim Along
Talk Jim Along, etc.

Old black Dan as black as tar,
He dam glad he was not dar.

Chorus

4

A CHRISTMAS SONG

Given as a song generally sung by slaves to white people who fail to give them a Christmas gift. Page 180 in *Incidents in the Life of a Slave Girl, Written by Herself* [Mrs. Harriet Jacobs]. Boston, 1861.

> Poor massa, so dey say;
> Down in de heel, so dey say;
> Got no money, so dey say;
> God A'mighty bress you, so dey say.

5

SLAVE JOCULARITY

A slave sings the following at his master's command to provide some amusement. Page 138 in *Clotel, or The President's Daughter, A Narrative of Slave Life in the United States.* By William Wells Brown, a Fugitive Slave, etc. London, 1853.

> The big bee flies high
> The little bee makes the honey.
> The black folks make the cotton
> And the white folks get the money.

6

SLAVE FLATTERY

An example of stanzas inserted by slaves in their songs to attract the master's favor. Page 98 in *My Bondage and My Freedom.* By Frederick Douglass. New York and Auburn. Miller, Orton and Mulligan, 1855.

> I am going away to the great house farm,
> O yea! O yea! O yea!
> My old master is a good old master,
> O yea! O yea! O yea!

7

"JUBILEE–BEATERS" SONG

An example of improvised song by "jubilee-beaters." Page 252 in *My Bondage and My Freedom.*

> We raise de wheat
> Dey gib us de corn;
> We bake de bread
> Dey gib us de cruss;

We sif de meal
Dey gib us de huss;
We peel de meat
Dey gib us de skin,
And dat's de way
Dey takes us in.
We skim de pot
Dey gib us the liquor
And say dat's good enough for nigger.

> Walk over! walk over!
> Tom butter and de fat;
> Poor nigger you can't get over dat;
> Walk over!

8

LITTLE MISS SALLY

One of the rowing chants in which slaves flatter their small mistress. In the same passage Fanny Kemble tells how she is often similarly flattered. Page 106 in *A Journal of a Residence on a Georgia Plantation, 1838–1839*, by Frances Anne Kemble, New York, Harper and Brothers, 1863.

> Little Missis Sally
> That's a ruling lady.

9

Another rowing chant, the tune of which "is a distinct descendant of 'Coming Through the Rye.'" Page 127 in Frances Anne Kemble's *Journal*.

> Jenny shake her toe at me
> Jenny gone away
> Jenny shake her toe at me
> Jenny gone away.
> Hurrah! Miss Susy, oh!
> Jenny gone away
> Hurrah! Miss Susy, oh!
> Jenny gone away.

10

A ONE–LINE SONG

Given by Frances Anne Kemble, *Journal*, p. 127, as an "original air," consisting of one line repeated with "a sort of wailing chorus."

> Oh my massa told me, there's no grass in Georgia.

II

FARE YOU WELL

Described by Fanny Kemble as a pretty and pathetic tune which "went off into nonsense verses about gentlemen in the parlor drinking wine and cordial and ladies in the drawing room drinking tea and coffee," etc. *Journal*, p. 127. Cf. no. 12 following.

> Fare you well, and good-by, oh! oh!
> I'm going away to leave you, oh! oh!

12

LADIES IN THE PARLOR

Given by a Southern slave-owner as a genuine Negro song, in contrast with the spurious ones of the minstrel stage. Evidently the song Fanny Kemble describes above. Page 77 in "Negro Minstrelsy, Ancient and Modern," *Putnam's Monthly*, January, 1855.

> De ladies in de parlor,
>   Hey, come a rollin' down —
> A drinking tea and coffee;
>   Good morning, ladies all.
>
> De genmen in de kitchen,
>   Hey, come a rollin' down —
> A drinking brandy toddy;
>   Good morning, ladies all.

13

CORN SHUCKING SONG

Page 78 in "Negro Minstrelsy Ancient and Modern," *Putnam's Monthly*, January, 1855, as sung while shucking corn.

> Cow boy on middle 'e island —
>   Ho, meleety, ho!
> Cow boy on middle 'e island —
>   Ho, meleety, ho!
>
> Missus eat de green persimmon —
>   Ho, meleety, ho! (*Repeat both lines.*)
>
> Mouf all drawed up in a pucker —
>   Ho, meleety, ho! (*Repeat both lines.*)
>
> Staid so till she went to supper —
>   Ho, meleety, ho! (*Repeat both lines.*)

14

PERSONAL COMMENT

One of the numerous and indefinitely continued autobiographic improvisations on matters of transient interest described in "Negro Minstrelsy, Ancient and Modern," *Putnam's Monthly*, January, 1855, p. 78.

> Ole Maus William, he gone to legislatur
> Ah chogaloga, chogaloga, chogalog
> Young Maus John, he done come home from college,
> Ah chogaloga, chogaloga, chogalog.

15

HIGH O

"An extemporaneous refrain," struck up by slaves en route from North Carolina to Louisiana. Page 77 in *The Master's House, a Tale of Southern Life*, by Thomas Bangs Thorpe, 1854.

> Master's going down de ribber
> High O, high O,
> Oh he's de man wid a hundred niggers,
> High O, high O,
> Walk along steam-boat what you waiting for?
> Whew–yaw, yaw, yaw.

16

EXTEMPORE BOAT SONG

As sung by a slave in *Frank Freeman's Barber Shop, A Tale*, by Rev. Bayard R. Hall, D. D. (New York, Charles Scribner, 1852), p. 17.

> Oh! how glad dis niggah are,
> Oh! he! yo! ho!
> Him see his lubby missis dare!
> Oh! he! yo! yo!
> Pull de oar and row her home —
> Oh! he! yo! yo!
> The lilly chiller see her come!
> Oh! he! yo! yo!
>
> Lord bless kind massa too!
> Oh! etc.
> You brush his coat, I clean his shoe!
> Oh! etc.

Good ole Diner kiss his hand!
  Oh! etc.
His lilly chiller by him stand!
  Oh! etc.

Dey both far have been away!
  Oh, etc.
Why so long from niggah stay?
  Oh! etc.
Bring home your fadder and your mudder
  Oh! etc.
We love de one just like tother!
  Oh! etc.

Unky Wardloe! come for missis!
  Oh! etc.
You tarcoal niggah! mind the missis!
  Oh! etc.
De big bags see! I gwyne to come!
  Oh! etc.
I gits de shirt! and you gits none!
  Oh! etc.

Pull! pull! pull quick oar!
  Oh! etc.
Pull! pull! dat is de shore!
  Oh! etc.
Dar run Carrie! dar sit Diner!
  Oh! etc.
The lilly chiller all ahind her!
  Oh! etc.

17

OLE VIRGINNY NEVER TIRE

Sung by Negro slaves in Williamsburg, Va., as reported in *A Second Visit to the United States*, by Sir Charles Lyell (New York, 1849). Also sung by slaves in *Uncle Tom's Cabin Contrasted with Buckingham Hall, The Planter's Home, or A Fair View of both sides of the Slavery Question*, by Robert Criswell, Esq. (New York, 1852), p. 69.

Ole Virginia never tire
Eat hog and hominy and lie by the fire.

18, 19

TWO CORN SHUCKING SONGS

Page 66 in *Uncle Tom's Cabin Contrasted with Buckingham Hall*, etc., by Robert Criswell, Esq., 1852.

"On the top of one of the heaps was mounted Uncle Cato, one of the principal slaves, and a great favorite of Eugene's. He was noted for his talent of improvisation. He would sing one or more lines of a song and the chorus would be repeated by all the others." One of his songs ran thus:

> The lubly Moon it shine so bright,
> We does n't want no oder light,

> *Chorus*

> Sing, darkeys, sing!

> De man up dare, he look at us,
> He tink we make a great, big fuss,

> *Chorus*

> Possum-dog he cotch a coon,
> Nigger skin him pretty soon,

> *Chorus*

> Sold de skin and got de chink,
> Berry sorry dat I drink.

> *Chorus*

"After this, whiskey was handed about by the overseers, and the slaves becoming very merry, began to caper more noisily than before."

———————

> Massa Eugene hab good whiskey,
> Makes de niggers bery friskey,

> *Chorus*

> Shucking ob de corn.

> O, ho! de niggers jolly!
> See dah, de pretty Polly!

> *Chorus*

Dat ar Jake, he sits beside her,
Will she hab dat big black spider?

Chorus

Jeff 's so mad, he look like tunder —
O-o-o-o! who dat hit me wid de corn dah?

Chorus

Jeff, he trew dat corn.

20

OLE SATAN

One snatch from nearly a dozen songs, "mixing religion, the parson, the great
city, the river," sung by Bishop Andrew's Negro boatmen in 1856. C. F. Deems,
ed., *Annals of Southern Methodism for 1856* (Nashville, Tenn., 1857), chap. 9.

Ole Satan you need n't to pick arter me for I not never gwine back no
more.

21, 22

TWO HYMN FRAGMENTS

Given as examples of hymn passages into which the slaves, according to Douglass, read a double meaning — "the North was our Canaan." Page 278 in *My
Bondage and My Freedom*, by Frederick Douglass, New York, 1855.

O Canaan, sweet Canaan
I am bound for the land of Canaan.

I thought I heard them say
There were lions in the way
I don't expect to stay
Much longer here.
Run to Jesus, shun the danger
I don't expect to stay
Much longer here.

23

A religious song sung by slaves. Page 108 in *Incidents in the Life of a Slave Girl.
Written by Herself* [Mrs. Harriet Jacobs], Boston, 1861.

Old Satan is one busy old man;
He rolls dem blocks all in my way;
But Jesus is my bosom friend
He rolls dem blocks away.

If I had died when I was young
  Den how my stam'ring tongue would have sung;
But I am ole and now I stand
  A narrow chance for to tread dat heavenly land.

24

Page 109 in *Incidents in the Life of a Slave Girl*. Sung by a congregation of slaves.

Old Satan thought he had a mighty aim;
He missed my soul and caught my sins.
Cry Amen, cry Amen, cry Amen to God!

He took my sins upon his back;
Went muttering and grumbling down to hell.
Cry Amen, cry Amen, cry Amen to God!

Old Satan's church is here below.
Up to God's free church I hope to go.
Cry Amen, cry Amen, cry Amen to God!

25

HYMN CALLED THE LAMB OF GOD

Page 50 in *A Narrative of the Life and Labors of the Rev. G. W. Offley, A Colored Man and Local Preacher. Written by Himself* (Hartford, Conn., 1860).

When I began I was but young
And now my race is almost run
Hosanna, hosanna, hosanna to the Lamb of God
Crying hosanna, hosanna, hosanna to the Lamb of God.

I never shall forget that day
When Jesus washed my sins away
Hosanna, etc.

I'm glad that I am born to die
From grief and woe my soul shall fly
Hosanna, etc.

Fight on, fight on, we're gaining ground;
Old Satan's kingdom must come down.
Hosanna, etc.

What makes old Satan hate me so?
He had me once and let me go.
Hosanna, etc.

I wish old Satan would be still
And let me do my Master's will.
Hosanna, etc.

We have come to make old Satan yield
Or die a fighting in the field.
Hosanna, etc.

What kind of shoes are these you wear
That you can walk upon the air?
Hosanna, etc.

On Jordan's waves I must go cross,
I hope to ride and not be lost.
Hosanna, etc.

26

Part of a song sung at a camp-meeting at Northampton, Mass. *Narrative of Sojourner Truth, Northern Slave, Emancipated from Bodily Servitude by the State of New York in 1828* (Boston, 1850), p. 116.

It was early in the morning — it was early in the morning
Just at the break of day
When he rose, when he rose, when he rose,
And went to heaven on a cloud.

27

Narrative of Sojourner Truth, etc., p. 119. Sung at the same meeting, to quiet interrupters.

I bless the Lord I've got my seal — today and today
To slay Goliath in the field — today and today.
The good old way is a righteous way,
I mean to take the Kingdom in that good old way.

28

Sung by Negro boatmen in 1860. Page 140 in W. H. Russell, *My Diary North and South*, Boston, 1863.

Oh your soul, oh my soul
    I'm going to the churchyard to lay this body down.
Oh my soul, oh your soul,
    I'm going to the churchyard to lay this nigger down.

29

Sung by West Indian Negro boatman. *The West India Sketch Book* (2 volumes, London, 1834), i, 241, with the air.

> Hurrah, my jolly boys, Fine time o' day.
> We pull for San Thamas, boys, Fine time o' day.
> San Thamas hab de fine girl, etc.
> Nancy Gibbs and Betsy Braid, etc.
> Massa cum fra London Town, etc.
> Massa is a handsome man, etc.
> Massa is a dandy-man, etc.
> Him hab de dollar, plenty, too, etc.
> Massa lub a pretty girl, etc.
> Him lub 'em much, him lub 'em true, etc.
> Him hunt 'em round de guaba bush, etc.
> Him catch 'em in de cane piece, etc. etc.

30

Sung by West Indian Negroes working at a cane mill. *The West India Sketch Book*, ii, 67, with the air.

> Shat-te-ray-nite aw cung la town
>   Chaun fine my deary hunney.
> Aw run roun da lemon tree,
>   Chaun, etc.
> Au look behine da guaba bush,
>   Chaun, etc.
> Aw wash my pot, aw wash um clean
>   Chaun, etc.
> Aw put in pease, aw put in poke
>   Chaun, etc.
> Aw boil my pot, aw boil um sweet,
>   Chaun, etc.
> Aw sweep my house, aw sweep um clean,
>   Chaun, etc.
> Aw clean my nife, aw clean um shine,
>   Chaun, etc.
> Aw mek my bed, aw mek um soft
>   Chaun, etc.
> Aw mek um up, aw shek um up,
>   Chaun, etc.

The same volume (p. 283) contains a Negro social song, with music.

31

From Matthew Gregory Lewis, *Journal of a Residence among the Negroes in the West Indies*, London, 1845. How one West Indian slave owner disposed of slaves who were about to die, according to a song heard by Monk Lewis.

> Take him to the Gully! Take him to the Gully!
> But bringee back the frock and board
> "O massa, massa, me no deadee yet!"
> Take him to the Gully! Take him to the Gully!
> Carry him along!

32

"A NEGRO SONG, FROM MR. PARK'S TRAVELS"

The words by the Duchess of Devonshire and music by G. G. Ferrari, prefixed to Mungo Park's *Travels in the Interior Districts of Africa*, etc., London, 1799. Park's literal translation (p. 198) is:

> The winds roared and the rain fell
> The poor white man, faint and weary
> Came and sat under our tree
> He has no mother to bring him milk, no wife to grind his corn.

Chorus

> Let us pity the white man, no mother has he, etc., etc.

> The loud wind roared, the rain fell fast
> The white man yielded to the blast
> He sat him down, beneath our tree
> For weary, sad, and faint was he
> And ah, no wife or mother's care
> For him the milk or corn prepare.

Chorus

> The White Man shall our pity share
> Alas, no wife or mother's care
> For him the milk or corn prepare.

> The storm is o'er; the tempest past
> And Mercy's voice has hushed the blast.
> The wind is heard in whispers low;

So far as I can discover, this is the first Negro song printed in English.

The White Man far away must go: —
But ever in his heart will bear
Remembrance of the Negro's care.

Chorus

Go, White Man, go — but with thee bear '
The Negro's wish, the Negro's prayer;
Remembrance of the Negro's care.

So far as I can discover, this is the first Negro song printed in English.

BIBLIOGRAPHY

BIBLIOGRAPHY

This bibliography owes a number of titles to the bibliographies printed in *The Negro Year Book* (1925–1926), *Negro Workaday Songs*, by Odum and Johnson, and Julius Mattfeld's *Folk Music of the Western Hemisphere.* However, I have examined and used most of the titles here listed.

I have not included in this bibliography books or articles which do not present or deal directly with the Negro folk-song. Accordingly, the numerous black-face-minstrel books and early religious songsters of the white people, though I have found frequent occasion to use them in studying Negro songs, are not here included.

Abbot, Francis H. *Eight Negro Songs* (from Bedford County, Va.), collected by Francis H. Abbot, edited by Alfred J. Swan. New York, Enoch & Sons, etc., 1924. 47 pp.

Adventure Magazine. The department "Old Songs That Men Have Sung," conducted by Dr. R. W. Gordon from July 10, 1923, to Nov., 1927, contains a number of Negro songs.

Allen, William Francis, comp. *Slave Songs of the United States.* 136 songs, including seven Creole songs. New York, A. Simpson & Co., 1867.

Armstrong, Mrs. Mary Frances (Morgan). *Hampton and its Students*, by two of its teachers, Mrs. M. F. Armstrong and Helen W. Ludlow. With 50 cabin and plantation songs, arranged by Thomas P. Fenner. New York, G. P. Putnam's Sons, 1874. 255 pp.

Backus, Emma M. "Negro Hymns from Georgia," in *Journal of American Folk-lore* (Boston, 1897–98), x, 202, 264; xi, 22.

Backus, Emma M. Negro song from Georgia, "I'se gwine on er journey," in *Journal of American Folk-lore*, 1897, x, 216.

Backus, Emma M. Negro song from North Carolina, "O my pious ole daddy, I done lub him dear," in *Journal of American Folk-lore*, 1898, xi, 60.

Ballanta, N. G. J. *St. Helena Island Spirituals.* 115 spirituals from Penn School, St. Helena Island. G. Schirmer, New York, 1925.

Barret, W. A. "Negro Hymnology," in *Musical Times* (London, 1871–1872), xv, 559–561.

Barrett, Harris. *Negro Folk Songs.* Hampton, Va., Press of the Hampton Normal and Agricultural Institute, 1912. Reprinted from the *Southern Workman* for April, 1912.

Barrow, David C. "A Georgia Corn-shucking," in *Century Magazine* (New York, 1882), xxiv (new series, ii), 873–878.

Barstow, M. "Singers in a Weary Lan'," in *World Outlook*, Oct., 1919.

Barton, William Eleazar. *Old Plantation Hymns; a collection of hitherto unpublished melodies of the slave and the freedman, with historical and descriptive notes.* 54 old hymns, 14 more recent. Boston, New York, etc., Lamson, Wolffe & Co., 1899. First published in *New England Magazine*, Dec., 1898, and Jan. and Feb., 1899. Noted down 1880–1887. Barton points out some connections with white hymns, but not all that his own songs show.

Benedict, Helen Dymond. *Belair Plantation Melodies*; eight real old Negro songs, arrangement by Helen Dymond Benedict. New Orleans, La., Helen D. Benedict, 1924. 17 pp.

"Black Art inspires White Artists," in *Literary Digest*, lxxxi, 30 (May 31, 1924).

"Black Voices," in *Nation*, cxix, 278 (Sept. 17, 1924).

Bond, Carrie Jacobs. *Old Melodies of the South*, compiled by Carrie Jacobs Bond, transcribed by Mary Gillen and Oliver Chalifoux. Chicago, The Bond Shop, Carrie Jacobs Bond & Son, 1918. 39 pp.

Broadwood, Lucy E. "English Airs and Motifs in Jamaica," in Walter Jekyll, *Jamaican Song and Story*. D. Nutt, London, 1907, pp. 285–288.

Brown, John Mason. "Songs of the Slave," in *Lippincott's Magazine* (1868), ii, 617–623.

Brown, Lawrence. Spirituals. Five Negro songs arranged by Lawrence Brown. London, Schott & Co., 1923. 19 pp.

Brown, Lawrence. *Steal Away*; Negro folk-song, arranged by Lawrence Brown. London, Winthrop Rogers, Ltd., 1922. 6 pp.

Burleigh, Harry Thacker. *Heav'n, Heav'n*; Negro spiritual arranged for mixed voices with piano accompaniment. New York, G. Ricordi & Co., 1921. 8 pp.

Burleigh, Harry Thacker. Negro folk songs (not spirituals). Four songs, with music. New York, G. Ricordi & Co., 1921.

Burleigh, Harry Thacker, arr. Negro spirituals arranged for solo voice by H. T. Burleigh. 43 volumes, each a separate song, in folio. New York, G. Ricordi & Co., 1917–1924.

Burlin, Mrs. Natalie Curtis, ed. *Songs and Tales from the Dark Continent, recorded from the singing and the sayings of C. Kamba Simango . . . and Madikane Cele*, by Natalie Curtis. New York, Boston, G. Schirmer, 1920. 170 pp.

Burlin, Mrs. Natalie Curtis. *Hampton Series Negro Folk-Songs*, recorded by Natalie Curtis Burlin. Four volumes. New York, Boston, G. Schirmer, 1918–1919.

Burlin, Mrs. Natalie Curtis. "The Negro's Contribution to the Music of America, etc.," in *The Craftsman* (1913), xxiii, 660–669.

Burlin, Mrs. Natalie Curtis. "Again the Negro," in *Poetry* (1917), ii, 147–151.

Burlin, Mrs. Natalie Curtis. "Negro Music at Birth," in *Musical Quarterly* (1919), v, 86–89.

Cameron, Ian. "Negro Songs" in *Musical Times* (London, 1923), lxiii, 431–432.

Campbell, Olive Dame, and Sharp, Cecil J. *English Folk Songs from the Southern Appalachians*. New York and London. G. P. Putnam's Sons, 1917. Contains a few lines and phrases found in Negro songs.

"Canning Negro Melodies." *Literary Digest* (New York, 1916), lii, 1556–1559.

Christensen, Mrs. Abigail M. Holmes. "Spirituals and 'Shouts' of Southern Negroes," in *Journal of American Folk-lore* (Boston, 1894), vii, 154–155.

Clarke, Mary Olmstead. "Song-Games of Negro Children in Virginia," in *Journal of American Folk-lore* (Boston, 1890), iii, 288–290.

Coleman, Z. A., ed. *The Jubilee Singers*, a collection of plantation melodies. Cincinnati, John Church & Co., 1883. 24 pp.

Coleridge-Taylor, S. *Twenty-Four Negro Melodies*, transcribed by S. Coleridge-Taylor. With a preface by Booker T. Washington. Oliver Ditson & Co., Boston, 1905.

Cox, John Harrington. *Folk-Songs of the South*. Cambridge, Harvard University Press, 1925. Mostly traditional songs of the whites. xxxi + 545 pp.

Curtis, Natalie. *See* Burlin, Mrs. Natalie Curtis.

D., C. W. "Contraband Singing," in *Dwight's Journal of Music* (Boston, 1861), xix, 182.

Dann, Hollis, ed. *Fifty-eight Spirituals for Choral Use*. Harmonized by Harvey Worthington Loomis. Boston, C. C. Birchard & Co., 1924.

Darby, Loraine. "Ring-Games from Georgia," in *Journal of American Folklore* (Lancaster, Pa., 1917), xxx, 218–221.

Davis, Henry C. "Negro Folk-lore in South Carolina," in *Journal of American Folk-lore* (Lancaster, Pa., 1917), xxvii, 241–254.

"Desecration of 'Spirituals.'" *Southern Workman* (Hampton, Va., 1922), li, 501–503.

Dett, R. Nathaniel. "Gently, Lord, O gently Lead us." Melody from *Bahama Songs and Stories* (American Folk-lore Society). Text from a hymn by R. Nathaniel Dett. Cincinnati, The John Church Co., 1924. 17 pp.

Dett, R. Nathaniel. "I'm a-goin' to see my friends again." Negro folk-song derivative, from the singing of Reverend J. Fletcher Bryant, Pueblo, Colorado. Cincinnati,The John Church Co., 1924. 5 pp.

Dett, R. Nathaniel. "A man goin' roun' takin' names." Negro folk-song derivative, from the singing of Captain Walter R. Brown. Cincinnati, The John Church Co., 1924. 5 pp.

Dett, R. Nathaniel, arr. *Negro Spirituals Arranged for Solo Voice*. Cincinnati, The John Church Co., 1919.

Dubois, W. E. B. "The Sorrow Songs" (chapter 14 of *The Souls of Black Folk*). Chicago, 1904.

Dvorak, Anton. "Goin' home," from the Largo of the symphony *From the New World*, op. 95. Music by Anton Dvorak, words and adaptations by William Arms Fisher. Boston, 1922. 10 pp.

Edwards, Charles Lincoln. *Bahama Songs and Stories. A contribution to folklore*. Forty songs, all but four containing phrases found in American Negro songs. No real difference except in dialect. Boston and New York, pub. for the American Folk-lore Society, by Houghton, Mifflin and Co., 1895. 111 pp.

Ende, A. von. "Die musik der amerikanischen Neger" in *Die Musik* (Berlin, 1906), Jahrg. 5, Heft 24, pp. 368–375.

Engel, Carl. *An Introduction to the Study of National Music, comprising researches into popular songs, traditions, and customs*. London: Longmans, Green, Reader and Dyer. 1866. 435 pp.

"Enigmatic Folksongs of the Southern Underworld" in *Current Opinion* (New York, 1919), lxvii, 165–166.

Farwell, Arthur, arr. Two Negro spirituals, "De rocks a-renderin'," and "Moanin' dove," recorded by Alice Haskell, harmonized by Arthur Farwell. Copyright 1905, by the Wa-Wan Press. 3 pp.

Fenner, Thomas P., arr. "Cabin and Plantation Songs as sung by the Hampton Students," arranged by Thomas P. Fenner, in charge of Musical Department at Hampton; in Armstrong and Ludlow, *Hampton and its Students* (1875), pp. 171–255.

Fenner, Thomas P., ed. *Cabin and Plantation Songs as Sung by the Students* (New York, G. P. Putnam's Sons, 1877), pp. 171-255.

Fenner, Thomas P., comp. *Cabin and Plantation Songs as sung by the Hampton Students*, arranged by Thomas P. Fenner, Frederick G. Rathbun, and Miss Bessie Cleaveland; third edition, enlarged by the addition of 44 songs. New York and London, G. P. Putnam's Sons, 1901. 166 pp. Includes a few songs "from Indian and other nationalities."

Fenner, Thomas P. *Religious Folk Songs of the Negro as sung on the Plantations*. New edition. Arranged by the musical directors of the Hampton Normal and Agricultural Institute from the original editions by Thomas P. Fenner. Hampton, Va., The Institute Press, 1909. 178 pp.

Ferrero, F. "La musica dei negri americani," in *Rivista Musicale Italiana* (Torino, 1906, anno 13), pp. 393-436.

Finger, Charles J., comp. *Frontier Ballads.* Woodcuts by Paul Honoré. Garden City, New York, Doubleday, Page & Co. Contains nine Negro songs. 181 pp.

Fisher, William Arms. "Deep River" (op. 19, no. 1), in Marcella Sembrich, *My Favorite Folk Songs* (Boston, 1918), pp. 6-9.

Fisher, William Arms, and others. *Ten Negro Spirituals*, arranged by William Arms Fisher, Harvey B. Gaul, J. Rosamund Johnson, Charles Fonteyn Manney. Boston, Oliver Ditson Company, New York, 1925. 32 pp.

Fisher, William Arms, ed. *Seventy Negro Spirituals*, edited by William Arms Fisher. Boston and New York, Oliver Ditson Company (*The Musicians Library*). Excellent historical and critical introduction, biographical sketches and notes. Versions carefully recorded. 1926. xxxiv + 212 pp.

Fletcher, John Gould. "Negro Folk-Poetry." (Review in *Nation*, London, 1922, xxxi, 763-764, of T. W. Talley, *q. v.*)

Frey, Hugo, comp. and arr. *A Collection of 25 selected famous Negro spirituals transcribed and arranged by Hugo Frey.* New York, Robbins-Engel, Inc., 1924. 47 pp.

Garnet, L. A. "Spirituals," in *Outlook*, cxxx, 589 (April 12, 1922).

Garrison, Lucy. "Songs of the Port Royal 'Contrabands,'" in *Dwight's Journal of Music* (Boston, 1862), xxii, 254-255.

Gaul, Harvey Bartlett. "Negro Spirituals," in *New Musical Review* (New York, 1918), xvii, 147-151.

Gaul, Harvey B., arr. *Negro Spirituals*, arranged by Harvey B. Gaul. Six volumes, six songs. Boston, Oliver Ditson Co., 1923-1924.

Gaul, Harvey B., comp. and arr. *Nine Negro Spirituals*, collected and arranged by Harvey B. Gaul. New York, The H. W. Gray Company, 1918. 25 pp.

Goldstein, Walter. "The Natural Harmonic and Rhythmic Sense of the Negro," in *Music Teachers' National Association Proceedings* (Hartford, 1918), series xii, pp. 29-39.

Gordon, R. W. *The Folk-Songs of America.* A series of eighteen articles in *The New York Times Sunday Magazine*, beginning Jan. 2, 1927. Those bearing most directly upon the Negro are "Work Chanteys" (Jan. 16, 1927), "The Spirituals" (Feb. 20, 1927), "Negro 'Shouts'" (April 24, 1927), "Negro Chants" (May 8, 1927), and "Jail Ballads" (June 19, 1927). See also under *Adventure*.

Graham, Alice. "Original plantation melodies as one rarely hears them," in *Etude* (Philadelphia, Pa., 1922), xl, 744.

Grant, Frances. "Negro Patriotism and Negro Music," in *Outlook* (New York, 1919), cxxi, 343–347.

Grant-Schaefer, G. A. *Songs from the South, adapted and arranged with pianoforte accompaniments.* Boston, New York, The A. P. Schmidt Co., 1925.

Guial, E. L. "Among the Sable Singers," in *Western Monthly* (Chicago, 1869), ii, 421–426.

Guion, David W. *Darkey Spirituals*, collected and arranged by David W. Guion. New York, M. Whitmark & Sons. 1918. Fourteen songs, each a separate volume.

Guion, David W. *Two Darkey Songs.* New York, G. Schirmer, 1918.

Hallowell, Emily. *Calhoun Plantation Songs*, collected and edited by Emily Hallowell. Boston, C. W. Thompson & Co., 1905.

Hallowell, Emily. *Calhoun Plantation Songs*, collected and edited by Emily Hallowell. 69 songs. Second edition. Boston, C. W. Thompson & Co., 1907.

Handy, William C., ed. *Blues;* an anthology, edited by W. C. Handy, with an introduction by Abbe Niles; illustrations by Miguel Covarrubias. New York, A. & C. Boni, 1926.

Hare, Maud Cuney. "The Drum in Africa, The Use of Music by a Primitive People," in *Musical Observer*, July, 1918.

Harris, Joel Chandler. "Plantation Music," in *Critic* (New York, 1883), iii, 505–506.

Harris, Joel Chandler. *Uncle Remus and his Friends; old plantation stories, songs and ballads, with sketches of Negro character.* Illustrated by A. B. Frost. Boston and New York, Houghton, Mifflin Co., 1892. 357 pp.

Harris, Joel Chandler. *Uncle Remus, His Songs and Sayings*, with an introduction by Thomas Nelson Page, and illustrations by A. B. Frost and E. W. Kemble. New York and London, D. Appleton and Company, 1920. 265 pp.

Haskell, Marion Alexander. "Negro 'Spirituals,'" in the *Century* (New York, 1899), lviii (new series, xxxvi), 577–581.

Hayes, Roland. *Sit Down*, Negro spiritual arranged by Roland Hayes. . . . High voice. New York. G. Ricordi & Co., 1923. 7 pp.

Higginson, Thomas Wentworth. "Negro Spirituals," in *Atlantic Monthly* (June, 1867), xix, 685–694. Contains 36 spirituals and two secular songs.

Higginson, Thomas Wentworth. *Army Life in a Black Regiment.* Chapter 9 contains Negro spirituals as sung in Col. Higginson's regiment during the Civil War. Boston, 1870.

"Higher Music of American Negroes," in *Literary Digest*, October 5, 1912.

Hobson, Anne. *In Old Alabama; being the chronicles of Miss Mouse, the Little Black Merchant*, illustrated by Carol McPherson. New York, Doubleday, Page & Company, 1903. 237 pp. (Words of 54 spirituals and plantation songs, pp. 157–236.)

Howard, John Tasker, Jr. "Capturing the Spirit of the Real Negro Music," in *The Musician* (New York, 1919), xxiv, no. 3, pp. 13, 41.

Howard, J. T. "Our Folk Music and its Probable Impress on American Music of the Future," in *Music Quarterly*, April, 1921.

Howard, J. T. "Rambling 'Round in Music Land," in *The Musician*, vol. xxix (June, 1924).

Howe, R. Wilson. "The Negro and his Songs," in *Southern Workman* (Hampton, Va., 1922), li, 381–383.

Jekyll, Walter. *Jamaican Song and Story.* London, D. Nutt, 1907. Publications of the Folk-Lore Society, London, vol. 55, 1904.

Jenks, F. H., and Frank Kidson. "Negro Music of the United States," in Grove's *Dictionary of Music and Musicians,* edited by J. A. Fuller Maitland (London, 1907), iii, 350–362.

Johnson, James Weldon, ed. *The Book of American Negro Spirituals,* edited with an introduction by James Weldon Johnson; musical arrangements by J. Rosamond Johnson, additional numbers by Lawrence Brown. 61 songs. New York, The Viking Press, 1925. 187 pp.

Johnson, James Weldon, ed. *The Second Book of Negro Spirituals,* edited with an introduction by James Weldon Johnson; musical arrangements by J. Rosamond Johnson. 61 songs. New York, The Viking Press, 1926. 189 pp.

"A Just Rebellion." New York, 1909–1910. Typewritten copies of two editorials from the New York *Sun,* Dec. 21 and 28, 1909, with two editorial replies from *Musical America,* New York, Jan. 1 and 8, 1910, on a question of Negro folk-songs, occasioned by the refusal of the students of Howard University to sing plantation melodies. (In New York Public Library, as described in Mattfeld Bibliography.)

Kennedy, Robert Emmet. *Black Cameos,* decorations by Edward Larocque Tinker. Interesting sketches, interspersed with songs. Good descriptions and understanding of Negro. Notes with songs. 20 songs, all but about five religious. New York, A. & C. Boni, 1924. 210 pp.

Kennedy, Robert Emmet. *Mellows, a Chronicle of Unknown Singers;* decorations by Simmons Persons. New York, A. and C. Boni, 1925. 183 pp.

Kennedy, Robert Emmet. "Poetic and Melodic Gifts of the Negro," in *Etude,* xli, 159–160 (March, 1923).

Kerlin, Robert Thomas. "Canticles of Love and Woe"; Negro spirituals, in *Southern Workman* (Hampton, Va., 1921), l, 62–64.

Kerlin, Robert Thomas. *Negro Poets and their Poems.* Washington, D. C., Associated Publishers, Inc., 1923. 285 pp. Chapter 1, "The Negro's heritage of song. Untaught melodies. The spirituals. The seculars" (pp. 1–20).

Kingsley, Walter. "Enigmatic Folksongs of the Southern Underworld," in *Current Opinion* (New York, 1919), lxvii, 165.

Krehbiel, Henry Edward. *Folk-Music Studies:* "Slave songs in America," pp. 1–11. Their origin and characteristics — growth of interest in them — the literature of the subject, in New York *Tribune,* Sept. 10 and 17, 1899.

Krehbiel, Henry Edward. "Lafcadio Hearn and Congo Music," in *The Musician* (Boston, 1906), xi, 544–545.

Krehbiel, Henry Edward. *Afro-American Folk-Songs; a Study in Racial and National Music.* New York and London, G. Schirmer, 1914. 176 pp.

Larremore, Thomas A. *Three Negro Spirituals,* arranged for men's voices *a capella* and dedicated to the K. U. Men's Glee Club. Lawrence, Kans., T. A. Larremore, 1924. 3 pp.

Leiding, Harriette Kershaw. *Street Cries of an old Southern City,* with music and illustrations. Charleston, S. C., The Daggert Printing Co., 1910. Unpaged.

Lemmermann, Karl. "Improvised Negro Songs," in *New Republic* (New York, 1917), xiii, 214–215.

Lockwood, L. C. "The Song of the 'Contrabands,' 'O Let my people go.'" Words and music obtained through the Rev. L. C. Lockwood, Chaplain of the

"Contrabands" at Fortress Monroe. Arranged by Thomas Raker. New York, Horace Waters, 1861. 7 pp.

Lomax, John Avery. "Self-Pity in Negro Folk-Songs," in *Nation* (New York, 1917), cv, 141–145.

Lomax, John Avery. "Some Types of American Folk-Song," in *Journal of American Folk-lore* (Lancaster, Pa., 1915), xxviii, 1–17.

Ludlow, Helen Wilhelmina, ed. *Tuskegee Normal and Industrial School, for training colored teachers, at Tuskegee, Alabama. Its story and its songs.* Edited by Helen W. Ludlow. Eighteen songs arranged by R. H. Hamilton, three not folk-songs, but by R. H. H. Hampton, Va., Normal School Press, 1884.

Macy, James C., ed. *Jubilee and Plantation Songs.* "Characteristic favorites, as sung by the Hampton students, Jubilee singers, Fisk University students, and other concert companies." Also, a number of new and pleasing selections. 104 songs. Boston, Oliver Ditson Co., 1887. 80 pp.

Manney, Charles Fonteyn, *Four Negro Spirituals*, arranged by Charles Fonteyn Manney. Boston, Oliver Ditson Co., 1922.

Marsh, J. B. T. *The Story of the Jubilee Singers; with their Songs.* Edited by J. B. T. Marsh. 7th ed., London, Hodder and Stoughton, 1877. 248 pp.

Mattfeld, Julius. *The Folk Music of the Western Hemisphere.* A list of the references in the New York Public Library, New York, 1925. 62 pp. Index. An indispensable bibliography.

McKay, Claude. *Songs of Jamaica.* Kingston, Jamaica. 1912.

McKim, J. "Negro Songs," in *Dwight's Journal of Music*, Boston, Aug. 9, 1862, p. 148.

McKim, J. A letter on Negro singing, in *Dwight's Journal of Music*, Boston, Nov. 8, 1862, p. 255.

Mees, Arthur, arr. *Six Authentic Negro Melodies*, by permission of Henry E. Krehbiel. Arranged for the Mendelssohn Glee Club by Arthur Mees. Copyright, 1899, by the Mendelssohn Glee Club. 27 pp.

Milhaud, D. "Jazz Band and Negro Music," in *Living Age* (Oct. 18, 1924), cccxxiii, 169–173.

Miller, George A. "Sounding a New Note of Freedom in Negro Music," in *Musical America* (New York, 1922), xxxvi, no. 8, p. 9.

Milligan, Harold Vincent. *Ain't gonna study war no more;* Negro spiritual for mixed voices. Boston, New York, The A. P. Schmidt Co., 1924. 8 pp.

Milligan, Harold Vincent. *Camp meeting;* Negro spiritual for mixed voices. Boston, New York, The A. P. Schmidt Co., 1924. 7 pp.

Milligan, Harold Vincent. *I Know the Lord's laid His hands on me;* Negro spiritual for mixed voices. Boston, New York, The A. P. Schmidt Co., 1924. 7 pp.

Mitchell, Humphrey. *Stay in de field, O warrior!* Old Negro spiritual arranged as a song by Humphrey Mitchell. High, in A. Boston, The Boston Music Co.; New York, G. Schirmer, 1918. 7 pp.

Mitchell, Mrs. M. L. *Songs of the Confederacy and Plantation Melodies.* Issued under the auspices of The Richard Hawes Chapter of Paris, Ky. Selected and arranged by Mrs. A. L. Mitchell, Paris, Ky. Cincinnati, The Geo. B. Jennings Co., 1901. Unpaged.

Moderwell, Hiram Kelley. "The Epic of the Black Man," in *New Republic* (New York, 1917), xii, 154–155.

Murphy, Jeannette Robinson. "Gawd bless dem Yankees!" in *Century* (New York, 1898), lvi (new series, xxxiv), 797–798.

Murphy, Jeannette Robinson. "Must the True Negro Music become Obsolete?" in Kunkel's *Musical Review* (St. Louis, 1905), xxx, no. 305, p. 10.

Murphy, Jeannette Robinson. "Southern Thoughts for Northern Thinkers," New York City, The Bandanna Publishing Company, 1904. 47 pp. 26 songs, mostly delivered in lectures, originally in 1898, then published in magazines.

Murphy, Jeannette Robinson. "The Survival of African Music in America." *Popular Science Monthly* (New York, 1899), lv, 660–672.

Murphy, Jeannette Robinson. "The True Negro Music and its Decline," in the *Independent* (New York, 1903), lv, 1723–1730.

Musical Directors of Hampton Institute, The. *The Religious Folk Songs of the Negro as sung on the Plantation*. Hampton, Va., 1909.

Myers, Charles Samuel. "Traces of African Melody in Jamaica," in Walter Jekyll, *Jamaican Song and Story* (London, D. Nutt, 1907), pp. 278–285.

National Jubilee Melodies. 161 songs. Nashville, Tenn. National Baptist Publishing Board. 191-? 15th ed.

"A Negro Explains Jazz," in *Literary Digest* (New York, 1919), lxi, no. 4, pp. 28–29.

"Negro Folk Songs; Acclaimed America's Musical Treasure," in *Musical America*, Aug. 3, 1918.

"Negro Minstrelsy, Ancient and Modern," in *Putnam's Monthly*, Jan., 1855, v, 72–79.

"Negro Songs, Indian and Negro in Music," in *Literary Digest*, June 29, 1912.

"Negro Spiritual," in *Etude*, xli, 678, Oct., 1924.

"Negro Spirituals," in *Living Age*, April 2, 1921.

Newton, Ernest, arr. *Twelve Negro Spiritual Songs*. Arranged, with new accompaniments, by Ernest Newton. London, F. Pitman Hart & Co., Ltd., 1925. 28 pp.

Niles, Abbe. "Blue Notes," in *New Republic*, xlv, 292–293.

Niles, John J., arr. *Impressions of a Negro Camp Meeting*. Eight traditional tunes adapted and arranged for voice and piano by John J. Niles. New York, Carl Fischer, Inc., 1925. 21 pp.

Niles, John J. *Singing Soldiers*, illustrated by Margaret Thornily Williamson. New York, Charles Scribner's Sons, 1927. 171 pp. Contains 29 songs, consisting of old songs sung at home, parodies of old songs to fit the new surroundings, impromptus on old models with a World-War setting, and imitations of the white soldier's songs, though not many of the latter.

Noble, Gilford Clifford. *The Most Popular Plantation Songs*. New York, Hinds, Noble and Eldredge, 1911.

"Objecting to the Negro Dialect," in *Literary Digest* (New York, 1916), liii, 1253.

O'Connell, L. "The Folk-Songs of Afro-America," in *The Musician* (Boston, 1906), xi, 503–504.

Odum, Anna Kranz. "Some Negro Folk-songs from Tennessee," in *Journal of American Folk-lore* (Lancaster, Pa., 1914), xxvii, 255–265.

Odum, Howard W. "Down that Lonesome Road," in *Country Gentleman*, May, 1926, pp. 18–19, 79.

Odum, Howard W. "Folk-Song and Folk-Poetry as Found in the Secular Songs of the Southern Negroes," in *Journal of American Folk-lore* (Lancaster,

Pa., 1911), xxv, 255–295 and 351–396. Largely repeated in Odum and Johnson's *Negro Workaday Songs, q. v.*

Odum, Howard W. "Religious Folk-Songs of the Southern Negro," in *American Journal of Religious Psychology and Education* (Worcester, Mass., 1908–1909), iii, 265–365. Largely repeated in Odum and Johnson's *The Negro and His Songs, q. v.*

Odum, Howard W., and Johnson, Guy B. *The Negro and His Songs.* Chapel Hill, The University of North Carolina Press, 1925.

Odum, Howard Washington, and Johnson, Guy B. *Negro Workaday Songs.* Chapel Hill, The University of North Carolina Press; London, H. Milford, Oxford University Press, 1926. 278 pp. "Selected bibliography" on pp. 265–270.

Owen, May West. "Negro Spirituals: their origin, development, and place in American folk-song," in *Musical Observer* (New York, 1920), xix, no. 12, pp. 12–13.

Parsons, Elsie Worthington (Clews). *Folk-lore of the Sea Islands, South Carolina.* Cambridge: American Folk-lore Society, 1923. xxx + 219 pp. (American Folk-lore Society, *Memoirs*, vol. xvi).

Peabody, Charles. "Notes on Negro Music," in *Journal of American Folk-lore* (Boston, 1903), xvi, 148–152.

Pearce, G. Wilfred. "Negroes and Negro Melodies." A letter in the New York *Sun*, Feb. 15, 1894.

"Percy Grainger's Tribute to the Music of the American Negro," in *Current Opinion* (New York, 1915), lix, 100–101.

Perkins, A. E. "Negro Spirituals from the Far South," in *Journal of American Folk-lore*, xxxv, no. 137 (July–September, 1922), 223–249. 47 songs.

Perrow, E. C. "Songs and Rhymes from the South," in *Journal of American Folk-lore* (1912–1915), xxv (1912), 137–155; xxvi (1913), 123–173; xxviii (1915), 129–190.

Peterson, Clara Gottschalk. *Creole Songs from New Orleans in the Negro Dialect*, set to music by Clara Gottschalk Peterson. New Orleans, The L. Grunewald Co., Ltd., 1902. 20 pp.

Peterson, Clara Gottschalk. *Creole Songs from New Orleans*, etc. New Orleans, The L. Grunewald Co., Ltd., 1909. 12 pp. "Revised edition."

Pike, Gustavus D. *The Jubilee Singers, and their Campaign for Twenty Thousand Dollars.* 61 songs. London, Hodder and Stoughton, 1873.

"Plantation Songs." *Southern Workman* (Hampton, Va., 1900–1921), vols. xxix–xxxii, xxxv–xxxvii, xli–xlii, xlv–xlvi, xlviii–l.

Porter, Grace Cleveland. *Negro Folk Singing Games and Folk Games of the Habitants.* Traditional melodies and text transcribed by Grace Cleveland Porter, accompaniments by Harvey Worthington Loomis. London, J. Curwen & Sons, Ltd., 1914. 35 pp.

Pound, Louise. "The Ancestry of a 'Negro Spiritual,'" in *Modern Language Notes* (Baltimore, 1918), xxxiii, 442–444. Traces one Negro spiritual to an early nineteenth-century camp-meeting song of white people.

Powell, Harold, and W. Elmer Keaton. "Brother, please don't let this harvest pass" (a favorite negro spiritual), arranged and revised by Harold Powell and W. Elmer Keaton. Kansas City, Mo., J. W. Jenkins Music Co., 1924. 3 pp.

Powell, Harold and W. Elmer Keaton. "Walk in Jerusalem jus' like John" (a favorite Negro spiritual), arranged and revised by Harold Powell and W. Elmer Keaton. Kansas City, Mo., J. W. Jenkins Sons, Music Co., 1924. 5 pp.

Pratt, Waldo Selden, and Charles N. Boyd. "Negro Music," in Grove's *Dictionary of Music and Musicians*. New York, Macmillan, 1920. American supplement, vi, 307.

Proctor, H. H. "The Theology of the Songs of the Southern Slaves," in *Southern Workman* (Nov. and Dec., 1907), xxxvi, 584–592, 652–656.

Puckett, Newbell Niles. *Folk Beliefs of the Southern Negro*. Chapel Hill, N. C., University of North Carolina Press, 1926. 644 pp. Analysis of Negro folk beliefs and practices, with incidental consideration of songs as connected therewith. Contains about 20 short songs or excerpts.

Redfearn, S. F. "Songs from Georgia," in *Journal of American Folk-lore*, xxxiv, 121–124. One secular and three religious songs.

Roberts, Helen H. "Possible Survivals of African Song in Jamaica," in *The Musical Quarterly* (New York, July, 1926), xii, no. 3.

Robinson, Frances. "Folk Music," in *Current Literature* (New York, 1901), xxx, 350–351.

Rodeheaver, Homer A. *Rodeheaver's Plantation Melodies*. A collection of modern, popular and old-time Negro songs of the Southland. Chicago, The Rodeheaver Company, 1916. 32 pp.

Saerchinger, César. "The Folk Elements in American Music," in *The Art of Music* (New York, 1915), iv, 277–330.

Sandburg, Carl, comp. *The American Song Bag*. New York, Harcourt, Brace & Co. 1927. Pp. xxiii + 495. Illustrated. Concerned mainly with folk-songs of white people, but contains words and music for a number of Negro songs.

Sawyer, J. J. *Jubilee Songs and Plantation Melodies* (words and music), specially arranged by Prof. J. J. Sawyer, and sung by the original Nashville students, the celebrated Colored Concert Co., H. B. Thearle, proprietor. Copyright, 1884. 13 pp.

Scarborough, Dorothy. *In the Land of Cotton*. New York, 1923. A novel containing a number of Negro songs.

Scarborough, Dorothy. *On the Trail of Negro Folk-Songs*, by Dorothy Scarborough, assisted by Ola Lee Gulledge. Cambridge, Harvard University Press, 1925. 289 pp.

Scherff, John C. "African Melodies." New York. 1844.

Seward, Theodore Frelinghuysen. *Jubilee Songs: as Sung by the Jubilee Singers, of Fisk University* (*Nashville, Tenn.*), under the auspices of the American Missionary Association. 24 songs. New York, Bigelow & Main, 1872. 28 pp.

Seward, Theodore F., and White, George L., comp. *Jubilee Songs: as Sung by the Jubilee Singers*. Part I enlarged. (Part II enlarged.) New York, Bigelow & Main, 1884. 2 vols. in 1. 160 pp.

Shepperd, E. (*pseud.*). See Young, Martha.

Smiley, Portia. "Folk-Lore from Virginia, South Carolina, Georgia, Alabama and Florida," in *Journal of American Folk-lore* (Lancaster, Pa., 1919), xxxii, 357–383.

Smith, De Loss, arr. *Little David; Old Negro Melody*. Cincinnati, Fillmore Music House, 1925. 5 pp.

Smith, Joseph H. "Negro Songs," in *Sewanee Review*, 1924.

Smith, N. Clark. *New Jubilee Songs for Quartette, Choir, or Chorus, Concert, Church and Home,* compiled and arranged by N. Clark Smith. Chicago, Smith Jubilee Music Co., 1906. 18 pp.

Smith, N. Clark. *New Plantation Melodies as sung by the Tuskegee Institute Quartette,* compiled and arranged by Capt. N. Clark Smith. The story of Booker T. Washington and Tuskegee Institute, as told by Charles Winter Wood. 1909. Unpaged.

Smith, N. Clark. *Favorite Folk-Melodies as Sung by Tuskegee Students,* compiled and arranged by N. Clark Smith. Wichita, Kansas (N. Clark Smith), 1914. 16 pp.

Smith, Reed. *Gullah.* Bulletin No. 190 of the University of South Carolina, Nov. 1, 1926. Columbia, S. C. Contains a section on spirituals. 45 pp.

Spaeth, Sigmund. *Read 'Em and Weep. The Songs You Forgot to Remember.* Doubleday Page & Co., Garden City, N. Y., 1926. 267 pp. Only two or three real Negro songs, but a dozen or more of the "coon songs" that have somewhat influenced Negro folk-songs.

Spaulding, H. G. "Under the Palmetto," in *Continental Monthly* (New York, 1863), iv, 188–203. Negro "shouts" and "shout songs," with five tunes, pp. 196–200.

Speers, Mary Walker Finley. "Negro Songs and Folk-Lore," in *Journal of American Folk-lore* (Boston, 1910), xxiii, 435–439.

Speers, Mary Walker Finley. "Maryland and Virginia Folk-Lore." Campmeeting hymn, "I uz dere win he walked in Galilee," in *Journal of American Folk-lore* (Lancaster, Pa.), xxvi, 190–191.

Stanley, May. "Foundation for Negro Music of Future," in *Musical America,* July 6, 1918.

Steward, T. G. "Negro Imagery," in *New Republic,* xii, 248.

Talbot, Edith Armstrong. "True Religion in Negro Hymns," in *Southern Workman* (Hampton, Va., 1922), li, 213–216, 260–264, 334–339.

Talley, Thomas Washington, comp. *Negro Folk Rhymes, wise and otherwise,* with a study by Thomas W. Talley. New York, The Macmillan Co., 1922. 347 pp. (*See* Gould, John Fletcher.)

Taylor, Marshall W. *A Collection of Revival Hymns and Plantation Melodies.* Musical composition by Miss Josephine Robinson; copied by Misses Amelia C. and Hettie G. Taylor. Cincinnati, Marshall W. Taylor and W. C. Echols. 1882. 262 pp. Makes no distinction between the religious songs of the white people and Negroes, nor can they be distinguished in most of the songs given.

Thanet, Octave. "Cradle Songs of Negroes in North Carolina," in *Journal of American Folk-lore,* vii, 310.

Thomas, Edna. *Negro Spirituals sung and arranged by Edna Thomas.* London, Keith Prowse & Co., Ltd., 1924, 6 vols.

Tiersot, Julien [Jean Baptiste Élisée Julien]. *La musique chez les peuples indigènes de l'Amérique du Nord (États-Unis et Canada).* Paris, Fischbacher; New York, Breitkopf et Haertel, 1911 (?). 231 pp.

Tonsor, Johann. "Negro Music," in *Music* (Chicago, 1892–1893), iii, 119–122.

Torrend, J. *Specimens of Bantu Folk-Lore from Northern Rhodesia;* texts (collected with the help of the phonograph) and English translations by J. Torrend. London, K. Paul, Trench, Trubner & Co., Ltd., New York, E. P. Dutton & Co., 1921. 187 pp.

Turner, Harriet. *Folk-Songs of the American Negro*, collected and harmonized by Harriet Turner. Boston, The Boston Music Co., 1925. 5 pp.

Wallaschek, Richard. *An Inquiry into the Origin and Development of the Music, Songs, Instruments, Dances and Pantomimes of Savage Races.* London, 1893.

Webb, W. Prescott. *Miscellany of Texas Folk-Lore.* Texas Folk-Lore Society Publications (Austin, Texas, 1923), no. 2, pp. 38–49.

Webb, W. Prescott. "Notes on Folk-Lore of Texas," in *Journal of American Folk-lore* (Lancaster, Pa., 1915), xxviii, 290–299.

White, Clarence Cameron. "Musical Genius of the American Negro," *Etude* (May, 1924), xlii, 305–306.

White, Clarence Cameron. "Negro Music a Contribution to the National Music of America," in *Musical Observer* (New York, 1919–1920), xviii, no. 11, pp. 18–19; xix, no. 1, pp. 16–17; no. 2, pp. 50–51; no. 3, p. 13.

White, James Cameron. "The Story of the Negro Spiritual 'Nobody knows the trouble I've seen,'" in *Musical Observer* (New York, 1924), xxiii, no. 6, p. 29.

White, Newman I. "Racial Traits in the Negro Song," in *Sewanee Review* (Sewanee, Tenn., 1920), xxviii, 396–404.

Wightman, Francis P., compiler. *Little Leather Breeches and Other Southern Rhymes.* Being a number of folk-lore songs, Negro Rhymes, Street Venders' Cries, etc., gathered from various parts of the South. New York, Taylor and Co., 1899. Unpaged.

Williams, Emily Harper. "The Emancipation of Negro Music," in *Musical America*, Jan. 5, 1918.

Wilson, H. J. "The Negro and Music," in *Outlook*, Dec. 1, 1906.

Wood, Clement, ed. *Negro songs, an anthology*, edited, with an introduction, by Clement Wood. Girard, Kans., Haldeman-Julius Company, 1924. 64 pp.

Work, Frederick J., ed. *Folk Songs of the American Negro.* Edited by Frederick J. Work. Introduction by John W. Work, Jr. 93 songs. Nashville, Tenn., Work Brothers, 1907. 48 pp.

Work, Frederick J. *New Jubilee Songs, as sung by the Fisk Jubilee Singers of Fisk University.* Nashville, Tenn., Fisk University, 1902. 48 pp.

Work, Frederick J. *Some American Negro Folk Songs.* Boston, 1909.

Work, John Wesley. *Folk Songs of the American Negro.* Nashville, Tenn., Press of Fisk University, 1915. 131 pp.

Work, John W. "Negro Folk Song," in *Opportunity*, October, 1923.

Work, Monroe N. "Some Parallelisms in the Development of Africans and other Races. Musical parallelisms," in *Southern Workman* (Hampton, Va., 1907), xxxvi, 106–111.

Young, Martha. *Plantation Songs for My Lady's Banjo, and other Negro Lyrics and Monologues*, by E. Shepperd (*pseud.*); with pictures from life, by J. W. Otts. New York, R. H. Russell, 1901. 150 pp.

INDICES

INDEX OF TITLES

			PAGE
Ain't Gonna Grieve My Lord No More	II	70	118
All My Sins Been Taken Away	II	3 C	62
Ante-bellum Chanted Prayer, An	II	81	126
Blue	V	20	207
Brother Eben's Got a Coon	V	37	223
Cemetery Blue	XIV	9	393
City of the Refuge	II	31	90
Climbing Jacob's Ladder	II	2	59
Cotton-Eyed Joe	XII	4	354
Creation	II	24 A	83
Delie	V	41 C	215
Den My Little Soul Will Shine	II	22 A, B	81
Don't You See	II	56	109
Eliza Jane	IV	28	172
Engineer Rigg	V	33	220
Er Clim'in' Up Thine Hill	II	26 A	86
Fragment of a Chanted Negro Sermon	II	82	126
Frankie and Albert	V	29	213
Git Along Liza Jane	IV	29 A	176
Gospel Pool, The	II	60	111
Great Titanic, The	XI	1	347
Hold Your Light	II	16	76
How It Tis-a With Me	II	62	114
I Got a Mother	II	63	114
I Got Shoes	II	8	69
I'm Climbin'	II	26 B	87
I'm Goin' t' Wear that Starry Crown Over There	II	20	79
It Ain't No Harm to Trust in Jesus	II	4 B	65
John Henry	V	1	189
John Henry	VII	23 A	260
Keemo Kimo	IV	29	175
Kingdom Coming	IV	27	170
L & N Special	VII	14	257
Little Black Train, The	II	6	65
Little Bunny Rabbit	VI	22	234
Little David, Play Yo' Harp	II	7	66
Lulu Gal	IX	43	305
Lynchburg Town	IV	33	178

Massa Had a Yaller Gal   IV   3   152
Most Done Suffering.   II   61   112
Mr. Frog Went a Courtin' He Did Ride   V   31   218
My Gal   V   27   212
My Liza Jane   IV   28 G   174

Oh, Mary, Don't You Weep!   II   1 B   59
Oh Suzanna   IV   34   178
Old Ship of Zion, The   II   34   93
Ole Massa Was a Stingy Man   IV   5   157

Pharaoh's Army   II   1   58
Pomp's Soliloquy   V   32   219

Redeemed   II   76   123
Roll, Jordan, Roll   II   27 A   87
Run, Nigger, Run.   IV   23   168

Shortnin' Bread   V   5   193
Show Me the Way   II   10   71
Simon Slick   IV   6   157
Simon Slick   VI   1   227
Sis Mary Wore Three Links of Chain   II   3   60
Some Folks Say   XII   39   370
Southern Jack, A   VII   91   280

That Gospel Train is Coming.   II   4   64
That Old-Time Religion   II   32   91
Theology in the Question   V   30   216
This Old Hammer   VII   23 B   261
Tim of This   II   86   129
Travelling Coon, The   XI   5   349

Uncle Ned   IV   21   164

Voodoo Man, The   V   19   206

Wake Nicodemus   V   12   200
We Gwineter Git Down an' Pray   II   65   116
What You Goin' to Do When the Rent Comes Round   . .   IV   43   182
Wheel, The   II   67   117
Where Shall I Be   II   21   80

Year of Jubilee, The   IV   28   173

ALPHABETICAL INDEX OF FIRST LINES

A

			PAGE
Aint gwine let you humbug me	VII	3	255
Ain't no hammer in this mountain	VII	24	262
Ain't no use in working so hard	IX	33	301
Alabama River, The	X	84	339
All the nigger is looking for is fat meat and sundown . . .	IX	2	293
Amy was a good woman, everybody knows	V	29 A	213
Angel rubber overcoat, patent leather shoes	X	61	331
Animals came in one by one, The	II	47	103
Animals came two by two	III	24 E	141
As I was goin' down de street	VII	44	267
As I went down the new-cut road	VI	49	247
As I wus goin' 'cross de field	VI	47	245
Ashes to ashes and dust to dust.	XIV	4	392
Ashes to ashes and dust to dust.	X	27 D	322
Ashes to ashes, dust to dust	X	27 B	322
Ashes to ashes, dust to dust	X	27 C	322
Ask Miss Liza to hab me	IV	28 A	172
Away down yonder in the forks of de branch	VI	40 B	243

B

Babe is a good little boy sometimes	XIV	15	396
Bake dem biscuits, bake 'em brown	IX	37	304
Baltimore for its oysters	VII	72	274
Banjo goes Ker-blank, ker-blank	VI	41	244
Been a great change since I been born (chorus)	II	66	116
Been working in the cotton and corn all day	X	73	335
Benny was arrested upon one Sunday afternoon	V	29 E	216
Big black nigger settin' on a log	V	4	192
Biggest fool I ever saw, The	IV	47	183
Bile them cabbage down	IX	36	303
Blondy woman, a blondy woman, A	X	5	314
Blues ain't nothin' but a good man feeling bad	XIV	13 C	396
Blues ain't nothing, De	XIV	13 A	395
Boat is up the river and she won't come down, The	VII	90	280
Boat's up the river, The	IX	49	307
Boll weevil, boll weevil	XI	10	352
Boll weevil told the farmer, The	XI	11	352
Boll weevil told the farmer, The	XI	12	353
Born all the way from Atlanta	III	33	147
Born in No'th Carlina	IX	5	293
Bottom bone, bottom bone	VI	44	244
Brother Eben's got a coon	V	37	223

"Brother, how did you feel dat day?" . . . . II 60 A, B 111
Brown gal she is a pretty queen . . . . X 21 319
Brudder, brudder, whar was you . . . . II 65 116
Buy me a ba'l of flour . . . . IX 34 302
Bye-bye, little black baby (chorus) . . . . XIII 15 384

C

Cap'n, cap'n, yo' must be cross . . . . IX 41 305
Cap'n says, hurry, I say take my time . . . . VII 2 255
Captain, Captain, don't you know . . . . VII 8 256
Captain, Captain, give me my time . . . . VII 17 258
Captain, Captain, I can't see . . . . VII 11 257
Captain, Captain, nothing but a man . . . . VII 12 257
Captain! Captain! yo' mules look fine . . . . VII 4 255
Captain, Captain, you must be cross . . . . VII 6 256
Captain, I'm drivin' (huh) . . . . VII 1 254
Carry dat load on your head . . . . IX 11 295
Chattanooga, Chickamauga . . . . V 3 192
Chicken, come down out of that sycamore tree . . . . . XII 44 373
Chicken in de tree . . . . VIII 6 284
Chicken in dis sack and de hounds is on my track. . . . XII 42 373
Chicken in dis tree and dere's nobody here but me . . . XII 41 372
Chicken in the bread tray . . . . VI 35 241
Chuck a luck, the more you lay down . . . . XII 22 B 365
Cindy went to meetin' . . . . IV 14 161
Clean that corn a coming . . . . XII 14 362
Climb up Jacob's ladder, higher and higher . . . . . . II 2 B 60
Cold cup o' coffee and the meat's mighty fat, A . . . . XIII 10 382
Come after breakfast . . . . XIV 25 400
Come all yaw rounders if you want to flirt . . . . . . VII 47 268
Come 'ere, chillun, an' listen to me . . . . II 39 98
Come here Jill wid yo' key . . . . IV 46 183
Come on, brother, let's go around the wall . . . . . . II 38 98
Come out of that kitchen . . . . IX 35 D 303
Come to the river . . . . V 7 194
Coming from my wife's house t'other Monday morning . IV 7 157
Coon's tail am a streaked tail, The . . . . VI 24 235
Coonshine, ladies, coonshine . . . . IV 41 181
Corn in de field . . . . XIV 2 391
Corn shuck fiddle and shoe string bow . . . . VII 57 270
Crow in de cornfield . . . . VI 37 241

D

Dark was the night and cold was the ground . . . . . . II 51 A 105
Dark was the night and cold was the ground . . . . . . II 51 B 105
Dat ole black gal . . . . VII 46 267
David had a harp with a thousand strings . . . . II 7 F 68
Daylight's a breakin', hear de rooster crowin' . . . . . VI 36 241
Delia! Delia! raise up yer head . . . . V 29 D 216

Delie, Delie, was a-goin' her last round   V   29 C   215
Dere was an old nigger by de name of Uncle Ned   IV   21 A, B   164
Dey mixed dem roun' an' stirred dem up   XII   37   370
Dey say dat spring is the loving time   X   63   332
Did you eber go afishin' on a hot summer day   XIV   27   400
Dis ain't no lie, jes' a natchel fact.   VII   70   273
Dis here hammer won't ring   VII   25   262
Dis mornin' I gets up and puts on my Sunday clothes . .   V   35   222
Doan you leave me here   XII   31   376
Doctor Cook's in town, Doctor Cook's in town   XI   15   354
Don' yo' leave me here (chorus)   XI   14   353
Don't go down that lonesome road.   IX   30   300
Don't min' workin'   VII   28   263
Down in de hen-house on my knees   XII   40   372
Down in the hollow, 'pon my knees   IX   55   308

E

Ef effer 'ligion wuz a thing dat money could buy   II   45 A   101
Eighteen hundred and forty-four   II   48   103
Engineer Rigg was a good engineer   V   33   220
Er a nigger'll be a nigger   XIII   4   379

F

Farmer said to boll weevil   XI   13   353
Father gwine to miss me in my walk   II   55   108
Fifteen cents in the panel of the fence   X   44   328
Fix me Jesus, fix me right   II   20   79
Forty days and forty nights the rain kept droppin' . . .   III   24 A   140
Four day blues ain't nuffin', De.   XIV   5 A   392
From ashes to ashes   XII   36   369
From ashes to ashes   X   27   321

G

Get up coon, let's go fishin'   VI   46   245
Gimme that old-time religion   II   32 A   91
Git up in de mawning and kill dat calf   IX   27   299
Give me that good ole time religion   II   32 B   92
Give me whiskey when I die   XII   24   366
Go ring dem bells, bells, bells at de Zion of Glory   II   23   82
Go to bed, children, and don't you cry   II   56   109
Goat one day was feeling fine, A   VI   12   231
God made a nigger   XIII   14 A   383
God made white man   XIII   14 B   384
Going to the race track   VII   56   270
Going up, going up, going up, going up   II   78   125
Gona get me a pistol with a shiny barrel   VII   64   272
Good lookin' woman   X   64   333
Good looking woman, A   X   2   313

Good looking woman, A   X   3   313
Good looking woman make a rabbit, A   X   I   313
Goodbye, darling, I am leaving   IX   13   295
Goodbye, Miss Eliza Jane   IV   28 D 173
Got on the dummy did n't mean no harm   V   16   204
Great big Negro black as tar . . . .   III 21   139
Great big nigger black as night   V   6   194
Gwine down by de parsnage   IV   28 E 174
Gwine up town and I 'se coming right back . . . . . .   XIV 29   400

H

Hallelujah, Hallelujah, we 'll jine the union band   II   33   92
Haunted mansion stood, A   V   18   205
Haven't been sober since the last October . . . .   XII 26   366
Haven't seen the like since I been born   II   7 B   67
He rambled and he rambled till the butchers cut him down   IV   50   184
He rambled, he rambled   V   14   201
Hello, Captain . . . .   VII 10   256
Hello Central!   X   35   325
Here comes Sal with a snicker and a grin   IV   12   160
Here I stand black and dirty   IV   36   179
Hey: Bull and Ben tally wham! . . . .   VII 37   265
Hey! my little man come a-ridin' by   IV   9   159
High brown rides a pullman car, The   X   23   320
Hikin' down the main line   IX   24   298
Hippercrits, de hippercrits, De   II   12 A   73
Ho! ho! and I wish my color would fade . . . .   XIII I   378
Hog in de 'taters   VI   30   239
Hol' my shaker an' hol' my shawl   II   84 A 128
Hold my bonnet and hold my shawl   II   84 B 128
Holy Ghost, I done done.   II   75   122
Honey, when I 'se had youse . . . .   VII 65   272
Hounds on my track . . . .   XII 42 B 373
How it 'tiz-a with me-a   II   62 A 114
Hypocrite, hypocrite, God despise.   II   12 B   74
Hypocrity, hypocrity, dress so fine   II   11 A   72

I

I ain't a gonna work a no mo'!   IX   7   294
I ain't no doctor . . . .   XIV 17   398
I ain't no miller . . . .   XIV 19   398
I ain't no preacher . . . .   XIV 18   398
I am climbing up Jacob's ladder   II   2 A   59
I am going back to Georgia   IX   6   294
I am so glad de cops dey don't know where I'm is . . . .   XII 16   362
I ask de captain — wham! . . . .   VII 14   257
I been 'buked and I been 'bused   II   15   75
I been hammering — Huh . . . .   VII 36   265
I can shimmy, she wabble, I can ball-the-jack   X   49   329

I carried old Raddler out	VI	16	232
I done called you	VII	21	260
I don't bother work and work don't bother me	IX	8	294
I don't like a black gal, I tell you the reason why	X	32	324
I don't mind race riding	VII	45	267
I don't play the dozen	XII	21	365
I don't want no jet black woman for my regular	X	42	327
I don't want to ride in no golden chariot	III	28	144
I give fifteen cents to see the elephant jump the fence	VI	52	249
I got a bull-dog in my back yard	VII	80	276
I got a long, tall yaller gal	X	29	323
I got a 'oman in de white folk's yard	IX	33 B	302
I got a southern jack	VII	91	280
I got de blues	XIV	8 B	393
I got de hesitation stockings and de hesitation shoes	XIV	1	391
I got peas in de pot ten days ol'	IX	28	300
I got shoes, etc.	II 8 A, B, C, D, E		69
I got the railroad blues, but I'm too damn mean to cry	XIV	8	393
I got up this morning and I wash my face	IX	54	308
I gotta woman, she lives down by the sea	X	30	323
I had a good lookin' 'oman	X	12	315
I had a good looking woman	X	13	316
I had a good woman, I had a good woman	XIV	11	394
I had a little dog an' his name was True	VI	18	232
I had a mule and he wouldn't gee	VI	5	229
I had a mule one time	VI	1	227
I had a sho-fly lady	X	59	331
I had a tall, long, kinky-headed woman	X	14	316
I had er good woman	VII	67	273
I had ole Irish potato	X	69	334
I have chiblings	III	10	135
I layed me head on de railroad track	IX	16	296
I love my wife, I love my baby	III	14	136
I lub dat 'oman	X	40	327
I peeped through de crack	IV	8	158
I rather be dead	X	85	340
I remember last summer	VII	20	259
I rose early one morning	IV	48	184
I saw a negro and a monkey	XIII	2	378
I stole dem breeches	V	32	219
I told you once and I told you twice	XII	20	365
I took my gal to a fancy ball	V	27	212
I waked up this morning	VII	51	269
I want to be ready	II	49	104
I want to century just one more time	XII	11	361
I want to go to Heaven and I want to go right	II	57	109
I was born about four thousand years ago	III	31	146
I was standing on the corner	XII	9	360
I went down in the valley one day	II	10 A	71
I went down in the valley to pray	II	10 B	71

I went down in the valley to pray.	III	1 A	132
I went down to a big crap game, went against my will	V	8 E	198
I went down to a coon crap game	V	8 A	195
I went down to de mill pond	VI	43	244
I went to de river	IX	17	297
I went down to de "slop" joint	X	36	326
I went down to my gal's house	X	68	334
I went down to my gul's house las' night	X	67	334
I went down to Sally's house	X	65	333
I went down that chicken roost	V	8 F	198
I went down to the cemetery	XIV	9	393
I went down to the old rock mill	XIV	22	399
I went on to Macon	X	81	338
I went out hunting on Sunday morn	XIV	20	399
I went to a Negro crap game	V	8 D	197
I went to a nigger crap game	V	8 B	196
I went to de ribber and I couldn't get across	VI	7	229
I went to the crap game the other night	V	8 C	197
I went to the ribber, but I did n't go to stay	III	1 B	32
I went to the smoke house to get a little toast	V	24	210
I wen' up a persimmon	VIII	19	287
I went up on the mountain.	X	82	338
I went up on the mountain to see de sun go down.	IX	56	309
I went up to town to get a cake of cheese	IV	29 C	176
I wish my captain would go blind	VII	15	258
I woke up early dis morning	VII	50	268
I woke up this morning with a knife in my hand	VII	13	257
I wonda where my brown gone	X	71	335
I wonder if my mother's on that train	V	34	221
I won't go to preaching, ain't got no shoes	VIII	10	285
I wore my knees up to the bone	II	26 A	86
I worked today, I worked mighty well	IX	4	293
I wouldn't marry a yaller gal	X	31	323
I wrote a letter	VII	63	272
I'd been married twenty-five years ago	XII	4	359
I'd rather be in the cotton field	VIII	25	289
If a horse had wool and a sheep had hair	VIII	4	283
If a white man kills a negro they hardly carry it to court	XIII	9	382
If de blues was whiskey	XIV	12 B	395
If de ribber was booze	XII	33	368
If de river was whiskey	XII	34	369
If de train goes and leaves me here	IX	46	306
If der river wus whiskey an' I was a duck	VII	76	275
If I die in de state of Arkunsaw.	VII	82 E	277
If I had a jug of rum	IV	20	164
If I had it you could get it	IX	59	309
If I had my rather I rather be a squirrel	VI	31	239
If I live and don't get killed	IX	57	309
If my mother wants to see me	II	59 B	111
If my wife comes home with whiskey on her breath	X	53	329

If my wife don't treat me right	X	52	329
If the ocean were whiskey and the seas were rye	XII	35	369
If the train breaks down, baby, I've got a mule to ride	VII	75	275
If the train go leave me	VII	74	274
If there ever was a Devil	XIV	26	400
If yo' house ketch on fire	IX	58	309
If you don't believe I'll treat you right	VII	66	272
If you don't believe I'm sinkin'	VII	89 B	279
If you don't believe I'm sinking down	VII	89 A	279
If you don't believe I'm sinking just look what a hole I'm in	X	48	328
If you don't know the panic's on	XI	7	351
If you don't let my brown-skin babe alone	VIII	20	287
If you get there before I do, all right, all right	II	59 A	111
If you goes and leaves me here	IX	25	299
If you in love and yo' gal don't treat you right	VII	55	270
If you think I'm goin' to	IX	38	304
If you want to go to Heaven	III	9	135
If you want to go to heben	III	26	144
If yo' bread is burning	IX	35	302
If you're in love and your gal don't treat you nice	X	51	329
If-a 'ligion was a thing that money could buy	II	45 B	101
If-a 'ligion wuz er thing that money could buy	XIII	5	380
I'll a'knowledge, Honey, I done wrong	VII	52	269
I'll just swear and swear to damn	VII	83	278
I'm Alabama Bound	IX	47	306
I'm Alabama Bound	IX	48	307
I'm climbin', I'm climbin', I'm climbin', bless God	II	26 B	87
I'm des a little nigger	IV	37	180
I'm from old Virginia wid a haid full of knowledge	III	25	143
I'm goin' far away	VII	84	278
I'm goin' ter live on de high	III	29 A	145
I'm going to der co'thouse	IX	45	306
I'm going to live anyhow till I die	III	29 B	145
I'm going to walk and talk wid my Jesus	II	72 B	120
I'm gonna roll dem dice	XII	18 B	364
I'm growing old and feeble now	IV	42	181
I'm gwain to town	XIV	21	399
I'm gwine back to Birmingham	XII	29	367
I'm gwine down town	IV	33	178
I'm gwine tell my loving Savior	II	72 A	120
I'm gwine ter leave on de mornin' train	II	3 H	63
I'm my mammy's Little Alabama coon	XIV	16	397
I'm on my way and I can't turn back	II	77 B	125
I'm on my way to the heavenly land	II	69	118
In come de animals two by two	III	24 F	142
In eighteen hundred and sixty-one	IV	27	170
In the Garden	VI	22	234
I'se de handsomest nigger in de county, O	VIII	17	286
I'se got a gal in Baltimo'	IX	14	296
I'se got a mule, I'se got a mule on de mountain	VI	2	228

I'se gotta gal in de white folk yard X   28   322
I'se gotter mudder in the promised land II   63   114
I'se gwina leave here, and I ain't coming back VII   58   270
I'se gwina save all of my nickels and dimes IX   15   296
I'se gwine to a nation, I'm goin' to ride the cannon ball . VII   59   271
I'se gwine to de race track XII   23   365
It ain't er gwine ter rain, it ain't er gwine ter rain . . . VIII   1   281
It ain't no lie, it's a natural fact III   23   140
It ain't no use a-pleadin' now lady, yo' done played your
   las' trump card. X   76   336
It takes a dark-skinned baby X   8   315
It takes a long, tall, slim, black man to make a German
   lay his rifle down XI   16   355
It takes a long, tall yaller gal to make a preacher lay his
   Bible down X   10   315
It takes a rubber ball to bounce III   32   146
It takes gravel and rock to make a solid road. VII   49   268
It takes the rock and gravel X   9   315
It was on one Monday morning just about one o'clock. . XI   1   347
It's a long way to old Kentucky XI   18   355
It's me, it's me, it's me, O Lord II   58 B   110
I've been hoodooed V   19   206
I've been to the 'Bama and I just got back VIII   13   285
I've been working on the railroad all the livelong day . . VII   71   274
I've got a brother in the snow-white fields II   71   119
I've got a woman and a sweetheart too VII   48   268
I've seen in my life some very funny folks V   36   222

J

Jack the rabbit! Jack the bear! VII   31   263
Jack's ole mule, Jack's ole mule VIII   9   284
Jesus lover of my soul III   3   133
Jesus lover of my soul III   4 A, B   133
John Henry had a little woman V   1 C   191
John Jasper was a man II   85   128
Jones, he's got my gal an' gone X   77   336
Jones, I got my butcher-knife and gattling gun XII   5   360
Juba dis and Juba dat IV   18   162
June, July, and August VII   32   264

K

Keep yo' hand on the Gospel plow II   64   115
Kentucky water drinks like sherry wine XII   25   366
Kill that chicken and give me wing VI   39   242

L

Laid in jail with my face turned to the wall VII   77   275
Las' year I was from Rack-en-sack IX   53   308
Lawd, Lawd, you hear dat, Captain? VII   5   255
Lickety splup, lickety splup XII   22   365

Listen white folks . . . . XIV 32 401
Little Bunny Rabbit . . . . VI 22 234
Little David, play on yo' harp, Hallelu (*chorus*) . . . . II 7 A 66
Little ole Liza Jane . . . . IV 28 B 173
Long come Noah . . . . III 24 C, D 141
Longest train I ever saw, The . . . . VII 73 274
Long-tailed rat an' a bowl er souse, A . . . . IV 29 B 176
Look here, nigger, do you figger on going up dar . . . . II 6 B 66
Look out, Sister Hannah, how you walk on the cross . . II 11 B 73
Look over yonder in the fields of green . . . . II 11 C 73
Look up yonder in the deep blue sky . . . . XIV 28 400
Looker yonder comin'! comin' down the track . . . . . XII 47 374
Lor' de hotter de sun shine de better I feel . . . . . . VII 29 263
Lor' Lor', if you're looking for Jesus you can rise and fly III 5 133
Lord he thought he'd make a man . . . . II 24 A 83
Lord, I put you in the shade . . . . X 56 330
Lord, I wish I wus in heaven . . . . II 54 108
Lord I'm on my way . . . . II 77 A 124
Lord made an elephant, The . . . . III 12 136
Lord said to his crowd, The . . . . II 80 125
Lord this old nega done done what you told me to do . . II 75 B 123
Lord, you work me so hard, Captain . . . . VII 9 256
Lord's train jus' got one track, De . . . . II 5 65
Lulu gal, Lulu gal . . . . IX 48 305

M

Mamie in the kitchen . . . . XI 17 355
Mary Bell, go ask yo' mama . . . . IV 32 177
Mary had a little lamb . . . . V 13 201
Mary Mack is dressed in black . . . . VIII 21 288
Mary, Martha, Luke, and John . . . . II 24 B, C, D 84
Mary wore a golden chain . . . . II 3 F 63
Mary wore an X-ray dress . . . . X 60 331
Mary wore three lengths of chain . . . . II 3 D 62
Massa bought a yaller gal . . . . IV 3 B 153
Massa had a yaller gal . . . . IV 3 C 154
Massa had an old black mule . . . . IV 6 157
Massa owned a yaller gal . . . . IV 3 D 154
Me an' my pardner . . . . VII 19 259
Me and my girl and the bob-tail dog . . . . V 28 213
Me and my pardner done made a plot . . . . VII 22 260
Me and my partner, partner Jack . . . . VIII 7 284
Me and my wife had a fallin' out . . . . III 16 137
Me an' my wife an' little fice dog . . . . VI 14 231
Milk in the dairy getting mighty old . . . . IV 29 A 175
Miss Mary, she did dream a dream . . . . VI 50 247
Mourner, mourner, you shall be free . . . . III 18 137
Mr. Frog went a-courtin' he did ride . . . . V 31 218
My baby needs a new pair shoes . . . . XII 18 A 363
My buggy it needs greasing . . . . VII 81 276

My chillans on de ground . . . . XII 18 c 364
My daddy drives a street car and my brother drives a hack XIV 24 399
My daddy had a rabbit dog . . . . VI 15 232
My daddy was a miller . . . . XIV 23 399
My love is like a red, red rose . . . . X 62 332
My marster had er little gray mule . . . . VI 3 228
My name is Sam . . . . IV 26 170
My old blue dog . . . . V 20 207
My old lady done gone an' lef me here . . . . III 15 137
My ole banjo hangin' on de wall . . . . IV 38 180
My ole missus dead an' gone . . . . IV 1 151
My ole mistis promised me . . . . IV 2 152

N

Near my God to the chicken in a cedar tree . . . . III 6 133
Negro and white man playing seven up . . . . XIII 17 B 385
Negro run, negro blew . . . . IV 23 c 169
Nickel worth of meal and a dime of lard, A . . . . XI 6 350
Nickodemus de slave was of African birth . . . . V 12 200
Nigger an' white man . . . . VI 13 231
Nigger and a white man playing seven up . . . . XIII 17 A 385
Nigger be a nigger, don't care what he do, A . . . . XIII 3 A 379
Nigger in de cotton patch picken' out cotton . . . . . . VIII 12 285
Nigger in de wild woods settin' on a log . . . . III 22 140
Nigger is happy, The . . . . VII 79 276
Nigger you better come out dose gymsampson weeds . . . XIV 30 401
Niggers in de cornfield, and li'l hogs in de yard . . . . . . III 34 147
Noah's hammer ring, Sinner repent . . . . II 31 90
No-eh built de ark . . . . II 43 100
Now I'se got a notion in my head . . . . V 30 216
Now look here woman, I can't stand . . . . X 47 328

O

O, a brunette woman . . . . X 6 314
O bear me away on your snowy white wing . . . . II 79 125
O Brother, don't you want . . . . II 14 75
O Christian hold up yo' light (chorus) . . . . II 16 B 77
O de rocks an' de mountains will all flee away . . . . . . II 21 B 81
O John, Jesus comin' . . . . II 83 128
O Mary don't you mourn . . . . II 1 B 59
O my brother when de world's on fier . . . . II 30 A 89
O my li'l sistah; I'm so glad . . . . II 9 70
O my loving pastor . . . . II 30 B 90
O police, police, turn me loose . . . . XII 12 361
O what ship is this that will take us all home . . . . . . II 34 B 95
O, what were you singing . . . . XI 2 C 349
O! who's gointa help dat missionary band . . . . II 44 100
Oh, a black headed woman . . . . X 7 314
Oh Babe! I smell your bread a-burnin' . . . . X 35 B 303

Oh brother! don't you want to go . . . . II 13 74
Oh, brother, what are you going to do when your lamp
  goes out?. II 37 97
Oh! Brudder can't you hol' out yo' light . . . . II 16 A 76
Oh crap-shooter, Oh crap-shooter . . . . II 17 77
Oh dat ole mule . . . . VIII 8 284
Oh! de rabbit on de log . . . . VI 20 233
Oh, dem golden slippers . . . . II 52 106
Oh! der blues ain't nothen' . . . . XIV 13 B 396
Oh, don't you cry, Suzannah . . . . IV 34 178
Oh! don't you hear that whistle blo'n' . . . . II 4 B 65
Oh! down in the valley where I was told. . . . . II 70 118
Oh, er yaller gal'll make er houn' dog quit his trail . . . . X 4 314
Oh, get away from the window . . . . X 34 325
Oh, goodbye, gal, honey, fare you well . . . . X 80 337
"Oh, how did you feel when you come out of the wilder-
  ness?". . . . . XII 15 362
Oh! if the blues was whiskey . . . . XIV 12 395
Oh! I'm goin' er way . . . . XII 38 370
Oh! I'm going on to Hebun anyhow . . . . III 27 144
Oh, it's rainin' here . . . . XIV 14 396
Oh let the sun go down, (hunk) . . . . VII 38 265
Oh, little nigger baby . . . . XIII 16 385
Oh Marster Jesus! Git on the swift flying horse of Zion . . II 81 126
Oh! Once I wuz a rich man and wore silks and satins . . . IV 30 177
Oh, the captain must er been drunk . . . . XI 4 349
Oh, the fat one and the lean one . . . . IV 39 180
Oh! The old gray mare she ain't what she used to be . . . VI 8 230
Oh, way down in South Carolina . . . . V 21 208
Oh we'll put John on the island . . . . II 35 96
Oh, well, it's raining here . . . . IX 22 298
Oh! where was you when the old Titanic went down . . . XI 2 348
Oh, yaller gal she drinks wine and champagne . . . . . . X 26 321
Ol' Aunt Dina drempt a dream . . . . XII 48 375
Old bee makes de honey-comb, The . . . . XIII 11 382
Old black gal is my living, old yellow gal is my home . . . X 11 315
Old Dan Cox rides a gray horse . . . . IV 35 179
Old folks better up and git to bed . . . . IX 26 299
Old Geneva . . . . VI 6 229
Old hawk flew up in the roof, The . . . . VI 32 B 240
Old hen sitten' in the fodder stack, An . . . . VI 32 A 239
Old Jonah got mad 'cause de rain kept a droppin' . . . . III 24 B 141
Old Kate, the garden gate . . . . IV 15 161
Old man Baker was a good old man . . . . IV 13 160
Old massa had a yaller gal . . . . IV 3 F 155
Old massa he done promised me . . . . III 8 134
Old master had a yellow gal . . . . IV 3 A 152
Old master had a story house, sixteen stories high . . . . VIII 22 288
Old Mother Pickapot, lying in the bed. . . . . IV 31 177
Old ship of Zion when she comes, when she comes, The . . II 34 C 95

Ole cow died in de head of de branch, De VI   40 C   243
Ole Eve was the first 'oman, Adams was the man V   26   211
Ole Marster bought a black man IV   3 G   155
Ole marster had a yaller gal IV   3 E   154
Ole marster was a stingy man IV   5   157
Ole master had a fine buggy IV   4   156
Ole master had a little grey mule VIII   23   288
Ole Mister beat me to the henhouse V   11   200
Ole Mr. Johnson, had a trouble of his own V   22   209
'Oman, 'oman, who can yo' reg'lar be?. X   39   327
On a Monday bright and fair the hearse come rolling by . VIII   24   289
Once there was a travelling coon XI   5   349
One morning soon death come creepin' in the room . . . II   19 B   79
One o' these days, 'bout twelve o'clock II   29   89
Only thing I ever done wrong, The VII   68   273
Other night down in the Lice Kill Club, The   V   2 A, B   191
Ought 's a ought and a figure's a figur' XIII   12   383
Our Brother is dead   II   82   126
Out on dat ocean XI   3   349
Over de fence and through de pasture VIII   11   285

P

Peas in the pot, hoecake a bakin' IX   39   304
Pharaoh army got drowned in the sea II   1 A   58
Pick, I 'll drive you VII   26   262
Po' gal take a warnin'. X   37   326
Po' morner, in de morn we shall be free III   17   137
Poor John Henry, (hic) VII   23 A   260
Pore ol' me, pore ol' me IX   44   305
Possum in gum stump. Cooney in the hollow   VI   27 B   238
Possum up a simmon tree, Raccoon on the ground . . . VI   26 C   237
Possum up the gum stump   VI   27 A   237
Preacher in de pulpit, De XII   30   376
Preacher in de pulpit put his bible down, De IX   52   308
Preacher in the pulpit. IX   51   308
Preacher went out hunting on one Sunday morning, The V   23   210
Put de dawgs on him VII   27   263

R

Rabbit is a cunning thing VI   19   233
Rabbit on de lawg, ... VI   21   233
Rabbit on the log   VIII   5   283
Raccoon am a cunnin' t'ing, De VI   29 B   238
Raccoon got a bushy tail   VI   23   234
Raccoon is a cunning thing, The VI   29 A   238
Raccoon up de gum stump, De VI   28   238
Raccoon up the simmon tree VI   26 A   236
Raccoon up the simmon tree VI   26 B   236
Railroad Bill did not know   XII   1   358

Redeemed, redeeemed, redeemed, redeemed (*chorus*). . . .   II   76   123
Rich gal drinks the snipped wine   X   25   321
Rich girl wears the ten dollar shoes, The   X   24   321
Rich man has a big fine house, The   XII   28   366
Rich man rides on a Pullman car   XIII   18   386
Richmond is no mo'   IV   25   170
Riding of the sheep, and leading of the goat   IX   31   301
Road is rocky, Lord, De   VII   33   264
Roborus was a mighty mean man   XII   2   359
Rock candy, my ladies (*chorus*)   IV   16   162
Rocks in de mountains, De   X   83   339
Rocks on the mountains   VII   62   271
Roll dat bale, roll dat cotton   IX   10   295
Roll, Jurding, roll, roll, Jurding, roll   II   27 A   87
Roll on, Jordan, roll   II   27 B   88
Rooster and de nigger got in a fight, De   VI   34   240
Rooster crowed in Paris and de hen she laughed in France .   VII   53   269
Rooster crows for midnight   VII   54   269
Rough rock road   II   61 B   113
Rough, rocky road, I'se most done suffering   II   61 A   112
Rufus, Rastus Johnson Brown   IV   43   182
Run here, Doctor, (*huh*)   VII   87   278
Run, nigga, run, or patrol will ketch you   IV   23 D   169
Run, nigger, run, paderow catch you   IV   23 A   168
Run nigger run, paderow catch you   IV   23 B   169
Run sinner, run, yo' house on fire   II   22 B   82

S

Sal's got a meat skin laid away   VII   60   271
Sally went to preachin', she shouted and she squalled . . .   VIII   3   282
Same train car'ed my papa   IX   42   305
Satan is mad and I am glad   II   68   117
Saturday night and Sunday too   X   75   336
Saturday night and Sunday too, pretty gals on my mind   .   IV   28 G   174
Save up yo' money   XI   8 A   351
Save up your money   XIV   31   401
Save yo' money   XI   8 B   351
Set to yo' pa'tner, dah, dah   IV   19   164
Shanghi-rooster ain't got no comb   XII   3   359
She cooks good cabbage   IX   40   304
She goes out fishin' ev'ry night   X   79   337
She is a long, tall yallow gal   IX   50   307
She went up the new cut road   IV   28 C   173
Sheep in the meadow don't you hear them bells   VI   11   231
She's my yaller gal   X   33   324
Shoot your dice and have your fun   XII   19   364
Shut your mouth and hold your breath   VIII   14   285
Sis Mary had three links of chain   II   3 E   63
Sis Mary wore three links ob chain   II   3 A   60
Sistah Mary, an' de bell done rung   II   22 A   81

Sister Mary wore three links ob chain	II	3 B	61
Sister Mary wore three links of chain	II	3 C	62
Snake bake a hoe-cake.	VI	48	246
Snappo-snap-peter, snap-nanny goat eater, snap-po	IV	10	159
So long, nigger, so long I say	VII	43	266
So low you can't crawl under	III	2	132
Som' ob dese mo'nin's I'm gwaine a git up an' wash my face	VIII	18	287
Some come cripple an' some come lame	II	24 E	85
Some come cripple and some come lame	II	7 G	68
Some folks say a negro won't steal	XII	39 A	370
Some folks say a Negro won't steal	XII	39 B	371
Some folks say dat de dummy won' run	V	15	202
Some folks say dat er preacher won't steal	XII	39 E	372
Some folks say dat niggers don't steal	XII	39 C	371
Some folks say that a negro won't steal	XII	39 D	371
Some folks say them four day blues ain't bad.	XIV	5 B	392
Some folks say-a de fo' day blues ain't bad	XIV	5 C	392
Some folks says dat dem St. Louis blues ain't bad.	XIV	6	392
Some folks says Memphis Blues ain't bad	XIV	7	393
Some o' these mornings and 'twon't be long	VII	16 A, B	258
Some says yellow	X	15	316
Somebody stole my old coon dog	VI	17	232
Sometimes I feel like a feather in the air	III	35	147
Sometimes up and sometimes down	II	62 B	114
Soon one mornin' Death come creepin' in de room	II	19 A	78
Squir'l he totes a bushy tail, De	VI	25	236
Stand back pork chops	VI	38	242
Standin' in some corner hongry as can be	XII	45	374
Standin' on de conah did n't mean no hawm	XII	10	361
Standing on a corner smoking a cheap cigar,	VII	78	275
Standing on de corner	X	72	335
Starch my jumper and patch my overalls	IX	23	298
Stick my head in a paper sack	IV	45	183
Sure as the vine grows up the wall	X	45	328
Susie went down to de bar room	V	29 B	214

T

'Taint my mother, 'taint my sister, but it's me, O Lord	II	58	110
'Taint no use to greab about it	X	58	330
Take my hammer	VII	18	259
Takes rock and gravel	VII	61	271
Takes two thousan' brick to top this kiln	VII	42	266
Talk about yo' gal but you ought to see mine	X	43	327
Tell me how long will I have to wait	IX	32	301
That gospel train am coming	II	4 A	64
That's all right	IX	18	297
There is no place in the height of Heaven	II	86	129
There is rest for the weary	II	50	104
There's a coon right down in the furniture room	V	25	211
There's a little black train a-comin'	II	6 A	65

There's a place prepared by my Savior's side . . . . . . II 73 121
There's one, there's two, there's three, there's four . . . . II 46 103
There was a Doctor by the name Peck, Peck . . . . IV 22 167
There was a man lived in our town . . . . VI 1 B 228
There was an old colored individual . . . . IV 21 D 167
There was an old negro and his name was Ned . . . . . . IV 21 C 165
There was an old nigger by de name of Uncle Ned . . . . IV 21 A 165
There was an old nigger whose name was Uncle Ned . . . IV 21 D 167
They give me coffee . . . . XII 17 363
Thirty-two special on a forty-four frame, A . . . . XII 7 360
This old hammer killed John Henry . . . . VII 23 B 261
This old hammer killed John Henry . . . . VII 23 D 261
This ole hammer, mos' too heavy, (grunt) . . . . VII 23 C 261
Thought I heard — Huh! . . . . VII 88 279
Thought I heard that K. C. whistle blow . . . . VII 69 273
Three weeks my head's been nappy . . . . IV 49 184
Thru de winder . . . . X 70 334
Times are hard and money is scase, The . . . . VIII 15 286
Took my gal to de milk-shake stand . . . . X 55 330
Train, train, train, train, run so fast. . . . . XIV 33 402
Tuesday mornin' after a shower of rain . . . . XII 46 374
'Twas in a hen coop one dark stormy night . . . . . . V 9 199
Two big horses hitched to a slide . . . . II 28 88
Two little niggers black as tar . . . . V 5 C 194
Two little niggers lay in bed . . . . V 5 B 194
Two little niggers lyin' in de bed . . . . V 5 A 193

U

Uster be er song er long time ago . . . . IV 40 181

W

Walk, talk, ginger blue . . . . XIII 6 380
Wash those clothes my honey child . . . . IX 9 294
Watch me whet my cradle, O! Alle! O! . . . . VIII 16 286
Water-boy, water-boy . . . . VII 34 264
Water Jack! you oughter been here and half way back . . VII 35 265
Way down yonder, and a long way off . . . . VI 40 A 242
Way down yonder in de fork ob de branch . . . . VI 40 D 243
'Way down yonder in de growin' corn . . . . VI 10 230
'Way down yonder, in the forks o' de creek . . . . . . VI 9 230
Way down yonder on Cedar street . . . . III 19 138
Way down yonder on Eagle Street . . . . III 20 138
'Way down yonder where I was born . . . . IV 11 160
Way down yonder where the wind blows cold . . . . . IX 3 293
Way up on the mountain top I gave my horn a blow . . . X 78 336
Way up yonder on the ole green lake . . . . VI 42 244
We'll ride the chariot wheel . . . . IX 29 300
We'll roll, we'll roll the chariot along (chorus) . . . . . . II 36 97
Well a white lady wears a hobble skirt. . . . . X 16 316

Well, de Good Book say dat Cain killed Abel . . . . . II 25 86
Well er workin' man . . . . IX 1 292
Well I wonder whut de po' nigger gwinder do. . . . . . XII 43 373
Well, it keeps on raining . . . . VII 7 256
W-e-ll Mr. Peckerwood . . . . VI 45 245
Well, my home ain't here . . . . IX 21 298
Well, the farmer told the merchant . . . . XI 9 351
Well the funniest thing I ever seen . . . . VII 85 278
Well the grave-yard must be an awful place . . . . . . XIV 3 391
Well they took him up on the smoky road . . . . VII 86 278
Went down to the rocks to hide my face . . . . II 74 121
Went to de chicken coop — chicken coop was locked . . V 10 199
Went to see my Susan Jane . . . . X 66 333
Went upon the mountain . . . . X 54 330
Whale swallowed Brother Jonah, The . . . . II 40 98
Whale swallowed Jonah . . . . III 30 145
Whar you goin', buzzard . . . . IV 17 163
What did the rooster say to the little red hen? . . . . . VI 53 240
What kind of clothes do the angels wear, Ugh! Ugh! . . IX 19 297
What kind of shoes you goin' to wear? Golden slippers . II 33 107
What ship is that will take us all home . . . . II 34 A 93
What you goin' to do when the meat gibs out . . . . . IV 44 181
What you gwina do when the world's on fire . . . . . . VIII 2 282
What's that yonder looks so black? . . . . III 11 135
When a woman takes the blues . . . . XIV 10 394
When I die. . . . . VII 82 D 277
When I die bury me deep . . . . VII 82 C 277
When I die bury me good and deep . . . . XII 32 B 368
When I die don't bury me a 'tal . . . . XII 32 A 368
When I die don't bury me deep . . . . VII 82 A, B 276
When I got good ole egg-nog an' simmon beer . . . . . XII 27 366
When I went to see Miss Liza Jane . . . . IV 28 F 174
When I leave here jumping . . . . IX 20 298
When John Henry was a baby . . . . V 1 A 189
When John Henry wuz er baby . . . . V 1 B 191
When my aporn tied in a bow . . . . X 38 326
When the rocks and the mountains flee away . . . . . II 21 A 80
When you git lazy and want ter lay off . . . . VII 39 266
When you see me coming . . . . IX 12 295
When you smell yo'r cabbage burnin' . . . . IX 35 C 303
Where wus you when the big Titanic . . . . XI 2 B 347
White child goes to school and learns to read and write, A XIII 7 381
White folks in the parlor eating ice cream . . . . . . XIII 8 B 381
White gal rides in an automobile . . . . X 19 318
White gal rides in automobile . . . . X 18 318
White gal rides on an automobile . . . . X 17 318
White gal sleeps in a folding bed, A . . . . X 22 320
White girl smell like Castile soap, De . . . . X 20 319
White man and the nigger, The . . . . XIII 13 383
White man in the dining room eating cake and cream . . XIII 8 A 381

White man in the parlor reading latest news   XIII   3 c   382
White man kill Muskogee duck   XIII   5   380
Who built the Ark? Noah built the Ark   II   42   99
Who dat knockin' at de do' belo'?.   XII   8   360
Who did, who did, who did swallow Jonah, Jonah   . . .   II   41   99
Whoa! Mule. Whoa! Mule, I holler   VI   4   228
Who's been here since I been gone?   II   7 D, E   68
Who's been here since I been gone   II   7 C   67
Willie the weeper was chimney sweeper   V   17 A, B   204
Woman I love is struck on a married man, The   X   41   327
Woman, woman, look what you done   X   57   330
Woo look er look er yonder   VI   51   248
Working on the railroad   VII   40   266
Working on the railroad at forty cents a day   VII   41   266

Y

Yankees they caught me, The   IV   24   169
Yonder comes a yaller gal   X   74   333
Yonder comes Bob Benson   XII   13   362
Yonder comes Noah stumbling in the dark   III   13   136
You can play the ace and tray   II   18 A, B   78
You got shoes, I got shoes . . . .   II 8 A, B, C, D, E   69
You gwine to kill yo' fool self a workin'   VII   30   263
You made me love you and now your man have come . .   X   46   328
You swing Sally and I'll swing Sue   X   50   329
You'll have to be de lover of an undertaker's daughter   .   III   7   134
You've been talking 'bout you coming, you going, you *gwine*   IX   60   310
You've got your big gun, and I've got mine   XII   6   360

Z

Zika made a wheel   II   67   117